May 19–21, 2011
San Antonio, Texas, USA

I0002765

Association for
Computing Machinery

SIGMIS CPR 2011

Proceedings of the 2011 ACM SIGMIS

Computer Personnel Research Conference

Sponsored by:
ACM SIGMIS

Supported by:
Baylor Business

Association for
Computing Machinery

Advancing Computing as a Science & Profession

The Association for Computing Machinery
2 Penn Plaza, Suite 701
New York, New York 10121-0701

Notice to Past Authors of ACM-Published Articles
ACM intends to create a complete electronic archive of all articles and/or other material previously published by ACM. If you have written a work that has been previously published by ACM in any journal or conference proceedings prior to 1978, or any SIG Newsletter at any time, and you do NOT want this work to appear in the ACM Digital Library, please inform permissions@acm.org, stating the title of the work, the author(s), and where and when published.

ISBN: 978-1-4503-0666-9

Additional copies may be ordered prepaid from:

ACM Order Department
PO Box 30777
New York, NY 10087-0777, USA

Phone: 1-800-342-6626 (USA and Canada)
+1-212-626-0500 (Global)
Fax: +1-212-944-1318
E-mail: acmhelp@acm.org
Hours of Operation: 8:30 am – 4:30 pm ET

ACM Order Number: 433110

Printed in the USA

Foreword

It is our great pleasure to welcome you to the 49th Annual Computer Personnel Research Conference - *ACM SIGMIS CPR 2011*. For forty-nine years, the conference has presented quality research on the themes of managing the information technology (IT) workforce. This year's theme is "Mind the Gap: Preparing, Recruiting, and Retaining IT Professionals in Today's Evolving Environment."

Today's information-based global society has created a gap between the available supply of IT professionals and the demand for their skills and talents. Subsequently, practitioners and researchers are challenged with addressing this gap through the preparation, recruitment and retention of IT professionals. From an individual perspective, questions remain about the abilities necessary to secure employment in an evolving environment (skills gap). From an educational perspective, programs are needed to increase student enrollments despite dwindling funding and the recent economic crisis (enrollment and funding gaps). From a profession perspective, organizations continue to struggle to manage their talent, provide career development paths and plan for succession as the baby boomers begin to retire (recruitment and retention gaps).

Given these many challenges, the ACM SIGMIS CPR 2011 conference proceedings consider how theory and research can help to elucidate influential factors, envision impacts and outcomes, and address the existing gaps. The papers, panel, tutorial and posters within the proceedings cover topics such as diversity and cultural issues in the attraction and retention of IT professionals, occupational commitment, curriculum issues and trends, and traditional CPR topics such as career development practices of IT professionals and the skills, and abilities required for the coming decade. We hope these proceedings serve as a valuable reference for computer personnel researchers and practitioners.

Putting together *ACM SIGMIS CPR 2011* was made possible by the work of many dedicated individuals. We first thank the authors for providing the content of the program, which continues to showcase exemplar work in the field. We are grateful to the program committee who worked diligently in reviewing papers and providing constructive feedback for authors. In addition, we would like to thank Andreas Eckhardt for organizing this year's doctoral consortium, which provides a glimpse of the exciting research on the horizon. We would also like to thank Indira Guzman for her role as Treasurer, Nita Brooks for publicity, and John Warren for local arrangements. Special thanks go to Lisa Tolles and her team from ACM-Sheridan Proceedings Service for their work in processing the proceedings in a timely manner. We also like to thank the San Antonio Convention & Visitors Bureau and Stuart Dee for the photograph included on the front cover of the proceedings. Finally, we thank our sponsor, ACM SIGMIS, the leadership of Janice Sipior, and our generous supporter Baylor University.

We hope that you will find this program interesting and thought-provoking and that the conference will provide you with a valuable opportunity to share ideas with other researchers and practitioners from institutions around the world.

Deborah J. Armstrong
Florida State University
Conference Co-Chair

Cindy Riemenschneider
Baylor University
Conference Co-Chair

Haiyan Huang
Michigan Technological University
Program Co-Chair

Jeria Quesenberry
Carnegie Mellon University
Program Co-Chair

Table of Contents

Session 6.2: Global Information Systems Development

Session Chair: Mike Gallivan *(Georgia State University)*

Session 7.1: Tutorial Session

Session 7.2: Diversity and Cultural Issues of IT Workforce

Session Chair: Eileen Trauth *(The Pennsylvania State University)*

Author Index

SIGMIS CPR 2011 Conference Organization

General Chairs: Deborah J. Armstrong (*Florida State University, USA*)
Cindy Riemenschneider (*Baylor University, USA*)

Program Chairs: Haiyan Huang (*Michigan Technological University, USA*)
Jeria Quesenberry (*Carnegie Mellon University, USA*)

Conference Treasurer: Indira Guzman de Galvez (*TUI University, USA*)

Doctoral Consortium Chair: Andreas Eckhardt (*University of Frankfurt am Main, Germany*)

Doctoral Consortium Mentors: Monica Adya (*Marquette University, USA*)
Damien Joseph (*Nanyang Technological University, Singapore*)
Norah Power (*University of Limerick, Ireland*)
Eileen Trauth (*The Pennsylvania State University, USA*)
Tim Weitzel (*University of Bamberg, Germany*)

Local Arrangements Chair: John Warren (*University of Texas, San Antonio, USA*)

Publicity Chair: Nita Brooks (*Middle Tennessee State University, USA*)

Program Committee: Monica Adya (*Marquette University, USA*)
M. Das Aundhe (*Louisiana State University, USA*)
Nita Brooks (*Middle Tennessee State University, USA*)
Orin Day (*RTI, USA*)
Jack Downey (*University of Limerick, Ireland*)
Andreas Eckhardt (*Goethe University Frankfurt, Germany*)
Thomas Ferratt (*University of Dayton, USA*)
Indira Guzman de Galvez (*TUI University, USA*)
Tracy Hall (*Brunel University, United Kingdom*)
Jafar Hamra (*University of Sydney, Australia*)
Damien Joseph (*Nanyang Technological University, Singapore*)
Michelle Kaarst-Brown (*Syracuse University, USA*)
Janet Kourik (*Webster University, USA*)
Sven Laumer (*University of Bamberg, Germany*)
Hsun-Ming Lee (*Texas State University, USA*)
Hyung-Koo Lee (*Georgia State University, USA*)
Diane Lending (*James Madison University, USA*)
Christian Maier (*University of Bamberg, Germany*)
Jo Ellen Moore (*Southern Illinois University, USA*)
Allison Morgan (*Howard University, USA*)
Gaetan Mourmant (*Paris Dauphine University, France*)

Program Committee
(continued): Fred Niederman (*Saint Louis University, USA*)
Stig Nordheim (*University of Agder, Norway*)
Lorne Olfman (*Claremont Graduate University, USA*)
Norah Power (*University of Limerick, Ireland*)
Gail Robin (*Baker College Center of Graduate Studies, USA*)
Sureerat Saetang (*University of South Australia, Australia*)
Mark Serva (*University of Delaware, USA*)
Nathan Sikes (*RTI, USA*)
Janice Sipior (*Villanova University, USA*)
Faye Teer (*James Madison University, USA*)
Eileen Trauth (*The Pennsylvania State University, USA*)
Karthikeyan Umapathy (*University of North Florida, USA*)
Irikefe Urhuogo (*Argosy University, USA*)
Faith-Michael Uzoka (*University of Botswana, Botswana*)
Xinwei Wang (*National University of Singapore, Singapore*)
Richard Woolridge (*University of Arkansas at Little Rock, USA*)
Susan Yager (*Southern Illinois University Edwardsville, USA*)

Sponsor:

Supporter: BaylorBusiness

Do Companies Look for Education, Certifications or Experience: A Quantitative Analysis

Gail J. Robin
Baker College Center for Graduate Studies
gail.robin@baker.edu

ABSTRACT
University degrees give a foundation education that can have long reaching application for both personal and professional purposes. However, will a degree lead to an information technology job, in today's competitive market place, for top rated IT company? This study will address education and experience (in years) requirements and whether a professional certification is required for job vacancies in "Information Technology" as advertised by the top eleven firms among the *Computerworlds Best 100 Places to Work in IT 2010*. The findings suggest that in those job vacancy postings less than one percent of the openings required a Masters. Though, bachelor's degrees are required for only 70 percent of the jobs while the remaining 11 percent required a bachelors or equivalent; 3 percent Associates and the final 15 percent did not specify any degree requirements.

Categories and Subject Descriptors
H.4.2 Types of Systems: Decision support (e.g., MIS); K.7.1 THE COMPUTING PROFESSION: Occupations.

General Terms: Human Factors

Keywords: IT education, IT certifications, work experience

1. INTRODUCTION
There is a plethora of both undergraduate and graduate degrees available in various information technology degrees. It is difficult to determine what type of degree program, if any, to pursue for future job considerations in the IT field. Arguably, experience in the field of IT is increasingly important and indicative of current knowledge of applications in part because certification is typically required, whereas a formal bachelors or masters' degree, once done, relies information that rapidly becomes outdated. This may in part explain why enrollment in IT degree programs has gone down while the need for IT professionals continues to rise across industries.

This research is an exploratory quantitative study reporting on whether a select group of companies are looking for a bachelor's degree for job consideration in this field or looking more for experience and certification. There are previous studies that have looked at various and related aspects that will be updated in this current study [1], [16], [21], [22], [27]. This study will examine the job qualifications for IT positions advertised by the "top 11" companies on *Computerworlds* list of the "Best 100 Places to

Work in IT 2010" [10]. This paper will address the current job vacancies of the subject companies for their current open positions. The more that is understood about the degrees and how they relate to the needs of industry the better served the communities of interest will become. The next section will briefly survey some of the educational requirements followed by certifications required for the IT field through an academic search. This paper then addresses the basic job requirements presented in job vacancies in "Information Technology," focusing on the required level of education, required professional certifications, and required years of work.

2. LITERATURE REVIEW
Current Industry Needs/Requirements
A 2009 report stated that those working in the IT field exceed three million workers [5]. IT professionals are needed for embedded positions in most aspects of purchasing, operations and training (9,para 1). Computerworlds' 2010 Salary Survey [11] shows that of the 2,090 manager level respondents; 47 percent indicated that would hire new IT personnel in the coming year. Anticipating top jobs between 2008 and 2018,BLS in December 2009 stated that at the Associates level there would be 235,000 job openings for computer support specialists; a need for 153,000 at the bachelors degree prepared for computer software engineers, systems software; 208,000 network systems and data communications analysts; 218,000 computer software engineers, applications and 223,000 computer systems analysts. At the graduate degree level there was no technology jobs listed in the top ten companies that were technology related.

An average of eight job seekers compete for every open position; and employers can be selective in who they choose for their vacancies [32]. "Chances are you don't possess all the criteria the hiring manager seeks in a candidate. This means you'll have to address your "deficiencies" during the job interview" (p. 10). Though it is possible that you will not get the opportunity to interview with the quantity of applicants; only those notified would know they were in consideration based on their resume.

Information World reported on The State of IT jobs early 2010 starting jobs continue to be Java, .Net and testing; IT admin support to servers, databases etc, web applications' development and help desk or general IT support. The hot jobs for 2010-2012 will include security, collaboration technologies', orchestration and virtualization (servers and storage currently and desktop projected). Some older skills were also identified to be needed in the next two years including ITIL, Six Sigma and Lean-IT management skills; project management, business analytics and business intelligence[14].

A study published by Partnership for Public Service in August 2010 reported on the assessment of governmental job applicants [23]

> Agencies view assessment too narrowly and miss out on good candidates. There is a tendency to think that assessment is confined just to the formal process of measuring applicant competencies. As a Partnership for Public Service result, HR and hiring managers may pay too little attention to other important parts of the process, including ensuring that job requirements are clear, that reference checks are conducted properly, and that they use the probationary period to validate hiring decisions. (Pages i and ii).

The value of an individual within any organization is influenced by various factors to include formal education, certifications and peer respect [15]. "In totality, we find that experienced IT professionals performed better than novices by providing a significantly larger repertoire of responses, taking significantly less time in generating this larger repertoire, and providing response that were of significantly higher quality" [17] , p 53. Many skill sets not only contain the technology skills but also gain more business skills as they become more important[18].

Infoworld.com reports that the IT managers need to grow within the business from the traditional operations, suggesting seven key skills for the new era which include [31]:

1. Balance specialization and cross-functional expertise
2. Become an arbiter of risk
3. Build strong working relationships
4. Embrace analytics
5. Embrace enterprise architecture
6. Move from project management to program management
7. Actively communicate

Education

There is a great deal of literature that deals with the various information technology programs available at all levels of formal education from bachelors to doctorate programs. Many IT professionals routinely state that the degree is not the key to their success, but they needed specific knowledge that that job requires. A bachelor's in a computer-related field usually is required for management positions as reported by Bureau of Labor Statistics [6], para 2)

"There is little empirical evidence to support the value of information systems education and training. While IS training is conducted because it is direct impact on the accretion of skills, the lack of empirical evidence for the value of information systems education limits resource allocation for it." [22] (p. 209).

Bureau of Labor Statistics [7] found that some managers of information systems can obtain these positions with an associates or trade school degrees, providing they have significant experience and continue to obtain skills on the job. A 2000 regional research reported that only 20 percent of IT job listings asked for college degrees, but identified that IT certification were increasing in popularity. Many individuals get into IT from the business side as well as move up though the technical side of the organization [1].

MBA provided the tools necessary to run IT like any other business using the skills gained in planning and execution that employ various managerial methodologies [19]. Demands for IT program graduates require in-depth technical skills; value added skills; and multidisciplinary awareness [24].

Professional Certifications

Professional certifications provide specialized skill sets; there some who feel it is important while others state it is more valued by human resource managers. Certification is coming to an age where it will be required for employability [25].

Employees need to demonstrate specific software or technology knowledge; many times this is demonstrated though professional certifications. "Although not required for most computer and information systems management positions, certification demonstrates an area of expertise, and can increase in applicant's chance of employment. These high-level certifications are often product specific, and are generally administrated by software or hardware companies rather than independent organizations" [5,Para 6].

According to the Global Knowledge and Tech Republic study [7], 12.9 percent of those surveyed received a raise through development of a new skill set or gained certifications. The study also reported that Project Management Professional (PMP) was among the most popular and could result in higher pay for this certification. Increased marketability in the workforce entry if they have a combination of education and IT certifications [2].

There exists a differing view on the importance of certifications between the needs of the hiring managers, who placed a greater efficiency on them, than do the IT professionals [8], [9]. Evaluation of the IT certifications should be addressed in the hiring practice [16]; certification programs can validate a specific skill set [15]. Certifications can also be viewed as a professional development activity to maintain job satisfaction [3],[12]. "For IT, diversity is a asset that has kept the organization fresh, engaged and ready to accomplish the rapid pace of change" [30, para 3]. Additionally the author stated that certifications are self limiting to the period of time received that change occurs too rapidly for long term value to be gained in the workplace environment [30]. Certification importance was reported to be on the decline [26], [28] [16]. Though you can easily find listings for what are the skills or certifications needed for the next six months. 25 certifications were found to increase value, but also states we continue to be in volatile market conditions [13]. This would make it difficult to evaluate the worth of certification actions used in the IT field. There is too much flexibility and fluidity in the IT field to stay within such narrow certification boundaries and limited long range usefulness [30].

Certifications reflect current skills knowledge beyond college degrees [12[, [15], [20]. It is not a question of getting a certification, but which one you should pursue [25]. Approximately 6.5 million people in the U. S. hold a computer certification; that number may exceed 20 million by 2010 [29] [16]. There are many IT teams without any certifications that are much more effective than certified practitioners; some certifications might be a matter of the ability to memorize; thus, limiting their value [26].

Technology changes occur rapidly and it is difficult to keep current with the skills necessary to be effective in a technology field [30]. IT certifications provide specific IT skills which meet some industry needs. Companies seek out professionals with these credentials [1]. A survey completed by mostly Society of Human Resources Managers (SHRM) members who were planning on hiring new IT personnel in the United States; the 240 represent the completed surveys reporting on certification needs. Of the 240 surveyed over 85 percent of the respondents in their study would request at least one certification for their next new IT employee while just over 50 percent would desire at least two IT certifications[16]; Figure One (1) shows some of the most popular in this study.

Certification (n = 240)	Number	Percentage
Microsoft Certified Professional (MCP)	67	27.9 %
Microsoft Certified Administrator (MCSA)	65	27.1%
Microsoft Certified Systems Engineer (MCSE)	51	21.3%
Microsoft Certified Database Administrator (MCDBA)	45	18.7%
Cisco Certified Networking Associate (CCNA)	41	17.1%
Network+	33	13.8%
Cisco Certified Networking Professional (CCNP)	25	10.4%
Oracle Certified Professional Database Administrator (OCP DBA)	23	9.6%
Certified Novell Administrator (CNA)	21	8.8%
Microsoft Certified Systems Developer (MCSD)	20	8.3%

Figure 1: IT Certifications Desired by Hiring Personnel [16,p 77]

The Partnership for Public Services [23] determined that human resource (HR) managers had limited ability to assist managers with their hiring and/or assessment needs. HR professionals value IT certifications more highly than IT professionals, [8].

The HR managers can use the certification documentation as a base line for IT related positions, [27]. It appears to be easy to evaluate certifications by both HR managers and technicians since it represents an easy to identify capability over what might evaluated for experience levels or even education.

3. RESEARCH METHOD

This is a quantitative study conducted using secondary data obtained from the Computer World 2010 Best Places to Work in IT [10]. The top eleven companies' data were **pulled in August, 2010 directionally from the career centers of the company sites to include: USAA, Booz Allen** Hamilton, JM Family Enterprises, Inc, General Mills, Inc, University of Pennsylvania, SAS Institute Inc, Quicken Loans Inc., Verizon Wireless, Securian Financial Group Inc, Salesforce.com Inc., and Kellogg Co.

Once at the career center for these eleven companies, the jobs were requested from a pick list and "information technology" was selected and limited to the United States for the data analysis.

Jobs were obtained by using the career search "Information Systems" for General Mills, Inc., SAS Institute Inc., and Securian Financial Group Inc and "technical" for Verizon Services Inc. Both JM Family Enterprises, Inc, and the University of Pennsylvania were excluded from this study only due to their lack of job postings that met the criterion.

From these sites there were specific fields evaluated for each of the jobs evaluate which include required educational level, professional certifications and years of experience.

4. RESULTS AND DISCUSSION

The information obtained from the corporate web sites were analyzed based on the information they placed in the "academic requirements" for the information technology positions. The total number of jobs evaluated were 403 separated into two different tables one including Booz Allen Hamilton (BAH) and then without N=117. BAH, given their large number of positions and their requirements skew the data; excluded from Table two (2) based on the large amount of jobs in IT from this one employer.

Degree Requirements:

Degree Requirements (including BAH) N=403

Degree Required	Raw Number	Percentage
No Degree Mentioned	61	15
Associates	13	3
Bachelors or Equivalent	43	11
Bachelors Required	**283**	**70**
Masters Required	2	0.5
Masters or Equivalent	1	0.25

Table 1: Degree Requirements

Degree Requirements (excluding BAH) N=117

Degree Required	Raw Number	Percentage
No Degree Mentioned	34	29
Associates	0	0
Bachelors or Equivalent	**42**	**36**
Bachelors Required	40	34
Masters Required	0	0
Masters or Equivalent	1	1

Table 2: Degree Requirements excluding BAH

The findings in Table One (1) suggest that while it is useful to have a master's degree that these companies have basic requirements in current postings only requiring a Masters at less than one percent of the openings. Likewise bachelor's degrees are required for 70 percent of the jobs while the remaining 11 percent required a bachelors or equivalent; 3 percent Associates and the final 15 percent did not specify any degree requirements.

Table Two (2) shows that for the current postings only requiring a Masters at one percent of the openings. Likewise bachelor's degrees are required for only 34 percent of the jobs while the remaining 34 percent required a bachelors or equivalent; 0 percent Associates and the final 29 percent did not specify any degree requirements.

Experience Requirements:

Experience was required in 85 percent of the jobs evaluated (Figure 3) for the evaluation with BAH which is very similar to the results without at a total of 82 percent (Table 4).

Experience Level in Years (including BAH) N= 344 of 403

Years	Number	Percentage
1	9	3
2	42	12
3	73	21
4	57	17
5	**76**	**22**
6	25	7
7	20	6
8	20	6
9	1	0.3
10	16	5
12	1	0.3
13	2	0.6
15	2	0.6

Table 3: Experience in Years N=403

Experience Level in Years (excluding BAH) N= 96 of 117

Years	Number	Percentage
1	1	1
2	10	10
3	16	17
4	**24**	**25**
5	21	22
6	9	9
7	5	5
8	4	4
9	0	0
10	4	4
12	1	1
13	0	0
15	1	1

Table 4: Experience in Years N=117

Certification Requirements:

The final analysis (figure 5) shows that certifications reflect current skills knowledge beyond college [12[, [15], [16], [20], [25]. "Investments in ... certifications are both cost and time-intensive, and school administrators and IT educators need valid data from which to make decisions" [27], p 302-303.

Certification Requirements (both with BAH and without)

Number	Number that require at least one form of certification	Percentage
N=403	58 of 403	14.4
N=117	16 of the 177	13.6

Figure 5: Certification Requirements

The results show that only 14.4 percent and 13.6 percent are designated in these job announcements. This has similar results to the Information ITAA Annual Workforce Development Survey (2004) results show that 14 percent required vender certifications [27].

5. LIMITATIONS

Although the job count totaled over 400 job opening descriptions; this was still a small sample for the type of question that is being addressed. Though many factors were listed in the job announcements, only the required degree, years of experience and if a professional certification was evaluated in this study for these top eleven companies. There are many more requirements and recommended skills from each posting that could be evaluated. Also, this study could be expanded to include the remaining 89 companies identified by Computer World or companies on the Fortune 100 listing.

Additionally, even for the companies evaluated there is more in-depth analysis that could be conducted to include both technology and soft skill requirements. An example would be to determine what types of business skills are necessary.

A question also remains is why individuals seek graduate level technology degrees considering the findings of this study do not support the need; aligning with the BLS (2009) report [9].

6. CONCLUSIONS AND FUTURE WORK

These results have important implications to the future analysis of IT researchers. First it should be the issue of designing IT programs to support the current needs of the industry while finding a way to allow new entrants into the field to gain the critical experience that is demanded in this field today.

Despite the fact this was a limited study of some of the "Top" companies to work for, the results might be indicative of the needs of a larger population of companies that, with rare exception, a graduate degree is not required to the extent that experience is deemed necessary as a basic requirement for employment. Perhaps this suggests that a successful candidate have a broader business knowledge including operational processes, finance, program management; which will need further investigation.

The results suggest that while a bachelor's degree is often necessary for these current job openings there is also a requirement to have a significant amount of experience. Most education programs only offer the foundational elements; so it would be difficult to get a job if you only obtained a bachelors degree; those with experience have greater likelihood of being considered for the job. With rare exception the need for a graduate degree was not found either in data analysis which supports the BLS report (2009). With increased competition for each job, it is more critical than ever for an applicant to provide a resume that matches or exceeds the basic education, experience and certification requirements requested by these industry leaders.

Further work that is significant to determine degree needs is to look at the specific degrees needed for each of the job openings; it this study that was not reported but noted in many cases the job advertisement would list just a bachelors or could be an IT or business degree.

Much work remains both in the quantity of companies looked at for these areas as well as additional details that can be extracted from these original top 11 companies.

REFERENCES

[1] Adelman, C. 2000. A parallel postsecondary universe: the certification system in information technology. *Office of Educational Research and Improvement, U.S. Department of Education.* Retrieved from the ACM Digital Library.

[2] Al-Rawl, A., Lansari, A., & Bouslama, F. 2005. Integrating sun certification objectives in to an IS programming course. *The Journal of Issues in Informing Science and Information Technology.* 2, 247-257.

[3] Barron, T. 1999. Wooing IT workers. *Training and Development, 53*(4), 21-24.

[4] Bureau of Labor Statistics 2009. May 2009 *National Occupational Employment and Wage Estimates: United States* http://www.bls.gov/oes/current/oes_nat.htm#15-0000

[5] Bureau of Labor Statistics 2009. Computer and Information System Managers. http://www.bls.gov/oco/ocos258.htm

[6] Bureau of Labor Statistics 2009. Overview of the 2008-2018 Projections. http://ww.bls.gov/occ/oco2003.htm

[7] Bureau of Labor Statistics 2010. Job openings and labor turnover- August 2010. *News Release, USDL-10-1392.* http://www.bls.gov/news.release/pdf/jolts.pdf

[8] Cegielski, C. G. 2004. Who values technology certifications? *Communication of the ACM.* 47(10). pp.103-105.

[9] Cervero, R. M. 2000. Trends and issues in continuing professional education. *New Directions for Adult Continuing Education, 86,* 3-13.

[10] Computerworld.com 2010. Overall Rankings for 2010. Retrieved from http://www.computerworld.com/spring/bp/2010/1

[11] Computerword.com. 2010. Salary Survey 2010. Retrieved from http://www.computerworld.com/s/article/9174032/Salary_Survey_2010

[12] de Reave, J. 2008. Why you need a certified IT specialist. *Cio.com* http://advice.cio.com/james_de_raeve/why_you_need_a_certified_it_specialist

[13] Foote, D. 2010. 50 hot IT skills on the rise. Retrieved from http://www.computerworld.com/s/article/print/351895/Career_Watch_50_Hot_Skills_on_the_Rise'?

[14] Gruman, G. 2009. The state of IT jobs: 2010. InforWorld.com Retrieved from http://www.infoworld.com/d/adventures-in-it/state-it-jobs-2010-506&current=9&last=8#slideshowTop

[15] Hoyle, T. 2010. Credentials for success: an evolution in the IT industry. T & D July 2010. 48-51.

[16] Hunsinger, D. S. and Smith M. A. 2009. IT certification use by hiring personnel. *Journal of Computer Information Systems.* 71-82.

[17] Joseph, D., Ang, S., Change, R. H. L. and Slaughter, S. A. 2010. Practical intelligence in IT: assessing soft skills of IT professionals. *Communications of the ACM* 53(2), 149-154.

[18] Lee, K & Mirchandani, D. 2009. Analyzing the dynamics of skill sets for the U. S. information systems workforce using latent growth curve modeling. *SIGMIS-CPR* 2009.

[19] MacKay, T. 2007. 10 reasons why you should get an MBA. *CIO.Com* http://www.cio.com/article/122508/10_Reasons_Why_You_Should_Get_an_MBA

[20] Mallard,S. 2008. The value of information technology certifications. Retrieved from http://www.brighthub.com/computing/enterprise-security/articles/18323.aspx

[21] Mason, J. 2003. Certifications – beat 'EM, join 'EM (or lose 'EM). *Journal of Computing Sciences in Colleges.* 18(6) 36-45

[22] Nosek, J. T. 2001) Justifying the business value of information systems education: a report on multi-cultural field experiments. *SIGCPR 2001* pp. 205-211.

[23] Partnership and PDRI. 2010The weakest link: how strengthening assessment leads to better federal hiring. Retrieved from http://ourpublicservice.org/OPS/publications/viewcontentdetails.php?id=148

[24] Peterson, M., Morneau, K. & Saad, A. 2003. Preparing the new information technology professional in Virginia. *Conference on Information Technology Education.* Pages 28-30

[25] Perkins, B. 2010. Certifications are no longer optional. Computerworld. March 8, 2010. Pg 31.

[26] Ragan, S. 2008. Which is most important to IT— certification or experience. The *Tech Herald.* Retrieved from http://www.thetechherald.com/article.php/200837/2000/Which-is-more-important-to-IT-

[27] Randall, M. H. and Zirkle, C. J. 2005. Information technology student based certification formal education settings: who benefits and what is needed. *Journal of Information Technology Education.* Volume 4, 287-306.

[28] Rothberg, D. 2006. Study shows downside of IT certifications. As reported in Hunsinger, D. S. and Smith M. A. 2009. IT certification use by hiring personnel. *Journal of Computer Information Systems.* 71-82.

[29] Tittel, E. 2001 are reported in Hunsinger, D. S. and Smith M. A. 2009. IT certification use by hiring personnel. Journal of Computer Information Systems. 71-82.

[30] Tillman, G. 2010. Why IT certification is a really, really bad idea. Retrieved from computerworld.com

[31] Weston, R. 2010. 7 skills every IT manager needs to survive the 2010's. *InfoWorld.com.* Retrieved from http://www.infoworld.com/d/adventures-in-it/7-skills-every-it-manager-needs-survive-the-2010s-072?page=0,0

[32] Whitcomb 2010. 8 ways a job interview can take a turn for the worse. Retrieved from www.computerworlduk.com as reported by Levinson, M.

Using an e-Book to Teach Technology: Effects on Student Performance

Susan E. Yager
Southern Illinois University Edwardsville
Department of Computer Management and
Information Systems, School of Business
Edwardsville, IL 62026-1106
1-618-650-2917
syager@siue.edu

Zsuzsanna Szabo
Marist College
Department of Education, School of Social
and Behavioral Sciences
Poughkeepsie, NY 12601
1-845-575-3000
zsuzsanna.szabo@marist.edu

ABSTRACT

This research in progress examines the effect of e-book use on students enrolled in a computer literacy course at a medium-sized, Midwestern university by comparing performance results of students using an e-book with students utilizing a traditional print textbook. Results from pre- and post-tests plus survey results are presented, as well as educational implications for teaching and student learning and for training users of technology.

Categories and Subject Descriptors

K.3.1 [**Computers and Education**]: Computer Uses in Education – *Computer-assisted instruction*
K.6.1 [**Management of Computing and Information Systems**]: Project and People Management – *Training*

General Terms

Human Factors, Performance

Keywords

E-Book, Electronic textbook, Student performance, Technology in education

1. INTRODUCTION

In today's information-based society, it is imperative that new generations of college graduates have the necessary technology-based skills to be competitive in the evolving job market of the 21st century. Whether considering college instructional materials or on-the-job training, technology is becoming more important in the education and training of the work force in today's job market. For this reason, many higher education institutions prepare students by offering computer literacy and advanced technology courses. More and more courses are technology-based and, consequently, require students to have computer literacy skills.

When instructors use technology, the two major questions related to teaching and learning focus on: 1) the type of technology used, and 2) the effect of use of technology on the teaching and learning process. With continuing opportunities to use innovative technology in education, and new possibilities of selecting publisher-provided Web-based textbooks, instructors may now choose to adopt electronic textbooks (e-books). But what effect does an e-book have on student learning and performance in a class designed to educate students about appropriate uses of technology? This research in progress examines the effect of e-book use on students enrolled in a computer literacy course at a medium-sized, Midwestern university by comparing performance results of students using an e-book with students utilizing a traditional print textbook.

2. LITERATURE REVIEW

2.1 Use of Technology in Education

Especially in the early 21st century, the focus in education is on critical thinking, higher-order thinking skills, and the development of lifelong learning skills. Koehler, Mishra, and Yahya [12] argue that technology should be used in a purposeful way in order to generate high levels of learning. The authors posit that "effective technology integration for teaching subject matter requires knowledge not just of content, technology and pedagogy, but also of their relationship to each other" [12, p. 746]. They introduced the concept of Technological Pedagogical Content Knowledge (TPCK). The model consists of four components: *Technology (T)* encompasses standard technologies used in educational setting, *Pedagogy (P)* includes the methods of teaching, *Content (C)* concerns the subject matter that is to be taught and learned, and *Knowledge (K)* consists of the information acquired by the student. Koehler, Mishra, and Yahya [12] stress that the TPCK model emphasizes the relationship between content, pedagogy, and technology. Each subject area domain has its own TPCK. The use of technology as pedagogy, or in conjunction with pedagogy, must be employed in a purposeful way in order to promote optimal learning. This idea is widely acknowledged in the literature and stressed by researchers, including Lei and Zhao [14].

Sivin-Kachala and Bialo [18], in a synthesis based on 86 research reviews, presented the effects of use of technology in education. Their analysis posited that the use of technology in teaching demonstrated a significant positive effect on achievement. They also showed that technology had positive effects on student attitudes toward learning and on student self-concept. In addition to effects on students, technology influenced teachers. Teachers employed more student-centered approaches to teaching when using technology, and the student-to-student and student-to-teacher interaction showed an increase when technology was used. The authors acknowledged, "It is not the technology that makes the difference but rather how teachers adapt and apply technology that makes the difference" [18, p. 389].

One component of using technology in education is related to the use of e-books. The electronic format of a textbook substantially reduces the expenses related to paper, printing, distribution, and recycling. In addition, Negroponte [17] draws attention to the availability of information once the information is transformed from atoms to bits; and with that, the entire spectrum of digital enhancements, such as hypertext and multimedia, become available. At the same time, the availability of e-books has an effect on the process of teaching and learning, forcing both instructors and students to alter the educational process.

2.2 Use of e-Books
A large amount of research has been conducted on the use of e-books, especially focusing on comprehension and improvement of literacy in students who used an e-book for learning purposes. Most of the research on e-books concentrates on the benefits to student learning or changes in the instructional process. However, it is possible that students employ different learning and test taking methods when using an e-book as compared to using a traditional printed textbook. Previous research reports conflicting results, covering the entire spectrum from the efficiency of e-books in learning to the lack of, or very small, effect on student learning.

Zucker, Moody, and McKenna [19] conducted a meta-analysis on 27 studies concerning the effect of e-books on literacy skills in the domains of comprehension and decoding for students in K-5th grade. Their results indicated that the effects of e-books on comprehension-related outcomes were small to medium in size. On the other hand, Cavanaugh [7] stressed the advantage of e-books, especially for teaching special needs children as well as exceptional children who need more challenging and richer information than a regular print book could offer. Aside from the effects of e-books on learning, Grimshaw, Dungworth, McKnight, and Morris [8] studied the effect of book medium presentation on students' motivation to read the e-book. Their results indicated that the type of medium did not significantly affect the children's enjoyment of the printed or electronic storybook. Their results also indicated that students obtained significantly higher comprehension scores when they only read the book, as compared to when narration was present (students were listening to narration at the same time they were supposed to read the printed text). Their research demonstrated that just because technology can offer many interesting features, the extra features were not always helpful.

Considerable data suggest that supportive digital text can help students who are experiencing difficulty in reading [1, 2, 3, 4, 5, 6, 9, 10, 11, 15, 16]. Korat, Segal-Drori, and Klien [13] observed the effects of e-books compared to printed books on reading comprehension. Results from their research indicate benefits of using e-books, specifically that using e-books increased literacy levels in low socio-economic status children.

3. RESULTS
In this exploratory research conducted in a computer literacy course, we observed the effect of using an e-book on student performance and potential changes in test taking skills. In three (3) sections of the course, students used an e-book and the teaching pedagogy incorporated expanded online materials. Similar content was covered, with the goal of students acquiring the same knowledge as students in ten (10) sections that used a printed textbook. The topics included were the same; however, the presentation format and detailed content was not.

3.1 The Course
This computer literacy course examines the interaction between information and methods of communication technology. It explores the impact that technology has on individuals and organizations and the effects of current technology infrastructure plus use, duplication, and transmission of information in our world. The course links technology with communication to provide consumers with access to a wealth of data and information, both locally and globally. Students will exhibit proficiency with Microsoft Office 2007 software applications (Word, PowerPoint, and Excel) and demonstrate knowledge of computer technology and components to aide in their understanding of data and information.

3.2 Pre-Test Results
We administered a pre-test to all students enrolled in thirteen (13) sections of the computer literacy course. The test consisted of objective questions covering basic computing concepts and Microsoft Office application skills. Instructor 4 taught using an e-book; all other instructors used a printed textbook. The results (see Table 1 below) were relatively consistent across sections and reinforced faculty assertions that students enrolled in the course did not understand computing basics nor did they possess the skills needed to successfully complete the course requirements.

Instructor	Number of Sections	Number of Students per Instructor	Average Score per Instructor
Instructor 1 (print text)	3	127	49.76
Instructor 2 (print text)	2	87	49.93
Instructor 3 (print text)	5	210	47.49
Instructor 4 (e-book)	3	98	51.37
Total	13	522	49.64

Table 1. Pre-test results by instructor

3.3 Post-Test Results
Prior to the end of the semester, students in all thirteen sections completed a post-test exam with the same questions as the pre-test exam. As usually occurs in a freshman-level course, student attrition and inconsistent attendance reduced the number of students completing the post-test assessment for instructors 1, 2, and 4.

Instructor	Number of Sections	Number of Students per Instructor	Average Score per Instructor
Instructor 1 (print text)	3	84	67.24
Instructor 2 (print text)	2	61	65.61
Instructor 3 (print text)	5	190	73.87
Instructor 4 (e-book)	3	62	66.52
Total	13	397	68.31

Table 2. Post-test Results by Instructor

As shown in Table 2, average scores for students of instructors 1, 2, and 4 are very similar. Students of Instructor 3 achieved a higher average score than the rest. Instructors 1, 2, and 4 administered the post-test during the week prior to final exams as an unannounced test. Instructor 3 chose to use the post-test as the final exam itself. That means that instructor 3's students had prepared for a comprehensive final exam while the other students were unaware that the post-test would be administered until they arrived for class. This situation explains both the higher attendance and higher post-test average scores for instructor 3's students.

A comparison of grade distributions for pre-test, post-test, and final course grades by instructor is presented in Table 3. Data listed in the table represent proportions of each respective grade from the total number of students in all sections of each individual instructor.

% grades	Instructor 1/print			Instructor 2/print			Instructor 3/print			Instructor 4/e-book		
Total number of students	131			87			208			111		
Test type	pre	post	final	pre	post	final	pre	post	final	pre	post	final
A	0.0	2.4	14.5	0.0	0.0	26.4	0.5	5.3	28.4	0.0	0.0	9.9
B	0.0	17.9	38.2	1.1	14.8	33.3	0.0	28.9	28.4	3.3	7.9	30.6
C	2.4	27.4	27.5	6.9	23.0	12.6	2.9	36.8	23.6	2.2	36.5	25.2
D	12.6	52.4	5.3	10.3	32.8	9.2	14.8	0.0	8.7	20.0	31.7	6.3
F	85.0	0.0	8.4	81.6	29.5	2.3	81.9	28.9	9.1	74.4	23.8	9.9
other	0.0	2.4	6.1	0.0	0.0	16.1	0.5	5.3	1.9	0.0	0.0	18.0

Table 3. Grade Distributions by Instructor

Comparing the pre-test, post-test, and final grade results by grade level across instructors, performance by students using the e-book was relatively similar to students using the printed book. The proportion of students who obtained grade of A in the e-book sections was lower than students taught by instructor 2 but comparable with results from instructor 1. As mentioned previously, instructor 3 used the post-test as the final exam. Since students prepared for that exam, A and B grades registered higher post-test proportions for students of instructor 3 than of instructors 1, 2, and 4.

The data in Table 3 allows for a comparison of results between sections and by textbook medium utilized. The performance of students using the e-book was comparable to that of students using the printed book. Since we did not have access to students' overall grade point averages (GPAs) by section, we cannot make any statement related to the knowledge level of students by instructor. For that reason, we can talk only about grades in the course and cannot argue that use of the e-book might have had an effect on overall grade distributions.

3.4 Survey Results

In addition to pre- and post-tests, all students were asked at the end of the semester to complete a survey about their experience in the course. The survey was administered to all sections taught by the four instructors. All students were asked to complete ten questions, and the results were compared across instructors. In addition, students using the e-book were asked to complete an additional 15 questions about their experience using the e-book and online study and training tools.

3.4.1 Results From Survey Across All Sections

Questions gathered student responses about their class attendance, time spent on the course outside of class, time spent reading the text, textbook preference (electronic versus printed), use of lecture slides, note-taking practices, exam preparation strategies, and time spent practicing skills. See Appendix 1 for a recap of response percentages from the survey items presented in this subsection.

Results show that the self-reported *class attendance* of students using the e-book was similar to reports from students using printed books. The students in the e-book sections also reported that they spent comparable study time *outside of class*, and a large majority of students in all sections spent between 1-2 hours on the course outside of class. When asked about their time *reading the textbook*, students using the e-book described comparable time as their counterparts using a printed book;

however, 50-86% of students spent less than one hour per week reading the textbook. Regarding their *textbook preference*, it is interesting to note that students using a printed book thought they would be better off with an e-book, while students using an e-book preferred a printed book.

Students in all sections reported that they used *lecture slides* in the classroom during lecture and in preparation for exams. Student-reported *note taking* behavior indicated that students took notes in class and when preparing for an exam. Of special interest was the distribution of note taking behaviors revealed by students using the e-book, which showed a more uniform note taking behavior across an assortment of activities when compared with their counterparts using the printed book. When *preparing for exams*, most students across all sections read the lecture slides. Students using the e-book also had the opportunity to take self quizzes and practice exams using the provided online tools, which a large majority stated that they did use for exam preparation. However, when asked more specifically if they used the self quizzes and practice exams, students stated that they used them sporadically for only a few (50%) or several (15%) topics. When asked how much time they spent *practicing the skills* required in the course, most students across all sections reported spending 1-2 hours per week.

3.4.2 Results From Survey of e-Book Sections

In addition to the survey items asked of all students, students using the e-book were asked additional questions about accessing the e-book at home, purchase of an optional printed form of the e-book, use of an online study aid, skill practice training, and skill practice exams. See Appendix 2 for a recap of response percentages from the survey items presented in this subsection.

The majority of e-book user students (51%) stated that they were able to *access the e-book at home* with few or no problems, while others could access it but with some difficulties (16%), or were unable to access it from home (14%). Despite their difficulties in accessing the e-book outside of the classroom, only 2% of the students stated that they purchased the *printed form* of the electronic textbook. Despite the fact that some students (22%) did not use or were unaware of the *online study aid*, most of them used it (55%), especially following lecture (21%) or in preparation for an exam (56%). Students who used the tool also stated that they had better performance on the exam because they used it (43%). Even though some students (13%) ignored the *skill practice training*, the majority of those who used it completed a few training practice tests (52%), while others completed several (21%) or most (12%) of the practice training made available. In general, students who used the skill practice training used all its features (observe – 36%, practice – 44%, and apply – 60%). More than half of all students (53%) stated that they completed a few of the **skill practice exams**, and 28% stated that they completed several or most of the skill practice exams.

4. DISCUSSION

Today, education goes beyond the classroom and beyond college into the work force. Colleges teach technology skills to their students, and businesses offer technology training to their employees. However, more research on technology is conducted within colleges, providing information and new ideas to shape on-the-job training practices. Since technology skills are important in today's work environment, colleges and employers offer similar instruction. With advantages of using e-books, including lower cost and smaller carbon footprint, we hope that our results will provide important information to employers who offer technology training courses.

We stress in this project the importance of "walking the walk." If we teach about technology, it is logical – and important – to integrate technology into our teaching practices. Following the TPCK model [12], when students learn about technology skills, the preferred pedagogical methods should also involve technology. In this exploratory study, we introduce content knowledge using e-books and use technology to teach productivity application skills. As can be seen from these results, students using e-books can demonstrate a level of course content knowledge similar to those students using a printed textbook. However, in addition to learning the content, the e-book users also develop skills related to using the e-book and other e-learning methods that accompany the e-book package.

We note that e-book users are not necessarily familiar with all the learning methods pertaining to using an e-book. E-book users can benefit from brief, informal training on use of the e-book and its accompanying learning opportunities. By using the self quizzes and online study tools, students can develop better learning skills while at the same time improving their technology use skills.

The advantage of using e-books is also reflected in more cost-effective education. Printed textbooks are more expensive than e-books, as well as a burden to acquire before and dispose of after a course has been completed. E-books are cheaper, do not require storage before, during or after use, allow for continuous updating of content and organic learning techniques, and may offer additional learning and testing opportunities. This cost effectiveness could be of great interest in organizations where employers target training that produces better marginal benefits. In a world where "green" products, living, and education are desired, the use of e-books – with equal performance effectiveness as printed textbook – can be welcomed.

Based on lessons learned from this exploratory study, we adopted the e-book for all sections of the course, and provided students with training to use all the features of the e-book. It is expected that by combining technology and good pedagogical methods, students will more effectively learn the content and develop better knowledge and technology skills.

5. REFERENCES

[1] Anderson-Inman, L., and Horney, M. 1997. Electronic books for secondary students. *Journal of Adolescent & Adult Literacy* , 40, 6, 486-491.

[2] Anderson-Inman, L., and Horney, M. 1998. Transforming text for at-risk readers. In D. Reinking, L. Labbo, M. Mckenna, and R. Kieffer, *Handbook of literacy and technology: Technological transformations in a post-typographic world* (15-43). Erlbaum, Mahwah, NJ.

[3] Anderson-Inman, L., and Horney, M. April, 1999. *Electronic books: Reading and studying with supportive resources.* Retrieved October 26, 2010 (http://www.readingonline.org/electronic/elec_index.asp?HREF=/electronic/ebook/index.html).

[4] Anderson-Inman, L., Horney, M., Chen, D., and Lewin, L. 1994. Hypertext literacy: Observations from the ElectroText project. *Language Arts* , 71, 4, 37-45.

[5] Boone, R., and Higgins, K. 1993. Hypermedia basal readers: Three years of school-based research. *Journal of Special Education Technology* , 12, 3, 86-106.

[6] Boone, R., Higgins, K., Notari, A., and Stump, C. 1996. Hypermedia prereading lessons: Learner-centered software for kindergarten. *Journal of Computing in Childhood Education* , 7, 1/2, 39-69.

[7] Cavanaugh, T. 2002. EBooks and accomodations: Is this the future of print accomodation? *TEACHING Exceptional Children* , 35, 2, 56-61.

[8] Grinshaw, S., Dungworth, N., McKnight, C., and Morris, A. 2007. Electronic books: Children's reading and comprehension. *British Journal of Educational Technology* , 38, 4, 583-599.

[9] Higgins, K., Boone, R., and Lovitt, T. 1996. Hypertext support for remedial students and students with learning disabilities. *Journal of Learning Disabilities* , 29, 4, 402-412.

[10] Higgins, K., Boone, R., and Lovitt, T. 2002. Adapting challenging textbooks to improve content area learning. In G. Stoner, M. Shinn, and H. Walker, *Interventions for academic and behavior problems (2nd ed.).* National Association of School Psychologists, Silver Spring, MD.

[11] Horney, M., and Anderson-Inman, L. 1995. Hypermedia for readers with hearing impairments: Promoting literacy with electronic text enhancements. In K. Hinchman, D. Leu, and C. Kinzer, *Perspectives on literacy research and practice* (448-458). National Reading Conference, Chicato, IL.

[12] Koehler, M., Mishra, P., and Yahya, K. 2007. Tracing the development of teacher knowledge in a design seminar: Integrating content, pedagogy and technology. *Computers & Education* , 49, 3, 740-762.

[13] Korat, O., Segal-Drori, O., and Klien, P. 2009. Electronic and printed books with and without adult support as sustaining emergent literacy. *Journal of Educational Computing Research* , 41, 4, 453-475.

[14] Lei, J., and Zhao, Y. 2007. Technology uses and student achievement: A longitudinal study. *Computers & Education* , 49, 2, 284-296.

[15] Lenz, B., and Hughes, C. 1990. A word identification strategy for adolescents with learning disabilities. *Journal of Learning Disabilities* , 23, 3, 149-163.

[16] MacArthur, C., and Haynes, J. 1995. Student assistant for learning from text (SALT): A hypermedia reading aid. *Journal of Learning Disabilities* , 28, 3, 150-159.

[17] Negroponte, N. 1995. *Being digital.* New York: Knopf.

[18] Sivin-Kachala, J., and Bialo, E. 1993. *The report on effectiveness of technology in schools 1990-1992.* Software Publishers Association, Washington, D.C..

[19] Zucker, T., Moody, A., and McKenna, M. 2009. The effects of electronic books on pre-kindergarten-to-grade 5 students' literacy and language outcomes: A research synthesis. *Journal of Educational Computing Research* , 40, 1, 47-87.

Question	Specific measure	Instructor/type of textbook			
		1 / print	2 / print	3 /print	4 /e-book
Attendance	Most times	44	40	37	49
frequency	Every class	45	53	60	45
Hours of study	Less 1 h	36	9	20	21
	1-2 h	51	46	45	45
	2-3 h	10	26	26	27
Hours of reading the	Less 1 h	86	47	79	62
textbook	1-2 h	10	35	15	27
	2-3 h	1	9	4	8
Preference of	e-book	44	32	44	32
textbook	Printed	25	29	23	45
	No preference	27	32	25	20
Use of power point	During lecture	87	57	83	62
lectures	Before lecture	18	4	14	6
	After lecture	26	16	32	27
	Exam prep	80	67	73	80
Note taking	In class	55	16	40	18
	Reviewing slides	27	11	19	18
	Reading txt	10	7	3	13
	Always for exam	36	11	27	14
	Sometimes not for exam	7	22	17	22
	Don't take	12	45	22	39
Exam preparation	Read notes	63	14	34	30
strategies	Read text	25	38	39	45
	Read text and notes	18	14	17	12
	Review slides	91	77	85	69
	Self quizzes	-	-	-	43
	Practice exams	-	-	-	61
Practice for learning	Less 1 h	42	21	31	33
content in this course	1-2 h	40	52	47	49
	2-3h	11	21	15	13

*Note: All data are response percentages; only larger proportions are presented in the table

Were you able to access the e-book at home?
Did you buy a print copy of the e-book?
Did you use the StudyMate Class tool to study for Exam 3? Please check all that apply.
When did you review the StudyMate Class games? Please check all that apply.
Do you believe StudyMate Class helped you to study for Exam 3?
Did you complete practice training in SAM 2007?
In the SAM 2007 practice training options, which of the three options did you use? Please check all that apply: Observe, Practice, Apply.
Did you complete the homework assignments (projects) in SAM 2007?

A Proposed Study Examining the Effects of Social Networking Use on Face-to-Face Communication

Mark A. Serva
University of Delaware
Alfred Lerner College of
Business and Economics
Department of Accounting & MIS
Newark, DE 19716
(302) 831-1795
servam@udel.edu

Michelle Barineau
University of Delaware
Alfred Lerner College of
Business and Economics
Department of Accounting & MIS
Newark, DE 19716
barineau@udel.edu

ABSTRACT
Although social networking tools have become pervasive, few studies have examined their potential downsides. In this proposed study, we examine the effects of Facebook on the friendship-making activities of college students. We hypothesize that increased social networking use will reduce the time that students spend face to face with their friends, as well as reduce the social connectedness with their friends. We also examine whether or not how students use social networking tools has a moderating effect on the hypothesized relationships.

Categories and Subject Descriptors
D.3.3 [**Programming Languages**]: Language Contructs and Features – *abstract data types, polymorphism, control structures.* This is just an example, please use the correct category and subject descriptors for your submission. The ACM Computing Classification Scheme: http://www.acm.org/class/1998/

General Terms
Human Factors.

Keywords
Social networking, friendship, social connectedness

1. INTRODUCTION
The social networking movement has taken the virtual world by storm. In July 2009, Facebook had 250 million users. By July 2010, it had doubled in size to 500 million users [1]. Although now among the most popular sites on the Internet, little is known about the effects of this almost addictive use of technology [3].

Previous research involving the trade-off between face-to-face (FTF) interaction and technological substitutes has focused primarily on the use of the Internet in general, without distinctly examining the effects of sites like Facebook that intend to serve as a new medium of online communication [15]. Recent evidence

suggests, however, that social networking use may reduce individuals' social connectedness even more than Internet or email use [3, 14]. Such findings require additional investigation, however, and this research proposes to examine how social networking use may inhibit one's proclivity to interact with others.

This research in progress paper examines the possible effects of social networking sites on the formation and maintenance of personal relationships. We focus our efforts on individuals that are at a junction point in their personal relationships—college freshmen. Because freshmen are transitioning from high school relationships to new relationships in college, we feel that this group may provide special insight into the potentially dysfunctional effects of social networking use. We present a new model that proposes that social networking use is negatively related to FTF interaction time. We take the position that this result is dysfunctional, based on previous findings that determine that humans require regular and rewarding FTF contact [4].

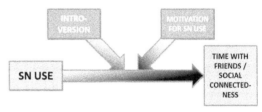

FIGURE 1

2. LITERATURE REVIEW
The model is presented in Figure 1. The model posits that social networking use will negatively affect the amount of time spent face-to-face with friends. The model also posits that two moderators will affect the strength of this relationship. This section discusses the previous research that has been conducted, along with the proposed hypotheses.

In perhaps one of the earliest studies of technology's effect on individuals' need for human contact, a study concluded that television viewing can in fact serve as a replacement for personal socialization [16]. More recently, Internet use has also been found to serve as a replacement for personal socialization. One recent study found that 58% of American adults reported that computers led them to spend less time with friends and family [9].

Facebook and other social networking sites may provide an even greater lure away from FTF interaction [10]. Unlike the web, Facebook's raison d'etre is creating a social community that encourages its users to interact with one another in an online setting. Although this functionality would seem to provide an adequate substitute for FTF interaction, previous theorists have proposed otherwise. Previous studies have found, for example, that humans not only desire FTF interaction, they also need FTF interaction and receive physiological benefits as a result [4]. No study has yet to be conducted, however, to examine how Facebook interaction affects actual FTF communication.

The above studies and arguments suggest that technology has been used as a surrogate for FTF human interaction. The results indicate that social networking has the potential to negatively impact the formation and maintenance of FTF interactions. Based on the above arguments, we hypothesize:

H1a: The more individuals use social networking for personal connection, the less time they will spend interacting FTF with their friends.

H1b: The more individuals use social networking for personal connection, the less they will feel socially connected with their friends.

Another factor that requires clarification is individuals' motivation for using social networking. Social networking sites such as Facebook provide a variety of capabilities. In a preliminary study, for example, one article [6] noted that Facebook is used for:

- *Keeping in touch*—contacting people who are away from home
- *Social surveillance*—passively checking out people; lurking
- *Reacquiring lost contacts*—reconnecting with people
- *Interactive communication*—chatting, poking, writing on walls, gaming
- *Photographs*—posting pictures, tagging pictures, sharing pictures
- *Design-related work*—changing privacy settings, changing defaults
- *Perpetual contact*—Updating one's status, communicating what one is doing now
- *Making new contacts*—Joining groups, finding new friends, talking to singles

We note that some of the above capabilities may or may not be used solely for connecting with others. As an example, the purpose behind posting photographs may be to connect with others, but it may also be to use the space as a storage location. In some cases, Facebook use may actually be *asocial*. The U.S. Justice Department recently admitted that it uses Facebook extensively to not only check up on crime suspects, but also to check up on suspects' friends and family [11]. Other reports have found that people create fake social networking accounts for the sole purpose of engaging in online bullying and fraud [11].

Because the purpose behind one's social networking use is important for understanding its effects, we hypothesize the following:

H2a: The relationship between social media use and time spent in FTF relationships will be stronger (i.e., more negative) for people who use social networking primarily to connect with other people.

H2b: The relationship between social media use and social connectedness will be stronger (i.e., more negative) for people who use social networking primarily to connect with other people.

Although previous research has examined technology's effect on FTF communication and social connectedness [13] little research has accounted for the importance of considering personality traits. In the Five-Factor Model (FFM), the extroversion-introversion dimension is characterized by levels of anxiety and volatility [2, 12], with extroverts having lower levels and introverts having higher levels of these two factors. Using social networking, introverts can immediately find others with similar interests, form relationships, and maintain those relationships all without physically interacting with others. People who are high in introversion, therefore, should find the detachment that is possible using computer mediated communication comforting, since the detachment allows for more time to consider a response and the technology shields them from the rich interaction required of FTF communication. Thus, the detachment provided by social networking sites should appeal to introverts [15].

But the sense of detachment that is intrinsic with social networking may have a downside. Previous research has determined that relationships formed and maintained using SNS are different from relationships formed through traditional FTF interaction [5]. Because SNS relationships tend to leverage the detachment that is possible over the Internet, SNS relationships are often characterized by more openness and disclosure of personal information than FTF relationships [17]. Other research has confirmed the apparent candidness of SNS-based relationships, finding that people are more likely to ask sensitive questions (e.g., one's sexual orientation) over SNS than in FTF relationships [17].

Although SNS-based relationship can allow for greater openness, this openness may inhibit the ability of introverts to form new relationships or even maintain existing relationships within the real world. When interacting face-to-face, introverts may find that the security and detachment that they found online cannot be duplicated in a FTF interaction. Introverts may therefore be more likely to increasingly rely on social networking for their relationships—even preferring them to FTF interactions. This dependence may continue to impede their ability to develop the necessary skills to maintain strong FTF relationships (e.g., failing to understand subtle verbal cues and body language). Hence, social media use for introverts may become a crutch, where they become more reliant on social media at the expense of FTF relationships. We therefore hypothesize:

H3a: The relationship between social media use and time spent in FTF relationships will be stronger (i.e., more negative) for people high in introversion than people high in extroversion.

H3b: The relationship between social media use and social connectedness will be stronger (i.e., more negative) for people high in introversion than people high in extroversion.

3. PROPOSED RESEARCH DESIGN

Data will be collected using a survey methodology. Although the questions have been omitted because of space concerns, the researchers will largely rely on existing scales for motivation for social networking use [6], introversion [7], and social connectedness [8]. Amount of social networking use will be collected using absolute time (in minutes), and percentage of time (relative to FTF interaction). Researchers will also control for gender and age.

4. CONCLUSION

The proposed study will examine the possible negative effects related to the social phenomenon of social networking. Previous research has shown that humans need the physiological benefits from personal interaction that online communication cannot provide [4]. This FTF interaction and its resulting benefits would play a vital role in the smooth transition for students graduating from high school into collegiate life. Therefore, the freshmen student sample in this study would be extremely vulnerable to the disadvantages created by a seeming addiction to social media that we expect limits their amount of essential FTF interaction.

5. REFERENCES

[1] *Facebook Membership Hits 500 Million Mark*. [website] [cited 2010 November 8]; Available from: http://www.physorg.com/news198941741.html.

[2] Bradshaw, S. D. Impression Management and the Neo Five Factor Inventory: Cause for Concern? *Psychological Reports*, (80) 1997, pp. 832-834.

[3] Cohen, E. *Five Clues That You Are Addicted to Facebook*. [website] 2009 [cited 2010 November 10]; Available from: http://articles.cnn.com/2009-04-23/health/ep.facebook.addict_1_facebook-page-facebook-world-social-networking?_s=PM:HEALTH.

[4] Hallowell, E. The Human Moment at Work. *Harvard Business Review*, January-February 1999, pp. 58-66.

[5] Jacko, A. S. a. J. A., ed. *The Human-Computer Interaction Handbook: Fundamentals, Evolving Technologies, and Emerging Applications*. 2 ed. 2008, CRC Press.

[6] Joinson, A. N., *'Looking at', 'Looking up' or 'Keeping up with' People? Motives and Uses of Facebook*, in *Conference on Human Factors in Computing Systems* 2008, ACM Press: Florence, Italy. p. 1027-1036.

[7] McCrae, R. The Five-Factor Model: Issues and Applications. *Journal of Personality*, (60:2) 1992.

[8] Milyavskaya, M., Reoch, J., & Koestner, R. Seeking Social Connectedness: Interdependent Self-Construal and Impression Formation Using Photographic Cues of Social Connectedness. *The Journal of Social Psychology*, (150:6) 2010, pp. 689-702.

[9] National Public Radio, K. F. F. a. K. S. o. G. *Survey Shows Widespread Enthusiasm for High Technology*. 2000 November 7, 2010]; Available from: http://www.npr.org/programs/specials/poll/technology/.

[10] Nie, N. H. Sociability, Interpersonal Relations, and the Internet: Reconciling Conflicting Findings. *American Behavior Scientist*, (45) 2001, pp. 420-430.

[11] Parrish, K. *Justice Department Doc Reveals Facebook Lurking*. 2010 November 8, 2010]; Available from: http://www.tomsguide.com/us/Justice-Department-Facebook-MySpace-Police,news-6155.html.

[12] Pervin, L. A., *Personality: Theory and Research*. 5 ed1989, New York: Wiley.

[13] Peter, V. a. Social Consequences of the Internet for Adolescents: A Decade of Research. *Current Directions in Psychological Science*, (18:1 2009, pp. 1-5.

[14] Roman, D. Internet Addiction: It's Spreading, but Is It Real? *Communications of the ACM*. (52:11), November 2009, pp. 12.

[15] Ross, C. Personality and Motivations Associated with Facebook Use. *Computers in Human Behavior*, 25 2009, pp. 578-586.

[16] Steiner, G. A. The People Look at Television: A Study of Audience Attitudes 1963.

[17] Tidwell, L. C. W., J.B. Computer-Mediated Communication Effects on Disclosure, Impressions, and Interpersonal Evaluations: Getting to Know One Another a Bit at a Time. *Human Communication Research*, 28 2002, pp. 317-348.

"In Times of Stress, Be Bold and Valiant": A Preliminary Exploration of the Psychosocial and Physiological Measures of Stress and Suggestions for Future MIS Research

Mark Serva	John "Skip" Benamati	Jon Blue	Jack Baroudi
University of Delaware	Miami University	University of Delaware	University of Delaware
Alfred Lerner College of Business and Economics	Farmer School of Business	Alfred Lerner College of Business and Economics	Alfred Lerner College of Business and Economics
Dept of Acct & MIS	Dept of Decision Sciences/MIS	Dept of Acct & MIS	Dept of Acct & MIS
Newark, DE 19716	Oxford, OH 45056	Newark, DE 19716	Newark, DE 19716
(302) 831-1795	(513) 529-4835	(302) 831-6002	(302) 831-6926
servam@lerner.udel.edu	benamajh@muohio.edu	jonblue@udel.edu	baroudi@lerner.udel.edu

ABSTRACT

Stress is a fact of life. Previous MIS research has examined stress, but has focused on the psychosocial aspects of stress, which are usually measures using self-reported metrics. This preliminary study examines the possible contrast between psychosocial and physiological stress—that is, the body's autonomic reaction to a potential threat. The study also examines the effectiveness of the Trier Social Stress Test (TSST), a protocol designed to induce stress in social situations. Using a sample of thirty-two students, the results indicate that the TSST protocol is an effectiveness mechanism for inducing both psychosocial and physiological stress. The results also indicate that psychosocial and physiological stress are indeed different metrics. The study concludes with recommendations for future MIS researchers to build on these findings.

Categories and Subject Descriptors:

K.6 .0 [MANAGEMENT OF COMPUTING AND INFORMATION SYSTEMS]; General

General Terms

Human Factors

Keywords

stress, physiological stress, biometrics, psychosocial stress

1. INTRODUCTION

"In times of stress, be bold and valiant."
  –Horace (65BC – 8BC), Roman lyricist and poet

"Stress is basically a disconnection from the earth, a forgetting of the breath. Stress is an ignorant state. It believes that everything is an emergency. Nothing is that important. Just lie down."
  –Natalie Goldberg (1948-), author

Stress is a fact of life. Everyone—regardless of their age, location, or career—experiences stress as a natural course of getting through one's day. In common usage, however, the term "stress" is imprecise. Implicit in the above quotes is the differentiation between the *physiological* and the *psychosocial* manifestations of stress. The quotes all reflect both an inner, physiological aspect to stress (how our physical body reacts when threatened) as well as an outer, psychosocial aspect to stress (how we perceive and subsequently choose to respond to that reaction). The quotes also illustrate the differences between how individuals perceive and manifest their stress. Some become "bold and valiant," and some choose to do nothing.

These different psychosocial responses to physiological stress should be a concern for MIS stress researchers. Stress among MIS professionals is common in systems development efforts as end dates loom and pressure of management and end users becomes more salient. MIS research has almost exclusively focused on the outer or psychosocial aspect of stress, but physiological stress and its implications have generated significant research outside of the MIS discipline [5, 10, 21]. Physiologically, the term "stress" refers to the human body's autonomic reaction that results from exposure to a hostile environment. The body reacts by increasing one's pulse, respiratory rates, adrenaline production, and blood pressure. Occasional exposure to stress typically results in minor symptoms (e.g., loss of appetite, sleeplessness), but persistent exposure can result in more serious consequences (substance abuse, depression, and even stroke or heart attack).

Clearly, therefore, both the psychosocial and physiological manifestations of stress have implications for MIS workers' effectiveness in their jobs. We contend that understanding the implications of physiological stress is especially important within the MIS discipline, given the MIS discipline's overreliance on the psychosocial approach to studying stress and the prevalence of stress in MIS jobs (e.g., end user support and systems development) [20]. The guiding research questions are:

- Can psychosocial and physiological stress effectively be induced?
- Do psychosocial (i.e., self-reported) measures of stress mirror the body's physiological reaction to stress?

2. LITERATURE REVIEW

Exploring the duality of stress is an important direction, given the important role that stress plays in MIS careers. Recent studies in other disciplines have acknowledged the differences between the psychosocial and physiological perspectives, and have found empirical support for each measure's unique theoretical role [10]. MIS research has also called for more attention to the effects stress has on MIS worker productivity [24].

2.1 The Psychometric Approach to Measuring Stress

Although most MIS studies have focused solely on the psychosocial aspect of stress [1, 22], some have conflated the psychometric and physiological aspects of stress, defining stress as "a *psychophysiological* response which deviates from a state of equilibrium" [emphasis added] [25: 29]. Although studies in other disciplines have recognized the importance of considering an individual's physiological response in their definition of stress [24], no MIS studies have actually empirically studied its effects.

Workers experience stress when the demands of their workplace exceed their capacity to meet them [20]. Previous MIS research has found, for example, that worker overload (a construct that incorporates aspects of stress) reduces one's tendency to innovate with IT [1]. Other MIS studies have identified workplace stressors, which are triggers that increase MIS employee stress [25]. Stressors that have been found to contribute to psychosocial stress include role ambiguity, role conflict, lack of feedback, keeping up with rapid technological change, and being responsible for other people [25].

Recent studies have focused on the psychosocial stress that results from the use of information and communication technologies (ICT), referred to as "technostress" [20, 22]. Technostress researchers posit that although ICT promises to make lives easier, it also has a considerable downside [27]. MIS workers increasingly find that they are expected to be "on the clock" beyond traditional work hours. ICT also increases opportunities for the clandestine monitoring of worker activities and raises the expectations of increased multitasking and worker productivity [20]. ICT also acts as a lifeline to critical data, other workers, and one's family. When ICT fails to operate as expected (which is still a too common occurrence), heightened feelings of frustration, helplessness, and stress can be considerable [20].

Psychosocial stress measures in MIS research are typically self-reported and collected using a survey instrument methodology (e.g., [1, 22, 25]). Self-reported measures have received increased scrutiny for potential bias [6, 11, 18]. Previous research has found, for example, that assessing one's stress level requires an amalgamation of one's psychological, sociological, contextual, and experiential situations [9, 14], which is a difficult and error-prone process. Environmental factors can also affect responses. Negative affectivity bias, for example, results from being exposed to negative environmental factors (e.g., lost your car keys, didn't sleep well, had an argument with a co-worker), which can significantly skew survey responses [3].

Although self-reported measures have their problems, they remain a valid perspective in understanding how perceived stress affects MIS workers. Indeed, the goal of using self-reported measures is to understand an individual's perceptions, which—in understanding the implications of stress—may be more important than one's autonomic physiological reaction. This paper posits, however, that MIS' sole focus on self-report measures has hampered the discipline's broader understanding of how stress affects MIS workers and what can be done to mitigate its effects.

Self-report measures may, for example, perform differently than physiological measures when examined within the context of causal models.

2.2 Physiological Measures of Stress

The measurement of physiological stress is fairly common in disciplines such as sociology and psychology, but we have found no use of these measures in MIS research. Hydrocortisone (more commonly called "cortisol") is produced in the adrenal gland when the body is exposed to distress, helplessness, or uncertainty [16]. The most common approach for collecting a physiological metric of stress is artificially exposing subjects to a hostile environment and then collecting individuals' cortisol levels by collecting saliva with a cotton swab. The swabs are then analyzed by a qualified lab. Because the human body generates cortisol only under high stress conditions, the physiological measurement of stress usually requires an experimental research design [4].

The most common approach for inducing stress is to use the Trier Social Stress Test (TSST) [4, 13]. Although the original TSST used only one subject at a time, the protocol has been adopted for use by two subjects simultaneously [4]. TSST first asks subjects to deliver a five minute presentation to a panel of "experts." The protocol recommends that the panel consists of one male and one female to mitigate possible gender effects [13]. The presentation topic is typically persuasive, for example, to convince the panel why the presenter should be hired for a job. To increase student self-awareness, subjects are told that the panel members will be watching them carefully, since the experts have been trained in reading body language and facial expressions.

During the persuasive speech, if the subject falters before the five minute time limit, an expert tells the subject that he or she has more time and asks them to continue. If the subject falters again, the expert panelists stare at the subject for twenty seconds without comment. If the subject falters yet again, he or she is then asked a generic question (e.g., "What characteristics would make you a valued employee?"). After exactly five minutes, the subject is cut off and not allowed to continue. After completing the speech, the subject is told he or she will be given a test of "mental acuity." The subject is asked to start with a high number and count rapidly backward by 13 for five minutes. Whenever an error is made, the subject is told to stop and start over. Subjects are videotaped throughout the protocol, and the camera is positioned very close to the participants to make the recording more salient [13].

Previous research has found that the TSST protocol is an effective method for instilling psychosocial stress [13], but the characteristics of the task suggests it will also be effective in inducing psychological stress. The presence of the video camera, public speaking requirement, and demonstration of math ability suggests that the participants will perceive a hostile environment. Such a perception should trigger their body's autonomic system, supporting the higher levels of physiological stress and the generation of cortisol. Although the protocol is typically used to measure physiological stress, it will also likely be effective in generating psychosocial stress. Given the social pressure to do well in front of a panel of experts, subjects should perceive higher levels of stress. This suggests that exposure to the protocol will result in higher levels of psychosocial stress as well as physiological stress. We therefore hypothesize:

H1: Psychosocial and physiological stress levels will be higher after the protocol than before the protocol.

2.3 Psychometric versus Physiological Measures of Stress

Although the question remains open regarding whether psychosocial and physiological stress reflect the same construct, differences between the two constructs have been found [10]. These differences may be attributable to methodological issues, however. As an example, studies have been fairly inconsistent in the timing of cortisol collection. To ensure that the same level of subject arousal is being tracked, the time period between administration of the swab and the collection of psychometrics is critical. The consensus is that cortisol levels manifest themselves in saliva fifteen to twenty-five minutes after exposure to the stress trigger [8, 12].

Another concern is the time of day that the cortisol is collected. Cortisol has a diurnal pattern [7] with levels varying over the course of a day. Therefore, the time period of the data collection must be held constant as much as possible across the sample [5]. The salience of the stress trigger may also vary across studies. Previous studies indicate that the trigger must be intense to trigger a significant increase in subjects' cortisol levels [23]. A number of external factors can also inhibit or enhance the production of cortisol. These factors include the use of oral contraceptives, alcohol, and prescription drugs [21]. Finally, studies have also varied in their care to reduce initial stress levels to an effective baseline. Subjects who have recently been exposed to an external stressful situation (e.g., missing the bus, arguing with a friend, disputing a test score with a teacher) may have an artificially enhanced baseline measure, which will reduce the chances that a stress manipulation will register a significant effect.

Beyond methodological concerns, there is some support for concluding that psychosocial and physiological stress actually measure different theoretical constructs. Previous studies have also found that while chronic exposure to workplace stressors can never be completely resolved, it can be psychologically managed [2, 17]. Hence, individuals who experience chronic stress may develop a psychological tolerance to its effects. In contrast, the body's physiological reaction to a hostile environment is autonomic—suggesting the individual's physiological response cannot be mitigated as easily as one's psychosocial response [7]. These differences suggest that an individual's reaction to psychosocial stress and physiological stress may differ.

Social desirability response bias [15] reflects subjects' tendency to respond how they *want* to be perceived, instead of how they *actually feel*. In a study of teenagers, subjects who scored high on social desirability [15] also reported lower levels of psychological distress [15], suggesting that a desire to be accepted affects one's openness regarding stress perceptions. Social desirability bias may be exacerbated when the expectations of peers is especially salient. Similar to the injured football player who refuses to exit the game because his teammates tell him to "Shake it off," MIS workers may feel pressure to "put on a positive face," even as they deal with helplessness and uncertainty on the job: "When an individual is commanded by an organization to reveal his innermost feelings, he has a duty to himself to give answers that serve his self-interest..." [26: 179].

Given these arguments, we hypothesize:

H2: Psychometric measures and physiological measures of stress will reflect different theoretical constructs.

3. RESEARCH METHODS

Students were recruited the week before the actual study. Students were told that they would be participating in a study that examined stress and that they would be paid $20 for their participation. No class credit was given and none of the students had ever had any of the researchers for a class. In all, 32 students participated in the study.[1] Students ranged in age from eighteen to twenty-seven years old. The average age was twenty. Five students were freshmen; five students were graduate students; one student was a junior; 3 students were seniors; and eighteen students were sophomores. Eleven out of thirty-two participants were female; the remainder were male (n=21). Because we solicited participants from the student body, we had no control over the gender makeup of the sample.

A number of steps were taken to control for potential bias in the cortisol collection procedure. All data were collected between 1:00pm and 4:00pm to control for diurnal effects [7]. Because alcohol consumption, prescription medications, and allergy medications can affect the validity of the physiological measures, students were asked upon enrollment to avoid these factors on the day of the study. Upon arrival, students were asked if they had consumed or taken any of the above within the last twelve hours. Oral contraceptives can also affect cortisol and testosterone levels, so students were also asked if they were using oral contraceptives (we note this restriction reduced the number of females who participated in the study). Students who confirmed consumption of any of the above items were paid and excused from further participation.

After admission to the study, additional steps were taken. Because students had a $20 incentive to lie (they might initially fear they would not be paid if they answered in the positive), after completion of the study and after being paid for their participation, students were again given the above questions and an envelope in which to seal their answers. Students were told the researchers would not review their answers until data analysis began. Students were also informed of the importance of answering the question honestly, because incorrect answers could affect the study's results. Students' answers for this final survey were all consistent with their initial answers.

For the physiological measures, researchers administered swabs at the following time periods: ten minutes after arrival (T1: 0:00); after an additional ten minute relaxation period (T2: +10:00); after a 5 minute preparation period and immediately before the TSST protocol (T3: +15:00); immediately after the TSST protocol (T4: +35:00); five minutes after the TSST protocol (T5: +40:00); and after a final 15 minute relaxation period (T6: +55:00).

For the psychometric measures, researchers administered surveys at T2 and at T5. These were determined to be key time periods

---

[1] Although n=32 can be considered a relatively small sample, we note that the costs associated with collecting the data were considerable. The cost of analyzing cortisol swabs is expensive ($13 per swab), and we collected swabs at six different time periods for each subject. We also paid each student $20, whether or not they passed our initial screening criteria. The total cost was therefore approximately $100 per student.

for understanding how psychometric responses differ when exposed the stressful situations. After students arrived, they were escorted into a small room with a table that contained reading material. After ten minutes (T2), the first survey was administered. This process was chosen for a number of reasons. Surveys were not administered upon student's arrival because the students may have been subject to external factors (e.g., arrived late, left a stressful class) which could increase the error level in the baseline stress measure. Researchers believed that collecting the data after a ten minute cool down period would establish a more consistent (i.e., less error-prone) baseline. The second survey was administered shortly after students completed the stress protocol (at T5), so that the differential effect of stress could best be examined. Because previous research suggests a fifteen to twenty-five minute delay before the cortisol appears in the body, the physiological cortisol readings from T3 and T6 were used.

3.1 The Trier Social Stress Test (TSST)

Researchers largely followed the TSST procedure outlined earlier in the paper, but adapted it slightly to achieve their research goals. We used the adaption of the TSST protocol which uses two students per manipulation instead of one [4]. At the start, each student first gave a 5 minute verbal presentation on why he or she deserved to be hired for a fictitious job. After both completed the presentation, students were then told to start counting backward by 13 from a very high number and to proceed as quickly as possible. Responses alternated between the two students. If a mistake was made, students were harshly told to stop and start over.

In addition, two different approaches were used to administer the protocol. In one group, subjects were subjected to the traditional TSST protocol—that is, they participated in a face-to-face interaction (FTF). In another group (i.e., computer mediation or CMC), subjects were alone in the room and interacted with the expert panel virtually—that is, through a computer monitor that used a video conferencing tool. A large 26 inch monitor was used to closely simulate an actual conference as best as possible. Students were assigned to the FTF or CMC group at random. Out of the n=32 participants, thirteen were assigned to the CMC group; Nineteen were assigned to the FTF group. To test for possible effects from the CMC/FTF conditions, we conducted a preliminary repeated measures ANOVA to check for possible group effects from the technology condition. Using cortisol levels from T3 and T6, no significant differences for the technology treatment were found (p=0.31). A similar analysis using the psychometric constructs from T2 and T5 also found no differences (p=0.63). The data were therefore pooled, and subsequent analyses will omit any further consideration of technology factors.

3.2 Measures

We measured stress using two different methods. The psychosocial constructs were measured using a psychometric scale consisting of one Likert scale item (T2: "I expect to experience a high amount of stress during the task"; T5: "I experienced a high amount of stress during the task) and three sliding scale items [19] (e.g., "How much tension do you feel?", etc.). For clarity, T2 stress levels will be referred to as "baseline self-reported stress"; T5 stress levels will be referred to as "treatment self-reported stress." Sliding scale questions are similar to Likert scales, but respondents instead place an "X" on a line to indicate their response. All psychometric questions are available

from the lead author. The physiological measures were collected using saliva swabs to gauge cortisol levels, which is the physiological marker of stress. To decrease the chances of error, each swab was assayed twice by the lab. The cortisol values that were used are the average of the two assay runs. None of the differences between the two runs for each swab exceeded the lab's guidelines for error tolerances, providing evidence of analysis reliability.

To confirm construct and discriminant validity for the psychometric measures, a factor analysis for the first survey collection was conducted. All measures were first standardized to a mean of zero and a standard deviation of 1 to control for scaling effects. The four psychometric and cortisol level were entered into a factor analysis. We retained factors using eigenvalues that were greater than 1.0. Varimax rotation was used to facilitate interpretation of the resulting two factors. The resulting analysis clearly indicates that the psychometric scores and the physiological score load on separate factors (see Table 1a). The Cronbach's alpha levels for the four psychometric stress questions (0.82) exceeded accepted levels of reliability. A factor analysis on the second survey results and cortisol level confirmed that the cortisol and psychometric scores load on differ factors (Table 1b). Cronbach's alpha levels for the psychometric scores were again acceptable (0.89). Given the results of the factor analysis and acceptable reliability levels, constructs for the stress measures were created by taking the mean of the four psychometric indicators.

Table 1: Factor Analysis

Table 1a: First Survey Factor Analysis

	Factor	
	1	2
CORTISOL	-.095	.919
STRESS1	.644	.369
STRESS2	.882	.033
STRESS3	.818	-.156
STRESS4	.859	-.320

Table 1b: Second Survey Factor Analysis

	Factor	
	1	2
CORTISOL	.043	.972
STRESS1	.620	.332
STRESS2	.944	.141
STRESS3	.957	-.107
STRESS4	.968	.055

4. RESULTS

Hypothesis 1 predicts that the Trier Stress Test will instill significant levels of stress. As stated in the data collection procedure section, we collected cortisol swabs at six different time periods. As mentioned earlier, cortisol manifests itself in the body only after a fifteen to twenty-five minute delay. For the purposes of examining our ability to instill stress, therefore, only two time periods are relevant: 1) The T3 cortisol measure reflects the subjects' baseline physiological stress level (i.e., fifteen minutes after their arrival), and 2). The T6 cortisol measure reflects the subject's stress levels twenty minutes after completing the Trier protocol. If successful, the stress levels for T6 should be significantly higher than the stress levels for T3. For clarity, these two periods will be referred to as the "baseline cortisol" and "treatment cortisol" levels.

To test H1, we conducted a pairwise t-test on the physiological measures and psychometric constructs. The pairwise difference between the average values for baseline cortisol (0.22) and for treatment cortisol (0.33) was 0.11 (p=0.002), indicating that cortisol levels significantly rose. For the psychometric values, the difference between treatment self-reported stress (3.81) and baseline self-reported stress (2.80) was also highly significant (p=0.004). Hypothesis 1 is therefore corroborated.

To analyze H2, we examined the correlations between the baseline self-reported and treatment self-reported constructs and the baseline and treatment cortisol measures. The purpose was to determine the amount of agreement between the two baseline and the two treatment measures of stress. The baseline self-reported stress measure correlation with the baseline cortisol level was -0.13 (p=0.75). For the post stress inducement measures, the correlation of treatment self-reported stress measure with the treatment cortisol level was 0.09 (p=0.32). These low levels contrast with the within-correlation values between the baseline and treatment values for cortisol (0.66; p<0.001) and the baseline and treatment values for the psychometrics (0.53; p<0.001), indicating that each metric is consistent across time. Both the earlier factor analysis and the correlation results support the prediction that the psychometric and physiological measures reflect different theoretical constructs.

5. DISCUSSION

The results of this preliminary investigation indicate that the TSST protocol can effectively induce stress in a controlled experimental environment when implemented through both face-to-face (FTF) and computer mediated communication (CMC). The results also indicate that psychosocial stress and physiological stress reflect different theoretical constructs.

Regarding the differences between the stress results, previous research has found that the convergence between the two measures has been inconsistent at best [10]. In one meta-analysis that examined fourteen studies that included psychosocial and physiological stress measures, two studies reported negative correlations; only four studies reported a positive correlation; and eight reported no correlation [10]. This study corroborates the latter findings, and provides a baseline for MIS researchers to examine the different roles each construct plays in the development of a broader theory of stress.

Previous research has found that external factors may have contributed to the lack of consistency between the psychosocial and physiological measures of stress. We took extensive measures to control for bias, however, so that we could provide a standard for future researchers to build on. The steps included:

- To control for the diurnal nature of cortisol, data were only collected between 1:00pm and 4:00pm.
- We took extensive steps to ensure that participants had not taken oral contraceptives, alcohol, and prescription medication—all of which have been found to affect subjects' cortisol levels.
- To elicit a strong stress response, we used the TSST protocol, which has been previously found to be effective in producing a cortisol reaction. Our results corroborated this finding.
- We incorporated the fifteen to twenty-five minute cortisol delay in our analysis by relating the T2 and T5 to the T3 and T6 physiological data.
- We took steps to establish an effective baseline stress level by allowing subjects to cool down for ten minutes before collecting any psychometric or physiological data.

We encourage other researchers to explore the implications of the sources of bias so that in the future the efficacy of cortisol measurement can continue to be improved.

5.1 Limitations and Future Research

Because of the significant costs involved when collecting cortisol measures, our sample size (n=32) was fairly low. The sample size may have reduced our power and possibly contributed to our insignificant results. We note, however, that even in the face of a much larger sample (and achievement of statistical significance), the magnitude of the determined correlations (0.09) was still extremely low. One was even negative (-0.13), when a positive correlation was expected. These levels would never be practically significant, nor pass even the most basic tests for measurement reliability and validity.

The lack of difference between experimental groups where stress was induced virtually (CMC) and face-to-face (FTF) could be attributed to the size of our sample. It is possible that physiological stress may be influenced by other factors such as personality traits, gender, or other demographic differences. It is also likely that the influence of these factors on stress may vary when stress is induced through FTF versus CMC methods. Future MIS research should focus on differences in stress experienced across these two delivery methods with larger samples.Additionally, we used adult students for our sample. Within the context and experimental nature of the study, however, we feel it is unlikely that students' physiological and psychosocial responses would differ greatly from the reactions of adults in the workplace. This question is an empirical one, however, and we encourage other researchers to further explore the nature of these two measures so that the implications of psychosocial and physiological stress can be better understood.

6. CONCLUSION

This preliminary study determined that the Trier Social Stress Test is an effective protocol for inducing stress within an experimental design. We also determined that psychosocial stress and physiological stress should be considered different measures. This study also provides a framework for other researchers to build on, so that a theory that incorporates both sources of stress can be developed.

7. REFERENCES

[1] Ahuja, M. & Thatcher, J. Moving Beyond Intentions and toward the Theory of Trying: Effects of Work Environment and Gender on Post-Adoption Information Technology Use. *MIS Quarterly*, (29:3)2005, pp. 427-459.

[2] Aldwin, C. M. & Brustrom, J., *Theories of Coping with Chronic Stress: Illustrations from the Health Psychology and Aging Literature*, in *Coping with Chronic Stress*, Gottlieb, B.H., Editor 1997, Plenum Press: New York. p. 75-103.

[3] Brief, A. P., et al. Should Negative Affectivity Remain an Unmeasured Variable in the Study of Job Stress? *Journal of Applied Psychology*, (73:1988, pp. 193-198.

[4] Childs, E., Vicini, L., & De Wit, H. Responses to the Trier Social Stress Test (Tsst) in Single Versus Grouped Participants. *Psychophysiology*, (43:2006, pp. 366-371.

[5] Clow, A., Hucklebridge, F., & Stalder, T. The Awakening Cortisol Response: Methodological Issues and Significance. *Stress*, (7:2009, pp. 29-37.

[6] Crowne, D. P. & Marlowe, D., *The Approval Motive: Studies in Evaluative Dependence*1964, New York: Wiley.

[7] Edwards, S., et al. Exploration of the Awakening Cortisol Response in Relation to Diurnal Cortisol Secretory Activity. *Life Sciences*, (68:2001, pp. 2093-2103.

[8] Gunnar, M. N., C. Event-Related Potentials in Year-Old Infants: Relations with Emotionality and Cortisol. *Childhood Development*, (65:1994, pp. 80-94.

[9] Harrison, D. A., McLaughlin, M. E., & Coalter, T. M. Context, Cognition and Common Method Variance: Psychometric and Verbal Protocol Evidence. *Organizational Behavior and Human Decision Processes*, (68:1996, pp. 246-261.

[10] Hjortskov, N., et al. Evaluation of Salivary Cortisol as a Biomarker of Self-Reported Mental Stress in Field Studies. *Stress and Health*, (20:2004, pp. 91-98.

[11] Kessler, R. C., *The Interplay of Research Design Strategies and Data Analysis Procedures in Evaluating the Effects of Stress on Health*, in *Stress and Health: Issues in Research Methodology*, Kasl, S.V. & C.L. Cooper, Editors. 1987, John Wiley & Sons: Chichester.

[12] Kimball, J., Lynch, K., & Stewart, K. Using Salivary Cortisol to Measure the Effects of a Wilbarger Protocol-Based Procedure on Sympathetic Arousal: A Pilot Study. *American Journal of Occupational Therapy*, (61:2007, pp. 406-413.

[13] Kirschenbaum, C., Pirke, K., & Hellhammer, D. The "Trier Social Stress Test"--a Tool for Investigating Stress Responses in a Laboratory Setting. *Neuropsychobiology*, (28:1993, pp. 76-81.

[14] Lanyon, R. I. & Goodstein, L. D., *Personality Assessment*. 3rd ed1997, New York: Wiley.

[15] Logan, D. E., Claar, R. L., & Scharff, L. Social Desirability Response Bias and Self-Report of Psychological Distress in Pediatric Chronic Pain Patients. *Pain*, (136:3), September 5 2008, pp. 366-372.

[16] Lundberg, U. Methods and Applications of Stress Research. *Technology and Health Care*, (3:3)1995, pp. 3-9.

[17] O'Brien, T. B., & DeLongis, A., *Coping with Chronic Stress: An Interpersonal Perspective*, in *Coping with Chronic Stress* Gottlieb, B.H., Editor 1997, Plenum Press: New York. p. 161-190.

[18] Paulhaus, D. L., *Measurement and Control of Response Bias*, in *Measures of Personality and Social Psychological Attitudes: Volume 1 of Measures of Social Psychological Attitudes*, Robinson, J.P., P.R. Shaver, & L.S. Wrightsman, Editors. 1991, Academic Press: San Diego, CA.

[19] Pierrehumbert, B., et al. The Influence of Attachment on Perceived Stress and Cortisol Response to Acute Stress in Women Sexually Abused in Childhood or Adolescense. *Psychoneuroendocrinology*, (34:2009, pp. 924-938.

[20] Ragu-Nathan, T. S., Tarafdar, M., & Ragu-Nathan, B. The Consequences of Technostress for End Users in Organizations: Conceptual Development and Empirical Validation. *Information Systems Research*, (19:4), December 2008, pp. 417-433.

[21] Sarkola, T. M., H.; Fukunaga, T.; Eriksson, CJ. Acute Effect of Alcohol on Estradiol, Estrone, Progesterone, Prolactin, Cortisol, and Luteinizing Hormone in Premenopausal Women. *Alcoholism, Clinical, and Experimental Research*, (23:6), June 1999, pp. 976-982.

[22] Tarafdar, M., et al. The Impact of Technostress on Role Stress and Productivity. *Journal of Management Information Systems*, (24:1), Summer 2007, pp. 301-328.

[23] Taverniers, J., et al. High-Intensity Stress Elicits Robust Cortisol Increases, and Impairs Working Memory and Visuo-Spatial Declarative Memory in Special Forces Candidates: A Field Experiment *Stress*, (13:4), July 2010, pp. 323-333.

[24] Thong, J. & Yap, C.-S. Information Systems and Occupational Stress: A Theoretical Framework. *Omega*, (28:2000, pp. 681-692.

[25] Weiss, M. Effects of Work Stress and Social Support on Information Systems Managers. *MIS Quarterly*, (7:1)1983, pp. 29-43.

[26] Whyte, W. H., *The Organization Man*1956, New York: Simon & Schuster.

[27] Zuboff, S., *In the Age of the Smart Machine: The Future of Work and Power.* :1988, New York: Basic Books.

Telecommuting Advantages and Challenges for IT Management and Staff

Nathan Sikes
RTI International
PO Box 12194
Research Triangle Park, NC
27709 USA
919-316-3320
sikes@rti.org

Kathy Mason
RTI International
PO Box 12194
Research Triangle Park, NC
27709 USA
919-541-7010
mason@rti.org

Suson VonLehmden
RTI International
PO Box 12194
Research Triangle Park, NC
27709 USA
919-316-3987
sfv@rti.org

ABSTRACT

Telecommuting for IT (information technology) staff has become a viable working alternative for both the organization and the employee. Since the advent of greater connectivity through hi-tech advancement, effective IT employees can work as efficiently remotely as from the confines of the organization's office buildings. Location in proximity to the office is less of a factor than ever before. More and more organizations, both in the private and public sectors, are taking advantage of telecommuting for a whole range of factors. Many employees see telecommuting as a valuable benefit if offered by the organization; likewise, some organizations use telecommuting as a benefit to retain IT employees. Even though the advantages of telecommuting are numerous, there are a number of challenges that exist for the organization, management, and the telecommuting IT employee. This paper will explore the advantages and challenges of telecommuting for the organization, the project, the telecommuting IT worker, and the telecommuting IT manager.

Categories and Subject Descriptors

K.7.0 [**The Computing Profession**]: General---Telecommuting

General Terms

Management, Human Factors.

Keywords

telecommuting, managing telecommuters, telecommuter advantages, telecommuter challenges, telecommuting employee characteristics.

1. INTRODUCTION

Telecommuting for IT staff can be a tremendous working alternative for both the organization and the employee. Since the advent of greater connectivity through hi-tech advancement, employees are able to work as efficiently remotely as they can from the confines of the organization's office buildings. More and more organizations, both in the private and public sectors, are

taking advantage of telecommuting for many reasons, including reducing office management expenses, increasing employee morale by recognizing the work-life balance, reducing or eliminating travel time and travel expenses for the employee, and helping diminish the impact on the environment of driving to work, because telecommuting reduces traffic congestion and pollution. Many employees see telecommuting as a valuable benefit if offered by the organization; likewise, some savvy organizations use telecommuting as a benefit to retain IT employees (Johnson 2001). An effective IT telecommuter's work can be just as successful from a remote location, most often their home, as from being physically located in the office. Even though the advantages of telecommuting are numerous, challenges exist for the organization, management, and the telecommuting employee. This paper explores both the advantages and challenges of telecommuting for IT employees as well as IT management.

Organizations can realize a great benefit by having a formal telecommuting policy (Kossek, Lautsch and Eaton 2006). Telecommuting policies include qualifications, a management strategy, and a robust security policy. The Federal government now requires by law that all Federal agencies have a telecommuting policy in place (Public Law 106-346, § 359). In 2008, nearly 103,000 Federal employees indicated that they telecommute on a regular basis at least one day per week with 61% of the agencies reporting an increase in the number of telecommuters among their work force resulting in improved morale, productivity increases, and performance improvement (Office of Personnel Management 2009).

Telecommuting for the typical IT employee can be an ideal situation. IT managers, software developers, help desk staff and many other IT employees conduct their work through the use of a desktop personal computer (PC) even when the IT environment includes the use of the "big iron" mainframe. Programmers, tech support staff and managers all use their PCs to conduct their work and effectively communicate to individuals and groups. Meetings may be often conducted over the telephone, program code is shared in code repositories, and project and organization documents are accessed over the network. Through the use of a virtual private network (VPN), web portals, terminal servers, and other connectivity means an employee can connect to the organization's network allowing the employee to often work remotely as easily as being on site.

Currently there exists an exhaustive set of tools that enrich the telecommuter's work and communication. Some of the essential tools include a connection to an organization's network, adequate bandwidth connectivity to the internet to meet the remote user's volume of data transfer, email, a telephone or "soft" phone, instant messaging, and, of course, a PC located at the point of telecommuting (Thissen *et al.* 2007). Even using these tools to make the telecommuting experience a productive one, the employee must possess certain attributes in order to be a good candidate for working in this environment.

2. IDEAL IT TELECOMMUTING ATTRIBUTES

The IT employee is the quintessential candidate for telecommuting (Baruch and Nicholson 1997, Guimaraes and Dallow 1999, Kepczyk 1998). Most computer programmers, if fully armed with knowledge and the right tools, can be given a set of program specifications and complete a task without too much interaction with a large number of people. Any misunderstanding or discrepancy in the specifications can be dealt with through email or over the telephone. Programmers proceed in a "heads-down" fashion and complete the tasks given to them. Completed program code is then tested and the test results logged where the programmer can review the results, apply the necessary updates and fixes to the program code, and release the program or application for another round of testing until it is ready to be implemented in production.

Technical support personnel are often good candidates as well. The ideal technical support person who telecommutes would not be involved with fixing hardware in a hands-on fashion but would be someone who receives communication such as email, telephone calls, or instant messaging which allow them to address issues with people's use of organizational software or escalates issues to others who can further deal with problems. Much infrastructure technical support can be administered remotely and does not require an on-site presence.

IT managers can successfully perform their job managing telecommuters and non-telecommuters alike and also function as telecommuters themselves. Communication and interaction are the keys to successful IT managing at the office but even more so if the IT manager telecommutes (Nunes *et al.* 2004). In many cases both managers and non-managers alike are much better communicators face-to-face than via any other mode. Such a person would not make an ideal telecommuter because non-visual communication plays such an important role in communication among remotely located staff.

IT managers must be effective and proactive, sometimes even aggressive, when communicating with telecommuting staffs to ensure that they are and remain on task. Some managers may not feel comfortable with this but it can be performed very effectively if the manager interacts with telecommuting staff as eagerly as if the IT manager were in person discussing matters face-to-face.

2.1 Desirable Traits for the IT Telecommuting Candidates

Based on our collective 34-plus years of managing IT staff, we offer the following set of traits which we find to be advantageous in IT staffing, particularly for telecommuting positions.

2.1.1 Self-Motivated

Programmers who function well as telecommuters often have a natural love for what they are doing. Their work is most often their reward. The programming profession is unique from other occupations in that the programmer typically has achievable milestones and their work often allows them to be creative which is highly fulfilling. A good IT manager will recognize this aspect of the programming job and exploit it to the fullest for his or her organization's success.

Responsible: A responsible programmer demonstrates that he or she can be given a task and will take the actions necessary to accomplish the task. The dependable programmer will look for avenues to accomplish their task on their own without a great deal of oversight.

2.1.2 Highly proficient in communications

Many IT employees often focuses so much on their work that they must be prompted to communicate by others who work with them. A successful IT telecommuter will overcome this "tunnel vision" and communicate effectively and frequently with their project peers and management, keeping all informed of the status of the tasks they are working on and have scheduled. The successful telecommuter will be proactive in communicating with other staff and clients (internal and external) and not wait to be asked to provide details of their work.

2.1.3 Assertive

When involved in communications, especially telephone calls, the IT telecommuter will be assertive and not remain passive in discussions with others. It is somewhat convenient for the telecommuter to remain "in the background" while discussions take place on teleconference calls and meetings. While in conference calls, the telecommuter must be an active participant in the conference call ready to speak up and contribute to the success of the conference call. They may even have to talk over an individual in order to get their points made.

2.1.4 Technically Sound

The IT telecommuter should be highly-proficient in the skills necessary to accomplish the task to which they are assigned (Baruch and Nicholson 1997, Guimaraes and Dallow 1999). When assigned a task that requires new skills, the IT telecommuter must have the wherewithal to learn these new skills when necessary. This may even require that the employee learn these skills on their own time. The self-motivated employee will not be afraid to take on a challenge that requires them to learn new skills. If an employee does not have the skills required to work on their own then they should not consider becoming a telecommuter.

2.1.5 Able to Work Independently

A programmer who requires a high degree of oversight and management may not be an ideal candidate for telecommuting (Harpaz 2002). The IT telecommuter must be able to work productively without continual oversight of their manager and other project staff. This should not be confused with working effectively as a team member on a project using good communications. The ability to work independently means that they can accomplish tasks without intervention and oversight by others, requiring minimal supervision (Baruch and Nicholson 1997, Kepczyk 1998).

2.1.6 Remote Location not a Hindrance

Ideal IT telecommuters will effectively turn their remote location into a satellite office with all the necessary hardware and software in order to make their telecommuting successful. Any programming challenges or obstacles that may arise are immediately dealt with by the employee and they often take pride in overcoming these temporary challenges and obstacles. The IT telecommuter will work to resolve all challenges as they arise and proactively if possible, including hardware and software issues as well as project personnel issues, scheduling issues, employee-management issues, and more.

2.1.7 Markets His/Her Abilities

IT telecommuters, if not careful, can be "out-of-sight, out-of-mind." Therefore telecommuting IT staffs should actively seek to market their abilities to other staff, especially managers, in order to maintain a viable presence within the organization. They must learn to "press the flesh" without actually being present in the flesh. Phone calls and emails to other staff, even those not on a current project, will remind others that the IT telecommuter is still a viable part of the organization. A good scenario will have the IT telecommuter partnering with his or her supervisor to maintain this presence with other IT staff and their clients (internal and external). This can be achieved by the supervisor speaking up for the telecommuter in discussions with other staff and by distributing emails when praise is deserved for a job well done.

3. ADVANTAGES OF TELECOMMUTING

Telecommuting has a number of advantages both from a business perspective and an individual perspective. From management's viewpoint, one huge advantage is that often it costs less to outfit an employee's home office than to pay for office space. This space saving option is especially important in areas such as large cities where space is costly. A second advantage is employee motivation. Telecommuting can be touted by management as a company benefit by stating that the company is willing to be flexible on work hours to allow its employees to manage their own schedules. For salaried employees, the key criterion is that the work be done regardless of the daily/weekly schedule. Another advantage these days is the environmental stance– a company can promote being "green" by allowing its workers to avoid driving into the office. Also telecommuting can provide significant strengths to a company's business continuity plan. Employees would be set up to seamlessly work from home in the event of a catastrophic event at the company's main facility or location.

The key advantage from the individual's perspective is the flexibility of the work arrangement (Harpaz 2002). Individuals in our fast-paced society are incredibly busy often with both parents working full-time, children in day care or school, volunteer activities, household duties, social responsibilities and the list goes on. Given the nature of software development work on or through the use of personal computers IT staffs are no longer constrained to being productive only during regular business hours. With honest assessment and careful planning by the IT Telecommuter other advantages to working outside the normal work environment can be increased productivity due to lack of interruptions, privacy vs. living in a cubicle world, and a better work/life balance (Duxbury, Higgins and Mills 1992).

4. CHALLENGES OF TELECOMMUTING

There are a number of challenges to be addressed in order to fully embrace telecommuting. The main business-side challenge involves monitoring work/productivity remotely. Many traditional managers find it difficult to evaluate employees unless they can observe and interact face-to-face. This technique obviously cannot be applied when the employee is working in a different physical location. Other specific challenges to telecommuting include the following:

4.1 IT security

Security is often cited as the number one concern of organizations regarding working remotely so an exhaustive security policy must be put in place to address issues such as computer security in the home, access and connection to the network, email, and other items (CDW-G. 2008). A good security plan requires a company to actively plan for alternate access to their business systems. There are a number of ways to guarantee security including VPNs, two-factor authentication and implementing more restrictive policies and procedures (e.g., requiring more frequent password changes). It's not insurmountable but does require additional thought and planning.

4.2 Managing a remote workspace

It's almost imperative that the telecommuter have a dedicated workspace at home so it is clear to the employee and others that live in the household that the space is for work only (Harpaz 2002) Otherwise the boundaries between work life and home life may get blurred. It is not uncommon to receive e-mails and phone calls far outside of normal busy hours so it's important to be able to "leave" work and participate in family life. An individual's family life and downtime should remain sacred. Some potential distractions may not be suitable for a telecommuting arrangement, such as a newborn baby which may require large chunks of time at variable times of day, whereas a distraction such as waiting for a repairman can more easily fit into a busy schedule.

4.3 Level of participation in meetings and multitasking

The solution to this challenge is to be not only assertive on conference calls but for the IT telecommuter to make him/herself known by being aggressive and participating fully. If a meeting is mostly in-person with just a few people on the phone, it is frequently difficult to get the attention of the group. Room participants often talk over each other so the telecommuter may have to raise his/her voice and be sure to enunciate clearly. The telecommuter may also need to be a champion for conference call etiquette. The absence of visual cues for the telecommuter can be overcome with periodic in-person meetings and/or videoconferencing. Multi-tasking while listening to conference calls may be a temptation in order to get more work done; however, based on our experience we recommend that telecommuters should not attempt to multi-task while on a conference call in order to be fully engaged with the task at hand.

4.4 Perception that career path growth and promotion opportunities are limited for telecommuters

There is a distinct negative perception in many companies about telecommuting, often despite company policies that support it (illegems and Verbeke 2004). Telecommuters may feel subtly discriminated against or they may feel overlooked for certain opportunities or advancements. To be successful, telecommuting employees should work with their managers to ensure they have well defined career paths and that they can participate in activities that will further them along their individual paths. This will ensure success for telecommuting IT staffs and the company.

4.5 Technical issues

This is probably the easiest challenge to address. The telecommuter simply needs to be solution-ready with appropriate and sufficient work area(s) and equipment such as a high speed connection dedicated phone and/or cell phone, printer, router, firewall, virus software, VPN software and the necessary office supplies (Fisher and Fisher 2010). Once the ideal telecommuting employee has been identified and the challenges associated with this atypical work situation have been addressed, management will need to review the implications this work arrangement might have on the organization as a whole was well as implications for specific project work.

5. ORGANIZATION AND PROJECT CHALLENGES

Companies in the last century have been reluctant to allow employees to work from home. Management had the impression that "if I can't see what my staff is doing then I assume I am not getting top value from them." However, advancement in IT communications and connectivity began to change the landscape significantly. With the emergence of the personal computer and global networking, we have greatly increased the employee's options of where they can work productively.

IT departments were often positioned to be on the forefront of the telecommuting movement as they were trying out new ideas and concepts in computer connectivity. As IT managers themselves began to experience liberation from their desks and could connect from their home to work 24/7, their staff were slowly encouraged to join the revolution as well. As the need for more 24/7 coverage in IT departments grew organizations began to embrace cutting edge technologies to afford their employees to work "on call" to fix problems from anywhere at any time. Now IT departments routinely employ telecommuting policies for all their staff as it is recognized as a viable alternative to an office presence. It is not uncommon now for employees to telecommute from the other side of the world from the organization's offices and computer center.

5.1 Managing Organizational and Project Challenges for the IT Telecommuter

Still challenges for the organization remain as they ensure that work is accomplished on time and on budget.

5.1.1 Ensuring Quality of Work

As with all employees who telecommute, it is extremely important for the IT telecommuter to establish high standards for producing quality work and for IT management to be convinced that the employee produces quality work prior to allowing the employee to telecommute. IT management should be intimately familiar with the employee's work habits and skill level. In a perfect world, management can study the employee on site to achieve this knowledge and then release the employee to work off site on a probationary period to determine if this will work for the project and organization. As with many things new and affecting a lifestyle change, an incremental transition over time to telecommuting may be best for all involved. In virtual organizations this may not be possible, so the IT manager must review the work remotely on a frequent basis from the beginning of the relationship to ensure that the quality of work promised by the employee lives up to the expectations of management. As trust grows between the telecommuting IT employee and the organization, review of their work, whether software development or technical support, can be less frequent. For example, the IT manager can assign a small task to the employee with an expected date to be completed and determine if the task was completed successfully with the quality expected and provide the appropriate feedback for the situation.

5.1.2 Achieving the Expected Quantity of Work

We recommend that expectations of the amount of work to be completed should not be relaxed for the IT telecommuter. If the employee has worked proficiently on site, they should continue to do so at the same level remotely. Often employees say they get more done remotely because they are not distracted with office interruptions and social exchanges. This is often part of the attraction of working as a telecommuter. Organization and project managers should convey project and organizational expectations to the IT telecommuter and non-telecommuter alike and hold them to these expectations.

5.1.3 Delivering the Work in a Timely Fashion

Managing software developers is more effective with clearly defined application specifications and goals (Illegems and Verbeke 2004). These should include expected milestone dates for different software objects developed. Managers should monitor the remote software developer just as much as one who is on site. Telephone calls and emails are effective in asking the programmer where they stand on tasks and the telecommuting software developer should give honest feedback as to where they are in development of software. Short frequent communication between these parties will usually allow the software developer to raise an issue if need be whether it is technical-related, scope-related, or if delivery dates will be affected.

5.1.4 Effective Communication with the Project Team

It is extremely important for the telecommuting IT employee to remain in frequent communication with project and organizational peers and management. This may be a natural trait of the employee or it may be one that has to be learned. IT managers should monitor the frequency and effectiveness of the communication of the telecommuting employee and provide realistic feedback (Hinds and Bailey 2003). Frequent and regular project meetings over the telephone are encouraged with an emphasis on having the telecommuting employee actively engaged in the discussions of software development or technical support. If the manager would normally drop by an employee's desk on site for discussion, they should telephone the telecommuting employee with the same frequency. Email can work as effectively and is generally easier to conduct but telephone conversations offer a more human touch that email cannot provide.

5.1.5 Resolving Software Development Issues

IT organizations should have tools and a culture in place to allow software developers to share issues easily with one another to help resolve problems when they arise. Sometimes a software developer is stretched beyond his or her level of knowledge and must overcome an obstacle in programming. The project manager should have established a culture in which the telecommuting software developer can feel free to ask for help from other developers and/or the manager on the project or in the organization. To help resolve issues, tools should be readily available in order to properly share the issue with other team or organizational members (remotely or on site). Hopefully the majority of issues can be worked out over the telephone or through email but often it may be useful to see what the programmer is seeing on their screen. For example, a desktop sharing tool can effectively allow others to view on the remote employee's computer the problem they are facing in their software development. If further interaction is needed, there should be common network storage to transfer software objects for other developers or the project manager to review the issue on their computer to eventually develop a solution.

5.1.6 Reporting Testing and Debugging Issues

The telecommuting software developer should be able to place their software in a location to be tested by others on the project team prior to releasing the software. Best practices suggest that an effective software project will implement a software solution that catalogs the test results of the project team member that can be communicated to the programmer whether they are on site or working as a telecommuter. Software cataloging of the test results can be a simple spreadsheet with accompanying screen shots, if necessary, or robust off-the-shelf software specifically suited to this task. While it may seem obvious, the telecommuting software developer should have easy access to the results and should be alerted when they are ready for review and correction, just as with a team of on-site developers; this type of sharing may take additional planning for a virtual team.

5.1.7 Hardware and Software Upgrades

It is important for the IT organization to have a strategy for synchronizing hardware and software upgrades for telecommuting IT staff. There are numerous approaches which can be followed. For example, organizations may simply have telecommuters who live in proximity to the organization's office bring their laptops or desktops to the office and make the appropriate upgrades. If the IT telecommuter is connected to the organization's network then software can be pushed to the telecommuter's PC. Another approach is to have these telecommuters connect to desktop PCs on site at the organization in order to more effectively manage the hardware and software updates. The remote IT employee would simply connect to the dedicated on-site computer using their home computer and running the computer as effectively as if they were on site.

An IT manager can successfully and effectively manage the issues as a telecommuter as easily as a manager on site at the office by consistently and proactively addressing any issues that may arise from working remotely instead of in the office. An effective telecommuting manager will try to mimic the relationship of the on-site employee and manager. They will proactively develop successful solutions to overcome any inhibiting factor that would not allow them to succeed in managing staff. All of the issues listed above can be effectively managed remotely by a telecommuting manager.

6. MANAGING TELECOMMUTERS

Another factor to ensure the telecommuting situation is a successful one is in how a manager addresses the challenges associated with telecommuting staff. Communication is absolutely vital to making this arrangement work for both the company and the employee (Nunes *et. al* 2004). Since a manager cannot stop by to "check in" on progress or conduct face to face meetings, it is vital that he/she maintains regular communication with the telecommuter. Employees should be clear about what their manager expects and frequent communication, setting

milestones, and providing timely responses are just some of the ways to make the telecommuting journey a success.

To ensure a good working relationship while telecommuting for either party, the employee should be responsive, and the manager should be flexible and adaptive when working in the telecommuting environment. It is important to set standards so that the employee is aware that "out of sight" does not translate to "out of mind" when it comes to dealing with co-workers. We are no longer looking to punching in and out with timecards to monitor when an employee is working. A better solution would be for managers to track progress by determining the employee's ability to meet deadlines and their ability to complete tasks and deliverables. It is very important to have milestones for work deliverables and regular virtual meetings to make sure that everyone has the same understanding of the task(s).

Work must be clearly defined, milestones must be identified, assigned tasks monitored, and feedback provided. So how does the IT manager monitor work performance of a telecommuter? There are several critical items to consider:

- Communication – Being reachable by phone, email or instant messaging during predefined hours will allow the employee to avoid frustrations often associated with telecommuting. If the employee needs to be away from their workspace for any reason, they need to set their out of office and/or leave a number where they can be reached if necessary.
- Quality of work – Work must be reviewed at regular intervals – daily, weekly, monthly as necessary.
- Visibility – If possible, occasional in-person meetings should be encouraged.
- Flexibility – Project leaders must be prepared with alternate plans if the telecommuting arrangement fails to meet expectations. Although infrequent, this can occur and must be addressed by the employee and manager.

7. CONCLUSIONS

Telecommuting is an attractive benefit for many IT employees. After becoming accustomed to working from home, a telecommuting employee may be reluctant to return to the confines of a cubicle in an office building for the entire work week. Maintaining a successful balance between work and life for employees ranks high as an enticing carrot for IT employees to remain with their current organization and telecommuting often helps meet that need (Bernthal and Wellins 2001).

Telecommuting may not be for everybody but it can be enjoyed by most to a large degree even if it is only for one afternoon during the work week. If at all possible, for the new telecommuter starting off, short stints in their remote location will aid in the transition to a more full-time telecommuting environment as they and management become comfortable with the situation. The employee should examine himself or herself to determine if they possess the attributes listed above and would therefore make a good IT telecommuter. Future directions could include surveying both telecommuters and non-telecommuters to verify and categorize other desired qualities as well as the state of satisfaction of telecommuting practitioners.

8. REFERENCES

[1] Baruch, Y. and Nicholson, N. 1997. Home, Sweet Work: Requirements for Effective Home Working, *Journal of General Management* 23,2, 15-30

[2] Bernthal, P.R. and Wellins, R.S. 2001. *Retaining Talent: A Benchmarking Study.* Development Dimensions International, Pittsburgh, PA.

[3] CDW-G. *2008 CDW-G Telework Report: Feds Stuck in Second Gear; Private Sector Puts the Pedal to the Metal.* DOI= http://www.telecommutect.com/employers/pr_4_1_08.pdf

[4] Duxbury, L.E., Higgins, C.A. and Mills, S. 1992. After-Hours Telecommuting and Work-Family Conflict: A Comparative Analysis. *Information Systems Research* 3,2, 173-190

[5] Fisher, K. and Fisher, M. 2010 *The Distance Manager: A Hands-On Guide to Managing Off-site Employees and Virtual Teams.* McGraw-Hill.

[6] Guimaraes, T. and Dallow, P. 1999. Empirically Testing the Benefits, Problems and Success Factors for Telecommuting Programmes. *European Journal pf Information Systems* 8,1 (March 1999), 40-54

[7] Harpaz, I. 2002. Advantages and Disadvantages of Telecommuting for the Individual, Organization and Society. *Work Study* 51,2, 74-80.

[8] Hinds, P.J. and Bailey, D.E. 2003. Out of Sight, Out of Sync: Understanding Conflict in Distributed Teams. *Organization Science* 14,6 (Nov/Dec 2003), 615-632.

[9] Illegems, V. and Verbeke, A. 2004. Telework: What Does it Mean for Management? Long Range Planning 37, 319-334.

[10] Johnson, N. J. 2001. *Telecommuting and Virtual Offices :Issues and Opportunities.* Idea Group Publishing, Hershey, PA.

[11] Kepczyk, R.H. 1998. Evaluating the Virtual Office. *The Ohio CPA Journal* (Apr/June), 16-17

[12] Kossek, E.E., Lautsch, B.A. and Eaton, S.C. 2006. Telecommuting, control, and boundary management: Correlates of policy use and practice, job control, and work–family effectiveness. *Journal of Vocational Behavior* 68,2 (Aug 2005), 347-367

[13] Nunes, S.T., Osho, S. and Nealy, C. 2004. The Impact of Human Interaction On the Development of Virtual Teams. *Journal of Business and Economics Research* 2,12 (Dec 2004), 95-100.

[14] Office of Personnel Management (OPM) 2009 "*Status of Telework in the Federal Government Report to Congress*", pp.1-31, DOI=http://www.telework.gov/Reports_and_Studies/Annual_Reports/2009teleworkreport.pdf

[15] Thissen, M. R., Page, J. M., Bharathi, M. C., & Austin, T. L. 2007. Communication tools for distributed software development teams. *Proceedings of the ACM-SIGMIS CPR '07 Conference: The Global Information Technology Workforce,* pp. 28-35.

Drivers, Challenges and Consequences
of E-Recruiting – A Literature Review

Stefan Lang
Centre of Human Resources Information Systems
University of Bamberg, Germany
+49 951 8632873
stefan.lang@stud.uni-bamberg.de

Sven Laumer
Centre of Human Resources Information Systems
University of Bamberg, Germany
+49 951 8632873
sven.laumer@uni-bamberg.de

Christian Maier
Centre of Human Resources Information Systems
University of Bamberg, Germany
+49 951 8632873
christian.maier@uni-bamberg.de

Andreas Eckhardt
Centre of Human Resources Information Systems
Goethe-University of Frankfurt, Germany
+49 69 79834659
eckhardt@wiwi.uni-frankfurt.de

ABSTRACT
Using a literature review of 80 journals and proceedings we identified 23 research papers discussing driver, challenges and consequences of e-recruiting. In total 14 drivers, 15 challenges and 9 consequences of implementing and using e-recruiting has been identified. Based on these results the paper introduces a model of drivers, challenges and consequences of e-recruiting and discusses implications for research and practice. The analysis reveals that e-recruiting will reduce costs for recruitment and selection, increase the number of suitable applicants, enable time savings for both organizations and applicants and improve the corporate image. These four consequences also have been identified as major drivers of e-recruiting projects. The identified challenges include the exclusion of potential applicants, the deception of applicants in e-assessment procedures, the security of applicants' data and low qualification of applicants.

Categories and Subject Descriptors

H.4.2 [Types of Systems] Decision support (e.g., MIS)

K.2 [HISTORY OF COMPUTING] Systems

General Terms
Management, Human Factors

Keywords
E-Recruiting, Literature Review, E-HRM, Drivers, Consequences, Challenges

1. INTRODUCTION
During the last three years the global economy struggled one of the major economic crisis and human resources management (HRM) has to change its focus from recruiting and developing employees to managing layoffs and other economic downturn issues [59]. In addition, the global demographic development, retirement of baby boomers [22] and changing values, norms and behavioral patterns influence HRM in organizations. In fact, these trends merely aggravate the challenges in many firms that have long suffered from a scarcity of qualified employees, or 'talent'. And the unavailability of certain candidates in many skill areas has long been identified as a major obstacle to firm success and growth even in times of economic downturns ([57]; [31]). For example, the German Federal Association for Information Technology, Telecommunications and New Media (Bitkom) reports that there were 45,000 open positions for IT workers at the end of 2008 and companies still cannot find appropriate IT staff even in a severe downturn[1]. In addition, an analysis with HR executives of 300 German IT organizations in 2010 showed that the scarcity of IT talent is one of the two most important trends HR executives have to deal with when managing the recruiting, developing and retention activities of IT organizations in the next years ([8]; [15]; [32]). As a consequence of this development during the last years the improved economic climate in Europe especially in Germany could make the scarcity of IT talent on the labor market an even worse challenge for organizations. At the same time, advances in information and communication technology and the ubiquity of the internet can offer substantially new ways to attract and recruit talent. E-recruiting can give a firm a substantial competitive edge in a tough market for skills by establishing a better talent management capability for scare profiles such as in the IT domain ([23]; [24]; [32]; [38]).

---

[1] More information about the situation in Germany could be found at http://www.bitkom.org/de/presse/62013_61645.aspx and http://www.bitkom.org/de/themen/54633_58438.aspx

In general, the scope of IT support for these recruiting activities ranges from attracting and identifying talent to selecting and retaining candidates ([5]; [16]; [21]; [29]; [30]; [44]; [49]; [53]; [54]; [58]). Recent research shows that the internet, in particular, has changed the way recruiting processes are managed ([9]; [19]; [33]; [48]). IT support for talent attraction could include online channels like internet job boards, social media applications or a firm's own career website [58]. For applicant selection organizations could use IT-based resumes and different forms of e-assessment systems [33]. In general, holistic e-recruiting systems can be used as suggested by Lee [37] to support the recruiting process from identifying a vacancy to closing the contract with the most suitable candidate and new applications like social media are potential e-recruiting tools.

In the context of e-recruiting in general, researchers have identified different reasons why organizations implement e-recruiting systems in the past (e.g. [2], [6]; see Figure 2). Moreover, prior research has discussed several challenges organizations have to address when implementing IT support for their recruiting activities (e.g. [13], [14]; see Figure 3). In addition to these drivers and challenges of e-recruiting, prior research also has provided insights into consequences of e-recruiting use and evaluated whether the expected benefits of e-recruiting could be realized (e.g. [12], [43]; see Figure 4).

In the course of the shift between generations and the maturation of the internet to what is often called a Web 2.0, the way the HR function in organizations is managed has significantly changed and is still changing [53]. Therefore, by reviewing 80 journals and proceedings relevant for information systems and e-recruiting research, the objective of our research is to provide an overview of drivers, challenges and consequences of e-recruiting in order to enable a more efficient and effective way of recruiting in the future when the global war for talents [11] returns.

Therefore, the reminder of this paper is as follows. In the next section we will describe the background of our research by discussing the recruiting process and IT support for these activities. Afterwards we will explain our methodology. Section 4 presents the results of our literature analysis. The paper concludes with a discussion of results and implications for future research.

2. RESEARCH BACKGROUND

As the purpose of this paper is to analyze drivers, challenges and consequences of e-recruiting this section summarizes research about the recruiting process and potential IT-support. Researchers from different disciplines introduced valuable approaches to discuss and research structure and standards of the recruiting process. Carroll et al. [10] introduced four stages of the recruiting process: an assessment if vacancies need to be filled, a definition and broad analysis of the job profile, the production of a job description and a person specification. In addition, Barber [3] sectioned the overall process into three steps: generating applicants, maintaining applicant status and influencing job choice decision. Breaugh and Starke [7] discussed the recruiting process as a combination of activities, variables and strategic measures to achieve a number of recruitment objectives. Faerber et al. [18] demonstrated in their model the relationship of each recruiting task, its activities and objectives. Therefore Faerber et al. [18] modeled the recruiting process based on prior work ([1]; [50]) as five main tasks (see Figure 1): short- and long-term candidate attraction, applicant management, pre-selection as well as the final selection of candidates [18].

Figure 1: Recruiting process ([1]; [18])

Lee [37] suggested an architecture for a holistic e-recruiting system to align all activities and IT tools supporting the recruiting process of an organization based on [36]. The main activities of the recruiting process are the publication of job ads and the management of applications. An overview of different measures that can be used for the different steps of the recruiting process is provided by Fernandez et al. [20] or recruiting in general and by Weitzel et al. [58] for IT professionals in particular. For each task at each step of the recruiting process an IT-based measure could be used. An organization expects several benefits by using different e-recruiting measures, has to address several challenges in order to realize the expected benefits and might gain some of these benefits after implementing e-recruiting. The following section describes the way we proceeded to identify driver, consequences and challenges of e-recruiting.

3. METHODOLOGY

In order to identify drivers, challenges and consequences of e-recruiting 80 journals were selected based on the Global Journal Ranking in JAIS [40], and of VHB[2] containing relevant journals and proceedings of e-recruiting research. In addition 60 potential search terms were generated to identify research papers dealing with e-recruiting. These potential search terms were pretested by searching 10 journals. As a consequence of these pretests we reduced the 60 potential search terms to 23 (see appendix for the list of 23 terms used), which provided comparable results. Based on these 23 search terms 80 journals and conference proceedings (see appendix for a list of the journals and conference) were scanned if they contain at least one search term in title, abstract or keyword. In this process, 23 publications – between 1990 and 2010 – could be identified. The 23 research papers discuss drivers, consequences and challenges regarding the introduction of an e-recruiting system and are the underlying base for our analysis. The identified publications were scanned and coded by one of the authors first and cross-checked by an additional author. The results were discussed with all authors afterwards. We will discuss and present the results of the literature analysis by discussing the identified drivers, challenges and consequence of e-recruiting in the following section.

4. RESEARCH RESULTS

Based on our literature analysis we identified several drivers, challenges and consequences of e-recruiting. Within this section we will highlight each identified driver, challenge or consequence and discuss the research results of the identified papers in more detail

4.1 Drivers of E-Recruiting

First of all, 14 drivers could be unfolded, which convince organizations to introduce an e-recruiting system. **Error! Reference source not found.** illustrates the 14 identified drivers

---

[2] http://vhbonline.org/service/jourqual/jq2/, Ranking of the German Academic Association for Business Research

and the research papers discussing them. In the following each driver will be discussed in more detail.

Drivers	References
Cost savings	Allen et al. 2007, Braddy et al. 2006, Eckhardt et al. 2007, Hogler et al. 1998, King et al. 2005, Laumer et al. 2009, Lee 2007, Lin et al. 2002, Malinowski et al. 2005, Panayotopoulou et al. 2007, Parry et al. 2008, Sylva et al. 2009
Time savings	Bartram 2000, Braddy et al. 2006, Chapman et al. 2003, Ibrahim et al. 2006, King et al. 2005, Lin et al. 2002, Malinowski et al. 2005, Musaa et al. 2006, Panayotopoulou et al. 2007, Parry et al. 2008, Stone et al. 2009, Sylva et al. 2009
Increased number of applicants	Allen et al. 2007, Chapman et al. 2003, Eckhardt et al. 2007, Hogler et al. 1998, Ibrahim et al. 2006, Keim et al. 2005, Parry et al. 2008
Improved employer image	Cronin et al. 2006, Ibrahim et al. 2006, King et al. 2005, Laumer et al. 2009, Sylva et al. 2009
Recruiting qualified staff more easily	Lee 2007, Lin et al. 2002, Parry et al. 2008, Stone et al. 2006
Independence of place and time	Bartram 2000, Chapman et al. 2003, Laumer et al. 2009
Usability	Chapman et al. 2003, Panayotopoulou et al. 2007, Stone et al. 2006
Providing additional workplace & organizational information	Braddy et al. 2006, Lee 2007, Stone et al. 2006
Efficient & effective personnel selection	Lin et al. 2002, Parry et al. 2008

Figure 2: Drivers of E-Recruiting

4.1.1 Cost savings

Costs often play a major role while introducing an information system in general and an e-recruiting system in particular. According to the papers identified and the results of several empirical studies discussed within these papers cost saving is the most important reason ([17]; [48]) or at least among the top three reasons [12] to establish an e-recruiting system. For example in 2001, 31.0% of 125 organizations tried to reduce costs of their personnel departments by using IT [12]. Parry and Tyson [48] identified that three of four organizations utilize job portals or corporate websites to find staff because of cost factors. Moreover, 71.0% of the companies surveyed named cost reduction as the main reason to introduce e-recruiting [48]. Malinowski et al. [43] highlighted that job advertisements could be posted with less cost on online channels such as internet job-boards compared to other channels like printed media. In addition Hogler et al. [25] argued that one third of the annual salary of a position is needed to fill a vacancy and Sylva and Mol [55] pointed out that up to 90.0% of the costs could be saved by using e-recruiting.

Furthermore different research endeavors demonstrated that both organizations ([4]; [28]; [47] ; [48]) and applicants ([2]; [6]; [37]) can save costs if an e-recruiting system is introduced and both use corporate websites or internet job portals for publish or searching

for job advertisements. According to Hogler et al. [25] an organization can reduce their costs up to 50% by utilizing internet job pages. The major reason for this is the cheaper access to applicants compared to printed media [37]. In addition the own website is also discussed as a method providing opportunities for cost savings within the recruiting process ([6]; [37]).

For the selection of candidates Laumer et al. [33] introduced e-assessments as a possibility to save cost in the recruiting process. If applicants take part in such an online-test instead of offline-procedure, they will save travel costs and the organization will spend less money for room, material and personnel costs which would be accrue in meetings with on-site attendance [33].

4.1.2 Time savings

In addition to monetary improvements, organizations expect time saving by recruiting new staff with the help of e-recruiting ([47]; [43]). Especially the time between publishing a vacancy and hiring staff (Time-to-Hire or Speed-to-Hire) is crucial for every second organization and therefore one reason to utilize e-recruiting [48]. If organizations need too much time for the whole application process and are responsible for delays, applicants could lose interest in taking up employments or signing a contract at a competitor [12]. Consequently, more than every second organization declared time saving aspects as Speed-to-Hire as one reason to use internet profile pages and is among most important reason [48].

The literature review unfolds three different issues why organizations use e-recruiting to save time by filling vacancy positions with suitable staff ([6]; [51]) as well as accelerating the whole recruitment process [28]. First of all, e-recruiting systems offer a fast possibility to publish job offers and applicants can search for them online immediately [45]. Second, according to Ibrahim and Ithnin [26] online application forms enable applicants to transfer their resume to the organization quickly. As a consequence organizations can start the selection of candidates afterwards without any time lag. Third, the recruiting processes could be managed automatic. Application systems could be used to check, analyze and evaluate applications automatically [12]. Moreover e-recruiting can provide standardized application forms on corporate website or internet job portals, whereby organizations receive only complete and perfect applications [39].

In addition, applicants also benefit as they have a faster access to job offers and can compare potential employers easily [55]. They deposit their applications online and organizations will receive them faster compared to paper-based applications sent by mail. Consequently, applications could save time by searching for potential employers and by using online applications ([39]).

4.1.3 Increased number of applicants

Several publications display that the enhancement of applicants is one reason to introduce an e-recruiting system ([17]; [12]; [26]; [25]; [27]; [48]). Hogler et al. [25] highlighted that because of the available internet access in households almost everyone can search job offers online and apply for jobs. As a consequence, it is expected that more potential staff can be addressed by publishing job offers on the own corporate website [2] or on extern internet job portal [39]. Based on empirical study Chapman and Webster [12] identified that every fourth organization implements an e-recruiting system to have access to more applicants. In addition by focusing on internet job portals, Parry and Tyson [48] identified that organizations utilize external service providers and their platform to receive more applicants.

4.1.4 Independence of place and time

Organizations implement e-recruiting system in order to provide access to the latest job advertisements for job seekers independent of place and time ([28]; [26]; [55]). In addition e-assessment methods are used to enable the applicant assessment in a time- and location-independent manner ([14]; [33]). Organizations might implement an online test for assessing the fit of applicants with the required skills of a vacancy. Using e-recruiting organizations have to implement these systems only once and candidates could perform the test without any time or location constraint [33].

4.1.5 Recruiting qualified staff more easily

Organizations implement e-recruiting with the expectation to fill vacant positions with suitable applicants more easily ([39], [52]). Especially organizations expect that with internet websites more qualified job seekers could be reached compared to classical methods liked printed media ([37]; [39]). Parry and Tyson [48] unfold that more than every second organizations (51%) intend to use internet job portals or the own corporate website to recruit well educated and trained staff more easily [48].

4.1.6 Improved employer image

The corporate website and the corresponding portal for applicants are expected to represent an essential aspect to develop a positive employer image [4]. A study by Chapman and Webster shows that 15.5% of the surveyed companies decide to utilize IS in human resources departments to enhance their own image [12]. Moreover, Laumer, von Stetten and Eckhardt [34] evaluated and discussed that organizations expect a relation between the operation of e-assessment procedures and the development of an attractive employer branding.

4.1.7 Efficient and effective personnel selection

Because of the high number of applications received by organizations human resource departments need suitable methods to select applications. The enhancement of effectiveness [12] and efficiency ([52]; [47]) of personnel selection processes is a driver to establish e-recruiting in an organization and to use IT-based selection measures.

4.1.8 Providing additional workplace & organizational information

In addition to the already mentioned reasons to establish e-recruiting Stone et al. [52] explain that organizations intend to use e-recruiting in order to provide additional information about a job position and the own organization to potential applicants and employees [52]. Organizations expect that most suitable for this objective is the own corporate internet site or the intranet. On the own website organizations can offer a higher extent of information with less costs compared to other channels like internet job portals [37] and traditional media [6]. Providing more information will enable candidates to make a better decision because more information is available [33].

4.1.9 Usability

E-recruiting methods are characterized by a high usability for organizations and applicants. A study by Parry and Tyson [48] showed that 52% of the surveyed companies expect an easy handling of internet job sites and 64% of the companies anticipate that applicants can derive benefits from such a user-friendliness application procedure. Lin and Stasinskaya [39] highlight that ease of navigation and operability of internet job portals are particular advantage of e-recruiting.

4.1.10 Target group orientation

Using internet channels for publishing job advertisement enable on the one side organizations to reach more job seekers compared to traditional media, but on the other side it is also possible to target job advertisement or image campaigns to a specific group of applicants only [43]. For example, if an organization is searching for an IT professional it could use IT portals only in order to attract the specific target group. Another example is the platform hrjobs.com, which addresses interested persons who want to work in a human resources department and therefore focuses on a particular profession. Weitzel et al. [58] highlighted that Siemens uses one specific blog in order to advertise a vacancy for the specific user group of this blog and filled the vacancy within a short period of time. As a consequence implementing target group oriented measures is one of the organizational drivers of e-recruiting use.

4.1.11 Updating of job and applicant data

Contrary to traditional job advertisements online job offers can be changed by the organization, even if the offer is published ([43]; [39]). As a consequence human resources departments can adapt advertisements quickly and change them easily. The same holds for applicants who have the possibility to modify their own applicant information [39]. As a consequence an easy way of updating relevant data is one reason why organizations and applicants intend to use e-recruiting.

4.1.12 Extending geographical scope of recruiting measures

Before using the internet human resources department got applicants almost from people living geographically close to the organization. With using internet job portals and the corporate websites organizations expect to address potential employees across geographical borders and also receive applications from regions not close to the organization [6].

4.1.13 Realization of competitive advantages

According to Parry and Tyson [48] internet job portals and the own corporate website are intended to use within the application process to gain a competitive advantage by 32% of the surveyed companies. This competitive advantage could be realized by a faster and cheaper recruiting process and by reaching more suitable candidates to select the best ones.

4.1.14 Corporate policy

As a last driver Parry and Tyson [48] identified the corporate policy as a driver to use e-recruiting. Every second organization proclaims that they want to make use of internet job portals and their own corporate website for recruiting issues because of their corporate policy [48].

4.2 CHALLENGES

Within the literature review 15 challenges could be identified which are associated with e-recruiting usage in organizations. Figure 3 illustrates these 14 challenges and the identified research paper dealing with these challenges. The following sections will explain each of them in more detail.

Challenges	References
User-friendly layout of e-recruiting systems	Bartram 2000, Cober et al. 2004, Cronin et al. 2006, Hogler et al. 1998, Panayotopoulou et al. 2007, Parry et al. 2008, Stone et al. 2006
Restricted standardization because of country-specific differences	Lin et al. 2002, Nickel et al. 2004
Identification of suitable evaluation criterions	Bartram 2000, Chapman et al. 2003, Cronin et al. 2006, Laumer et al. 2009
Restricted effectiveness of IT-based methods to choose staff	Cronin et al. 2006, Laumer et al. 2009, Lee 2007
Restricted control of content in job advertisements	Bartram 2000, Lee 2007
Restricted possibility of providing organization- & job-specific information	Lee 2007, Lin et al. 2002
Processing a variety of file formats	Cronin et al. 2006, Chapman et al. 2003
Identification of suitable applicants	Bartram 2000
Unauthorized usage of contents of online-tests	Lin et al. 2002
Choice of suitable internet job portals	Braddy et al. 2006
Effort & costs of e-recruiting projects	Lee 2007
Low qualification of applicants	Lin et al. 2002
Security of applicants' data	Bartram 2000
Deception of applicants in e-assessment procedures	Tixer 1996
Exclusion of potential applicants	Bartram 2000

Figure 3: Challenges of E-Recruiting

4.2.1 Exclusion of potential applicants

A first challenge for organizations associated with e-recruiting is the unintentional exclusion people who are not able to use the internet for their job searching activities. As a consequence organizations might not get the best candidates available as they might not use e-recruiting [14]. For example, if social relationships are of major importance for persons they will not use e-recruiting to the same degree as others. They would prefer application processes which allow a direct and personal interaction with the organization [52]. Another reason not to apply for a job with the help of e-recruiting could be a missing internet access. As a consequence no application could be transferred online [48] and some applications could not take part in e-assessments [14].

Furthermore, several of the identified research papers focus on factors influencing the availability of internet access. The most important aspects are age, income and professional group of job seekers. One factor of the phenomenon "Digital Divide" describes differences regarding the access and the use of technologies as the internet. As companies try to enhance the number of applicants they have to address this issue. According to a study by Cober et al. [13] elderly applicants use internet within the application process much fewer than young ones and are more reserved in offering information via this channel [13]. Such a behavior was also confirmed by a case study [48] illustrating organizations that argue that e-recruiting is not appropriated for everyone. Especially elderly people are not able to use e-recruiting because of their lower extent to use the internet in general. In particular organizations can reach more easily younger job-seekers, who are between 25 and 34 years old ([25]; [52]). Apart from that e-recruiting is particularly suited for hiring persons for the middle

management as pointed out by Parry and Tyson [48]. Moreover, if organizations search employees in management positions, e-recruiting is as improper as for hiring production workers [47]. In addition Hogler et al. [25] argued that the probability to use IT-based application methods increases if people earn more money. One reason for this is according to Bartram [4] the non-existence of e-recruiting methods for low-earning jobs, since potential employees have worse access to internet.

4.2.2 Security of applicants' data

Data security is the second most important challenge associated to e-recruiting according to our literature analysis. Applications, which are transmitted over the internet, contain highly sensitive personal data and organizations have to ensure data security for all applications received [4]. By using internet job portals organizations have to ensure high security mechanism to protect applicants' data ([37]; [39]). A lack of data security in internet job portals or the corporate career website depicts a competitive advantage, because stolen data could be used abusive ([37]; [39]) and lead to a situation that applicants will not reveal personnel data in future [46]. Moreover data security is of major importance in the context of e-assessments. E-assessment results have to be treated confidentially and no third party may gain access to these data [33].

4.2.3 Deception of applicants in e-assessment procedures

E-assessment methods as online-simulations or online-tests have a lot of advantages but these methods also include significant challenges as identified by our literature analysis. Hence, as it is not necessary for applicants to appear personally organizations have to ensure that candidates themselves take part in the e-assessment. Theoretically an applicant could be substituted by a third person to achieve a better result ([4]; [12]; [14]; [33]). Moreover applicants could obtain access to the test questions before the real e-assessment starts. Consequently, the validity and the comparability of results are questionable and objectively impossible [14].

4.2.4 Effort & costs of e-recruiting projects

By publishing job offers in internet job portals or by developing and implementing a portal at the own corporate website organizations have to handle costs as well as the effort of the project [37]. Especially the implementation of an own portal is time-intensive and expensive, because IT experts are necessary to design the portal and respect organizational particularities ([14]; [37]). According to Laumer, von Stetten and Eckhardt [34] the same holds for e-assessment methods. The reason therefore is, because these systems have to be implemented on the own corporate site, meet specific organizational requirements and requires many resources. As a consequence e-recruiting projects have to be managed as any IT project within the provided cost and time objectives of the project what remains one of the most important challenges while implementing e-recruiting.

4.2.5 Low qualification of applicants

Another challenge for organizations as identified by the literature analysis is the low qualification of applicants, which can be observed in internet job portals. Frequently, the skills of applicants do not fit with the job profile [4]. This is – compared to other e-recruiting methods – particularly highlighted for internet job portals [37]. Organizations have to implement measures that will on the one side increase the number of qualified applicants as discussed above, but on the other side with an increase amount of applications in general also the number of unqualified applicants increases.

4.2.6 Choice of suitable internet job portals

By deciding to use internet job portals organizations have to choose in a next step which particular portals they want to use to publish job offers. Thereby it is important to consider the relation of candidates to number of job offers on a job portal and that this ratio is balanced [39]. Moreover, the internet job portal should be well known and highly used by the applicants an organization is looking for [37] to be able to reach and to recruit well qualified staff. Finally, data security as already discussed is another important point that should be regarded by organizations before choosing an arbitrary internet job portal ([39]).

4.2.7 Unauthorized usage of contents of online-tests

Once an organization allows applicants to access an online-test, the organization cannot protect the content from abusive use [14]. Within the literature review two unauthorized usage behaviors could be revealed. First, applicants can complete the test and pass the contents of the online-tests to another applicant. Hereby the expressiveness of the results of these two applicants would be limited and would not reflect the real skills ([12]; [14]). Second, other organizations might access the content of such online-tests and integrate aspects into their own test procedure [12].

4.2.8 Identification of suitable applicants

As already described organizations have to manage more applications if they utilize e-recruiting. As a consequence human resources departments have to scan hundreds of applications and select suitable candidates [4]. Implementing effective and efficient approaches for identifying suitable applicants remains as an important challenge while using e-recruiting.

4.2.9 Processing a variety of file formats

Applicants can upload their application by using different file formats. Hence, organizations should implement an IT system which is in the position to read and handle these formats [39].

4.2.10 Restricted possibility of providing organization- & job-specific information

By publishing job offers on the own corporate website it is essential to provide different information about the organization, the position to be filled and the skills involved. Nonetheless, if jobs are promulgated in one or more internet job portals, organizations have to pay a fee to the operator, dependent on the space required [6]. Consequently, organizations can provide a lot of data in internet job portals combined with high costs or go the other way around.

4.2.11 Restricted control of content in Internet Job Portals

Another challenge related with e-recruiting and especially internet job portals is the restricted control of the content that will be published by internet job portal provider [37]. As a user of these portals one has only control about the own generated content, but not over additional content published on these portals. Especially with the introduction of social media and user generated content this challenge becomes more and more important [58].

4.2.12 Restricted effectiveness of IT-based methods to choose staff

As organizations try to use IT to select personnel it should be noted that some methods are merely limited suitable. For example internet based interviews have only limited effectiveness compared to personal interviews, because employers could not get a full picture of potential applicants and their skills. Besides, no perfected search and filter functions are available to select suitable applicants [39]. Weitzel et al. [58] discussed that e-recruiting is not using exclusively IT-based measures, but a combination of both online and offline methods to attract, select and hire suitable candidates.

4.2.13 Identification of suitable evaluation criterions

Furthermore, to evaluate applicants and their skills, evaluation criterions are essential for human resources departments to select good-qualified people. Therefore selection criterions have to be defined by organizations and if necessary modeled within IT-based selection systems. However, after performing an existing IT-based evaluation a high number of appropriate applicants should remain and the human resources department has to select the best applicants [4].

4.2.14 Restricted standardization because of country-specific differences

As a consequence of the globalization organizations recruit people in different countries and therefore standardized IT systems would be necessary, but the application process can vary for different countries as different countries have different legal requirements for the recruiting process. Consequently such differences represent a challenge for introducing and using a standardized and transnational e-recruiting system [56].

4.2.15 User-friendly layout of e-recruiting systems

According to Bartram [4] operative tasks within the context of human resources management will be executed more and more decentralized and thus every business location is responsible for recruiting and selecting personnel itself. Thus, several persons have to handle the e-recruiting system but have no special education for such systems. Hence, organizations should develop an e-recruiting system which can be handled easily by the own employees [4]. Moreover, e-recruiting systems will be visited by a lot of applicants whereby the system should also be characterized by a high user-friendliness for these potential staff to provide a fine first attitude. Bartram [4] demonstrates that 74% of all researched applicants had problems with using an application portal because of the low and poor usability.

4.3 Consequences

Finally, our literature analysis revealed nine consequences which occur after introducing an e-recruiting system and are identified by prior research. Figure 4 summarizes these nine consequences and the identified research paper. The following section will introduce each consequence in more detail.

Consequences	References
Reducing costs for recruitment & selection	Chapman et al. 2003, Malinowski et al. 2005, Musaa et al. 2006
Increasing number of suitable & unsuitable applicants	Chapman et al. 2003, Parry et al. 2008
High implementation costs for e-recruiting system	Chapman et al. 2003
Time savings for organization & applicant	Malinowski et al. 2005
Misuse of applicants' data	Linz et al. 2002
Perceived fairness of IT-based personnel selection	Chapman et al. 2003
Reduced contact or perceived loss of individuality	Chapman et al. 2003
Improved corporate image	Parry et al. 2008
Higher independence of other methods in personnel recruitment	Parry et al. 2008

Figure 4: Consequences of E-Recruiting

4.3.1 Reducing costs for recruitment & selection

By the use of e-recruiting systems personnel recruiting and selection costs could be reduced as shown by prior research. According to Musaa et al. [45] e-recruiting lowers costs by up to 90.0%. Moreover, Innovex – an organization in the health-care sector – diminished their personnel selection costs up to 50% by the use of IT-based recruiting measures ([12]).

4.3.2 Increasing number of suitable and unsuitable applicants

Previous sections discussed that organizations introduce e-recruiting to reach more applicants as well as the expectation of receiving an increasing number of applications by unskilled people. These two aspects are addressed as consequences within previous literature. Several publications illustrate the rise of applications after introducing e-recruiting ([12]; [48]). According to Chapman and Webster [12] a company received 5,000 applications per week and another one got 40,000 in four months. The reason for such a high number of applications is the cheap and fast possibility to apply for a job [12]. Nonetheless there are also a lot of incoming applications that do not fit the required skills of the posted job ([12]; [48]). This aspect is of particular importance for companies, who have no technologies to filter out low-skilled persons and therefore need more time to select staff [12].

4.3.3 High implementation costs for e-recruiting system

Before realizing cost savings organizations have to spend money to establish and introduce an e-recruiting system. Furthermore, an e-recruiting system has to be implemented and maintained across its life cycle. To demonstrate the staff how to handle the new system requires high expenses ([12]). According to prior research identified e-recruiting systems come along with high implementation cost, however, as discussed above, during the life cycle of the system organizations are also able to save money.

4.3.4 Time savings for organizations & applicants

In addition to the illustrated consequences of utilizing e-recruiting Malinowski et al. [43] analyzed within a case study that organizations as well as applicants saved time after the introduction of such a system. Once an applicant prepared his profile in an internet job portal, he/she could use it for further applications [43]. In addition organizations can communicate faster – internally as well as externally – with the help of an e-recruiting system. Consequently data of applicants will be sent from one department to the other a lot faster. Moreover, an applicant management system reduces administrative tasks in each phase of the applicant recruiting process and therefore enables a faster processing of applications [43]. The time organizations save by using e-recruiting varies according to the literature identified. Sylva and Mol [55] quoted an existing value and assume that 25% of the time could be saved. Two other researchers announced assumptions by determining the saving potentials to 50% [4] or even 66% [45].

4.3.5 Misuse of applicants' data

Applicant data could be misused as a consequence of using electronic applications. For example, Lin and Stasinskaya [39] reported that resumes were downloaded from ComputerJobs.com, an internet job portal, by a concurrent and published on another side [39]. In addition to such a misuse organizations do not only use internet job portals for searching new staff they also try to find their own employees to discover if they are looking for a new job and a new challenge. When organizations recognize of such activities they also fired their staff as shown by Lin and Stasinskaya [39]. Therefore using e-recruiting might lead to a misuse of the data required to manage the recruiting process with the help o e-recruiting systems.

4.3.6 Perceived fairness of IT-based personnel selection

Chapman and Webster [12] analyzed how e-recruiting systems are perceived by applicants. Thereby, their study reveals that participants perceive that IT-based selection methods operate not in an efficient way and are not trouble-free. Therefore IT-based personnel selection systems are perceived as less fair than other measures.

4.3.7 Reduced contact or perceived loss of individuality

Another consequence of using e-recruiting is the reduction of personnel contact between applicants and organizations within personnel recruitment and selection. Chapman and Webster [12] confirm the fact that HR staff searches applicants in a database of candidates instead of holding talks. In addition, applicants perceive that they will lose their individuality and the personal contact to organizations while using e-recruiting.

4.3.8 Improved corporate image

Parry and Tyson [48] confirm that using e-recruiting will positively influence how applicants perceive an organization. Their case study indicates that organizations reported that applicants appreciate them as an attractive employer.

4.3.9 Higher independence of other methods in personnel recruitment

According to Parry and Tyson [48] an organization can reduce the dependence of personnel recruiting methods by introducing e-recruiting. The underlying case study showed, that less job offers were published in the public employment agency after the change [48].

5. DISCUSSION

Using a literature analysis of 80 journals and proceedings relevant for e-recruiting and information systems research this paper identifies 23 papers discussing 14 drivers, 15 challenges and 9 consequences of implementing and using e-recruiting. Figure 5 summarizes the results by introducing a model of drivers, challenges and consequences of e-recruiting. The model indicates that cost savings, time savings, an increased number of applicants, an improved employer image, recruiting qualified staff more easily, independence of place and time, usability, providing additional workplace and organizational information, efficient and effective personnel selection, updating of job and applicant data, target group orientation, extending geographical scope of recruiting measures, realization of competitive advantages and the corporate policy are drivers of e-recruiting as identified and discussed by prior research.

In addition the articles found confirm that e-recruiting will reduce costs for recruitment and selection, increase the number of suitable and suitable applicants, enable time savings for both organizations and applicants and improve the corporate image. These four consequences were already expected and the analysis of consequences discussed by prior research confirms that e-recruiting will met these expectations. However, there are some unexpected consequences as well. The literature analysis reveals high implementation costs for e-recruiting system, misuse of applicants' data, perceived fairness of IT-based personnel selection, reduced contact or perceived loss of individuality and higher independence of other methods in personnel recruitment as additional consequences of e-recruiting. Moreover, prior research as identified in our literature analysis does not provide evidence that e-recruiting makes recruiting qualified staff more easily, improves the usability, will provide additional information, enables an efficient and effective personnel selection, and enables the realization of competitive advantages. Our literature analysis reveals that no research so far has shown that these expectations could also be met by using e-recruiting.

However, our research has identified different challenges an organization has to address to enable positive consequences of e-recruiting. These challenges include the exclusion of potential applicants, the deception of applicants in e-assessment procedures, the security of applicants' data, low qualification of applicants, effort and costs of e-recruiting projects, the choice of suitable internet job portals, unauthorized usage of contents of online-tests, identification of suitable applicants, processing a variety of file formats, restricted possibility of providing organization- and job-specific information, restricted control of content in job advertisements, restricted effectiveness of IT-based methods to choose staff, identification of suitable evaluation criterions, restricted standardization because of country-specific differences and user-friendly layout of e-recruiting systems

Our proposed model of drivers, challenges and consequences of e-recruiting is merging the identified research results into one model (Figure 5) summarizing prior e-recruiting research within one model.

The proposed model could be the basis for future research. First of all, future research might identify additional divers, challenges and consequences not discussed in prior research. Especially social media usage in recruiting might bring up additional drivers, challenges and consequences. Moreover, future research might provide evidence for drivers that has not been identified as consequences already that also these expectations could be met by

e-recruiting. Especially social media applications will be a promising area of research to discuss drivers, challenges an consequences of e-recruiting as social media is expected to change the way recruiting is managed again [58].

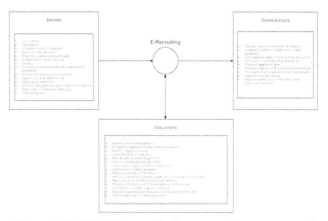

Figure 5: Model of Drivers, Challenges and Consequences of E-Recruiting

Besides the discussed implications for e-recruiting research the results of our literature review also have some implications for practitioners. The identified drivers, consequences and challenges of prior e-recruiting projects are indicators of future projects as well. The proposed model shows what the consequences are when an organization uses e-recruiting. The analysis reveals that these consequences could be positive (e.g. reduced cost, time saving, increasing number of suitable applicants, improved corporate image), but also negative (e.g. increasing number of unsuitable applicants, high implementation costs, possible misuse of applicants' data). As prior research shows e-recruiting will enable a lot of positive effects, but there are also negative consequences organizations have to deal with. Another important implication for practice is the summary of challenges of e-recruiting. The list of 15 challenges gives organizations an overview of possible pitfalls while implementing and using e-recruiting. Organizations might address these challenges when setting up the project and implementing measures to address these challenges in order to enable more positive effects of e-recruiting. Therefore, the conducted literature analysis and the proposed model are suitable for researchers as well as practitioners as it summarizes e-recruiting research conducted in the last 20 years and published in one of the 80 research journals or proceedings.

6. REFERENCES

[1] Albert, G. *Betriebliche Personalwirtschaft* Kiehl, Ludwigshafen a.R., 1998.

[2] Allen, D. G., Mahto, R. V., and Otondo, R. F. 2007. Web-Based Recruitment: Effects of Information, Organizational Brand, and Attitudes Toward a Web Site on Applicant Attraction. *Journal of Applied Psychology* (92:6), 1696–1708.

[3] Barber, A.E. Recruiting employees Thousand Oaks, CA: *Sage Publications*, 1998.

[4] Bartram, D. 2000. Kissing Frogs to find Princes. *International Journal of Selection and Assessment* (8:4), 261–274

[5] Berthel, J., and Becker, F. G. 2010. *Personal-Management - Grundzüge für die Konzeption betrieblicher Personalarbeit*, Stuttgart: Schäffer-Poeschel Verlag.

[6] Braddy, P. W., Meade, A. W., and Kroustalis, C. M. 2006. Organizational recruitment website effects on viewers' perceptions of organizational culture. *Journal of Business and Psychology* (20:4), 525–543.

[7] Breaugh, J.A., and Starke, M. Research on Employee Recruitment: So Many Studies, So Many Remaining Questions. *Journal of Management* (26:3) 2000, pp 405-434.

[8] Broderick, R., and Boudreau, J. W. 1991. Human Resource Management, Information Technology, and the Competitive Edge. *Center for Advanced Human Resource Studies*, 1–18.

[9] Bussler, L. and E. Davis 2001. Information Systems: The Quiet Revolution in Human Resource Management. *Journal of Computer Information Systems* 42(2): 17.

[10] Carroll, M., Marchington, M., Earnshaw, J., and Taylor, S. Recruitment in small firms: processes, methods and problems, *Employee Relations* (21:3) 1999, 236-250.

[11] Chambers, E. G., F. Foulon, H. Handfield-Jones, S. M. Hankin and E. G. Michaels (1998). The War for Talent. *The McKinsey Quarterly* 1.

[12] Chapman, D. S., and Webster, J. 2003. The Use of Technologies in the Recruiting, Screening, and Selection Processes for Job Candidates. *International Journal of Selection and Assessment* (11:2-3), 113–120.

[13] Cober R. T., Brown, D. J., Keeping, L. M., and Levy, P. E. 2004. Recruitment on the Net: How Do Organizational Web Site Characteristics Influence Applicant Attraction?, *Journal of Management* (30:5), 623–646.

[14] Cronin, B., Morath, R., Curtin, P., and Heil, M. 2006. Public sector use of technology in managing human resources. *Human Resource Management Review* (16:3), 416–430.

[15] Dolan, A. F. 2004. *Recruiting, Retaining, and Reskilling Campus It Professionals. Technology Everywhere: A Campus Agenda for Educating and Managing Workers in the Digital Age.* B. L. Hawkins, J. A. Rudy and W. H. Wallace, Jossey-Bass: 75-91.

[16] Eckhardt, A. and Laumer, S. 2009. An IT-Architecture to Align E-Recruiting and Retention Processes. *International Journal of E-Services and Mobile Application*s, 1(2), 38-61;

[17] Eckhardt, A., Weitzel, T., Koenig, W., and Buschbacher, J. 2007. How to Convince People Who Don't Like IT to Use IT: A Case Study on E-Recruiting. *Americas Conference on Information Systems (AMCIS)* (13), pp. 1–12.

[18] Faerber, F., Keim, T., and Weitzel, T. An Automated Recommendation Approach to Personnel Selection. 2003 *Americas Conference on Information Systems*, Tampa, 2003.

[19] Feldman, D. C. and B. S. Klaas (2002). Internet Job Hunting: A Field Study of Applicant Experiences with on-Line Recruiting. *Human Resource Management* 41(2): 175-192.

[20] Fernández-Aráioz, C., Groysberg, B. and Nohria, N. 2009. A Definitive Guide to Recruiting in Good Times and Bad, *Harvard Business Review*,

[21] Festing, M., and Eidems, J. 2009. Transnationale Personalmanagementsysteme - Prozessanalyse auf Basis der Dynamic-Capabilities-Perspektive und Fallstudie, in *Management der Internationalisierung*, S. Schmid (ed.), Wiesbaden, 370–394.

[22] Frank, F. D., R. P. Finnegan and C. R. Taylor 2004. The Race for Talent: Retaining and Engaging Workers in the 21st Century. *Human Resource Planning* 27(3): 12-25.

[23] Gottwald, M., and Schambach, A. 2008. Human Resources Software - Der Praxisratgeber für Personal-Entscheider. Arbeit und Arbeitsrecht - *Die Zeitschrift für den Personalprofi* .

[24] Gueutal, H. 2009. HR and Our Virtual Business World. *Journal of Managerial Psychology* 24(6).

[25] Hogler, R. L., Henle, C., and Bemus, C. 1998. Internet recruiting and employment discrimination: A legal perspective, *Human Resource Management Review* (8:2), 149–164.

[26] Ibrahim, O., and Ithnin, N. M. N. A. 2006. The Acceptance Behavior of Online Recruitment Users in Malaysia. *Pacific Asia Conference on Information Systems* 10, 685-696.

[27] Keim, T., Malinowski, J., and Weitzel, T. Bridging the Assimilation Gap: A User Centered Approach to IT Adoption in Corporate HR Processes. *Americas Conference on Information Systems (AMCIS)* 1162–1170.

[28] King Tong, D., and Sivanand, C. N. 2005. E-recruitment service providers review: International and Malaysian. *Employee Relations* (27:1), 103–117.

[29] Laumer, S. and A. Eckhardt 2009. Help to Find the Needle in a Haystack: Integrating Recommender Systems in an It Supported Staff Recruitment System. *Proceedings of the special interest group on management information system's 47th annual conference on Computer personnel research. Limerick, Ireland, ACM.*

[30] Laumer, S. and A. Eckhardt 2009. What Makes the Difference? Introducing an Integrated Information System Architecture for Employer Branding and Recruiting. Handbook of Research on E-Transformation and Human Resources Management Technologies: Organizational Outcomes and Challenges. T. Bondarouk, E. Oiry, K. Guiderdoni-Jourdain and H. Ruel, *Information Science Reference.*

[31] Laumer, S. and A. Eckhardt 2010. Analyzing It Personnel's Perception of Job-Related Factors in Good and Bad Times. *Proceedings of the 2010 Special Interest Group on Management Information System's 48th annual conference on Computer personnel research on Computer personnel research.* Vancouver, BC, Canada, ACM: 95-99.

[32] Laumer, S., Eckhardt, E., and Weitzel, T. 2010. Electronic Human Resources Management in an E-Business Environment, *Journal of Electronic Commerce Research*, (11:4)

[33] Laumer, S., A. Eckhardt and T. Weitzel 2009. Status Quo and Trends in E-Recruiting - Results from an Empirical Analysis. *International Conference on Information Resources Management (CONF-IRM).* Dubai, United Arab Emirates.

[34] Laumer, S., A. Von Stetten and A. Eckhardt 2009. E-Assessment. *Business & Information Systems Engineering* 1(3): 263-265.

[35] Laumer, S., Stetten, A. von, and Eckhardt, A. 2009. E-Assessment, *Wirtschaftsinformatik* (51:3), 306–308.

[36] Lee, I. An integrated economic decision and simulation methodology for e-recruiting process redesign, *International Journal of Simulation and Process Modelling* (1:3/4) 2005, 179-188.

[37] Lee, I. 2007. An Architecture for a Next-Generation Holistic E-Recruiting System. *Communications of the ACM* 50(7): 81-85.

[38] Lee, I. 2005. The evolution of e-recruiting: A content analysis of Fortune 100 career Web sites. *Journal of Electronic Commerce in Organizations* (3:3), 57-68

[39] Lin, B., and Stasinskaya, V. S. (2002). Data warehousing management issues in online recruiting, *Human Systems Management* (21:1), pp. 1–8.

[40] Lowry, P.B., Romans, D. and Curtis, A. 2004. Global Journal Prestige and Supporting Disciplines: A Scientometric Study of Information Systems Journals, *Journal of the Association for Information Systems* 5 (2), 29–77.

[41] Luftman, J. and R. Kempaiah 2008. Key Issues for It Executives 2007. MIS Quarterly Executive 7(2): 99-112.

[42] Luftman, J., and Ben-Zvi, T. 2010. Key Issues for IT Executives 2009, *MIS Quarterly Executive* (9:1), pp. 151–159

[43] Malinowski, J., Keim, T., and Weitzel, T. 2005. Analyzing the Impact of IS Support on Recruitment Processes: An E-Recruitment Phase Model. *Pacific Asia Conference on Information Systems* (9), 977–988.

[44] Malinowski, J., T. Weitzel and T. Keim 2008. Decision Support for Team Staffing: An Automated Relational Recommendation Approach. *Decision Support Systems* 45(3): 429-447.

[45] Musaa, N., Junaini, S. N., and Bujang, Y. R. 2006. Improving Usability of E-recruitment Website: A Preliminary Study on Sarawak Government Website. *Pacific Asia Conference on Information Systems* (10) 507-515.

[46] Nickel, J., and Schaumburg, H. 2004. "Electronic Privacy, Trust and Self-Disclosure in E-Recruitment," ACM Transactions on Computer Human Interaction (22), 1231–1234.

[47] Panayotopoulou, L., Vakola, M., and Galanaki, E. 2007. E-HR adoption and the role of HRM: evidence from Greece. Personnel Review (36:2), 277–294.

[48] Parry, E. and S. Tyson 2008. An Analysis of the Use and Success of Online Recruitment Methods in the Uk. *Human Resource Management Journal* 18(3): 257-274.

[49] Pfeffer, J. 2005. "Producing Sustainable Competitive Advantage Through the Effective Management of People," Academy of Management Executive (19:4), 95–108

[50] Schneider, B. Personalbeschaffung Peter Lang Europäischer *Verlag der Wissenschaften*, Frankfurt a. Main, 1995.

[51] Stone, D. L., and Lukaszewski, K. 2009. "An expanded model of the factors affecting the acceptance and effectiveness of electronic human resource management systems," *Human Resource Management Review* (19:2), 134–143.

[52] Stone, D. L., Sonte-Romero, E. F., and Lukaszewski, K. 2006. "Factors affecting the acceptance and effectiveness of electronic human resource systems," *Human Resource Management Review* (16:2), 229–244.

[53] Strohmeier, S. 2007. "Research in E-Hrm: Review and Implications." *Human Resource Management Review* 17: 19-37.

[54] Strohmeier, S. 2009. "Concepts of E-Hrm Consequences: A Categorisation, Review and Suggestion." *The International Journal of Human Resource Management* 20(3): 528 - 543.

[55] Sylva, H., and Mol, S. T. 2009. E-Recruitment: A study into applicant perceptions of an online application system, *International Journal of Selection and Assessment* (17:3), 311–323.

[56] Tixier, M. 1996: Employers' recruitment tools across Europe, Employee Relations, Vol. 18, No. 6, pp. 69-80.

[57] Trevor, C. O. and A. J. Nyberg 2008. Keeping Your Headcount When All About You Are Losing Theirs: Downsizing, Voluntary Turnover Rates, and the Moderating Role of Hr Practices. *Academy of Management Journal* 51(2): 259-276.

[58] Weitzel, T., A. Eckhardt and S. Laumer 2009. A Framework for Recruiting It Talent: Lessons from Siemens" *MIS Quarterly Executive (MISQE)* 8(4): 175-189.

[59] Welbourne, T.M., *Hrm in Tough Times*. Human Resource Management, 2009. **48**(2): 181-182.

7. APPENDIX

An overview of the used search terms and included journals could be found at http://isdl.uni-bamberg.de/chris/e-recruiting/cpr20-lang.pdf

Software Practitioners Dropping-out: A Research Proposal

Jack Downey

Lero, the Irish Software Engineering
Research Centre
University of Limerick
Ireland
+ 353 61 213072
jack.downey at lero.ie

ABSTRACT

This paper proposes an exploratory study to determine why some computer science or software engineering graduates abandon their careers in software to pursue radically different paths. While these people may be experiencing a generic mid-life crisis, is it possible that the tremendous technical focus of their work means they are ill-prepared for the senior roles on offer, roles that involve inter-personal as opposed to technical skills?

Categories and Subject Descriptors

K.7.1 [Occupations]:

General Terms

Human Factors, Theory.

Keywords

Careers in software, mid-career crisis, social cognitive theory

1. INTRODUCTION

For university educators in the computer science and information systems fields, the need to produce employable graduates is vital. To that end, much work has gone into understanding the skills potential employers require of graduates [1-5]. The impression given by industry is that it wants graduates who can hit the ground running and be productive as soon as possible.

As well as canvassing industry directly, researchers have also studied the job adverts for computer personnel. These adverts emphasize the technologies required without much regard for the soft skills or the potential of the candidate to develop into senior roles [6-8]. Given the emphasis placed on specific technologies by industry, it is no surprise to find that computer science and software engineering programs are weighted towards technical subjects.

However, there seems to be little concern for software developers in the years following graduation. Studies in traditional engineering disciplines show how important hands-on technical work is to engineers. For instance, Bailyn and Lynch [9] report

that "the unambiguous and immediate gratifications obtainable from solving concrete technical problems" (p.281) are key motivators. This love of technical work has also been seen in the software world [10-11]. In fact, so strong is the interest in technical aspects that none of the managers interviewed in Downey's study [11] expressed any staff motivation issues.

However, Allport's warning that "[w]hen skills are mastered they have no longer any motivational character" [12, p.247] is very relevant to software developers. Once expertise is acquired in a particular language or technology, the developer will want to move on to a new area This is shown by a tendency towards what Schein [13] calls a 'circumferential' career path. Thus software developers have been seen moving from group to group within an organization in order to learn new technologies [11]. If such opportunities do not exist within the organization, then software developers will move to other companies. For instance, Gallagher et al discovered that if their informants "had to do the same work for an extended period, they would rather change jobs or even work for another firm" [10, p.17].

Unfortunately, such a circumferential career path is not sustainable. Although "[i]n most professional fields experience makes a difference" [14, p.169], there is a perception in the software industry that experience in previous equipment, languages or operating systems is not valuable [15]. Thus a middle-aged programmer learning a new language or software package will be perceived as offering similar value to the organization as a graduate developer. As well as being in competition from recent graduates, the software developer who stays too long in a programming role will also find competition from experienced people in low-wage economies.

Therefore highly skilled technical workers are forced into managerial or customer-facing roles that they are ill-prepared for or which do not suit their personalities [11]. For instance, people with Asberger's syndrome can make excellent programmers, but lack the people skills needed for the other roles [16]. Alternatively, software developers leave the industry, returning to academia or embarking on radically different career paths.

Given this general agreement that a technical role only lasts through what Dalton, Thompson and Price [17] call stages I and II of their careers, there seems to be a problem in the transition to stage III. In other words, software people have difficulty going from achieving through their own efforts, to achieving through the efforts of others.

Of course this stage transition problem may simply be a generic mid-life crisis. According to Golembiewski [18] this "is a pivotal time between two more stable periods, which period usually peaks in the early 40's. The transition can be smooth or turbulent. The central issue is the disparity between what has been achieved and what is desired" (p.217).

However, Golembiewski cites rapidly changing technology as contributing to the confusion experienced at this point, so software developers, being close to these technology shifts, may have an increased "sense of being out of control over central life events, of being the acted-upon rather than the actor" (p.218).

Given the lack of research on mid-career software developers, this paper proposes an exploratory study of people with computer science or software engineering degrees who have dropped out of the industry and are now occupied in totally different ways. The research question being: why do well-educated software developers leave the profession?

2. THEORETICAL BACKGROUND

Because this is an exploratory study, interviews are suggested to gain insights into this phenomenon. This is one of Lethbridge, Sim and Singer's "inquisitive techniques" [19]. A grounded theory approach will be followed in that no pre-conceived hypothesis is postulated that might bias the findings. Or as Strauss and Corbin [20] advise, the process will be one of building rather than testing theories.

Following Miles and Huberman's [21] recommendation that a data collection instrument must be designed and, at the same time must not be completely prescriptive, a semi-structured interview seems a sensible compromise. However, there is a serious issue: how to design an interview instrument that captures all the necessary data, without knowing precisely what data needs to be collected.

Downey's [11] previous work on software skills also used interviews to elicit data. In that study, Bandura's social cognitive theory [22] provided the theoretical framework on which the interviews were based. Given that this new study also concerns individuals, it is expected that social cognitive theory will be applicable here as well. This theory postulates that a person is influenced by three factors: their personality, their behaviors and their environment, with these factors affecting each other reciprocally. Designing an appropriate interview instrument, based on this theory, involves identifying aspects of personality, behavior and environment relevant to the overall research question: why do well-educated software developers leave the profession?

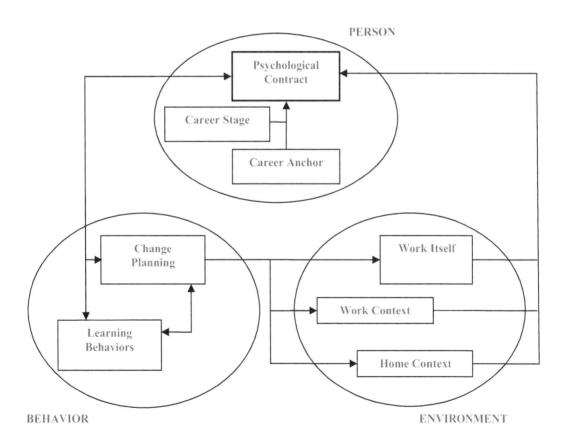

Figure 1 Social Cognitive Theory

2.1 Personality

Why does someone leave an organization? An important factor could be a perceived breach in that person's psychological contract with the organization [23]. A psychological contract concerns the expectations an employee has of the place s/he works as well as the expectations the employer has of the employee.

Such a contract is implicit and can be quite dynamic [24]. Agarwal and Ferratt's [25] research suggests that a person's career anchor [13] as well as their career stage [17] will influence the psychological contract. For instance, it has been observed that people with a technical career anchor are "often found in systems programming, applications programming, and software engineering positions" [26, p.162], whereas those with a managerial career anchor tend "to cluster in such positions as systems analyst, project leader, and computer manager" (p.162). Thus the move from a programming to a project leader role may cause two changes in the person's psychological contract. In one sense, the move could upset someone with a strong technical career anchor while, at the same time, fulfilling a need to move to the next career stage.

For the purposes of this research, the psychological contract between the individual and the software industry in general, as well as the person's perception of self need to be explored. Thinking of this in terms of Maslow's hierarchy of needs [27]: was work in the software sector contributing to the person's sense of esteem or feelings of self-actualisation? Or had it simply become a way of paying the bills?

Another useful area to explore would be the person's original career motivation – this would also help to understand any subsequent breaches in the psychological contract.

2.2 Behavior

"As open systems, human beings as well as work organizations, need to grow and develop" [28, p.64]. Despite this, change is difficult and people tend to resist it. According to Schein [29], there are three steps to making a change. Firstly, the motivation for change must be created – the person must realize that something is wrong with the status quo. There must be a feeling of survival anxiety, where the person feels s/he will not survive unless s/he changes; or a feeling of guilt, where s/he feels that important goals will not be achieved without change. Change tends to be resisted and the person needs to build up the confidence to overcome anxiety about learning new ways.

The second step is learning new concepts and new meanings for old concepts. This is done by identifying new role models and starting to imitate them. A lot of trial and error learning is required at this stage. Finally, the new concepts and meanings have to be internalized – i.e. incorporated into the person's self concept and identity, as well as into ongoing relationships. In some occupations, the person may be expected to undergo some sort of rite of passage before being admitted into the new role [30].

Thus changing careers is something that requires planning. Handy [31] argues that change cycles span two or three years and recommends research into the next cycle well before action needs to be taken. So it would be expected that anyone who has made a major career change has planned it. The interview needs to explore the point where the person has realized that something is wrong with the status quo and has experienced survival anxiety or guilt. Then the steps taken to research their new career have to be teased out.

Learning behaviors may also offer insights into the person's willingness to change occupations. It has been shown that people who lack confidence in their ability to do one job will be less likely to abandon it for another, different form of occupation [32]. However, if the person receives training in the new role (perhaps by attending a night class or signing up for a distance learning course) they might gain the confidence to make the transition. Similarly, exploring a possible career change might cause the person to re-evaluate their psychological contract and conclude that there are worse things out there than their current role.

2.3 Environment

There is widespread agreement that it is the work itself that provides the main motivation for employees [33-36]. A decision to leave the software industry could come about because of boredom with the work (the person has achieved mastery of a particular technology and there are no opportunities to move to different technical work [12]) or a change to a new role that does not engage the employee as much as technical work (e.g. management or sales roles).

Other work-related factors could be a lack of training and continuous professional development [37], or even the lack of social supports – i.e. supervisor and co-worker supports [38]. However, an increasing concern, at least in the information systems world, is the affect of burnout on the individual [39]. Therefore, both the work itself and the work environment need to be explored to identify factors contributing to the person's decision to leave the industry.

Of course the person's home environment can come into play as well [9, 40]. Changes in family circumstances, such as marriage, the birth of children, divorce, or the need to care for sick or elderly relatives can all influence a person's decision to change career – particularly if the career places significant demands in terms of long hours and extensive travel. Indeed, Heppner and Heppner's research [41] suggests that the stress associated with traditional male roles may contribute to the seven-year shorter lifespan men can expect on average.

3. THE INTERVIEW INSTRUMENT

The people selected for interview will be those who have:

1. Obtained a third-level degree in a software-related discipline – e.g. computer science, software engineering or information technology. This study is concerned with people who have made significant educational investments in their software careers [42]. Because the barriers to obtaining software employment are low, unqualified individuals who have knowledge of a particular technology can easily obtain a software development role. However, because of their limited educational investment, leaving the industry at a later stage is not a significant issue for them [43]. Such a person "is characterized by retraining, continuing education, and transitions to

different occupations" [32]. This is called a 'protean' career path – the "term is derived from the Greek god Proteus, who could change shape at will" [44]. These people - who have dipped into the industry for a time - are not of interest here.

2. Taken the above course because it is their first choice. The reason for this is an attempt to control against generic mid-life crises. If a person was unable to do what s/he really wanted – because of parental pressure or being unable to meet the entrance requirements – then s/he is more likely to decide later in life to pursue the original goal. The people required for our study should have had a genuine interest in computing at the very start.

3. Worked as software developers. This reflects another investment in a software career – the apprenticeship, or experiential learning phase.

4. Are now working in a totally different area, both in terms of role and business – i.e. they no longer work in the software development arena.

It is anticipated that these people will be found through the network – former colleagues who have moved on to non-software work. Preliminary investigation reveals stories of software developers becoming house husbands, working as porters or being employed in the leisure industry. These people will be approached to take part in the study.

The key behavioral event in this study is the transition from being a software developer to something else. Thus, we need to understand the personal and environmental circumstances of the informants before and after the change. To make the interview flow in a logical fashion, a chronological approach is appropriate. The interviewees will be guided through three stages of their lives as follows:

1. **Original Career Choice**

   - What attracted you into software development in the first place?
     - Did you think you had an aptitude for this sort of work?
   - Did you consider other alternatives?
     - What would you have really liked to do?
   - Did early work experiences live up to expectations?
     - What sort of goals did you have back then?
     - What was it about software work that you liked?
     - Were there any sacrifices involved – long hours, travel?

2. **Decision to Change**

   - Roughly how long were you working in software when you decided you needed a change?

   - Was there a moment or specific incident that made you re-evaluate your career?
     - Change of role at work?
     - Change of boss, key co-workers?
     - Redundancy?
     - Changes in family circumstances?
     - Gradual dissatisfaction with the job?
   - How did you go about making the change?
     - What options did you feel you had?
     - Did you have any support in deciding what to do next?
     - Did you expect that a time would come when you would have to consider a career change?
   - Why did you choose a non-software role?

3. **Current Role**

   - How does your current role fulfil expectations?
   - How does it compare with your original role?
     - Financially?
     - Socially (work-life balance)?
     - In terms of personal satisfaction?
   - If you could rewind the clock, would you have been better off opting for this role at the start of your career?
   - Do you feel qualified for your new role?
     - Have you completed formal courses?
     - Have you gone through any rites of passage?
   - How have your ambitions changed over time?
   - Is this a temporary position?
     - Do you foresee other changes in the future?

Relating the questions above to the theoretical background given earlier, it can be seen that the psychological contract is being explored at both the original (software) career stage and at the current stage. Also, some feeling for the person's career anchor should be obtained by comparing the attractions of software work to those of the new role.

The only behavior the study is concerned with is the actual career change event and this is explored in depth. It will be interesting to see if this change is time-related – a gradual realization that software work is not satisfactory – or due to a cathartic event, such as redundancy or a change in family circumstance. Another important insight concerns how the person went about exploring the options available and preparing for the change.

The environment is crucial to this study. It is likely that the decision to change will be influenced by changes in either the work or domestic environments. Indeed, an environmental upheaval might just be the catalyst to set the person on a new path. For instance, employment in a secure, well paying software role might be enough to offset growing feelings of discontentment with the job. However, if that company shuts down, the option to change careers may be a viable alternative to finding a similar role in another company. In other words, a situation may arise that creates "survival anxiety" [29] and triggers the change process.

Once the decision to change is made, how the person chooses a new path and makes the steps to become qualified for that path are of interest. How easy is it for someone to change career? Is it necessary to make a similar investment in preparing for this new career as they did for their original, software developer role?

Finally, the sense of self after the transition must be related back to the psychological contract and the person's career anchor. Is this new role a better fit for that person? Or is this only an intermediate step to an ultimate goal? Was the interviewee in control of the change process – resigning from software development because the role was not fulfilling their higher-level needs [27]? Or was s/he forced into change through environmental circumstances – the need to care for relatives, redundancy, job stressors, etc. In these latter circumstances, it is possible that the new role is not ideal for the person, but is the best possible in the circumstances.

4. POSSIBLE OUTCOMES

Being an exploratory study, we cannot be sure of the outcomes of this study. The hope is to learn why the informants have made a radical change in their career paths or as Patton [45] put it: "[t]he mandate of qualitative methods is to go into the field and learn about the program firsthand" (p.17). In the worst case scenario, it might become obvious that radically different environmental factors triggered these changes. However, it would be interesting if there is something inherently lacking in the software developer's career that prompts people to leave the profession, despite having invested so much in getting into it in the first place.

If there are particular criticisms of the software career coming out of the study, these can be fed back into both academia and industry, in order to address possible deficiencies in undergraduate curricula and to inform companies on how software people need to be developed throughout their careers. Golembiewski [18], for instance, recommends that the person's employer needs to "assume primary responsibility for helping directly with the mid-life transition, and especially for funding ameliorative efforts" (p.221). Fast-paced software organizations might not appreciate this and, as a result, not give sufficient support to their staff as their needs change.

Similarly the outcomes can help individuals make early career choices. For instance, it might be the case that particular career anchors are totally unsuited for software work.

Another possibility is that people could be ideally suited to technical work, but are not compatible with senior roles in the computing industry. Transitions to people-oriented roles, like management and sales, may not suit those who lack communication and collaboration skills. It would be interesting to learn what choices those with strong technical/functional

career anchors make to avoid management roles. It has been seen that opportunities on the technical career ladder in subsidiaries to large multi-nationals involve extensive people-interaction and sometimes management responsibility [46]. The findings of this study could inform a revised technical career path that would suit technical people better.

If there is a common thread to these interviews and a plausible theory emerges, it will not be easy to follow up with a quantitative study. For instance, to poll a representative sample, researchers would need to know how many people have given up professional software employment. While universities should have figures relating to their software graduates, their alumni associations may not have as accurate a picture of what all these graduates are doing today.

Such a study would also need to consider other professions. Are the factors identified for software people also relevant for those in other professions, or are software people unique in some way?

5. ACKNOWLEDGEMENT
This work is partially supported by Science Foundation Ireland (SFI) under grant number 03/CE2/I303-1.

6. REFERENCES
[1] D. M. S. Lee, E. M. Trauth and D. Farwell, Critical Skills and Knowledge Requirements of IS Professionals: A Joint Academic/Industry Investigation, *MIS Quarterly*, **17**, 313-340 (1995)

[2] E. M. Trauth, D. W. Farwell and D. Lee, The IS Expectation Gap: Industry Expectations Versus Academic Preparation, *MIS Quarterly*, **17**, 293-307 (1993)

[3] N. Shi and D. Bennett, Critical Success Factors for IS Executive Careers - Evidence from Case Studies, *ACM SIGCPR Computer Personnel*, **19**, 34-54 (1998)

[4] C. L. Noll and M. Wilkins, Critical Skills of IS Professionals: A Model for Curriculum Development, *Journal of Information Technology Education*, **1**, 143-154 (2002)

[5] S. Sawyer, K. R. Eschenfelder, A. Diekema and C. R. McClure, Corporate IT Skill Needs: a Case Study of BigCo, *ACM SIGCPR Computer Personnel*, **19**, 27-41 (1998)

[6] C. R. Litecky, K. P. Arnett and B. Prabhakar, The Paradox of Soft Skills versus Technical Skills in IS Hiring, *Journal of Computer Information Systems*, **45**, 69-76 (2004)

[7] J. Downey, An Artifact-centric Method for Creating Job Descriptions, D. J. Armstrong and C. Riemenschneider, Eds., 2008 ACM SIGMIS CPR, Charlottesville, Virginia, ACM Press, 2008, p. 12-21

[8] J. Downey, Designing Job Descriptions for Software Development, C. Barry, M. Lang, K. Conboy, W. Wojtkowski and G. Wojtkowski, Eds., 16th International Conference on Information Systems Development (ISD2007), Galway, Ireland, Springer, 2007, p. 447-460

[9] L. Bailyn and J. T. Lynch, Engineering as a life-long career: its meaning, its satisfactions, its difficulties, *Journal of Occupational Behaviour*, **4**, 263-283 (1983)

[10] K. P. Gallagher, K. Kaiser, K. Frampton and V. C. Gallagher, Best Practice for Grooming Critical Mid-Level

Roles, ACM SIGMIS CPR, St. Louis, Missouri, ACM Press, 2007, p. 15-19

[11] J. Downey, Career Paths for Programmers: Skills in Senior Software Roles, Cambridge Scholars Publishing, Newcastle, England, 2009.

[12] G. W. Allport, Pattern and Growth in Personality, Holt, Rinehart and Winston, Cambridge, Massachusetts, 1937.

[13] E. H. Schein, Career Anchors: Discovering Your Real Values, Pfeiffer & Co, San Diego, 1990.

[14] A. Shapero, Managing Professional People: Understanding Creative Performance, The Free Press, New York, 1985.

[15] P. McGovern, HRM, Technical Workers and the Multinational Corporation, Routledge, 1998.

[16] S. Silberman, The Geek Syndrome, *Wired Magazine*, **9**, 1-10 (2001)

[17] G. W. Dalton, P. H. Thompson and R. L. Price, The Four Stages of Professional Careers - A New Look at Performance by Professionals, *Organizational Dynamics*, **6**, 19-44 (1977)

[18] R. T. Golembiewski, Mid-Life Transition and Mid-Career Crisis: A Special Case for Individual Development, *Public Administration Review*, **38**, 215-222 (1978)

[19] T. C. Lethbridge, S. E. Sim and J. Singer, Studying Software Engineers: Data Collection Techniques for Software Field Studies, *Empirical Software Engineering*, **10**, 311-341 (2005)

[20] A. Strauss and J. Corbin, Basics of Qualitative Research, Sage Publications, Inc., Thousand Oaks, California, ed. 2nd, 1998.

[21] M. B. Miles and A. M. Huberman, Qualitative Data Analysis, Sage Publications, Thousand Oaks, California, ed. 2nd, 1994.

[22] A. Bandura, Social Foundations of Thought & Action: A Social Cognitive Theory, Prentice Hall, Englewood Cliffs, New Jersey, 1986.

[23] H. Meland, R. P. Waage and M. K. Sein, The Other Side of Turnover: Managing IT Personnel Strategically, J. E. Moore and S. E. Yager, Eds., 2005 ACM SIGMIS CPR Conference, Atlanta, Georgia, ACM Press, 2005, p. 67-74

[24] D. A. Kolb, I. M. Rubin and J. M. McIntyre, Organizational Psychology: An Experiential Approach, Prentice-Hall Inc., Englewood Cliffs, New Jersey, ed. 2nd, 1974.

[25] R. Agarwal and T. W. Ferratt, Retention and the Career Motives of IT Professionals, ACM SIGCPR conference on Computer personnel research, Chicago, Illinois, ACM Press, 2000, p. 158-166

[26] M. Igbaria, J. H. Greenhaus and S. Parasuraman, Career Orientations of MIS Employees: An Empirical Analysis, *MIS Quarterly*, **15**, 151-169 (1991)

[27] A. H. Maslow, Motivation and Personality, Harper & Row, New York, ed. 2nd, 1970.

[28] D. J. O'Connor and D. M. Wolfe (1986) Career crises at midlife are more than they are cracked up to be, pp. 60-64.

[29] E. H. Schein, The Corporate Culture Survival Guide, Jossey-Bass, San Francisco, 1999.

[30] H. M. Trice and D. A. Morand (1989) Rites of passage in work careers, ed. M. B. Arthur, D. T. Hall and B. S. Lawrence. Cambridge, Cambridge University Press, pp. 397-416.

[31] C. Handy, The Empty Raincoat, Random House, ed. 1, 1994.

[32] K. Otto, D. E. Dette-Hagenmeyer and C. Dalbert, Occupational Mobility in Members of the Labor Force: Explaining the Willingness to Change Occupations, *Journal of Career Development*, **36**, 262-288 (2010)

[33] F. Herzberg, B. Mausner and B. B. Snyderman, The Motivation To Work, John Wiley & Sons Inc., ed. 2nd, 1959.

[34] J. R. Hackman and G. R. Oldham, Work Redesign, Adison-Wesley, Reading Massachusetts, 1980.

[35] V. H. Vroom, Work and Motivation, John Wiley and Sons Inc, New York, 1964.

[36] J. B. Thatcher, Y. Liu and L. P. Stepina, The Role of the Work Itself: An Empirical Examination of Intrinsic Motivation's Influence on IT Workers' Attitudes and Intentions, SIGCPR '02, Kristiansand, Norway, ACM, 2002, p. 25-33

[37] M. Sumner, A Report on Industry-University Roundtable Discussions on Recruitment and Retention of High-Tech Professionals, ACM SIGCPR Conference on Computer Personnel Research, 2001, p. 139-143

[38] J. Yoon and S. Thye, Superviser Support in the Workplace and Positive Affectivity, *The Journal of Social Psychology*, **140**, 295-316 (2000)

[39] J. E. Moore, Job Attitudes and Perceptions of Exhausted IS/IT Professionals: Are We Burning Out Valuable Human Resources?, SIGCPR, Boston, ACM Press, 1998, p. 264-271

[40] D. Scholarios and A. Marks, Work-life balance and the software worker, *Human Resource Management Journal*, **14**, 54-75 (2004)

[41] M. J. Heppner and P. P. Heppner, On Men and Work: Taking the Road Less Traveled, *Journal of Career Development*, **36**, 19 (2009)

[42] G. S. Becker, Human Capital, The University of Chicago Press, Chicago, ed. 2nd, 1975.

[43] D. Joseph, S. Ang and S. Slaughter, Identifying the Prototypical Career Paths of IT Professionals: A Sequence and Cluster Analysis, J. E. Moore and S. E. Yager, Eds., 2005 ACM SIGMIS CPR Conference, Atlanta, Georgia, ACM Press, 2005, p. 94-96

[44] D. T. Hall, Protean Careers of the 21st Century, *Academy of Management Executive*, **10**, 8-16 (1996)

[45] M. Q. Patton, How to Use Qualitative Methods in Evaluation, SAGE Publications, Inc., Newbury Park, California, 1987.

[46] J. Downey (2010) Careers in Software: Is there Life after Programming?, ed. J. Downey and D. Joseph. Vancouver, Canada, ACM Press, pp. 1-7.

IT Workforce Planning:
A Modular Design Science Approach

Monica Adya
Department of Management
Marquette University
Milwaukee, WI 53201, USA
+1 (414) 288-7526
monica.adya@marquette.edu

Fred Niederman
Shaughnessy Professor of MIS
St. Louis University
St. Louis, MO 63108, USA,
+1 (314) 977-3845
niederfa@slu.edu

ABSTRACT
Strategic benefits offered by well-executed investments in information technology (IT) have been acknowledged extensively. Among other factors, successful return on IT investments depends upon timely availability of quality of IT personnel. IT workforce planning necessitates active projections of a firm's workforce transformation from both known technology evolutions such as shifting among platforms, and personnel transition scenarios such as retirement, turnover, and other career decisions. Using a design science approach, we propose the development of a modular workforce planning system that captures current workforce inventory, projected personnel transitions, and projected skill evolutions to generate future workforce states. This proposed system has implications for development and design of systems for succession, transition, training, and hiring/exit decisions for an IT workforce environment.

Categories and Subject Descriptors
K.6.1 [**Project and People Management**]: Staffing

General Terms
Human Factors

Keywords
IT human resources, Forecasting personnel demand, Forecasting personnel supply, IT Personnel Transition Evolution Model, Staffing support systems.

1. INTRODUCTION
The strategic benefits and competitive advantages offered by mature and well-executed investments in information technology (IT) are acknowledged and undeniable [2] [8]. Successful IT investments are reliant on numerous factors such as quality of existing infrastructure, clarity of project planning, maturity and abilities of end users, and skilled IT personnel to manage and deliver well engineered and correct systems [1]. It is this last element, the skill and availability of qualified IT workforce, which forms the foundation of this study.

IT environments are typically dynamic, necessitating a systematic and deliberate approach to attracting, developing, and retaining IT professionals ([10] [11]. Most critically this translates into better identification of personnel needs and a planned evolution of current skill sets to future desirable states [1]. Workforce needs in the IT area are particularly vulnerable to both technical and economic shifts in the business world. New technologies routinely, and sometimes unexpectedly, replace traditional ones. The recent emergence of social networks, for example, is having demonstrated and significant effect on organizational communication, information sharing, and knowledge management. Furthermore, economic shifts tend to impact the green-lighting of IT projects during a downturn and the choice of new project types during recovery.

IT workforce planning, therefore, compels active projections of a firm's workforce transformation from both known technology evolutions (such as shifting among known platforms or moving to new versions of ERP software) and personnel transition scenarios such as retirement, intra-organizational transition, and other significant career decisions. It presents a complex or, as Hevner, March, Park, and Ram [7] suggest, a "*wicked*" problem (pg. 81). Such problems are characterized by unstable and ill-defined requirements environment, complex interactions between subcomponents, and significant reliance on human cognition and social abilities to define a fitting solution [7]. Yet, a robust solution for this problem can provide significant value and utility to IT organizations through the development and design of systems for succession, transition, training, and hiring/exit decisions for an IT workforce environment. From this perspective, workforce planning, which is constantly in flux because of personal, professional, and environmental churn, lends itself well to a design science approach that produces and applies "knowledge of tasks and situations to create effective artifacts" (pg. 252) [13] as opposed to creating theoretical knowledge.

In this study, we propose the development and evaluation of a modular workforce planning strategy that captures current workforce inventory, projected personnel transitions, and projected skill evolutions to generate future workforce states. Each of these elements can be developed as separate components as described in this paper. Propositions in this paper build upon the IT Personnel Transition Evolution Model (ITPTEM) proposed in Andrews & Niederman [1]. In the next section, we review IT workforce planning and the ITPTEM model within this context. Next, we describe the proposed workforce planning system and its elements, discuss its variant implementations, and propose a research agenda based on the design science paradigm. The paper concludes with the potential applications, implications, and research needs in this domain.

2. BACKGROUND AND MOTIVATION

Effective job analysis lies at the heart of meaningful workforce planning initiatives [14]. Job analysis captures work-related information for jobs as they currently exist or have existed in the past within an organization [12]. However, in todays' dynamic IT environment characterized by rapidly evolving technologies, shortened product life cycles [14], and globalized IT functions, the knowledge, skills, and abilities (KSAs) demanded of IT professionals experience a more rapid churn. Further, ongoing shortages in the IT talent pool [9] and bidding wars between competing organizations for talented workers has created a volatility in the IT workforce environment that could potentially be mitigated by effective workforce planning. Firms looking to leverage IT initiatives for strategic advantage must place significant consideration towards management of its IT human resources (HR) [3].

Recommendations for strategic and systematic workforce management have primarily emerged from the HR literature. Most notably Schneider & Konz [12] suggested an eight step approach to workforce planning : (1) collect information about current jobs; (2) specify job tasks and build task clusters; (3) develop and administer task surveys; (4) analyze task survey responses; (5) conduct the KSA process; (6) develop and administer KSA surveys; (7) gather information about the future; and (8) revise tasks and/or task clusters and KSA or KSA clusters in light of future changes. In recent years, Singh [14] recognized the ambiguity around individual and job skills and modified Schneider & Konz model to propose an alternative framework that encompasses: (a) environmental analysis / job scan; (b) focused internal analysis of current jobs; (c) gap analysis and preparation for future jobs through selection, staffing, and other HR functions; and (d) evaluation of planning process effectiveness.

In the IT literature, Andrews & Niederman [1] provide a conceptual foundation for a systematic approach to IT workforce planning, the ITPETM model, which suggests that a firm's current KSA state, captured as a skills/personnel inventory, can be transitioned to a future desirable skills state through systematic execution of specific HR programs such as training and hiring. The model highlights the complex interplay of skill gains (e.g. hiring, retention, training), skill losses (e.g. retirement, turnover), and continuous learning for fulfilling future state skill gaps.

The organizational-level perspective reflected in the studies discussed above highlight three areas of workforce planning that warrant further attention. First, KSAs are typically examined through the lens of skill *sets* and skill *clusters*, thereby assuming that sufficient staff is on payroll to support the formation of such sets and clusters. Small and mid-sized organizations where skills sets and personnel counts are limited may find limited utility for these approaches. This can be a more critical issue in IT where a smaller internal talent pool, and hence skill clusters, may be largely supplemented by contractual and temporary workers. Second, these models overlook the explicit connection between KSAs and organizational work needs represented via projects and ongoing work assignments. IT work, in contrast, is largely and explicitly structured around strategic projects, tactical demands from day-to-day organizational IT activities that "keep the lights on," and from operational demands that stem from management of IT assets [15]. Each of these imposes differential demands on workforce planning. For instance, closure of existing projects, initiation of new ones, steady-state operations, and evolving tactical assignments will trigger planned KSA changes. KSA changes may also occur because of personal factors such as upcoming retirement, change in career direction, and turnover. A VB.net developer, for example, may enhance her skills by adding Java and php for continued engagement in upcoming projects. Such progressive expansion of her skill sets may occur with some certainty based on her career plans, upcoming project needs, and other personal and professional factors. In sum, while KSA expansions are uncertain, they are not random or static. Most traditional workforce planning models only implicitly address this uncertainty and explicit link between current and future states of IT work. Consequently, we propose that the explicit integration of projects and ongoing engagements be a crucial component of any IT workforce planning system.

Finally, most existing empirical studies, such as Dawes & Helbig [4], do not directly utilize existing corporate data to develop and evolve workforce planning scenarios. Rather, they rely upon surveys of IT employees and leaders to determine current and future workforce needs and plan for transition between the two states. Although the value of such domain expert knowledge is undeniable, it is best combined with patterns captured in historical trends and knowledge of environmental factors to lend objectivity to the forecasting process.

In this paper, we propose a Workforce Planning Strategy (WPS) with the intent of addressing the limitations highlighted above i.e. (a) recognition of individual level KSAs as opposed to KSA sets and clusters, and (b) predicting future workforce needs based on active recognition of project and operational assignments, and (c) combining organizational data with domain knowledge. The next section describes in detail the proposed workforce planning strategy and later, discusses how design science paradigm will inform our future research.

3. WORKFORCE PLANNING STRATEGY

Figure 1 illustrates the conceptual framework for the WPS. We propose this as a *modular* approach since each of its components – workforce inventory, work assignments inventory, future supply and demand forecasts, and fit-gap analysis - can be developed and matured as separate components such that the model evolves with the organization. Key outcome from the WPS is a recommended strategy towards fitting the gap between projected supply of and demand for IT KSAs.

3.1 Enumerate and Categorize Current Workforce Inventory

Current workforce inventory [5] is comprised of people currently employed by the organization, their KSAs, and demographic information. Most organizations today maintain active databases where such information is captured, although efforts must be invested in standardizing data and its organization. For instance, one organization may list "programming" as a skill, another may distinguish ability to devise algorithms from ability to translate requirements into code; some may list ability to deal with "middleware" while others may specify particular middleware languages. Because such inventory is likely organized primarily for compensation and assignments to career hierarchies, many

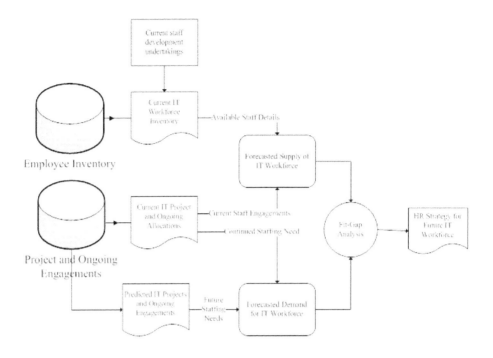

Figure 1: IT Workforce Planning System

different kinds of work activity may be counted within the same grouping.

We propose use of the following measures for each individual IT employee as a base line of current status relevant to calculating future supply: personnel type such as contract, permanent, and part-time, age to determine factors such as retirement or risk of transition, time at organization, time in position, number of company positions held (from which average time to promotion can be calculated), and each KSA. Ideally, an evaluation of the accomplishment level for each KSA should also be present. Table 1 illustrates a simulated IT personnel environment for Firm A.

Although much of this information may exist in HR Information Systems (HRIS) or other databases, massaging the data into a usable format, normalizing it across departments, and filling gaps in data may constitute a significant task. For instance, IT employees assigned to user functions may be technically assigned to the functional area rather than IT. Accepted security and privacy measures should be applied. Additionally, assessing performance and skill levels may require human interpretation and triangulation. Self-surveys, for example, might be supplemented with supervisor surveys and/or actual performance evaluations.

3.2 Enumerate and Categorize Current Projects/Ongoing Requirements

We use Symons' [15] categorization of IT work as consisting of three broad types – *projects* aimed at creating specific changes or outcomes, *tactical engagements* that provide day-to-day support for business IT, and *operational engagements* that support maintenance of IT assets such as infrastructure. From this perspective, projects are viewed as having a defined start and end while tactical and operational (i.e. ongoing) engagements employ workers in sustained manner.

At a given point in time, it might be expected that all employees are involved in some combination of project and ongoing activities. An inventory of such engagements should, in principle, be derivable by enumeration and summation of work assignments of all current personnel. Table 2 provides a simplified illustration of this concept for Firm A. Thus, if a particular programmer has responsibility for the maintenance of a particular application and is also assigned to the development of a new application, we can derive the first portion of an enumerated portfolio by listing these two applications. When such an enumeration is completed for all employees, a portfolio of projects and ongoing engagements can be derived as the sum of assignments (for example 8 programmers on a project with an average of 50% time would suggest that such a project is currently staffed at 4 FTEs). Such a portfolio could be laid out, for example, using an ITIL type set of services to organize them by common types. Table 3 illustrates outcome of the process described above.

Work requirements determined as above can be mapped against listings derived from personnel to identify skill needs and gaps. It is possible that some assets are not assigned any regular supervision, that they are informally handled, or that their service is contracted out (e.g. printing). Performance of such an analysis may be unlikely to turn up large numbers of mission critical applications that are not "owned" by one or another responsible party, but clusters of smaller applications/assets may suggest additional assignments for improvement of overall governance.

In practice, such enumeration will identify additional tasks and responsibilities beyond those listed. Such clarification of gaps could allow more deliberate allocation of responsibilities and accurate compensation for actual work and responsibilities. Additionally, current assignments can help distinguish between temporary and ongoing needs for specific employees and their KSAs. Combined with information from the current workforce

Table 1: Example of Current Workforce Inventory for Firm A

Personnel (who)	Personnel Type	Age[1]	Time at Firm A[2]	Yrs. in Position	# of Positions	Primary KSA	Skill Level
A	Consultant	34	2	2	1	Bus. Analyst	100
B	Permanent	45	8	3	3	RDBMS	75
C	New Hire	23	0.5	0.5	1	Windows	50
D	Consultant	28	1	1	1	Oracle	75
E	Contract	42	1	1	1	PeopleSoft	90
F	New Entrant	21	0.5	0.5	1	JAVA	75
G	Permanent	57	15	5	4	COBOL	100
H	Employee	59	20	5	5	Mainframe	80
I	Consultant	29	2	1	2	C++	80
J	New Hire	22	0.5	0.5	1	Visual Basic	80
K	Consultant	31	1.5	1	2	Oracle	75
L	Permanent	48	4	2	2	RDBMS	95
M	Permanent	38	8	4	3	Project Mgmt.	80
N	Permanent	42	8	3	4	Project Mgmt.	95

Table 2: Example of Project and Ongoing Assignments for Firm A

Personnel (who)	Work Assignment	Project?	Start of Assignment	End of Assignment	Time Allocation
A	CRM Module Design	Y	Jan 2010	Jan 2011	50%
A	HRIS Requirements	Y	Jan 2010	Mar. 2010	50%
B	CRM Database	Y	Jan 2010	March 2011	25%
B	Customer Database Support	N	-	-	50%
B	HR Data Support	N	-	-	25%
C	End User Support	N	-	-	100%
D	CRM Oracle	Y	Jan 2010	June 2011	100%
E	CRM Development	Y	Jan 2010	June 2011	100%
F	CRM Development	Y	June 2010	Dec 2011	50%
F	Corporate Web	N	-	-	50%
G	Legacy Systems Maintenance and Phase-out	N	-	June 2011	100%
H	Legacy Systems Maintenance and Phase-out	N	-	June 2011	100%
I	HRIS Development	Y	June 2010	May 2011	50%
I	Legacy Maintenance	N	-	-	50%
J	End-user Support - reports	N	-	-	100%
K	CRM Development	Y	Jan 2010	May 2010	50%
K	HRIS Development	Y	June 2010	May 2011	50%
L	Database Support and Maintenance	N	-	-	100%
M	CRM Project Management	Y	Jan 2010	Dec 2011	100%
N	HRIS Project Management	Y	June 2010	June 2011	100%

Table 3: Example of Summarized Project and Ongoing Assignments for Firm A

Assignment	KSAs	Current FTE	Required FTE	FTE Gap[1]	Estimated End of Requirement[2]
CRM Module	Oracle	1	2	1	Dec 2011
	PeopleSoft	1	2	1	
	Analyst	0.5	1	0.5	
	Developers	2	2	0	
	RDBMS	0.25	1	0.75	
	Project Mgmt.	1	1	0	
HRIS Application	Requirements	0.5	0.5	0	June 2011
	Development	1	2	1	
	Project Mgmt.	1	0.5	-0.5	
End-User Support	Database Support	0.75	1	0.25	-
	Custom Reporting	1	0.5	-0.5	-
Legacy Systems	Legacy Systems Maintenance and Phase-out	2.5	2.5	0	Dec. 2011
Corporate Web	Web development and maintenance	0.5	1	0.5	-

inventory, current engagements will facilitate prediction of projected workforce supply. Further, they can identify skills nearing obsolescence that might need replenishment. Finally, these provide a more objective measure of employee engagement when calculated using techniques such as Markov and network analysis [6].

Where an organization has readily available data regarding assignments, much of this analysis should be systematically derivable. However, it is unrealistic to expect such data to be available in electronic form within an evolving environment. For example, projects of more than three months may be formally connected to work assignments while teams working sequentially on short term projects may be viewed as more generally assigned to a work area. Additional triangulation may be available in organizations that have independent inventories of projects and assets (e.g. hardware and software).

3.3 Enumerate and Categories Future Projects/Ongoing Engagements

Projecting expected IT work for firms even a few months in the future can be challenging. Rapid evolution of technologies and business needs necessitates flexibility and innovation. To some extent this can be built into job design. Java developers, for instance, will maintain their Java skills as language and compiler upgrades emerge. Similarly, a project manager can be assumed to manage future IT projects despite uncertainty about what these projects will be. However, we would argue that a substantial amount of ongoing engagements can be expected to continue into the future. Some must be responsible for desktop computing, running help desks, data centers, security, eliciting user requirements, and product and vendor evaluations at all times. Many new application projects may be initiated, but a plan for upgrading enterprise systems to new releases on a three year cycle will still be in place. Perhaps only 80% of the workforce needs in three to five years is predictable but this suggests liberal application of "what if" scenarios and ranges rather than abandoning the potential benefits of planning.

Traditional workforce planning methodologies have suggested use of techniques such as Delphi to determine future workforce needs [6]. These techniques essentially rely on predicting the future state of an organization and tie workforce needs to these future states. We endorse these approaches particularly in application to the 80/20 rule - while "20%" of workforce needs are likely to be a surprise, "80%" will be a continuation of current trend. This 80% can be drawn from interviews and surveys of current managers.

We propose that each organization define best its own planning horizon. The approach we recommend for overall workforce planning can be applied at 1, 2, 3, or 5 year planning horizons. As established empirically in forecasting literature, accuracy of forecasts decline progressively over the forecast horizon and amount of "expected surprise" is expected to increase.

3.4 Forecast Workforce Supply

Employee workforce characteristics are their measurable and concrete aspects that are critical for organizational success [5] and can be influenced over time by HR policies and practices. With the proposition that future state of IT engagements may be a better predictor of future workforce needs than unstructured workforce assessments, the WPS considers a linkage between

current and expect future work demand as well as demographic adjustment in forecasting future workforce configurations.

Several steps must be executed in this phase. First, for each employee, probabilities will be generated regarding their exit or retention within the organization. These will rely on factors such as age and tenure within the organization, desirability of the skill set to reflect opportunities for cross-organizational transfer, projected engagement in current projects, and potential for upward or lateral movement within the organization. Historical retention data can be used to determine probabilities. For instance, assuming that past demographic records show different turnover rates for those ages 50 and above, those between 35-50, and those under 35, we can calculate an expected retention for entry-level programmers. These probabilities are then aggregated across job titles to yield projected workforce supply across skill categories.

Numerous other factors can impact probability estimations in these categories. First, factors such as performance evaluation, engagement in current projects, and promotion potential can result in varied projections. For instance, if 20 programmers are spread over 10 departments, turnover and other demographics may lead to varied retention probabilities for the category for different departments. Second, workforce mix – contractor, full time, part-time, and other arrangements – can be an important component. Assuming that a firm is currently staffed with 50% contractors and 50% full-time employers and that this is viewed as a strategically important mix, one might discover that expected retention would be 60% contractor and begin taking actions over the time horizon to encourage selected movement of contractors to full-time employees. Further, current operational and project assignments, ongoing training initiatives, and self-learning from current engagements will be used to determine both quantity of personnel and their projected KSAs.

3.5 Forecast Workforce Demand

Under the assumption that most IT organizations generate projections of ongoing and planned projects as well as operational engagements one to three years out, we propose that these projections be used to develop scenarios of future state workforce and skill demands. Further, we propose that future state projections be generated independently of current workforce inventory to support the fit-gap analysis proposed next.

3.6 Conduct Fit-Gap Analysis

Fit-gap analysis attempts to reconcile the gap between projected workforce demand and its projected supply. At this stage, the analysis specifically identified KSAs that need additional staffing, training, and development since these will be identified as gaps. Additionally, it will provide an indication of obsolescence wherein transition to newer skills and or exit strategies may need to be defined depending upon projections of obsolescence. We further suggest use of Bayesian approaches to generate workforce projections as newer workforce and project information becomes available.

3.7 Recommendations for Future HR Needs

An assessment of fit-gap analysis can help define more coherently the specific HR and staff development initiatives necessary to transition an organization from current to future state. These initiatives can include training (in-house, on-the-job, self); exit, hiring, and retention decisions; use of technology champions; project-related temporary acquisitions; technological assimilation; technology push/pull; and radial advice [1]. HR initiatives can result in several potential outcomes - adding a new skill to the inventory (skill shift), enriching existing skills (skill enhancement), loss of skill e.g. through turnover (skill loss), or intentional depletion of skill sets (skill obsolescence).

4. FUTURE RESEARCH AGENDA

Our proposed work on WPS fits within the design science paradigm since it attempts to provide a useful and workable technology-based solution to the complex IT workforce planning problem. March & Smith (1995) suggest that design science undertakings engage in iterative build and evaluate cycles with the intent of delivering constructs, model, methods, and implementations. We use components of their framework for directing future research efforts.

Artifact Design: In keeping with the design science paradigm, the study will deliver a design artifact i.e. the proposed model and its technological implementation. The WPS will be developed and validated initially on simulated data. Training data will be used to develop and evolve the two forecasting components and fit-gap modules. This, in itself, will be an extensive undertaking in that simple workforce scenarios will need to be evolved to more complex ones using progressive elaboration. The permutations and combinations are numerous and for a robust system, these must be adequately captured and utilized for artifact enhancement.

Design Evaluation: The next phase of this project will test the system in live settings where data from participating organizations will be used to further mature the artifact based on pragmatic constraints from real-world scenarios. This level of engagement brings a new level of complexity since each test organization will have its own unique characteristics such as the mix of in-house versus contract staff, nature of projects that are outsourced, build versus buy preferences among others. Incremental improvements will be tested using out-of-sample testing strategies using historical data. The challenge lies in our ability to evaluate effectiveness of this proposed artifact in real-time setting since this would require a lag of 2 to 3 years before forecast accuracy becomes evident.

Design Evolution: With the understanding that design is an iterative and evolutionary process [7] and that an artifact may be unable to address all possible solutions [13], we propose to utilize an iterative approach to maturing the WPS to a point that it captures a most useful set of solutions to the planning problem. A progressively more complex set of conditions will be used to evolve the WPS. Beyond that, our focus will shift to identifying conditions under which this matured WPS works effectively and identifying solutions for those that it does not.

5. IMPLICATIONS AND CONCLUSIONS

The WPS as proposed is preliminary and conceptual work. It is intended to add consideration of the dynamic nature of MIS work requirements into a broad workforce planning approach. Several elements of this proposal need to be further delved into. Specifically, the following issues require further consideration:

Role of Skill Enhancement: What is the impact of skill enhancement on the personnel environment and how can this be captured? A possible solution may entail using a third element i.e. personnel "quality" which can be reflected in our classification of a particular individual her skill level and skill enhancements. Therefore, a person undergoing on-the-job training is probably enhancing current skills through its application. In the future state, this individual's skill enhancement efforts should have resulted in improved skills in the same area and greater experience, yielding higher skill ranks.

Leveraged Skills: Leveraged skills such as continuous learning, presence of technology champions, and organizational assimilation are expected to play a more indirect role in our proposed model. These are part of the organizational environment and will often result in more tangible and direct initiatives such as on-the-job and in-house training. These variables can serve as global parameters and organizations that possess one or more of these can expect to transition to future states faster and/or more efficiently.

Role of IT Strategy: IT strategy may also be perceived as a global variable that can define how rapidly a division can define and obtain its future workforce state. On the one hand, it can be argued that IT strategy will define the sort of hiring, retention, training, and other initiatives undertaken for future state.

Organizational Perspective on Retention: Not all organizations are equivalent in how they view relationship with IT personnel. Organizations taking a long term view of IT investments seek sustained and productive relationships with IT personnel (Agarwal and Ferrat, 2001). On the other hand, those that view IT investments as short term initiatives, must convincingly balance recruitment and compensation of IT contractors (Agarwal & Ferrat, 2001) while developing a sustainable skill set for potential shifts to more strategic directions. The specific organizational perspective can significantly impact the execution and evolution of this model.

This discussion is presented as a framework and approach to an IT specific future workforce planning model. We view this as a modular framework in that each segment provides an opportunity as a standalone activity to provide benefits. We would expect that future research will address each of these modules through simulations of the underlying mathematical relations, and through design science and action research in implementing particular pieces of this in business settings.

6. REFERENCES

[1] Andrews, A., & Niederman, F. (1998). A Firm-level Model of IT Personnel Planning. *SIG MIS Computer Personnel Research*, 274-285.

[2] Bhardwaj, A., Bhardwaj, B., & Konsynski, B. (1999). Information technology effects on firm's performance as measured by tobin's q. *Management Science*, 45 (6), 1008-1024.

[3] Byrd, T.A. & Turner, D.E. (2001). An exploratory analysis of the value of the skills of IT personnel: Their relationship to IT infrastructure and competitive advantage. *Decision Sciences*, 32(1), 21-54.

[4] Dawes, S., & Helbig, N. (2007). Building Government IT Workforce Capacity: A Competency Framework.

Proceedings of the 8th International Conference on Digital Government Research , 254-255.

[5]   Emmerichs, R., Marcum, C., & Robbert, A. (2004). *An Operational Process for Workforce Planning.* Santa Monica, CA: RAND Corporation.

[6]   Greer, C. (2000). *Human Resource Management: A General Managerial Approach.* Upper Saddle River, NJ: Prentice Hall.

[7]   Hevner, A.R., March, S.T., Park, J., and Ram, S. (2004). Design science in Information Systems research, *MIS Quarterly*, 28(1), 75-105.

[8]   Im, K., Dow, K., & Grover, V. (2001). Research report: A reexamination of IT investment and the market value of the firm - An event study methodology. *Information Systems Research* , *12* (1), 103-117.

[9]   Luftman, J., Kempaiah, R. (2007). The IS organization of the future: The IT talent challenge, *Information System Management*, 24(2), 129-138.

[10] Luftman, J., Kempaiah, R., and Nash, E. (2006). Key issues for IT Executives 2005. *MIS Quarterly Executive*,

[11] Luftman, J., Kempaiah, R., and Rigoni, E.H. (2009). Key issues for IT Executives, 2008, *MIS Quarterly Executive*,

[12] Schneider, B., and Konz, A. (1989). Strategic Job Analysis. *Human Resource Management*, 51-63.

[13] Simon, S.T., and Smith, G.F. (1995). Design and natural science research on Information Technology, *Decision Support Systems*, 15, 251-266.

[14] Singh, P. (2008). Job Analysis for a Changing Workplace. *Human Resource Management Review* , 87-99

[15] Symons, C. (2006). How IT must shape and manage demand. White Paper, Project Management Institute, http://www.pmi.it/file/whitepaper/000071.pdf, last accessed 2/16/2011

Role of Professional Associations in Preparing, Recruiting, and Retaining Computing Professionals

Karthikeyan Umapathy
School of Computing
University of North Florida
Jacksonville, FL 32224, USA
k.umapathy@unf.edu

Albert D. Ritzhaupt
School of Teaching & Learning
University of Florida
Gainesville, FL 32611, USA
aritzhaupt@gmail.com

ABSTRACT

The purpose of this preliminary study is to investigate an under-explored topic, specifically, the role of professional associations in preparing, recruiting, and retaining computing professionals. Drawing on relevant literature, we identified a comprehensive list of services that should be provided by professional associations in order to prepare, recruit, and retain professionals. Then we assessed several computing professional associations to determine whether they offer those identified services. Our findings show that ACM has better coverage of services, followed by IEEE-CS, AITP, and AIS. This study indicates that computing professional associations have considerable influences on higher educational institutes by establishing curriculum guidelines to prepare professionals, on organizations by organizing career fairs and placement websites to recruit professionals, and on retention by providing professional development opportunities. We propose that more research is needed to gain an in-depth understanding of the role of computing professional associations and to identify unique ways they can influence preparation, recruitment, and retention of computing professionals.

Categories and Subject Descriptors

K.3.2 [**Computers and Education**]: Computer and Information Science Education, K.4.2 [**Computers and Society**]: Social Issues, K.7.m [**The Computing Profession**]: Miscellaneous.

General Terms

Management

Keywords

Computing Professional Associations, Computing Professionals, ACM, AIS, AITP, IEEE-CS, Preparing Professionals, Recruiting Professionals, and Retaining Professionals.

1. INTRODUCTION

Computing Personnel Research (CPR) scholars have investigated the issue of preparing professionals from various viewpoints, including skills need for graduates to be well-prepared for the job market [1-3], strategies to prepare the millennial generation for the workforce [4], and accreditation process to evaluate education programs [5]. CPR scholars have extensively examined the issue of recruiting professionals from various viewpoints, including definition of information technology (IT) workforce [6], impact of the skills gap [7], gender issues in the workplace [8, 9], diversifying the workforce [10], cross-cultural influences [11],

career anchors [12, 13], compensation [14], and increasing the number entrants into the workforce [15]. CPR scholars have addressed the issue of retaining professionals from various viewpoints, including turnover [16], industry certifications [17], and professional development activities [18]. These literatures indicate a broad spectrum of computing personnel topics addressed by scholars. However, a significant area remains under researched the role of professional associations.

Professional associations can play a significant role in preparing, recruiting, and retaining computing professionals (inclusive of software engineering, information systems (IS), and IT). For example, associations can help with preparing professionals by providing access to peer-reviewed journals, help with recruitment by publishing employment listings, and with retention by providing training workshops. In this paper, we address this critical gap in the literature. Thus, the objective of this preliminary study is to gain initial understanding of the role of computing professional associations (CPAs). Towards that, first, we identified services that can be offered by associations for preparing, recruiting, and retaining professionals based on review of relevant literature. Then, we assess four CPAs against those identified services by examining services offering descriptions provided in their websites. We hope findings from this paper inspire discussion among CPR scholars to study various facets of professional associations relevant to computing personnel's.

2. REVIEW OF PRIOR WORKS ON ROLE OF PROFESSIONAL ASSOCIATIONS

Prior works relevant to the role of professional associations are limited. From computing profession context, there has been studies on roles of professional association with technology diffusion [19], socio-cultural factors affecting online communities within a professional association [20], investigations on using virtual communities to bolster their relationship with association members [21], motivations and needs of computing professionals joining professional associations [22], factors affecting CPA membership [23], demographics of Society for Management Information Systems (SIMS) [now the Association of Information Systems (AIS)] membership [24], and role of professional associations with establishing and guiding ethical behaviors of computing professionals [25, 26].

From the context of preparing, recruiting, and retaining professionals, there has been studies examining the role of associations with educating and training UK professionals [27], relationships between students, managers, and curriculum development by associations [28], and impacts of associations on career growth of professionals [29]. In the next section, building on existing literatures, we identify potential services that can be offered by professional associations.

3. SERVICES PROFESSIONAL ASSOCIATIONS CAN PROVIDE

The primary purpose of professional associations is to offer educational and informational services [30]. Professional associations exist to aid advancement of its members, set educational and other standards governing the profession, advance professional practice by disseminating relevant information, provide avenues for interaction among members, and promote interests of the profession [31, 32]. In this section, we identify from existing literatures a comprehensive set of services that can be offered by professional associations for preparing, recruiting, and retaining professionals.

3.1 Preparing Professionals

Higher education institutes require guidelines to develop curricula that produce graduates meeting current workforce needs. Professional associations establish educational standards for curriculum and provide instructional resources to aid higher education institutes in producing a consistent workforce that meets the needs of organizations [33]. Access to resources such as peer-reviewed journal articles and conference proceedings are crucial for professionals to keep pace with current advancement in their field [34]. Professional associations can provide access to dissemination sources like magazines, reports, and white papers to update its members with best practices and trends in the field [35]. Professionals are expected to perform their duties complying with ethical standards [36]. Professional associations can disseminate information on professional practice standards, etiquette, and guidance on ethical matters [37]. Table 1 provides listing of services identified for preparing professionals.

3.2 Recruiting Professionals

Professional associations are a good source for organizations to advertise their job openings and recruiting professionals. Organizations can utilize various resources such as Web posts, listservs, journals, and magazines provided by professional associations to publish job openings [38]. By organizing career fair events along with their annual conferences and conventions, professional associations can provide organizations access to a large pool of potential candidates. Professional associations can help professionals with their job search by providing general tips, guides, and advice [39]. In regard to developing relationships, professional associations can be helpful by organizing social and networking events at local, regional and international levels [40]. Professional associations can utilize online social networking tools to assist professionals develop their network. In regard to ensuring continued growth of the workforce, professional associations can also play a role with encouraging high school and college students to major in the profession. To help recruiters raise awareness about careers in the profession among high school students, professional associations can develop resources such as videos, classroom materials, and posters [41]. Professional associations are well positioned to ensure workforce is diversified by taking initiatives to address minority and gender issues [41]. Table 1 provides listing of services identified for recruiting professionals.

Above literatures indicate that professional associations can play a substantial role in preparing, recruiting, and retaining professionals. In the next section, we assess services offered by four major CPAs against to above identified services.

Table 1. Listing of identified services

Service	Description
Preparing Professionals	
Develop educational standards	To aid generation of consistent workforce
Access to journals and conference proceedings	To disseminate information on latest advancements
Access to magazines, reports, and whitepapers	To disseminate best practices and current trends
Access to code of conduct and ethics	To aid professionals comply with practice and ethical standards
Recruiting Professionals	
Publish employment listing	To allow organizations advertise open positions
Organize career fair events	To allow organizations recruit potential candidates
Access to career enhancing tips	To aid professionals with job search
Organize networking events	To help professionals develop professional relationships
Access to online networking tools	To allow professionals build relationships remotely
Access to recruitment resources	To allow recruiters raise awareness about careers in the profession
Initiatives to diversify workforce	To ensure professionals workplace environment concerns are addressed
Retaining Professionals	
Topic specific workshops	To provide in-depth training on a technical skill
Soft skills workshops	To provide training on soft skills
Establish peer-reviewed publication avenues	To provide forum for exchanging knowledge
Organize social events	To provide forum for interaction and informal knowledge exchanges
Organize guest speaker events	To update professionals with current advancements
Access to mentors	To help professionals develop professional development plans
Access to industry certifications	To certify professionals with modernized skill sets
Establish recognition awards	To distinguish professionals who make valuable contributions to the growth of the profession
Access to online tutorials	To provide access to self-study courses and tutorials
Remote access to events and seminars	To provide access for those who cannot be physically present
Access to online communities	To allow exchange of ideas, information, and knowledge among peers

3.3 Retaining Professionals

Professional associations can play an influencing role with retention by providing career advancement programs. Professional associations are well placed to ensure a professional's competence by helping them with gaining new skills to advance their careers [40]. Local/ regional chapters can offer training workshops on specialized knowledge [42] and soft skills required for career progression [43]. Professional associations can provide a forum for exchange of formal knowledge (via conferences and journals) and informal knowledge (via social events) [44]. Local/ regional chapters can invite experts to speak on special topics and provide access to guest speaker presentation files to help professionals learn more about current advancements in the field.

Professional associations can assist professionals establish mentoring relationship with senior members to develop a strategic approach to their professional development [45]. By establishing competence criteria for each specialty with a profession, professional associations can certify individuals who satisfy those criteria [46], thus recognizing those individuals with modernized skill sets satisfying workforce demands. Professional associations can provide recognition awards to professionals who make valuable contributions to the continued growth of the profession [47]. Access to self-study resources such as online tutorials and Web-based streaming of seminars of experts can help professionals learn new skills on their own timeline. Professional associations can create online communities to encourage professionals share their professional development experiences, challenges, plans, and strategies. Table 1 provides listing of services identified for retaining professionals.

4. ASSESSMENT OF SERVICES OFFERED BY COMPUTING PROFESSIONAL ASSOCIATIONS

We assess four major computing professional associations (CPAs): Association for Computing Machinery (ACM), IEEE Computer Society (IEEE-CS), Association for Information Systems (AIS), and Association of Information Technology Professionals (AITP). The objective of the assessment is to examine services offered by the CPAs to prepare, recruit, and retain IT professionals. During the study, each CPAs website was assessed to determine whether or not services identified in the previous section are offered. If a service was offered, then nature and scope of the service were further analyzed to determine the kind of support provided, i.e., whether the service supports most varieties of functionalities identified in the literature (Full Support), only supports some of the identified functionalities (Partial Support), or no service offered (No Support). For example, in regard to *Develop educational standards* service, if an association offers services that provide curriculum guidelines and instructional material recommendations, then it would be considered as providing Full Support. However, if an association offers service that provided only curriculum guidelines for higher educational institutes, then it would be considered as Partial Support.

4.1 Association for Information Systems (AIS)

AIS is the premier association for IS educators and researchers. AIS states that their main purposes are to "create and maintain a professional identity for IS educators, researchers and professionals", "promote communications and interaction among members", "improve curricula, pedagogy, and other aspects of IS education", "create a vision for the future of the IS field and profession", "create and implement a modern, technologically sophisticated professional society", and "establish standards of practice, ethics, and education where appropriate" among other things [48]. Towards that AIS provides various services such as special interest group (SIG) service, Research resource service, Listserv service, Pedagogy service, e-library service, Journals and Conference service, and Code of Research Conduct service. Table 2 provides a summary of assessment of relevant services offered by AIS.

AIS is better at aiding preparation of IS professionals than with recruitment or retention of professionals. AIS provides either Full or Partial support for all the identified services for preparing professionals. In regard to "*Develop educational standards* service", it is well known that AIS works along with other CPAs such as ACM and AITP to create curriculum guidelines for IS programs. Conversely, we were not able to find any curriculum guideline information on their website. One can argue that for *Develop educational standards* service, AIS provides Full Support. However, we assessed it as Partial Support, since we were not able to retrieve it from AIS website.

AIS provides either Full or Partial support for about 50% of identified services for recruiting and retaining professionals. AIS can improve its support for recruiting professionals by providing career enhancement guides for interviews, salary negotiation, and resume writing; providing recruitment toolkits for organizations to recruit potential candidates and for higher education institutes to promote IS programs; by developing initiatives to ensure diversity issues are well addressed in IS workforce; and by utilizing social networking tools to aid professionals strengthen their network. AIS can improve its support for retaining professionals by offering soft skills workshops; developing mentorship programs where in senior member's aid junior members with professional development plans; recommending IS professionals appropriate industry certificates to gain competitive advantage; and providing access to real-time streaming or videos of invited talks. AIS can improve its support for recruiting and retaining professionals by creating local chapters. AIS has regional chapters, however, it does not have chapters to aid professionals develop relationships at the local level or provide opportunities to socialize with local leaders. Effort such as AIS student chapter initiative could help AIS develop local presence.

4.2 IEEE Computer Society (IEEE-CS)

IEEE-CS envisions being a leading service provider of technical information, community services, and professional development for computing professionals. Strategic goals of IEEE-CS [49] include services that provide resources to professionals for achieving success, provide educational services to improve competencies of students and professionals, provide professionals access to expertise, products, and information among other goals. To achieve these goals, IEEE-CS provides various services such as IEEE-CS Digital library, Career Watch, e-Learning Campus, Education Activities, Software Development Certifications, and Women in Computing. Table 3 provides assessment of relevant services offered by IEEE-CS.

IEEE-CS is better in aiding preparation and recruitment of computing professionals as it provides Full or Partial support for at least 80% of the identified services. IEEE-CS can improve its support for retaining professionals by conducting workshops and tutorials on soft skills and by incorporating a mentorship program with its Build Your Career service. IEEE-CS can improve its support for recruiting and retaining computing professionals by allowing its members with similar interests develop online communities to interact with their peers and build their network.

Table 2. Summary of relevant services offered by AIS

Service	Support	Remarks
Preparing Professionals		
Develop educational standards	Partial Support	Through Pedagogy service, AIS has created wikis for instructors to share resources such as syllabus. However, AIS website does not provide curriculum guidelines.
Access to journals and conference proceedings	Full Support	Journal and conference proceeding supported by AIS are made available to its members through e-Library service.
Access to magazines, reports, and whitepapers	Partial Support	MIS Quarterly Executive Journal is exclusively used for publishing articles relevant for IS practitioners. However, AIS does not publish any magazines or whitepapers on specific topics.
Access to code of conduct and ethics	Partial Support	AIS provides code of conduct for IS researchers but not for IS practitioners.
Recruiting Professionals		
Publish employment listing	Full Support	Organizations can post their open positions in AIS Career Placement Service website as well as AIS listserv.
Organize career fair events	Full Support	AIS provides separate space for organizations to recruit potential candidates during their international conferences such as ICIS and AMCIS.
Access to career enhancing tips	No Support	Neither AIS website nor Career placement service provide tips for career enhancement.
Organize networking events	Partial Support	Social networking events are held during international conferences. AIS regional conferences also held to assist professionals develop their regional networks. However, AIS does not have any local chapters to aid members develop relationships in their local community.
Access to online networking tools	Partial Support	Through SIG service, AIS allows creation of listserv and wikis for their community. AIS does not utilize any other social networking tools to assist its members build their relationships.
Access to recruitment resources	No Support	AIS does not provide any recruitment materials for higher education institutes.
Initiatives to diversify workforce	No Support	AIS does not have any initiatives to address diversity issues.
Retaining Professionals		
Topic specific workshops	Partial Support	AIS organizes topic specific research workshops, however, does not organize hands-on training workshops relevant for IS professionals.
Soft skills workshops	No Support	AIS does not organize soft skills workshops for IS professionals.
Establish peer-reviewed publication avenues	Full Support	AIS has several peer-reviewed Journals and conferences publication avenues such as MISQ, JAIS, CAIS, ICIS, and AMCIS.
Organize social events	Full Support	AIS SIGs organize social events during conferences to encourage interaction among its members.
Organize guest speaker events	No Support	AIS does not have local chapters to organize guest speaker events.
Access to mentors	No Support	AIS does not have any mentorship program to help its members develop their professional development plan.
Access to industry certifications	No Support	AIS does not provide any information regarding industry certifications.
Establish recognition awards	Full Support	AIS have established several awards such as Leo Award, Fellow Award and Education Award to recognize contributions made by most valuable members.
Access to online tutorials	Partial Support	AIS provides online tutorials on specific topics such as IS theories, design research, quantitative and qualitative methods.
Remote access to events and seminars	No Support	AIS does not provide Web streaming or video access to speaking events.
Access to online communities	Partial Support	SIGs and listserv for special topics are created, however, AIS does not provide online community presence for SIG members to interact with each other.

4.3 Association for Computing Machinery (ACM)

ACM is well recognized educational and scientific society for computing professionals. ACM aims to provide computing professionals [50]: access to original research and perspective articles on computing technologies; and opportunities for professional development, career enhancement, and networking. ACM aims to strengthen the computing profession by providing strong leadership, inspiring dialogue among members on important issues, addressing challenges faced by the profession, promoting high standards for conduct and ethics, and supporting scientific advancement through conferences and journal publications. To achieve its objective, ACM offer services such as ACM Digital Library, Educational Activities, Online Book & Courses, and Career & Job Center to name a few. ACM provides

Table 3. Summary of relevant offered by IEEE-CS

Service	Support	Remarks
Preparing Professionals		
Develop educational standards	Full Support	IEEE CS Educational Activities Board provides curriculum guidelines, instruction material, and accreditation information for various computing programs.
Access to journals and conference proceedings	Full Support	Member can subscribe to IEEE-CS Digital library and IEEExplorer.
Access to magazines, reports, and whitepapers	Full Support	IEEE CS publishes various magazines such as Computer, IT Professional, and Internet Computing to disseminate current trends and best practices to its members.
Access to code of conduct and ethics	Full Support	IEEE Code of Ethics is made accessible to IEEE CS members.
Recruiting Professionals		
Publish employment listing	Full Support	IEEE CS allows organizations to publish their openings through Jobs Board service.
Organize career fair events	Full Support	Certain IEEE CS conferences hold career fair events such as ICWS and SCC.
Access to career enhancing tips	Full Support	IEEE CS through their Career Watch service provides a variety of career development articles.
Organize networking events	Full Support	IEEE CS organizes networking events during their conferences. IEEE local chapters also organize networking events to help its members develop their network at the local level.
Access to online networking tools	No Support	IEEE CS does not provide any online medium to assist members develop their professional relationships.
Access to recruitment resources	Full Support	IEEE CS provides recruitment toolkits for organizations. However, it does not provide any recruitment resources for higher education institutes.
Initiatives to diversify workforce	Full Support	IEEE CS addresses diversity issues through initiatives such as Image of Computing and Women in Computing.

Retaining Professionals		
Topic specific workshops	Full Support	IEEE CS organizes various workshops and conference for specific topics, where in hands on tutorial on latest topics are provided. IEEE local chapters also organize hands on training workshops.
Soft skills workshops	Partial Support	IEEE CS through Build Your Career services does provide articles on soft skills, however, do not offer workshops.
Establish peer-reviewed publication avenues	Full Support	IEEE CS has several peer-reviewed Journals and conferences publication avenues such as IEEE Software, IEEE Transactions for Software Engineering, and Service Computing Conference.
Organize social events	Full Support	Social events are organized around conferences to encourage interaction among members. IEEE local chapter as well organizes social events to encourage interaction within the local community.
Organize guest speaker events	Full Support	IEEE local chapters organize guest speaker events.
Access to mentors	No Support	IEEE CS does not have a mentorship program to assist members with professional development.
Access to industry certifications	Full Support	IEEE CS has established certificates for software engineering professionals: Certified Software Development Associate (CSDA) and Certified Software Development Professional (CSDP).
Establish recognition awards	Full Support	IEEE CS recognizes its outstanding members by providing awards in various categories of technical, education, and service.
Access to online tutorials	Full Support	IEEE CS members can access various online courses and online books through e-Learning Campus service.
Remote access to events and seminars	Full Support	Through IEEE.tv services members have access to event videos and other vast array of special interest videos.
Access to online communities	No Support	IEEE CS does not provide online community presence for its members to interact with each other.

full support for all the services identified for preparing, recruiting, and retaining professionals, except it provides Partial Support for *Soft skills workshop* service. Table 4 provides a summary of assessment of relevant services offered by ACM.

ACM aims to provide computing professionals [50]: access to original research and perspective articles on computing technologies; and opportunities for professional development, career enhancement, and networking. ACM aims to strengthen the computing profession by providing strong leadership, inspiring dialogue among members on important issues, addressing challenges faced by the profession, promoting high standards for conduct and ethics, and supporting scientific advancement through conferences and journal publications. To achieve its objective, ACM offer services such as ACM Digital Library, Educational Activities, Online Book & Courses, and Career & Job Center to name a few. ACM provides Full support for all the services identified for preparing, recruiting, and retaining professionals, except it provides Partial Support for *Soft skills workshop* service. Table 4 provides a summary of assessment of relevant services offered by ACM.

Table 4. Summary of relevant services offered by ACM

Service	Support	Remarks
Preparing Professionals		
Develop educational standards	Full Support	ACM Education Activities service makes curriculum guidelines for different computing disciplines.
Access to journals and conference proceedings	Full Support	ACM provides access to a variety of journal articles and conference proceedings through its Digital Library.
Access to magazines, reports, and whitepapers	Full Support	ACM publishes magazines such as CACM and interactions, which provide viewpoints and informative news.
Access to code of conduct and ethics	Full Support	ACM Code of Ethics and Professional Conduct are made accessible to its member.
Recruiting Professionals		
Publish employment listing	Full Support	ACM allows organizations to publish their openings through Career and Jobs Center service as well as in their leading magazines such as CACM.
Organize career fair events	Full Support	Certain ACM conferences such as SIGMETRICS and SIGGRAPH holds career fair events.
Access to career enhancing tips	Full Support	ACM provides career enhancement tips such as interview tips and sample resumes through their Career and Jobs Center service.
Organize networking events	Full Support	ACM organizes networking events during their conferences. ACM local chapters also organize networking events to help members develop their network at local level.
Access to online networking tools	Full Support	ACM has created listservs and blogs for specific topics. ACM also utilizes other social networking tools such as Facebook, Linkedin, and Twitter to help members contact their peers.
Access to recruitment resources	Full Support	ACM provides recruitment toolkits for organizations and for higher education institutes to recruit students for ACM student chapter. ACM also provides workshops and instructor materials for high school teachers to create interest in computing topics among high school students.
Initiatives to diversify workforce	Full Support	ACM addresses diversity issues relevant through ACM-W Council committee.

Retaining Professionals	Support	Remarks
Topic specific workshops	Full Support	ACM organizes various workshops and conference on special topics, where in hands on tutorial on latest topics are provided. ACM local chapters also organize hands on training workshops.
Soft skills workshops	Partial Support	ACM through its Career Content library provides articles on soft skills, however, do not offer workshops.
Establish peer-reviewed publication avenues	Full Support	ACM has several peer-reviewed Journals and conferences publication avenues such as ACM SIGMIS Database, Transactions on Information Systems, SIGMIS CPR Conference and ACM SIGSOFT conference.
Organize social events	Full Support	Social events are organized around conferences to encourage interaction among members. ACM local chapter as well organizes social events to encourage interaction within the local community.
Organize guest speaker events	Full Support	ACM local chapters organize guest speaker events.
Access to mentors	Full Support	ACM through its Career Coach and Ask the Experts services provide members mentorship with their professional development.
Access to industry certifications	Full Support	ACM recommends Institute for Certification of Computing Professionals (ICCP) certificates for its members.
Establish recognition awards	Full Support	ACM recognizes its outstanding contributions made by professionals through awards such as A. M. Turing and Software System awards.
Access to online tutorials	Full Support	ACM members can access various online courses and online books through online courses and books service.
Remote access to events and seminars	Full Support	Through ACM e-store members can purchase proceedings and videos for certain conferences.
Access to online communities	Full Support	ACM provides support for its chapters and SIGs to create website, wikis, blogs, and listserv to allow its members interact with each other.

4.3 Association of Information Technology Professionals (AITP)

AITP is a leading professional society for IT professionals. The mission of AITP [51] is to be a leader in delivering relevant education, research, information on technology and business issues, and forums for networking and collaboration. To achieve its mission, AITP offers services such as Model Curriculum, Education Special Interest Group, InfoCenter Jobs Search, and aitpNetwork. AITP provides either Full or Partial support for at least 80% of the services identified for preparing, recruiting, and retaining professionals. AITP can improve its support for recruiting professionals by providing resources for higher education institutes to encourage students to take IT majors and establish initiatives to diversify IT professional workforce. AITP can improve its support for retaining professionals by providing real-time streaming and videos of the speaker presentations, and by supporting members of similar interests to form online communities to interact with each other. Table 5 provides a summary of assessment of relevant services offered by AITP.

Table 5. Summary of relevant services offered by AITP

Service	Support	Remarks
Preparing Professionals		
Develop educational standards	Full Support	AITP through its Model Curriculum service makes curriculum guidelines for available for IS programs.
Access to journals and conference proceedings	Full Support	AITP provides access to journal articles and conference proceedings through Education Special Interest Group.
Access to magazines, reports, and whitepapers	Full Support	AITP publishes newsletters, magazines, and reports; which provide informative articles.
Access to code of conduct and ethics	Full Support	AITP Code of Ethics and Standard of Conduct are made accessible to its member.
Recruiting Professionals		
Publish employment listing	Full Support	AITP allows organizations to publish their openings through InfoCenter Jobs Search service.
Organize career fair events	Full Support	AITP holds career fair events during Annual National Collegiate Conference.
Access to career enhancing tips	Full Support	AITP provides career enhancement tips for resume writing and interviews through their InfoCenter service.
Organize networking events	Full Support	AITP organizes networking events during their conferences. AITP local chapters also organize networking events to help members develop their network at the local level.
Access to online networking tools	Full Support	AITP through its aitpNetwork service allows its members to have peer-to-peer interactions.
Access to recruitment resources	Partial Support	AITP through its InfoCenter service provides recruiting strategies for organizations. However, AITP does not provide recruiting resources for higher education institutes.
Initiatives to diversify workforce	No Support	AITP does not have any initiatives to address diversity issues.

Retaining Professionals		
Topic specific workshops	Full Support	AITP local chapters organize hands on training workshops.
Soft skills workshops	Full Support	AITP local chapters organize hands on training workshops.
Establish peer-reviewed publication avenues	Full Support	ACM has several peer-reviewed Journals and conferences publication avenues such as JISE, ISEDJ, JISAR, ISECON conference and CONISAR conference.
Organize social events	Full Support	Social events are organized around conferences to encourage interaction among members. AITP local chapter as well organizes social events to encourage interaction within the local community.
Organize guest speaker events	Full Support	AITP local chapters organize guest speaker events.
Access to mentors	No Support	AITP does not have any mentorship program to help members develop their professional development plan.
Access to industry certifications	Full Support	AITP recommends Institute for Certification of Computing Professionals (ICCP) certificates for its members.
Establish recognition awards	Full Support	AITP recognizes its outstanding contributions made by professionals through awards such as Educator of the Year and EDSIG Fellows awards.
Access to online tutorials	Full Support	AITP members can access various online tutorials and online books through Microsoft Resource Center service.
Remote access to events and seminars	No Support	AITP does not provide Web streaming or provide video access to events.
Access to online communities	Partial Support	AITP through its aitpNetwork service allows members to interact with other peers with similar interests. However, AITP does not provide support for members with similar interests to develop online communities.

5. DISCUSSION

Examination of service descriptions at the professional associations' websites indicates that ACM has better coverage of services as it provides Full Support for all identified services, except for *Soft skills workshops* service. Second best coverage of services is provided by IEEE-CS as it provides Full Support for 18 out of 22 services. Third best coverage of services is provided by AITP as it provides Full Support for 17 services. AIS has least coverage of services as it provides Full Support for only six services. However, it should be noted here that AIS focuses on IS educators and researchers and not on IS practitioners. In this research, we focus on services that influence practicing professionals; this may be a factor for substantial differences between AIS and rest of the associations. More research is needed to gain better understanding on service offering differences for educators, researchers, and practitioners.

Although professional associations do not directly work towards preparing, recruiting, and retaining professionals; our assessment indicates they can strongly influence practices and attitudes followed to prepare, recruit, and retain computing professionals. The role of professional associations in preparing the professional is well known, as by definition, professionals are those trained through formal education–governed and regulated by professional associations [46]. CPAs have established curriculum guidelines to ensure higher education institutes produce a consistent workforce that can satisfy current and future needs. CPAs are preparing professionals to be competent by providing them access to peer-reviewed articles, reports, articles on current trends and issues, code of conduct, and ethical standards.

CPAs help organizations recruit professionals by creating career placement website and recruitment toolkits to advertise their open positions. CPAs organize career fair events as part of their conferences to help organizations recruit skilled professionals. CPAs assist professionals with their job search by providing career enhancement tips, organizing networking events, and online networking tools.

CPAs help with retention of professionals by providing technical training workshops on specific topics, establishing peer-reviewed publication avenues, organizing socializing events to develop professional relationships, organizing guest speaker events on current topics, and recognizing contributions made by professionals. CPAs help professionals increase their potential by providing access to industry certifications to counter deprecating skill sets, online tutorials for self-paced learning, and online communities to exchange knowledge with their peers.

In addition to their existing range of services, CPAs can consider offering professional development services such as discounts for continuing education courses and vendor-supplied training. Prior research has indicated that these services can be effective means for professional development [52]. CPAs can address the shortage of skilled workers by taking initiatives to ensure that working environment for computing professionals are conducive for minorities and underrepresented groups. CPAs can address misconceptions of the profession and enrollment drop in computing majors by taking initiatives to improve the image of the profession and providing necessary resources such as videos for high schools and higher education educators to encourage students to take computing majors. Currently, ACM and IEEE-CS have initiatives to diversify the workforce and improve the image of computing profession, but AIS and AITP do not have any diversity or image improvement initiatives.

The main limitation of this study is that the assessment was performed by documenting the presence or absence of a service. Simply noting presence or absence of a service does not enable researchers to perform in-depth analysis on services offered or differentiate effectiveness of services offered among professional associations. Despite the limitation, this paper contributes by exploring an uncharted territory, namely, the role of professional of associations by assessing whether those associations recognize and provide much needed professional services and supports. As part of future work, researchers plan to conduct content analysis to gain understanding about how professional associations are offering services, determine service quality, and how professional associations differentiate their services.

In conclusion, we argue that professional associations can facilitate the preparation, recruitment and retention of computing professionals. Through this paper, we hope to start a discussion on how to enhance the influence of professional associations within computing community. We encourage other researchers to investigate the role of professional associations and identify best practices with respect to how to offer quality services using limited resources such as volunteer time and cost.

6. REFERENCES

[1] Sumner, M. and Yager, S. E. *An investigation of preparedness and importance of mis competencies: research in progress.* ACM, City, 2008.

[2] Benamati, J. S. *Current and future entry-level IT workforce needs in organizations.* ACM, City, 2007.

[3] Huang, H., Kvasny, L., Joshi, K. D., Trauth, E. M. and Mahar, J. *Synthesizing IT job skills identified in academic studies, practitioner publications and job ads.* ACM, City, 2009.

[4] Beard, D., Schwieger, D. and Surendran, K. *Preparing the millennial generation for the work place: how can academia help?* ACM, City, 2008.

[5] Lending, D. and Mathieu, R. G. Workforce preparation and ABET assessment. In *Proceedings of the Special Interest Group on Management Information System's annual conference on Computer personnel research* (Vancouver, BC, Canada, 2010). ACM, [insert City of Publication],[insert 2010 of Publication].

[6] Kaarst-Brown, M. L. and Guzman, I. R. Who is "the IT workforce"?: challenges facing policy makers, educators, management, and research. In *Proceedings of the ACM SIGMIS CPR conference on Computer personnel research* (Atlanta, Georgia, USA, 2005). ACM, [insert City of Publication],[insert 2005 of Publication].

[7] Aken, A. and Michalisin, M. D. *The impact of the skills gap on the recruitment of MIS graduates.* ACM, City, 2007.

[8] Adya, M. P. *Work alienation among IT workers: a cross-cultural gender comparison.* ACM, City, 2008.

[9] Buche, M. W. *Influence of gender on IT professional work identity: outcomes from a PLS study.* ACM, City, 2008.

[10] Tapia, A. H. and Kvasny, L. *Recruitment is never enough: retention of women and minorities in the IT workplace.* ACM, City, 2004.

[11] Trauth, E. M., Quesenberry, J. L. and Huang, H. *Cross-cultural influences on women in the IT workforce.* ACM, City, 2006.

[12] Sumner, M., Yager, S. and Franke, D. *Career orientation and organizational commitment of IT personnel.* ACM, City, 2005.

[13] Quesenberry, J. L. *Career anchors and organizational culture: a study of women in the IT workforce.* ACM, City, 2006.

[14] Wang, C. *Building a theory of IT compensation.* ACM, City, 2007.

[15] Joseph, D. *Increasing the number of entrants into the IT profession: the role of experiential training.* ACM, City, 2008.

[16] Meland, H., Waage, R. P. and Sein, M. K. *The other side of turnover: managing IT personnel strategically.* ACM, City, 2005.

[17] Hitchcock, L. *Industry certification and academic degrees: complementary, or poles apart?* ACM, City, 2007.

[18] Mahatanankoon, P. *The effects of post-educational professional development activities on promotion and career satisfaction of IT professionals.* ACM, City, 2007.

[19] Swan, J., Newell, S. and Robertson, M. The diffusion, design and social shaping of production management information systems in Europe. *Information Technology & People*, 13, 1 2000), 27-46.

[20] Yu, Y., Kumar, N. and Lang, K. *The Impact of Cultural Distance on the Internationalization of Online Professional Communities --An Empirical Investigation of ISWorld.* City, 2007.

[21] Cox, A. and Morris, A. *Information dynamics and discourse in a distributed professional community*. City, 2004.

[22] Ritzhaupt, A. D., Umapathy, K. and Jamba, L. Computing Professional Association Membership: An Exploration of Membership Needs and Motivations. *Journal of Information Systems Applied Research (JISAR)*, 1, 4 2008), 1-23.

[23] Umapathy, K., Jamba, L. and Ritzhaupt, A. D. Factors that Persuade and Deter Membership in Professional Computing Associations. *Journal of Information Systems Applied Research (JISAR)*, 3, 14 2010), 1-11.

[24] Ball, L. and Harris, R. SMIS Members: A Membership Analysis. *MIS Quarterly*, 6, 1 1982), 19-38.

[25] Oz, E. Ethical Standards for Information Systems Professionals: A Case for a Unified Code. *MIS Quarterly*, 16, 4 1992), 423-433.

[26] Sandy, G. A., Hall, M. J. J. and Bellucci, E. *Indicative Markers of Leadership provided by ICT Professional Bodies in the Promotion and Support of Ethical Conduct*. Association of Information Systems (AIS), City, 2007.

[27] Watkins, J. Educating Professionals: the changing role of UK professional associations. *Journal of Education and Work*, 12, 1 1999), 37 - 56.

[28] Turner, R., Fisher, J. and Lowry, G. *Describing the IS Professional with a Structural Model*. City, 2004.

[29] Corbin, J. C. The role of the professional society in the career development of engineers. *IEEE Aerospace and Electronic Systems Magazine*, 3, 3 1988), 12-16.

[30] Andreasen, N. C., Brown, T. L., Chayes, J., Cohen, S., Cole, J. R., Conn, R., Dresselhaus, M., Holton, G., Kalil, T., Kates, R. W., Killeen, T. L., Molina, M., Suppes, P., Bemmel, J. H. v., Warnow, T., White, R. M. and Zoback, M. L. *The Role of Professional Societies*. National Academy of Sciences, City, 2004.

[31] Sheather, G. *A History of the Australian Society for the Study of Intellectual Disability (ASSID)*. Unpublished Honours Thesis, University of Newcastle, Newcastle, 2002.

[32] Jones, C. Legal status of software engineering. *Computer*, 28, 5 1995), 98-99.

[33] Collins, A. National Science Education Standards: A political document. *Journal of Research in Science Teaching*, 35, 7 1998), 711-727.

[34] Dodgen, D., Fowler, R. D. and Williams-Nickelson, C. *Getting Involved in Professional Organizations: A Gateway to Career Advancement*. Springer, City, 2003.

[35] Arndt, T. *Backpack to briefcase : steps to a successful career*. Life After Graduation, LLC Bainbridge Island, WA, USA, 2006.

[36] Bowman, J. S. Towards a Professional Ethos: From Regulatory to Reflective Codes. *International Review of Administrative Sciences*, 66, 4 (December 1, 2000 2000), 673-687.

[37] Pater, A. and Gils, A. V. Stimulating Ethical Decision-making in a Business Context:Effects of Ethical and Professional Codes. *European Management Journal*, 21, 6 2003), 762-772.

[38] Heiberger, M. M. and Vick, J. M. *The Academic Job Search Handbook*. University of Pennsylvania Press, Philadelphia, 2001.

[39] Rosenberg, R. S. *Beyond the code of ethics: the responsibility of professional societies*. ACM, City, 1998.

[40] Casillas, C. A. and Shields, P. M. *The Value of Association Membership: An Evaluation of the Central Texas Chapter of the American Society for Public Administration*. American Society for Public Administration (ASPA), City, 2009.

[41] Elfrink, J. A. and Woodruff, G. S. Recruiting the Best and the Brightest: The Role of Accounting Societies. *The CPA Journal*, 78, 2 2008), 68-71.

[42] Brindley, G. *Language assessment and professional development*. Cambridge University Press, City, 2001.

[43] Turner, R., Lowry, G. and Fisher, J. *A Structural Model of the Information Systems Professional*. Springer, City, 2005.

[44] Newell, S., Swan, J. A. and Galliers, R. D. A knowledge-focused perspective on the diffusion and adoption of complex information technologies: the BPR example. *Information Systems Journal*, 10, 3 2000), 239-259.

[45] Watkins, J. UK professional associations and continuing professional development: a new direction? *International Journal of Lifelong Education*, 18, 1 1999), 61 - 75.

[46] Denning, P. J. The profession of IT: who are we? *Communications of the ACM*. 44, 2 2001), 15-19.

[47] Gruen, T. W., Summers, J. O. and Acito, F. Relationship Marketing Activities, Commitment, and Membership Behaviors in Professional Associations. *Journal of Marketing*, 64, 3 2000), 34-49.

[48] AIS *Association for Information Systems (AIS)*. AIS, City, 2010.

[49] IEEE-CS *IEEE Computer Society (IEEE-CS)*. IEEE, City, 2010.

[50] ACM *Association for Computing Machinery (ACM)*. ACM, City, 2010.

[51] AITP *Association of Information Technology Professionals (AITP)*. AITP, City, 2010.

[52] Schambach, T. and Blanton, J. E. The professional development challenge for IT professionals. *Communications of the ACM (CACM)*, 45, 4 2002), 83-87.

Designing an E-Mentoring Application for Facebook

Hsun-Ming Lee
Dept. of Computer Information
Systems and Quantitative Methods
Texas State University – San Marcos
San Marcos, Texas

samlee@txstate.edu

Ju Long
Dept. of Computer Information
Systems and Quantitative Methods
Texas State University – San Marcos
San Marcos, Texas

julong@txstate.edu

Mayur R. Mehta
Dept. of Computer Information
Systems and Quantitative Methods
Texas State University – San Marcos
San Marcos, Texas

mayur_mehta@txstate.edu

ABSTRACT
Facebook is the most popular social networking site, with more than 500 million active members. It has brought new opportunities for the learning and career development of students that live with technology and networked communications. This study explores the design of an e-mentoring Facebook application intended to bring together students, faculty, and Information Technology (IT) professionals as mentors and mentees.

Categories and Subject Descriptors
J.1 [**Computer Applications**]: Administrative Data Processing

General Terms
Design, Experimentation

Keywords
Social Networking, E-Mentoring, Facebook, Computer Mediated Communication, Career Development.

1. INTRODUCTION
Social network sites (SNSs) such as such as Facebook, LinkedIn, and MySpace allow individuals to present themselves, articulate their social networks, and establish or maintain connections with others [11]. All the benefits and amusements of online social networking have led to a tremendous increase of SNS usage in the past several years. An example would be Facebook. In July 2010, Facebook was reported to have more than 500 million active users. In addition, more than one million developers and entrepreneurs from more than 180 countries engage in developing applications based on the Facebook platform. Currently, more than 550,000 applications are active on the platform. Further, 70% or more of Facebook users engage with these applications each month (Facebook statistics 2011). The communication opportunities within the SNSs are boundless. It therefore presents a fertile ground for initiating a career mentoring program.

Researchers have emphasized the need to investigate non-traditional modes of mentoring [6]. One alternative that is gaining in popularity and usage is electronic mentoring (e-mentoring) [9].

E-mentoring is the act of providing and receiving guidance and support through computer-mediated technology, such as e-mail, electronic chat, and message boards. With the development of technology, particularly the increased access to the Internet among all segments of society, e-mentoring has become more common in recent years [8, 24]. Given the well-documented shortage of adults who are both capable of serving as traditional face-to-face (F2F) mentors and willing to do so, e-mentoring is likely to continue to grow in the foreseeable future [21].

According to DiRenzo et al. [9], most mentoring relationships today are characterized by at least some degree of computer-mediated communication (CMC). As technologies are evolving, younger generation college students tend to use online social networks rather than interacting through the traditional CMC. Thus, our study is set to address this trend. Several e-mentoring programs, such as MentorNet [3], GEM-Nursing, GEM-SET [20], have been created with certain degrees of success. However, to our best knowledge, little development and research have been done on e-mentoring through online social networks (except the proprietary IBM MentorMe Networking Program on Facebook). We developed a mentoring program in which mentor–mentee association was conducted entirely within Facebook. A very important design aspect, which involves building and sustaining mentoring relationships, is studied in a pilot program during the spring 2011 semester. This single aspect already presents a complex problem that requires solutions of recruiting, matching, monitoring, and training mentors to minimize problematic relationships [7].

The rest of the paper is organized as follows: in the second section, we review the theoretical literature on e-mentoring. In the third section, we present the design of the e-mentoring program structure. In the fourth section, we list the future research questions and conclude the paper.

2. THEORETICAL BACKGROUND AND RESEARCH MOTIVATION
E-mentoring is still relatively new and under-researched [12, 13, 15, 17, 23]. Research has examined many advantages of the e-mentoring. First, e-mentoring provides a flexibility and easy access that are not limited by geographical or organizational boundaries. This is especially beneficial to mentors and mentees when they are located in different geographical locations [4]. Second, e-mentoring can facilitate both synchronous and asynchronous communication, which adds to the richness and variety of the interactions. The flexibility offered by e-mentoring's asynchronous communication methods also means that it would not have to interfere with other daily commitments [16]. Third, e-mentoring can help support a reflective learning environment,

where mentoring pairs can explore their values, feelings and objectives at their own pace and more freely than in F2F communication, which can be pressurized through the need to respond immediately [16]. Fourth, the mentees are able to take responsibility for initiating contact and play an active role in e-mentoring. Fifth, e-mentoring offers the opportunity to set up dynamic multi-dimensional learning networks. Sixth, e-mentoring has egalitarian characteristics [1]. It is argued that virtual relationships make gender, race and status relatively invisible [13]. Thus, e-mentoring creates fewer barriers and access to senior mentors and is more open than traditional mentoring programs, which tend to have more rigid hierarchies [18]. A further benefit of e-mentoring is that there is usually a record of interactions both between pairs and among groups [18].

Mentoring is associated with a wide range of favorable behavioral, attitudinal, health-related, relational, motivational, and career outcomes [10]. E-mentoring may provide career development functions, which give the mentee the tools and skills required to advance in his/her chosen career path [18]. Although e-mentoring is promising, very little is known about the best practices for the development and implementation of e-mentoring programs [21]. A basic e-mentoring program is field-based and developmental, using the framework of Karcher et al. [21]. It refers field-based mentoring to programs in which a sponsoring agency coordinates and supports mentor-mentee matches, but mentors and protégés typically interact at mutually convenient times and locations (online). In developmental mentoring, the primary focus is on facilitating the relationship between mentor and mentee as a way of promoting the students' academic and career development. It is pointed out that developmental mentoring processes are viewed as the mediator of subsequent, distal achievements of more specific goals or skills.

Mentoring occurs through the form of meetings of peers, groups, and virtual communities [20, 22, 26, 34]. This research aims to design and test a new mentoring structure that takes advantage of the availability of special populations of mentors (e.g., computing professionals) and social networking technology. Recently the study of the similarity between pairs of friends in online social networks found no evidence of gender homophile but significant evidence of homophily for interests, ethnicity, religion, age, country, and marital status [32]. Since mentors offer friendships [25, 29], the same results of homophily may exist to some degree in the matching between mentors and mentees on online social networks. Thus, a Facebook mentoring application may require different designs than those in traditional e-mentoring. As we discussed earlier, some studies suggest no preference of demographic backgrounds for e-mentors.

3. RESEARCH QUESTIONS AND METHODS

This research is to: (1) implement the design of e-mentoring on Facebook to engage college students in making career choices; and (2) examine the factors that impact the relationships between mentors and mentees. The design guides the mentors, who are seen to drive the relationships, to meet and support their mentees.

To validate and test the design of e-mentoring on social networks, a Facebook application, named as Apprenticebook, has been developed (http://apps.facebook.com/apprenticebook, see Figure 1). It implements the design of (1) matching mentors and college students (mentees) according to genders, experiences of mentors,

and professional interests; (2) allowing them to ask and answer questions; and (3) giving mentors the tools to promote professional events and post internship/job opportunities. An administrator has set up the basic program information, such as the school name and the areas of professional interests that the program concentrates on. Several mentors have been invited to join the program by the administrator, who sent a key to each new mentor to activate and update his/her profile. The mentors are IT experts from businesses, faculty, recent graduates, or senior students with internship experiences. A class of students has been informed of the existence of this program. They just needed to open this application, when visiting Facebook, to start using it. It is convenient for them to create profiles, find their mentors, and start sending and receiving messages. The mentors have the options to review the students' profiles before accepting or denying the requests from the students (potential mentees).

Figure 1. An e-mentoring application on Facebook.

Using Apprenticebook, we intend to test the homophiy of pairs of mentors and mentees on online social networks.

Do the students prefer the mentors of the same gender?

Do the students prefer the mentors of similar ages?

Do the students develop closer relationships with the mentors of the same gender?

Do the students develop closer relationships with the mentors of similar ages?

Do the students develop closer relationships with the mentors of more professional interests in common?

4. SUMMARY AND FUTURE RESEARCH DIRECTION

We implement a basic program structure for e-mentoring, which uses the Facebook site as the underlining infrastructure. It is to allow mentors to engage a large population of college students to develop their careers in IT. Although some researchers have addressed individual mentee attributes, such as the influence of demographic characteristics [27, 28, 30, 31], mentee personality [33], and goal orientations [14], there remains a number of unexplored questions as to how mentor and mentee differences might impact mentoring relationships [9].

The pilot study particularly investigates the design of building and maintaining relationships through online social networking. In our Facebook mentoring application, mentees select their mentors based on their genders, years of experiences in IT, and professional interests. The pilot study will generate data for analysis to find out good matching practices to improve or verify the design. The results will indicate the priorities of running e-mentoring programs, such as those for building the pool of mentors. For example, the recruitment of recent graduates is important if the age homophily is significant. In that case, we should invest our efforts to apply Facebook in the design of advancing mentees to mentors [19]. However, the students may prefer experienced experts; then, it becomes a priority to address the privacy concerns and their reluctance to use Facebook. A possible solution to get the experts' involvement is the development of separate mobile clients using Blackberry or iPod/iPhone that are becoming popular among professionals.

The design of instrumental mentoring is also under pursuit. The instrumental approach targets the achievement of prescribed goals or skills as the proximal or immediate goal of mentoring [21]. The idea is that mentors can help mentees create and follow plans of preparation for certifications or competitions in IT. The Facebook application will allow us to customize the practices of e-mentoring programs easily. After it is used by several colleges, we will be able to collect a large amount of data and to test many variables simultaneously in the design (customization) that has potentials to lead to improved outcomes in IT student recruitment, retention, and job placement.

5. ACKNOWLEDGMENTS

Our thanks to the anonymous reviewers for their valuable comments.

6. REFERENCES

[1] Algiere Kasprisin, C., Boyle Single, P., Single, R., and Muller, C. 2003. Building a better bridge: Testing e-training to improve e-mentoring programmes in higher education. *Mentoring & Tutoring: Partnership in Learning*, 11, 1, 67-78.

[2] Allen, T. D., Eby, L. T., Poteet, M. L., Lentz, E., and Lima, L. 2004. Career benefits associated with mentoring for protégés: A meta-analysis. *Journal of Applied Psychology*, 89, 127-136.

[3] Bailey M. W. 2007. ACM partners with MentorNet. *ACM SIGPLAN Notices*. 42, 11, 1-1.

[4] Bierema, L. L. and Hill, J. R. 2005. Virtual mentoring and HRD. *Advances in Developing Human Resources*, 7, 4, 556-568.

[5] Bierema, L. L. and Merriam, S. B. 2002. E-mentoring: Using computer mediated communication to enhance the mentoring process. *Innovative Higher Education*, 26, 3, 211-227.

[6] Byrne, Z. S., Dik, B. J., and Chiaburu, D. 2008. Alternatives to traditional mentoring in fostering career success. *Journal of Vocational Behavior*, 72, 429-442.

[7] Chao, G. T. 2009. Formal mentoring: lessons learned from past practice. *Professional Psychology-Research and Practice*, 40, 3, 314-320.

[8] Cravens, J. 2002. Online mentoring: Programs and suggested practices as of February 2001. *Journal of Technology in Human Services*, 21, 85–109.

[9] DiRenzon, M., Linnehan, F., Shao, P., and Rosenbery, W. L. (2010). A moderated mediation model of e-mentoring. *Journal of Vocational Behavior*, 76, 2, 292-305.

[10] Eby, L. T., Allen, T. D., Evans, S. C., Ng, T., and DuBois, D. L. 2008. Does mentoring matter? A multidisciplinary meta-analysis comparing mentored and non-mentored individuals. *Journal of Vocational Behavior*, 72, 2, 254-267.

[11] Ellison, N. B., Steinfield, C., and Lampe, C. 2007. The benefits of Facebook "friends:" Social capital and college students' use of online social network sites. *Journal of Computer-Mediated Communication*, 12, 4, Article 1.

[12] Ensher, E. A., Heun, C., and Blanchard, A. 2003. Online mentoring and computer-mediated communication: New directions in research. *Journal of Vocational Behavior*, 63, 2, 264-288.

[13] Fagenson-Eland, E. A., and Lu, R. Y. 2004. Virtual mentoring. In Clutterbuck, D. & Lane, G. (Eds.). *The situational mentor: An international review of competences and capabilities in mentoring* (pp. 148-159). Aldershot: Gower Publishing.

[14] Godshalk, V. M. and Sosik, J. J. 2003. Aiming for career success: The role of learning goal orientation in mentoring relationships. *Journal of Vocational Behavior*, 63, 3, 417-437.

[15] Headlam-Wells, J. 2004. E-mentoring for aspiring women managers. *Women in Management Review*, 19, 4, 212-218.

[16] Headlam-Wells, J., Craig, J., and Gosland, J. 2006. Encounters in social cyberspace: e-mentoring for professional women. *Women in Management Review*, 21, 6, 483-499.

[17] Headlam-Wells, J., Gosland, J., and Craig, J. 2005. 'There's magic in the web': E-mentoring for women's career development. *Career Development International*, 10, 5, 444-459.

[18] Headlam-Wells, J., Gosland, J., and Craig, J. 2006. Beyond the organisation: the design and management of e-mentoring systems. *International Journal of Information Management*, 26, 5, 372-385.

[19] Holmes, D. R., Hodgson, P. K., Simari, R. D., et al. 2010. Mentoring making the transition from mentee to mentor. *Circulation*, 121, 2, 336-340.

[20] Kalisch B. J., Falzetta L., and Cooke J. 2005. Group e-mentoring: A new approach to recruitment into nursing. *Nursing Outlook*, 53, 4, 199-205.

[21] Karcher, M. J., Kuperminc, G. P., Portwood, S. G., Sipe, C. L., and Taylor, A. S. 2006. Mentoring programs: A framework to inform program development, research, and evaluation. *Journal of Community Psychology*, 34, 6, 709-725.

[22] Karcher, M. J. 2009. Increases in academic connectedness and self-esteem among high school students who serve as

cross-age peer mentors. *Professional School Counseling*, 12, 4, 292-299.

[23] Megginson, D., Clutterbuck, D., Garvey, B., Stokes, P., and Garrett-Harris, R. 2006. *Mentoring in action: A practical guide* (2nd ed.). Kogan Page, London.

[24] Miller, H. and Griffiths, M. 2005. E-mentoring. In DuBois, D.L. & Karcher, M.J. (Eds.), *Handbook of youth mentoring*. (pp. 300–313). Sage, Thousand Oaks, CA.

[25] Murphy, C. A., Cupples, M. E., Percy, A., et al. 2008. Peer-mentoring for first-time mothers from areas of socio-economic disadvantage: A qualitative study within a randomised controlled trial. *BMC Health Services Research*, 8, Article 46.

[26] Pololi L. H., Knight S. M., Dennis K., Frankel R. M. 2002. Helping medical school faculty realize their dreams: An innovative, collaborative mentoring program. *Academic Medicine*, 77, 5, 377-384.

[27] Ragins, B. R. 1997. Diversified mentoring relationships in organizations: A power perspective. *Academy of Management Review*, 22, 482-521.

[28] Ragins, B. R. and Cotton, J. L. 1999. Mentor functions and outcomes: A comparison of men and women in formal and informal mentoring relationships. *Journal of Applied Psychology*, 84, 529-550.

[29] Resvanis, L. K. 2003. My friend and mentor Tom - reminiscing a twenty five year long friendship. *Nuclear Instruments & Methods In Physics Research Section A*, 502, 1, 26-27

[30] Scandura, T. A. and Ragins, B. R. 1993. The effects of sex and gender role orientation on mentorship in male-dominated occupations. *Journal of Vocational Behavior*, 43, 251-265.

[31] Scandura, T. A. and Williams, E. A. 2001. An investigation of the moderating effects of gender on the relationships between mentorship initiation and protégé perceptions of mentoring functions. *Journal of Vocational Behavior*, 59, 342–363.

[32] Thelwall M. 2009. Homophily in MySpace. *Journal of the American Society for Information Science and Technology*, 60, 2, 219-231

[33] Turban, D. B. and Dougherty, T. W. 1994. Role of protégé personality in receipt on mentoring and career success. *Academy of Management Journal*, 37, 688–702.

[34] Whitbeck, C. 2001. Group mentoring to foster the responsible conduct of research. *Science and Engineering Ethics*, 7, 4, 541-558.

Occupational Commitment of IT Students:
A Social Cognitive Career Theory Perspective

Christine Siew Kuan Koh
Nanyang Technological University
50 Nanyang Avenue S3-01C-96
Singapore 639789
+65 67906153
askkoh@ntu.edu.sg

Damien Joseph
Nanyang Technological University
50 Nanyang Avenue S3-B2C-99
Singapore 639789
+65 67904831
adjoseph@ntu.edu.sg

ABSTRACT

The shortage of IT professionals remains a critical concern today, with fewer IT students entering the workforce compared to IT professionals leaving or retiring. While research has examined factors contributing to the declining of IT enrollments, it is unclear why some IT students choose to go on to an IT career while others eschew IT. To address this gap, this paper examines students' commitment to the IT profession as students' attitudes towards the profession begin to form. We draw on and extend the social cognitive career theory (SCCT) by examining factors that affect IT students' occupational commitment. We tested our model using survey data from a large sample of students majoring in computer science and information systems related fields. Results from structural equations modeling indicated that students with higher interests, self-efficacy, outcome expectations and social support report higher occupational commitment. This study contributes to theory by extending prior research on occupational commitment by providing insights into factors that shape occupational commitment prior to entering the IT workforce.

Categories and Subject Descriptors

K.7.1 [**Occupations**]

General Terms

Management, Theory.

Keywords

Information Technology Students, Occupational Commitment, Social Cognitive Theory, Career.

1. INTRODUCTION

There are fewer information technology (IT) students entering the workforce compared to IT professionals leaving or retiring. According to the latest statistics by the National Science Foundation, 41.1% of IT graduates in a given year do not go on to pursue an IT career [16]. Combined with IT professionals voluntarily leaving the IT profession and with baby boomers

retiring [9], there is a potential impending shortage of IT labor. As IT is strategically and operationally critical for an organization, the impending shortage of IT labor is fueling a fear in the broader economy that the shortage of IT professionals would lead to a loss of competitive advantage [16].

Although the IT discipline has undertaken considerable research addressing the declining enrollments in IT [e.g. 1], we still lack a clear understanding of why IT graduates are not entering the IT workforce from an IT related major. The extant literature on career choice in IT and vocational psychology assumes that enrolling in an academic major is a career choice [e.g. 1, 13].

The widely used social cognitive career theory [SCCT, 12, 13] utilized to examine career choice remains silent as to why some IT students go on to a career in IT while other IT students eschew an IT career. To fill this gap in the literature, this study examines occupational commitment within the SCCT framework that may explain why some IT students go on to a career in IT while other IT students eschew an IT career.

Occupational commitment is defined as the "psychological link between an individual and his/her occupation that is based on an affective reaction to that occupation" [11 p. 800]. Little is known about the commitment of IT students to the IT profession (with the exception of Guzman and Stanton [5]). Most studies on occupational commitment relate to employees currently in the workforce, even though "occupational socialization begins prior to employment in an organization" [11 p. 806].

So, this paper aims to enhance our understanding of factors affecting occupational commitment of IT students. While there has been some work on occupational commitment to IT [e.g. 5], little is known about the interference of occupational demands on the personal life of IT students.

2. THEORY AND HYPOTHESES

Social cognitive career theory (SCCT) aims to understand the processes through which individuals develop occupational interests, choices and pursuits [12]. The theory examines the interplay of personal agentic cognitions (e.g. self-efficacy, interests), behaviors and contextual factors (e.g. barriers, support systems) that may either facilitate or constrain individuals' career pursuits. Central in the social cognitive theory of occupational choice is the role played by career self-efficacy. The theory posits that self-efficacy and outcome expectations predict occupational interests, which in turn, predict occupational choices [12].

2.1 Career Interests

Career interests refer to "patterns of likes, dislikes, and indifferences regarding career-relevant activities and occupations" [12 p. 88]. The theory posits that individuals who pursue their career interests generally require less mental resources to remain attached to their chosen occupation. By contrast, individuals who pursue a career in which there is less interest tend to expend more cognitive, emotional and physical resources to remain engaged. Consequently, working in an occupation that is congruent with one's interests can lead to satisfactory outcomes such as greater satisfaction and success at work, and tenure in the organization [6]. Hence:

H1: Career interests are positively related to occupational commitment.

2.2 Self Efficacy

Self-efficacy refers to a person's belief or confidence in his or her ability to perform a given behavior or set of tasks [3]. In other words, self-efficacy relates to "beliefs about one's ability to successfully perform particular behaviors or courses of action" [14 p. 53]. SCCT theory proposes that self-efficacy facilitates persistence toward their goals by maintaining towards achieving outcomes. Especially in the context of occupational commitment, where there is potential for remaining in the same occupation throughout a person's working life, the notion of persistence is of key salience. The available empirical evidence supports the relationship between self-efficacy and persistence in one's career [10]. Hence:

H2: Self-efficacy is positively related to occupational commitment

2.3 Outcome Expectations

Outcome expectations refer to one's beliefs about the consequences of engaging in a task or set of behaviors [12]. In other words, it addresses the question - "If I do this, what will happen?" Outcome expectations in SCCT research typically focus on positive outcomes resulting from a particular choice behavior, including both extrinsic outcomes and intrinsic outcomes. Prior studies [e.g. 12] have demonstrated that outcome expectations are central to choice of occupation. In the same vein, we argue that outcome expectations should similarly be associated with occupational commitment because students who hold positive outcome expectations of working in the IT profession are more likely to remain committed to the IT occupation. Therefore:

H3: Outcome expectations is positively related to occupational commitment

2.4 Social Support

Social support represents individuals' perceived contextual factors that sustain them [13]. The SCCT posits that social support can render a career choice more appealing based on the subjective appraisals of one's environment. The perception of having more social support helps allay tensions and uncertainty associated with continuing in the IT profession. Conversely, the perception of less social support and more barriers increases the strain experienced by staying in the profession. Therefore:

H4: Social support and barriers is positively related to occupational commitment

3. METHOD
3.1 Sample and Procedures

We tested the hypotheses on survey data collected from students majoring in IT related courses. Data was gathered via a web-based survey. We obtained a total of 1,034 completed responses, representing a response rate of about 7%.

Respondents were predominantly male (66%), pursuing a course of study in information systems/technology or computer science (57% IS/IT, 43% computer science).

3.2 Measures

Occupational commitment was measured with four items (1 = strong disagree; 7 = strongly agree) adapted from Blau [4].

Interests in an IT Career was measured with four items (1 = strong disagree; 7 = strongly agree) adapted from Guzman and Stanton [5].

Self-efficacy was measured with five items from Marakas et al. [15]. Respondents were asked to indicate the extent of their confidence in completing a set of IT related tasks

Outcome expectations was measured with five items adapted from Lent et al. [14]. Respondents were asked to indicate the importance of a set of factors relating to a career in IT.

Social support was measured with three items adapted from Lent et al. [13].

Research has shown that perceptions towards and interests in IT differ between males and females (Adya and Kaiser 2005; Barker and Aspray 2006; Bartol and Aspray 2006; Brown et al. 2006). Thus, we controlled for gender and discipline of study (1=computer science, 0= IT specialization).

4. ANALYSES AND RESULTS

We tested our hypotheses with structural equations modeling using LISREL 8.80 [8]. Following recommended practice [2], we used a two-step analytic approach by first evaluating the measurement model to assess the validity and reliability of the measures. Next, we test the structural model to assess the strength and significance of the hypothesized links among the variables.

To assess the measurement model, we modeled a correlated factor model in which we allowed each item to load on their associated underlying latent variable. Given that all our measures were self-reported, we controlled for common method bias using the approach recommended by Podsakoff et al. [17]. Specifically, each item is an indicator not only of its substantive factor, but also of an unmeasured latent method factor.

The measurement model showed good fit as indicated by all fit indices above recommended values [7]. Composite reliabilities for all constructs were above 0.70. All factor loadings were significant (t values range 7.90 - 38.22, all $p < 0.001$).

Results of the structural model showed support for all hypothesized relationships. Occupational commitment was significantly related to interests in IT, self-efficacy, outcome expectations and social support.

5. DISCUSSION AND CONCLUSION

Current theories of career choice are silent in explaining why some IT students go on to a career in IT while other IT students eschew an IT career. Addressing this gap in the literature, this study examines occupational commitment as a factor within the SCCT framework to explain why some IT students go on to a career in IT while other IT students eschew an IT career. Drawing on social cognitive career theory, we tested our hypotheses on a sample of 1,034 students majoring in computer science and information systems related majors.

The results obtained in this study provide strong support for all hypotheses, consistent with evidence on SCCT for career choice. Specifically, results showed that students with higher interests, self-efficacy, outcome expectations and social support report higher occupational commitment.

In doing so, our study contributes to theory by extending prior research on occupational commitment by providing insights into factors that shape occupational commitment prior to individuals entering the workforce.

6. REFERENCES

[1] Ahuja, M., et al., *Gender and Career Choice Determinants in Information Systems Professionals: A Comparison with Computer Science*, in *Human Resource Management of IT Professionals*, F. Niederman and T.A. Ferratt, Editors. 2006, Information Age Publishing: Greenwich, CT. p. 279-304.

[2] Anderson, J.C. and D.W. Gerbing, *Structural Equation Modeling in Practice: A Review and Recommended Two-Step Approach.* Psychological Bulletin, 1988. 103(3 (Fall)): p. 441-423.

[3] Bandura, A., *Social Foundations of Thoughts and Action: A Social Cognitive Theory.* 1986, Englewood Cliffs, New Jersey: Prentice Hall.

[4] Blau, G., *Testing the Generalizability of a Career Commitment Measure and Its Impact on Employee Turnover.* Journal of Vocational Behavior, 1989. 35(1): p. 88-103.

[5] Guzman, I.R. and J.M. Stanton, *IT Occupational Culture: The Cultural Fit and Commitment of New Information Technologists.* Information Technology & People, 2009. 22(2): p. 157-187.

[6] Holland, J.L., *Making Vocational Choices: A Theory of Vocational Personalities and Work Environments.* 1997, Odessa, FL: Psychological Assessment Resources.

[7] Hu, L.T. and P.M. Bentler, *Cutoff Criteria for Fit Indexes in Covariance Structure Modeling: Conventional Criteria Versus New Alternatives.* Structural Equations Modeling, 1999. 6: p. 1-55.

[8] Jöreskog, K. and D. Sörbon, *Lisrel for Windows 8.80.* 2006, Scientific Software International: Lincolnwood, IL.

[9] Joseph, D., et al., *Careers of the Information Technology Workforce: An Analysis of Career Sequences, Mobility and Objective Career Success.* MIS Quarterly, In Press.

[10] Judge, T.A. and J.E. Bono, *Relationship of Core Self-Evaluations Traits-Self-Esteem, Generalized Self-Efficacy, Locus of Control, and Emotional Stability-with Job Satisfaction and Job Performance: A Meta-Analysis.* Journal of Applied Psychology, 2001. 86(1): p. 80-92.

[11] Lee, K., J.J. Carswell, and N.J. Allen, *A Meta-Analytic Review of Occupational Commitment: Relations with Person- and Work-Related Variables.* Journal of Applied Psychology, 2000. 85(5): p. 799-811.

[12] Lent, R.W., S.D. Brown, and G. Hackett, *Toward a Unifying Social Cognitive Theory of Career and Academic Interest, Choice and Performance.* Journal of Vocational Behavior, 1994. 45: p. 79-122.

[13] Lent, R.W., et al., *Career Choice Barriers, Supports, and Coping Strategies: College Students' Experiences.* Journal of Vocational Behavior, 2002. 60(1): p. 61-72.

[14] Lent, R.W., et al., *Social Cognitive Career Theory and the Prediction of Interests and Choice Goals in the Computing Disciplines.* Journal of Vocational Behavior, 2008. 73(1): p. 52-62.

[15] Marakas, G.M., R.D. Johnson, and C. P.F., *The Evolving Nature of the Computer Self-Efficacy Construct: An Empirical Investigation of Measurement Construction, Validity, Reliability, and Stability over Time.* Journal of the Association for Information Systems, 2007. 8(1): p. 15-46.

[16] National Science Board, *Science and Enginering Indicators 2006.* 2006, National Science Foundation: Arlington, VA.

[17] Podsakoff, P.M., et al., *Common Method Biases in Behavioral Research: A Critical Review of the Literature and Recommended Remedies.* Journal of Applied Psychology, 2003. 88: p. 879-203.

The Trend is Our Friend –
German IT Personnel's Perception of Job-related Factors Before, During and After the Economic Downturn

Sven Laumer
Centre of Human Resources Information Systems
University of Bamberg, Germany
+49 951 8632873
sven.laumer@uni-bamberg.de

Christian Maier
Centre of Human Resources Information Systems
University of Bamberg, Germany
+49 951 8632873
christian.maier@uni-bamberg.de

Andreas Eckhardt
Centre of Human Resources Information Systems
Goethe-University of Frankfurt, Germany
+49 69 79834659
eckhardt@wiwi.uni-frankfurt.de

Tim Weitzel
Centre of Human Resources Information Systems
University of Bamberg, Germany
+49 951 8632871
tim.weitzel@uni-bamberg.de

ABSTRACT
With the bankruptcy of Lehman Brothers the global economic crisis has reached one of its summits. Before that time CIO's challenged high turnover rates of IT personnel and recruiting, developing and retaining the IT workforce was one of the most important concerns of CIOs [21]. However, the global economic development has changed on the one side the challenges of organizations [22], and on the other side also the perception of job-related factors of IT talent [17]. Based on this development we compare major IT turnover constructs using three empirical surveys in 2008, 2009 and 2010 in order to discuss how the global economic development influences the perceptions of job-related factors and turnover intentions of German IT personnel. The analysis showed that job satisfaction and organizational commitment is decreasing since 2008, perceived job alternatives are increasing compared to 2009 and turnover intention has reached a maximum in 2010 compared to the two other years in question.

Categories and Subject Descriptors
K.7.1 [THE COMPUTING PROFESSION] Occupations

General Terms
Management, Measurement, Human Factors

Keywords
IT Personnel, Economic Downturn, Job Perception, Job Alternatives, Job Satisfaction, Organizational Commitment, Turnover Intention

1. INTRODUCTION
In 2009, the global economy experienced one of its worst crises. The crisis started with financial problems of one particular bank, continued as an essential issue for financial institutions and finally reached every company in every industry sector worldwide. One summit of the crisis was the bankruptcy of Lehman Brothers in September 2008. Two years and different state interventions later the situation especially in Germany seems to be improving as the economy is growing again and is reporting promising business opportunities [40]. Before that crisis the IT industry had to face the challenge of hiring suitable IT personnel and retaining them with the organizations [21]. Before 2008 CIOs identified recruiting, developing and retaining IT talent as the most important issue for IT organizations and the scarcity of IT talent represented a crucial problem in almost every industry, not only in US but also in Europe and other states. In the 2009 SIM survey, recruiting, developing and retaining IT talent left the ranking of CIO's ten most important concerns. In 2009 *"companies have experienced IT budget and salary reductions, projects and purchases put on hold, and hiring freezes"* [22]. However, an analysis with HR executives of 300 German IT organizations in 2010 showed that the scarcity of IT talent is one of the two most important trends HR executives have to deal with when managing the recruiting, developing and retention activities of IT organizations in the next years [16]. In addition, the German Federal Association for Information Technology, Telecommunications and New Media reports that there were 45,000 open positions for IT workers at the end of 2008 and companies still cannot find appropriate IT staff even in a severe downturn[1]. As a consequence of this development during the last years the improved economic climate in Europe especially in Germany could make the scarcity of IT talent on the labor market an even worse challenge for organizations. In addition, the

---

[1] More information about the situation in Germany could be found at http://www.bitkom.org/de/presse/62013_61645.aspx and http://www.bitkom.org/de/themen/54633_58438.aspx

improved economic climate could initiate people again to leave their current organizations and look for a new employer. A comparison of job-related perceptions and turnover behavior of IT personnel of 2008 and 2009 showed that there are no differences for job satisfaction, organizational commitment and turnover intentions of IT personnel comparing 2008 and 2009. However, the study reveals differences for perceived job alternatives and turnover behavior of German IT personnel in 2008 and 2009 [17].

Based on these results and the expectations for the IT labor market this paper aims at extending the analysis of job-related perceptions, turnover intentions and turnover behavior by providing a one year update and a comparison of the years 2008, 2009 and 2010. Thus, the focus of this paper is to analyze IT personnel's job-related perceptions and behaviors regarding the development of the global economy over the last three years by asking the following research question:

Do the ups and downs of the economic development during the last 3 years influence IT personnel's perception of job satisfaction, organizational commitment, job alternatives and turnover intention?

Therefore, the paper extends the results of the 2008 and 2009 comparison. In order to answer the research question an additional empirical survey with German IT personnel has been conducted in 2010. To scrutinize this publication the reminder is as follows. Section 2 explains the theoretical background of turnover intention and the relevance of the economic climate. Afterwards, the research methodology will be presented. The following section 4 presents the research results and finally section 5 discusses the findings.

2. THEORETICAL BACKGROUND

This section highlights important models of an individual's turnover intention from organizational as well as information system literature in order to explain the job-related factors used in this research.

2.1 Turnover Intention of IT Personnel

2.1.1 Organizational Behavior Literature

According to Hom et al. [9] turnover intention are influenced by job satisfaction, job alternatives and search intentions. Job satisfaction was investigated the first time in the 1930s and has been investigated within more than 12,400 studies since 1991. The research about job satisfaction reveals a negative correlation between job satisfaction and turnover intention. The correlation was approved in different meta-analyses as for example in Joseph et al. [12].

Another more detailed model of voluntary turnover is the Job Investment Model. This model posits that job satisfaction and organizational commitment determine turnover. Job satisfaction is influenced by job rewards as well as job costs and organizational alternatives. Investments in the organization determine organizational commitment [6]. Similar to job satisfaction, organizational commitment is also highly investigated and prior research revealed a negative correlation with an individual's turnover behavior [35]. Nonetheless, if an employee leaves an organization to accept another job, he/she is not necessary less satisfied with the actual job than other employees, who do not change their employer, but other factors might determine his/her decision. According to an analysis by van Dam job satisfaction is negatively related to organizational commitment [38].

2.1.2 Information Systems Literature

Next to turnover models in organizational behavior literature several authors focused on IT professionals and their turnover intention. Based on a literature review and a meta-analytic structural equation model Joseph et al. [12] identified job satisfaction as the most examined determinant of IT personnel turnover [12]. Thereby, each study - considered in the meta-analysis by Joseph et al. [12] - detected a negative relationship with turnover. On position two ranks organizational commitment. Therefore organizational commitment and job satisfaction are the most important job-related factors influencing turnover intentions of western IT professionals ([8]; [12]). Based on these results Lacity et al. [14] developed the basic model of Western IS Professionals turnover intention explaining turnover intention and actual turnover behavior by job satisfaction, organizational commitment and perceived alternatives [14].

2.2 IT personnel turnover and times of economic downturns

"More importantly, if there are many (or few) leavers from an organization because local labor market conditions are excellent (or very poor) and the base rate for turnover in the organization is extremely high (or low) then turnover will be poorly predicted by job satisfaction" [10]. This is one of the basic assumptions of the influence of the economic environment on the intention to leave an organization. However, as Trevor and Nyberg pointed out *"researchers know very little about downsizing effects on the critical employee behavior (...), perhaps the most telling of these behaviors is voluntary employee turnover"*. In general downsizing has been found to negatively affect organizational commitment ([4]; [13]), job satisfaction ([23]; [2]) and perceived job alternatives [10].

The development of the last three years provides the possibility to analyze these effects as within three years the economy went down and is starting to grow again. Before the bankruptcy of Lehman Brothers in September 2008 the economic booms and IT personnel were highly coveted [21]. Just one month later, almost every industry got financial problems, whereby IT professionals like others were afraid to lose their job [17]. As a consequence, IT personnel did not consider quitting their job, because they did not see job alternatives [17]. In this period a lot of employees supported their employer to avoid the insolvency by reducing their salary or without getting salary increases.

According to the economic development over the last year we assume that downsizing due to the economic environment will affect the turnover intention of IT personnel as described by prior research for downsizing in general. In our approach we will test for the effect of the economic crisis in the last three years on the perception of IT personnel regarding their turnover intention, job satisfaction, organizational commitment and perceived alternatives. Therefore, the following section describes our research methodology.

3. RESEARCH METHODOLOGY

In order to extend the comparison of IT personnel perception of job-related factors from 2008 and 2009, one additional empirical survey was conducted in June/July 2010. In 2010 the same measurement models were used as in 2008 and 2009 and the survey was targeted at the same group of German IT personnel as in 2008 and 2009.

As the research aims at providing information of turnover intentions of IT personnel from different companies, age, gender, and tenure an online survey was evaluated as the most appropriate form of data collection ([34]). The surveyed IT personnel were registered in an online platform for business purpose and got an e-mail invitation to take part in the online study. Demographic information about the participating IT personnel in 2008, 2009 and 2010 is summarized in Table 1.

Table 1. Demographic information of survey participants

		2010		2009		2008	
Gender	Male	1068	84.9%	291	81.5%	309	79.4%
	Female	187	14.9%	65	18.2%	80	20.6%
Age	<25	38	3.0%	9	2.5%	16	3.1%
	25-29	224	17.8%	65	18.2%	72	18.5%
	30-34	271	21.5%	70	19.6%	103	26.5%
	35-39	225	17.9%	59	16.5%	72	18.5%
	40-44	254	20.2%	54	15.1%	58	14.9%
	45-49	141	11.2%	53	14.8%	40	10.3%
	>50	101	8.0%	46	12.9%	28	7.2%
Tenure *	Young Professional	204	16.2%	68	19.0%	78	20.1%
	Professional	639	50.8%	197	55.2%	184	47.3%
	Manager	151	12.0%	52	14.6%	38	9.8%
	Other	264	22.0%	40	11.2%	70	18.0%
Total		1258		357		389	
* Young Professional (<5 years), Professional (>=5 years)							

Based on IS and organizational literature different measures were selected to measure job-related factors and turnover intentions of IT personnel. The used measurement items can be seen in the construct result tables in the results section. Four items were used to measure the turnover intention. Such a measurement is consistent with prior practice in human resources and IS literature [36] and the items used by Thatcher et al. [36] were adapted for this study. As suggested by Thatcher et al. [36] the Organizational Commitment Questionnaire ([25]; [29]) was used to measure organizational commitment. To measure job satisfaction of IT personnel literature suggests different measurement items ([3], [19], [32]). The Cornell Job Descriptive Index [32] uses several job situation facets which were selected within this study to capture IT personnel's job satisfaction. To measure job alternatives different items are available as used by prior research, however these measurement models include limitations ([34]; [21]; [33]; [11]). For the research presented in this paper, the perceived job alternatives measurement model as developed by Thatcher et al. [36] were used to control for perceived job alternatives of IT personnel [36]. The surveyed IT personnel were asked to report their perceptions of job-related factors using these measurement items. The result of the three empirical studies in 2008, 2009 and 2010 are presented in the following section.

4. RESEARCH RESULTS

In order to understand the turnover intention of IT personnel in more detail, this section focuses on three related aspects – job satisfaction, organizational commitment and perceived alternatives – to three different points in time and at intervals of 12 months. Consequently, the presented data offer insights on the perceptions of job-related factors of IT personnel before, during and after the economic crisis.

4.1 Job Satisfaction

According to Locke the "*overall job satisfaction is the sum of the evaluations of the discrete elements of which the job is composed*" [20]. Therefore, the extent of satisfaction of German IT professionals was captured with an instrument developed by Smith et al. [32] in the years 2008, 2009 and 2010. In addition, the results were investigated with the help of an analysis of variance (ANOVA) and are illustrated at **Error! Reference source not found.**. The results show that significant differences could be unfolded for 'way to work' and 'department' in the years 2008 and 2010. Moreover the perceived career expectations varied in 2008 – compared to 2009 and 2010. The same holds for the other decomposed aspects of the overall job satisfaction. Nonetheless, even if only a few statistical significant changes could be observed, almost every decomposed job satisfaction aspect is lower in 2010 than in the past 2 years. Only the exchange of information increases a little and the perception of the employer takes the same value as in 2008.

Table 2. Job satisfaction

	YEAR	N	MEAN	STR. DRV	Sig.(ANOVA)	multiple comparison	
						2009	2008
supervisor	2010	749	3.40	1.289	0.073	0.421	0.090
	2009	342	3.51	1.285			0.774
	2008	371	3.58	1.193			
company as an employer	2010	740	3.34	1.180	0.557	0.736	0.630
	2009	342	3.40	1.123			0.991
	2008	371	3.42	1.120			
career expectations	2010	748	2.54	1.169	0.001*	0.850	0.001*
	2009	343	2.59	1.159			0.032*
	2008	368	2.82	1.148			
rewards	2010	748	2.92	1.121	0.495	0.497	0.957
	2009	344	3.01	1.143			0.738
	2008	371	2.94	1.081			
colleagues	2010	747	4.02	0.875	0.292	0.560	0.360
	2009	344	4.08	0.900			0.963
	2008	373	4.10	0.845			
working conditions	2010	747	3.56	1.077	0.048*	0.137	0.132
	2009	344	3.69	1.029			1.000
	2008	371	3.69	0.974			
way to work	2010	747	3.39	1.171	0.018*	0.471	0.019*
	2009	344	3.48	1.153			0.416
	2008	370	3.59	1.016			
department	2010	741	3.64	1.049	0.013*	0.122	0.029*
	2009	342	3.78	1.002			0.895
	2008	371	3.82	0.977			
public perception of your employer	2010	744	3.36	0.993	0.149	0.180	1.000
	2009	342	3.48	1.041			0.276
	2008	370	3.36	1.058			
international orientation	2010	745	3.30	1.053	0.156	0.450	0.203
	2009	340	3.39	1.196			0.918
	2008	369	3.43	1.089			
exchange of information	2010	744	2.83	1.182	0.283	0.990	0.349
	2009	344	2.82	1.130			0.399
	2008	370	2.94	1.146			

4.2 Organizational Commitment

As discussed, job satisfaction subsumes every emotion towards one's job and moreover it has an influence on organizational commitment [6]. Organizational commitment describes the extent to which an employee is loyal to a particular organization ([26]; [30]). To measure the construct the Organizational Commitment Questionnaire ([25]; [29]) was used in this research and the results of the measurement items are illustrated at **Error! Reference source not found.**. Over the last 3 years no significant changes could be discovered apart from a small variation in the item that the employee is glad to work for the organization they choose. Noticeable is the fact that in 2010 each value is lower than in 2008 and 2009.

Table 3. Organizational Commitment

	YEAR	N	MEAN	STR DRV	Sig.(ANOVA)	multiple comparison	
						2009	2008
I really care about the fate if this organization	2010	742	5.67	1.450	0.208	0.289	0.439
	2009	341	5.81	1.353			0.954
	2008	387	5.78	1.310			
I feel high loyalty to this organization	2010	739	5.30	1.588	0.363	0.376	0.780
	2009	338	5.44	1.521			0.816
	2008	384	5.36	1.462			
I am willing to put in a great deal of effort beyond that normally expected in order to help this organization to be successful	2010	737	4.71	1.716	0.611	0.993	0.625
	2009	337	4.72	1.723			0.776
	2008	386	4.81	1.581			
I talk up this organization to my friends as a great organization to work for	2010	739	4.36	1.825	0.128	0.539	0.144
	2009	339	4.49	1.778			0.793
	2008	386	4.58	1.748			
I find that my values and the organization's values are very similar	2010	735	4.25	1.673	0.526	0.628	0.680
	2009	337	4.36	1.739			0.994
	2008	385	4.35	1.694			
I am extremely glad that I choose this organization to work for	2010	732	4.26	1.709	0.047*	0.256	0.073
	2009	340	4.45	1.785			0.892
	2008	385	4.51	1.723			

4.3 Perceived Job Alternatives

Another job-related aspect that influences job satisfaction and turnover intention is perceived job alternatives. Thau et al. [37] view this perception as the probability to find another job on the labor market. Using the measurement items provided by Thatcher et al. [36], **Error! Reference source not found.** illustrates the results of this research. In the last three years employees' attitude changed regarding the possibility to get another job. In 2010 more participants expect attractive job opportunities on the national as well as the international market compared to 2009. Even if there is no significance, the mean-value is also better than in 2008. Nonetheless, the possibility to find a job is not as high as in 2008. Summing up, most of the reported opinions in 2010 towards job alternatives are better than in the economic crisis last year, but worse than in the economy boom 2008.

Table 4. Perceived job alternatives

	YEAR	N	MEAN	STR DRV	Sig.(ANOVA)	multiple comparison	
						2009	2008
There are many jobs available similar to mine	2010	743	4.43	1.445	0.221	0.988	0.239
	2009	325	4.44	1.497			0.434
	2008	351	4.58	1.403			
I can find another employer easily where I can do exactly what I am doing now	2010	741	4.11	1.545	0.123	0.876	0.227
	2009	326	4.06	1.601			0.166
	2008	349	4.29	1.561			
There are many alternative job opportunities including some that are different from what I do now	2010	741	4.96	1.338	0.043*	0.651	0.155
	2009	324	4.88	1.360			0.000*
	2008	348	5.13	1.295			
There are many possibilities to find a job doing satisfying work	2010	739	4.14	1.495	0.000*	0.338	0.006*
	2009	326	3.99	1.505			0.000*
	2008	350	4.46	1.560			
It is easy to get a new job offer	2010	738	4.00	1.606	0.005*	0.107	0.224
	2009	325	3.77	1.593			0.005*
	2008	352	4.18	1.723			
Due to my current job situation it is promising to find a new job	2010	734	4.25	1.508	0.000*	0.000*	0.000*
	2009	320	3.70	1.625			0.000*
	2008	351	4.66	1.571			
There are attractive opportunities on the internal job market	2010	725	3.52	1.508	0.042*	0.502	0.214
	2009	315	3.37	1.996			0.046*
	2008	335	3.75	1.849			
There are attractive opportunities on the national job market	2010	733	4.86	1.398	0.005*	0.005*	0.623
	2009	316	4.55	1.520			0.150
	2008	332	4.77	1.365			
There are attractive opportunities on the international job market	2010	731	4.93	1.415	0.044*	0.044*	0.811
	2009	312	4.69	1.619			0.277
	2008	332	4.87	1.399			

4.4 Turnover Intention

In 2008 and 2009 the turnover intention was constant and comparable. This changed in parts, as in 2010 more employees think of quitting their job and searching a new employer. This becomes obvious as people do not only think about leaving the employer but also about quitting their job. Comparing the mean value for all turnover indicators, the analysis shows that the mean is already higher in 2010 compared to 2008. Last year a decrease could be measured, however the analysis also shows that the development hits the bottom last year.

Table 5. Turnover intention

	YEAR	N	MEAN	STR DRV	Sig.(ANOVA)	multiple comparison	
						2009	2008
I think often about quitting my job at my current employer	2010	756	3.12	1.407	0.084	0.378	0.628
	2009	357	2.93	1.432			0.921
	2008	396	3.13	1.350			
I intend to quit my actual job	2010	753	2.80	1.427	0.023*	0.044*	0.628
	2009	356	2.56	1.438			0.389
	2008	395	2.78	1.298			
I think about leaving my actual employer	2010	750	3.29	1.428	0.044*	0.029*	0.978
	2009	356	3.06	1.411			0.097
	2008	390	3.20	1.319			
I will look for a new job within the next months	2010	752	3.48	1.437	0.329	0.117	0.997
	2009	356	3.35	1.453			0.166
	2008	394	3.39	1.365			

After analyzing each construct of the basic model of western turnover intentions in more detail, the following section summarizes the development over the last three years.

4.5 IT Personnel's perception of job-related factors in 2008, 2009 and 2010

After illustrating the results of each measurement item for turnover intention and the three basic antecedents in the previous sections, **Error! Reference source not found.** summarizes the results for each construct of the basic model of western IT personnel. As the results indicate, there are no significant differences for organizational commitment and turnover intention. Nonetheless, the mean of turnover intention reached its highest value in 2010 which also outranges the turnover intention in 2008. In addition organizational commitment takes the lowest value in 2010.

Job satisfaction and perceived job alternatives varied significantly over the last three years. After the economic slump in 2008 job satisfaction decreases year by year and culminates in the lowest value in 2010. The mean value is significantly different compared to the time before the crises started. Moreover, the perceived number of alternative jobs is increasing compared to 2009, but still less than 2008 according to the mean as illustrated by **Error! Reference source not found.**.

Table 6. Summary of results

	YEAR	N	MEAN	STR DRV	Sig.(ANOVA)	multiple comparison	
						2009	2008
Job Satisfaction	2010	756	3.30	0.734	0.014 *	0.247	0.019*
	2009	345	3.38	0.720			0.648
	2008	375	3.43	0.693			
Organizational Commitment	2010	748	4.76	1.422	0.166	0.388	0.244
	2009	341	4.89	1.426			0.980
	2008	390	4.91	1.350			
Perceived Job Alternatives	2010	751	4.37	1.086	0.000*	0.024*	0.053
	2009	327	4.17	1.088			0.000*
	2008	358	4.54	1.137			
Turnover Intention	2010	759	3.17	1.317	0.052	0.056	0.906
	2009	357	2.98	1.308			0.219
	2008	401	3.14	1.213			

In addition, Figure 1 illustrates the mean development of the four constructs during the last three years. In 2010, IT personnel have the highest turnover intention over the last three years. Moreover, IT employees perceive more job alternatives compared to the last year, however, still less than 2008. Furthermore, the results indicate that the crisis has a long-ranging effect on the relationship between organization and employees, because employees are not able to sustain the identification people had with the organization during and before the crisis. Finally, the most important turnover intention predictor, job satisfaction, is also declining over the last years.

5. DISCUSSION

Our research investigates the individual turnover intention and the perception of job-related factors of German IT personnel over the last three years. Notably, these are job satisfaction, organizational commitment and perceived alternatives ([36]; [12]). The results show a higher willingness to quit the actual job in 2010 compared to 2009 and 2008. Parallel to an increasing turnover intention job satisfaction and organizational commitment is decreasing. In addition, employees feel that other organizations also search for IT personnel, so that the job market offers several new possibilities and the situation improved compared to 2009.

Since more employees will quit their job in 2010 compared to 2008 and 2009 this has essential implications for organizations. On the one side organizations have to retain IT personnel who are willing to leave and on the other side, when employees are leaving, new IT talent has to be attracted for the organization. Therefore, one can expect for Germany that retaining, developing and recruiting IT talent will return as one of the major challenges for CIOs.

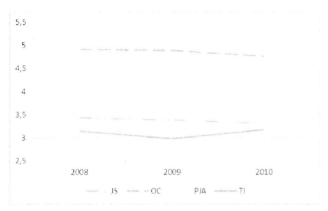

Figure 1. IT personnel perception of job-related factors

Moreover, the results indicate that the improved economic situation will accentuate the challenge of recruiting IT talent and will renew the "War for Talent" [5]. This development requires new approaches for retaining IT staff over a long period. Literature suggests different approaches which could be useful in future as well; however organization might focus on retaining IT talent again ([15]; [27]; [28]). Furthermore, it is also essential to hire new qualified IT staff. For this purpose, literature contains diverse suggestions, strategies and frameworks ([18]; [39]; [1]; [31]; [24]).

Contrary to the implications for organizations, employees have good prospects for the future as results of our analysis indicate. If the demand of organizations for IT personnel increases, employees will get more job offers, can choose between different employers – actually they can still feel this process – and will

have a better negotiating position. Therefore the trend on the job market as perceived by the research German IT personnel during the last three years will be the friend of IT employees.

Furthermore, the results of the analysis indicate that the crisis has a long-ranging effect on the relationship between organizations and IT employees. IT employees show a decreasing commitment with the organization and satisfaction with their job. Therefore, one could conclude that employees need time to build up trust again, especially after difficult economic situations with dismissals.

Further research can develop more detailed strategies, how organizations could fulfill the challenges of economic fluctuations. Moreover, the descriptive analysis of the development in 2008, 2009 and 2010 could be represented in another way like structural equation modeling to analyze if turnover intention can be determined by job satisfaction, perceived job alternatives and organizational commitment in good and bad times equally.

6. REFERENCES

[1] Agarwal, R. 2002. Enduring practices for managing IT professionals. *Communications of the ACM* (34:9)

[2] Armstrong-Stassen, M. 2002. Designated Redundant but Escaping Lay-Off: A Special Group of Lay-Off Survivors. *Journal of Occupational & Organizational Psychology* **75**(1): 1-13

[3] Bartol, K. M. 1983. Turnover among Dp Personnel: A Casual Analysis. Communications of the ACM (26:10), pp. 807–811

[4] Brockner, J., S. Grover, T. Reed, R. Dewitt and M. O'malley 1987. Survivors' Reactions to Layoffs: We Get by with a Little Help for Our Friends. *Administrative Science Quarterly* **32**(4): 526-541

[5] Chambers, E. G., Foulon, F., Handfield-Jones, H., Hankin, S. M., and Michaels, E. G. 1998. The War for Talent, *The McKinsey Quarterly* (1)

[6] Currivan, D. B. 1999. The Causal Order of Job Satisfaction and Organizational Commitment in Models of Employee Turnover, *Human Resource Management Review* (9:4), pp. 495–524

[7] Farrell, D., and Rusbult, C. 1981. Exchange variables as predictors of job satisfaction, job commitment, and turnover: The impact of rewards, costs, alternatives, and investments, *Organizational Behavior and Human Performance* (28:1), pp. 78–96

[8] Gallivan M.J. 2004. Examining It Professionals' Adaptation to Technological Change: The Influence of Gender and Personal Attributes, *SIGMIS Database* (35:3), pp. 28–49

[9] Hom, P. W., Caranikas-Walker, F., Prussia, G. E., and Griffeth, R. W. 1992. A Meta-Analytical Structural Equations Analysis of a Model of Employee Turnover, *Journal of Applied Psychology* (77:6), pp. 890–909

[10] Hom, P. W., R. Katerberg Jr and C. L. Hulin 1979. Comparative Examination of Three Approaches to the Prediction of Turnover. *Journal of Applied Psychology* **64**(3): 280-290

[11] Igbaria, M., and Greenhaus, J. 1991. Determinants of Mis Employees' Turnover Intentions: A Structural Equation Model. *Communications of the ACM*, pp. 34–49

[12] Joseph, D., Kok-Yee, N., Koh, C., and Soon, A. 2007. Turnover of Information Technology Professionals: A Narrative Review, Meta-Analytic Structural Equation Modeling, and Model Development, *MIS Quarterly* (31:3), pp. 547–577

[13] Knudsen, H. K., J. Aaron Johnson, J. K. Martin and P. M. Roman 2003. Downsizing Survival: The Experience of Work and Organizational Commitment. *Sociological Inquiry* **73**(2): 265-283

[14] Lacity, M., Iyer, V., and Rudramuniyaiah 2008. Turnover Intentions of Indian Is Professionals, *Information Systems Frontiers* (10:2), pp. 225–241

[15] Laumer, S. 2009. Non-Monetary Solutions for Retaining the It Workforce. *Americas Conference on Information Systems* (AMCIS 2009), San Francisco

[16] Laumer, S., Eckhardt, E., and Weitzel, T. 2010. Electronic Human Resources Management in an E-Business Environment, *Journal of Electronic Commerce Research*, (11:4)

[17] Laumer, S., and Eckhardt, A. 2010. Analyzing IT Personnel's Perception of Job-related Factors in Good and Bad Times. *Proceedings of SIGMIS CPR 2010*. Vancouver

[18] Lee, I. 2007. An Architecture for a Next-Generation Holistic E-Recruiting System, *Communications of the ACM* (50:7), pp. 81–85

[19] Lee, T. W., Mitchell, T. R., Holtom, B. C., McDaniel, L. S., and Hill, J. W. 1999. The Unfolding Model of Voluntary Turnover: A Replication and Extension, *Academy of Management Journal* (42:4), pp. 450–462

[20] Locke, E. A. 1969. What is job satisfaction? *Organizational Behavior and Human Performance* (4), pp. 309–336

[21] Luftman, J., and Kempaiah, R. 2008. Key Issues for IT Executives 2007, *MIS Quarterly Executive* (7:2), pp. 99–112

[22] Luftman, J., and Ben-Zvi, T. 2010. Key Issues for IT Executives 2009, *MIS Quarterly Executive* (9:1), pp. 151–159

[23] Luthans, B. C. and S. M. Sommer 1999. The Impact of Downsizing on Workplace Attitudes: Differing Reactions of Managers and Staff in a Health Care Organization. *Group Organization Management* **24**(1): 46-70

[24] Maier, C., Laumer, S., and Eckhardt, A. 2009. An Integrated IT-Architecture for Talent Management and Recruitment. *Proceedings of the 3rd International Workshop on Human Resource Information Systems*

[25] Mowday, R. T., Porter, L. W., and Steers, R. M. 1982. Employee-organization linkages. The psychology of commitment, absenteeism, and turnover/ Richard T. Mowday; Lyman W. Porter; Richard M. Steers, New York: Academic Press

[26] Mueller, C. W., Wallace, J. E., and Price, J. L. 1992. Employee commitment: Resolving some issues, *Work and Occupations* (19), pp. 211–236

[27] Murray, J. P. 1999. Successfully hiring and retaining IT personnel, *Information Systems Management*

[28] Pare, G., Tremblay, M., and Lalonde, P. 2001. Workforce retention: what do IT employees really want? *Proceedings of the 2001 ACM SIGCPR conference on computer personnel research*

[29] Porter, L. W., Steers, R. M., Mowday, R. T., and Boulian, P. W. 1974. Organizational Commitment, Job Satisfaction, and Turnover among Psychiatric Technicians. *Journal of Applied Psychology*, pp. 603–609

[30] Price, J. L. 1997. Handbook of Organizational Measurement, Bradford, UK: MCB University Press

[31] Rao, H. and Drazin, R.. 2002. Overcoming resource constraints on product innovation by recruiting talent from rivals: A study of the mutual fund industry, 1986-94, *Academy of Management Journal* (45:3), pp. 491–507

[32] Smith, P. C., Kendall, L. M., and Hulin, C. C. 1969. The Measurement of Satisfaction in Work and Retirement: A Strategy for the Study of Attitudes, Chicago: Rand-McNally.

[33] Steel, R. P., and Griffeth, R. W. 1989. The Elusive Relationship between Perceived Employment Opportunity and Turnover Behavior: A Methodological or Conceptual Artifact? *Journal of Applied Psychology* (74:6)

[34] Tan, C. W., Benbasat, I., and Cenfetelli, R. T. 2007. Understanding the Antecedents and Consequences of E-Government Service Quality: An Empirical Investigation. *International Conference on Information Systems*

[35] Tett, R. P., and Meyer, J. P. 1993. Job Satisfaction, Organizational Commitment, Turnover Intention, and Turnover: Path Analyses Based on Meta-Analytic Findings, *Personnel Psychology* (46:2), pp. 259–293

[36] Thatcher, J. B., Stepina, L. P., and Boyle, R. J. 2002. Turnover of Information Technology Workers: Examining Empirically the Influence of Attitudes, Job Characteristics, and External Markets, *Journal of Management Information Systems* (19:3), pp. 231–261

[37] Thau, S., Bennett, R. J., Stahlberg, D., and Werner, J. M. 2004. Why should I be generous when I have valued and accessible alternatives? Alternative exchange partners and OCB, *Journal of Organizational Behavior* (25:5), pp. 607–626

[38] van Dam, K. 2005. Employee Attitudes toward Job Changes: An Application and Extension of Rusbult and Farrell's Investment Model, *Journal of Occupational & Organizational Psychology* (78:2), pp. 254–272

[39] Weitzel, T., Eckhardt, A., and Laumer, S. 2009. A Framework for Recruiting IT Talent: Lessons from Siemens, *MIS Quarterly Executive* (8:4), pp. 175–189

[49] Wirtschaftswoche 2010. Die Wirtschaft zieht weiter an, http://www.wiwo.de/politik-weltwirtschaft/die-wirtschaft-zieht-weiter-an-435017/ (last access 7th Nov. 2010)

Exponential Random Graph Modeling of Communication Networks to Understand Organizational Crisis

Jafar Hamra
Center for Complex Systems
Research, Project Management
Graduate Programme, The University
of Sydney
NSW 2006, Australia
+61 2 93515229
jafar.hamra@sydney.edu.au

Shahadat Uddin
Center for Complex Systems
Research, Project Management
Graduate Programme, The University
of Sydney
NSW 2006, Australia
+61 2 93515229
shahadat.uddin@sydney.edu.au

Liaquat Hossain
Center for Complex Systems
Research, Project Management
Graduate Programme, The University
of Sydney
NSW 2006, Australia
+61 2 9036 9110
liaquat.hossain@sydney.edu.au

ABSTRACT

In recent social network studies, exponential random graph models have been used comprehensively to model global social network structure as a function of their local features. In this study, we describe the exponential random graph models and demonstrate its use in modeling the changing communication network structure at Enron Corporation during the period of its disintegration. We illustrate the modeling on communication networks and provide a new way of classifying networks and their performance based on the occurrence of their local features. Among several micro-level structures of exponential random graph models, we found significant variation in the appearance of A2P (Alternating k-two-paths) network structure in the communication network during crisis period and non-crisis period. This finding could also be used in analyzing communication networks of dynamic project groups and their adaptation process during crisis which could lead to an improved understanding how communications network evolve and adapt during crisis.

Categories and Subject Descriptors

H.1.1 Systems and Information Theory, J.4 Social and Behavioral Sciences, K.4.3 Organizational Impacts, H.4.3 Communications Applications

General Terms

Measurement, Design, Experimentation, Human Factors.

Keywords

Social networks; Email Communications; Exponential random graph models; p* models; Statistical models for social networks; Organizational Disintegration.

1. INTRODUCTION

In this paper, we attempt to analyze the changing communications structure for investigating the patterns associated with the final stage of organizational disintegration. This study is made possible by the fact that Enron Corporation went through the final phase of

disintegration during the period early 2000 to late 2001, and the entire set of email communications exchanged by Enron employees during this period was made available for research by the Federal Energy Regulatory Commission (FERC).

The goal of social network is to understand the functioning of organization's communication which, in large part, depends on their complex underlying structure. Summarizing an organization's communication into a network representation allows us to study the complex structure via the interactions among its components and the simple frequent patterns, or features, which they form. Thus, when studying the systemic nature of organizations' communication, many modeling approaches focus on simple, but prominent, structural features, as they are easier to understand than the global networks and, once identified, can be used as building blocks to briefly describe the network [17].

One class of approaches, statistical network modeling, has recently earned interest from the social network community, and a number of methods and models have been proposed as frameworks for investigating networks. Based on recent social network modeling efforts, this article discusses modeling communication networks using a family of statistical models called exponential random graph models, also known as p* models. Exponential random graph models provide a way to support our understanding of the network interactions in communication systems. We are particularly interested in studying the way that a network's global structure and its function depend on its local structure. How does one use an understanding of local features or attributes such as employee-employee interaction or even node degree to understand the more global notion of the function of a network system?

In this article, we introduce exponential random graph models for communication network exploration, and then we discuss the process of modeling communication networks using exponential random graph models, including the choice of explanatory variables. Finally, we illustrate the modeling on email communication network and provide a new way of classifying networks and their performance based on the occurring of their local features. The paper addresses the following research questions:

(i) How communication patterns and local structure are affected by organizational crisis?

(ii) Do we find any significant differences in the changes of structural properties of communications network based on the intensity of increasing crisis?

(iii) How can exponential random graph modeling be used to understand (ii), which may lead to exploring the correlation between evolving and adaptation of communications network during the phase of organizational disintegration?

There are very few systematic studies found in the current literature about organizational disintegration. In one such study, which was about the turmoil of a school that survived only for four years, ideographic methodology and dialectical analysis was applied to understand the ideological and structural contradictions among school members and collectivists. Ideology constrained structural and process changes that contributed to the school's disintegration. Organization leaders and members were unaware of the contradictions, and hence they could not be rectified [7]. However, in our research, we use different approach to understand organizational disintegration, which is based on statistical network modeling.

The rest of this article is organized as follows. In Section 2, we discuss the theory of exponential random graph models. Section 3 contains the description of the network data sets that we used to evaluate the exponential random graph modeling. Section 4 covers the method used to analyze the data. Section 5 covers the results of our analysis. Finally, Section 6 summarizes our conclusions, presenting the benefits of exponential random graph models for communication networks.

2. EXPONENTIAL RANDOM GRAPH MODELS

Most of the research about exponential random graph modeling (ERGM) focuses on building the theory of ERGM. Only few studies have applied ERGM in practice. In one of those few studies, ERGM was used to fit the models to a data set from an Australian government organization. In that study, which has the main objective to deal with missing data using ERGM [15], ERGM was used to find whether external connections beyond the department are important to the understanding of departmental structure. Researchers also applied ERGM in other context such as students' networks in junior high school classes [11], and communication among genes in biological networks [17]. All those studies have applied ERGM in practice; however no study has tried to use ERGM to understand organizational disintegration. In this paper, we model organizational communication network using ERGM to understand organizational disintegration in terms of the prevalence of micro-structures within the network.

Exponential random graph (p*) models are probabilistic models that can effectively identify structural properties in social networks [25]. It simplifies a complex structure down to a combination of basic parameters. The advantage of this approach is that it is very general and scalable as the architecture of the graph is represented by locally determined explanatory variables, and the choice of explanatory variables is quite flexible and can be easily revised. This theory-driven modeling approach also allows us to test significance of structural parameters. The disadvantage of this approach is the difficulty in estimating the

execution time, complex interpretations when multiple parameters are considered and the difficulty to get convergence sometimes.

We use the notation and terminology described in [14]. For each pair i and j of a set N of n actors, Xij is a network tie variable with Xij = 1 if there is a network tie from i to j, and Xij = 0 otherwise. We specify xij as the observed value of Xij with X the matrix of all variables and x the matrix of observed ties of the network. X may be directed or non-directed. A configuration is a set of nodes (usually small) and a subset of ties among them. For example, an edge is a subset of two nodes in which one node is connected by a tie to other, and a three-star is a subset of four nodes in which one node is connected by a tie to each of the other three. Configurations are defined hierarchically, so that a triangle also includes three 2-stars.

The general form of the class of (homogeneous) exponential random graph models is as follows [16]:

$$Pr(X = x) = (1/\kappa) \exp\{\Sigma_A \eta_A g_A(x)\} \dots \dots \dots (1)$$

where:
(i) the summation is over configuration types A; different sets of configuration types represent different models (e.g. dyadic independence or Markov random graph);
(ii) η_A is the parameter corresponding to configuration of type A;
(iii) $g_A(x)$ is the network statistic corresponding to configuration A (for homogeneous Markov graph models this is the number of configurations of type A observed in the network: for example, the number of triangles);
(iv) κ is a normalizing quantity to ensure that (1) is a proper probability distribution.

The model presents a probability distribution of graphs on a fixed node set, where the probability of observing a graph is dependent on the presence of the various parameters expressed by the model. One can explain the structure of a typical graph in this distribution as the result of a combination of these particular local configurations. With suitable constraints on the number of configurations, it is possible to estimate parameters for a given observed network. The parameters then provide information about the presence of structural effects observed in the network data [16].

2.1 Markov Random Graphs

The Markov random graphs are a particular sub-class of exponential random graph models in which a possible tie from i to j is assumed conditionally dependent only on other possible ties involving i and/or j [5]. An example of a Markov random graph model for non-directed networks, with edge (or density), 2-star, 3-star and triangle parameters, is given in

$$Pr(X=x) = (1/\kappa) \exp \{\theta L(x) + \sigma_2 S_2(x) + \sigma_3 S_3(x) + \tau T(x)\} \dots (2)$$

In Eq. (2), θ is the density or edge parameter and L(x) refers to the number of edges in the graph x; σ_k and $S_k(x)$ refer to the parameter associated with k-star effects and the number of k-stars in x; while τ and T(x) refer to the parameter for triangles and the number of triangles, respectively [14]. For a given observed network x, parameter estimates indicate the strength of effects in the data. For instance, a large and positive estimate for σ_2 suggests that, given the observed number of edges and stars, networks with more two-stars are more likely. One of the strengths of these models is the explicit inclusion of transitivity effects, which are of course widely observed in social networks, but rarely successfully modeled [21]. The configurations and parameters of Markov a random graph model is shown on figure 1.

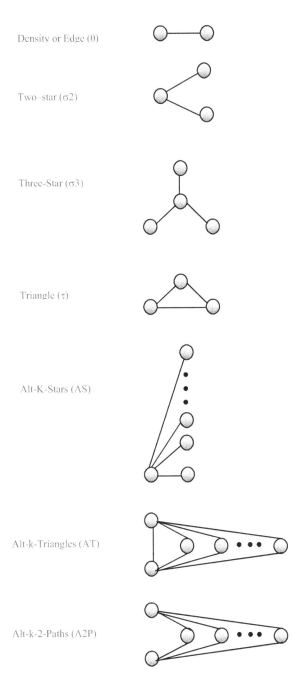

Density or Edge (θ)

Two–star (σ2)

Three-Star (σ3)

Triangle (τ)

Alt-K-Stars (AS)

Alt-k-Triangles (AT)

Alt-k-2-Paths (A2P)

And Other Higher Order Configurations

Figure 1. Configurations and parameters for exponentials random graph models. SOURCE: Robins, Pattison, Kalish and Lusher 2006: 28.

When the star and triangle effects are set to zero, then the edge parameter θ is the only non-zero effect in the model which results a Bernoulli random graph distribution, often called the simple random graph. For graphs in this distribution, edges occur independently of each other with a constant probability across the graph. Bernoulli random graphs are poor models for social networks, in part because they tend to have low levels of triangulation [16].

It is, in principle at least, relatively straightforward to simulate the distribution of graphs expressed in (2) for a given set of parameter values (and a fixed number of nodes), using for instance the Metropolis–Hastings algorithm. Strauss [22] was the first to simulate Markov random graph distributions; more recent simulation results and additional descriptions of algorithms for simulation are in [8, 19].

2.2 Higher Order Models:

Recently, three new configurations have been proposed that can be included in specifications for exponential random graph models: alternating k-stars, alternating k-triangles and alternating independent two-paths [21]. Researchers typically refer to these parameters, and their associated models, as higher order because they include configurations with more than three nodes. In this section, we focus on higher order parameters for non-directed graphs [16]. The configurations and parameters of higher order model are shown on figure 1.

2.2.1 Alternating k-stars

Technically, a model with an alternating k-star parameter alone remains within the class of Markov random graph models. If the alternating k-star parameter is positive, then highly probable networks are likely to contain some higher degree nodes ("hubs"), whereas a negative parameter suggests that networks with high degree nodes are improbable, so that nodes tend not to be hubs, with a smaller variance between the degrees. More particularly, a positive alternating k-star parameter (together with a negative density parameter) implied graphs that exhibit preference for connections between a larger number of low degree nodes and a smaller number of higher degree nodes, akin to a core–periphery structure [21]. But once a node reaches a certain degree, the attainment of additional degrees adds little to its "popularity". Loosely, a node finds its way into the core once it has achieved a certain degree, with no particularly strong pressure for much higher degrees. At the same time, other nodes of lower degree remain outside the core. So the global implication is for a "loose" core–periphery structure, with few or any core nodes having particularly high degrees [16].

2.2.2 Alternating k-triangles

The alternating k-triangle assumption moves beyond the dependence assumptions underlying Markov random graph models, utilizing instead the partial dependence concept proposed by Pattison and Robins [13]. The underlying dependence assumption is presented in [21]. Broadly, a positive k-triangle parameter can be interpreted as evidence for transitivity effects in the network. More particularly, a positive k-triangle parameter suggests elements of a core–periphery structure (dependent on other effects in the model), but in this case due to triangulation effects rather than to popularity (degree) effects, as was the case for the alternating k-star effects. We can imagine the star-based core–periphery structure as arising from the degree distribution, a natural outcome of a process whereby a subset of actors are more popular; whereas for the triangle-based core–periphery process, the degree distribution is itself one of the outcomes of the process, in which a core is built from overlapping triangulations [16].

2.2.3 Alternating k-two-paths

Another parameter that was proposed is a lower order configuration for a k-triangle, namely a k-two-path [21]. These configurations represent the number of distinct two-paths between a pair of nodes. They can be thought of as k-triangles without the base. The motivation is to introduce a parameter that, when used in conjunction with k-triangles, will enable researchers to distinguish between tendencies to form edges at the base, or at the sides of a k-triangle. We should note that the sides of a k-triangle in the absence of the base represent a type of edge clustering that is only the precondition to transitivity, while the presence of the base edge reflects transitive closure. So, this combination of parameters can provide evidence for pressures to transitive closure [16].

2.3 Estimation

There are two methods commonly used in the statistics and social networks communities to estimate the maximum likelihood fit to exponential random graph models, Markov chain Monte Carlo maximum likelihood estimation and maximum pseudo-likelihood estimation. They can also be used for network simulation. These techniques have been recently discussed by various authors [10, 14, 19], so we restrict our comments here to summary remarks. To date, the most common form of estimation for Markov random graph models has been maximum pseudo likelihood [23]. The properties of the pseudo-likelihood estimator are not well understood, the pseudo-likelihood estimates can at best be thought of as approximate, and it is not clear from existing research as to when pseudo-likelihood estimates may be acceptable.

Monte Carlo Markov chain maximum (MCMC) likelihood estimation, when available, is the preferred estimation procedure. The different Monte Carlo techniques of Snijders [19] and Hunter and Handcock [10] are both based on refining approximate parameter estimates by comparing the observed graphs against a distribution of random graphs generated by a stochastic simulation using the approximate parameter values. If the parameter estimates never stabilize (converge), the model is likely to be degenerate. When convergent estimates are obtained, then simulation from the estimates will produce distributions of graphs in which the observed graph is typical for all of the effects in the model. One of the advantages over maximum pseudo-likelihood estimates is that one can also obtain reliable standard errors for the estimates [16]. The number of edges can be conditioned when estimating parameters, that is, the number of edges is fixed in Monte Carlo estimation procedures [5, 20-21]. In such models there are no density parameters. Fixing the number of edges is designed to diminish the risk of degeneracy problems and will have minor effects on other parameter estimates (except perhaps for star parameters). Based on the experience of network scholars, that at least with smaller networks, conditioning on edges may not be necessary, and estimation procedures may successfully converge for the new specifications with density parameters included.

3. DATA

We explore Enron email communications dataset during organization disintegration. Enron Corporation was an American energy trading, natural gas, and electric utilities company based in the Enron Complex in Downtown Houston, Texas that employed around 22,000 people in late 2001. After a wave of accounting scandals, the company filed for bankruptcy on the end of 2001. The US Justice Department investigated whether Enron defrauded investors by hiding information about its finances and released the email communication records to the public. In October 2003, over half a million emails sent by Enron employees were made public and posted on the Internet by the Federal Energy Regulatory Commission (FERC) during its investigation.

We used the Enron email corpus for various reasons. Firstly, it is a large scale collection of actual emails from a real organization. Secondly, the email corpus spans a period of three and a half years. Thirdly, the dataset allows for content, attribute and social network data analysis. Finally, the corpus appeal to researchers who have adopted social networks approach to explore organizational design-performance [1-2].

We start with the premise that email networks establish a useful reference for the underlying communication networks in existing organizations. A study by Smith et al. [18] investigated how different age groups managed their personal networks and what types of technology-mediated communication tools they used. They found that people around their 30s (25-35 years) used email with most of their social network contacts (81%). The 60% of older age groups (50-60 years) also tended to keep in touch with their personal contacts primarily by using the email. As a modern and technologically advanced organization, we know that Enron employees used email as a significant medium of communication. Wellman [26] has argued that computer supported social networks (CSSNs) sustain strong, intermediate and weak ties that provide information and social support in both specialized and broadly-based relationships. CSSNs support and foster both formal and informal workplace communities. In a subsequent work, the author also reported that work groups in organizations using computer mediated communications tend to achieve higher levels of communication than those who do not, although this may reduce the use of face-to-face communication. Moreover, "forward-and copy" feature of email communication (which is also inexpensive to maintain) provides indirect connections between previously disconnected people and organizations and promote weak ties. Some of the examples include: work teams that spans boundaries, inter-organizational coordination of joint projects, linking of buyers and sellers in different organizations etc [12].

Our goal in this study is to explore the changing communication network structure at Enron Corporation during the period of its disintegration using exponential random graph models. We further explore the differences between the best fitted models and parameters for each of several networks. Thereby, we can learn which variables characterize which classes of networks at the early period of disintegration and possibly identify groups of networks at the late period of disintegration.

4. METHODS

Social networks change over time, cross-sectional analyses may miss the important change in networks, and its effects. To that end, we evaluated exponential random graph modeling using different networks at different times of the year. Figure 2 shows the transition of Enron network from April 2001 to October 2001.

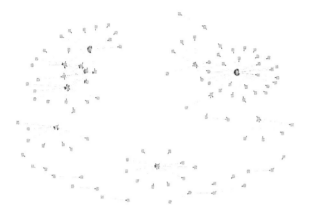

April 2001

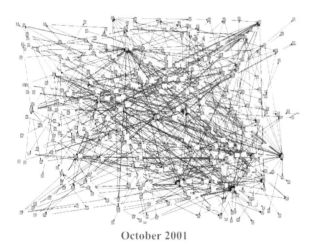

October 2001

Figure 2. The Enron network in April 2001 and October 2001.

In developing the social network, the correspondences between the employees were used as the source of data. The data was collected for the year 2001. Then the actor-by-actor matrix was formed by using Excel spreadsheet for each month of year 2011 except December as Enron filed for bankruptcy on December 2, 2001. This kind of structure is, by definition, a "two-dimensional," and "square" (the number of rows and columns are equal) [9]. The information in each cell provides the volume of communication between a particular pair of actors. The data sets are moved from Excel into UCINET data file. Graphs are then produced using Netdraw to represent social network data as shown in figure 2. Graphs are very useful ways of presenting information about social networks. However, when there are many actors and/or many kinds of relationships, they can become so visually complicated that it is very difficult to see patterns [9]. So in order to analyze the social network data, the matrix form was used as a basis for the analysis. Representing the information in this way also allows the application of mathematical and computer tools such as Pnet to summarize and find patterns using exponential random graph models. Using Pnet, we estimate the parameters which describe changes in a network from tk-1 to tk. We fitted a number of different models to the different networks described above and investigated the relative importance of many different explanatory variables in these networks. We then try to approach our goal which is to try to find which variables characterize which classes of networks at the early period of disintegration and possibly identify groups of networks at the late period of disintegration.

5. RESULTS AND DISCUSSION

Using Pnet, we performed the iterative model fitting procedure described above, fitting every model to the Enron network using Monte Carlo Markov chain maximum (MCMC) likelihood estimation. We have first fitted the network with (edge, 2-star, 3-star, Triangle) model. This model did not converge. To help convergence for parameter estimation, we assumed that the graph density is fixed, which means that the number of arcs/edges will not change during estimation. Fixing graph density may help convergence for parameter estimation, especially for large networks. Note, as the number of arcs/edges has been fixed, the arc/edge parameter should not be selected for estimation.

We then fitted the Enron Network with (2-star, 3-star, Triangle) model, (Alternating k-stars, Alternating k-triangles, Alternating k-two-paths) model and (2-star, 3-star, Alternating k-stars, Alternating k-two-paths) model after fixing the graph density. The results for the last model are shown on table 1. In contrast to pseudo-likelihood estimation, the standard errors here are meaningful, so a parameter estimate that is more than twice its standard error can be considered significantly different from zero. The estimates for each parameter divided by the standard error throughout the year of 2001 are shown in figure 3.

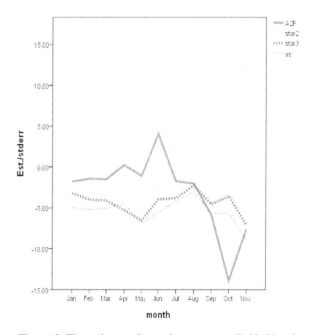

Figure 3. The estimates for each parameter divided by the standard error throughout the year of 2001

Table1. The results from (2-star, 3-star, Alternating k-stars, Alternating k-two-paths) model

effects	Jan			Feb			Mar			Apr		
	Est.	stderr	Est./stderr	Est.	stderr	Est./stderr	Est.	stderr	Est./stderr	Est.	stderr	Est./stderr
2-star	2.80	0.61	**4.61**	2.15	0.38	**5.59**	1.18	0.19	**6.19**	0.54	0.19	**2.88**
3-star	-0.27	0.09	**-3.18**	-0.22	0.06	**-3.99**	-0.09	0.02	**-4.10**	-0.03	0.01	**-5.25**
AS(2.00)	-4.58	0.93	**-4.93**	-3.87	0.74	**-5.23**	-2.31	0.46	**-5.03**	-1.35	0.30	**-4.45**
A2P(2.00)	-0.62	0.34	**-1.81**	-0.28	0.20	**-1.43**	-0.19	0.13	**-1.52**	0.05	0.18	**0.27**

effects	May			Jun			Jul			Aug		
2-star	1.56	0.27	**5.84**	-52.88	13.87	**-3.81**	1.41	0.27	**5.32**	2.50	0.72	**3.49**
3-star	-0.10	0.02	**-6.54**	-0.50	0.13	**-3.97**	-0.06	0.02	**-3.79**	-0.22	0.10	**-2.25**
AS(2.00)	-3.96	0.57	**-6.92**	-7.30	1.31	**-5.59**	-2.65	0.65	**-4.07**	-3.17	1.05	**-3.01**
A2P(2.00)	-0.22	0.20	**-1.09**	56.64	13.87	**4.08**	-0.40	0.23	**-1.76**	-0.67	0.33	**-2.02**

effects	Sep			Oct			Nov			Dec		
2-star	1.17	0.15	**7.89**	0.49	0.06	**8.27**	0.84	0.06	**13.03**	-1.82	17.02	**-0.11**
3-star	-0.05	0.01	**-4.55**	-0.02	0.00	**-3.56**	-0.05	0.01	**-7.12**	-0.62	0.14	**-4.42**
AS(2.00)	-2.29	0.40	**-5.67**	-1.28	0.23	**-5.64**	-2.06	0.23	**-8.94**	-6.80	1.11	**-6.12**
A2P(2.00)	-0.39	0.07	**-5.85**	-0.13	0.01	**-13.91**	-0.16	0.02	**-7.58**	5.78	16.99	**0.34**

Our interpretation of the parameters is as follows. In the (2-star, 3-star, Triangle) model, the triangle parameter is not significant, as is the alternating k-triangle parameter in the higher order model. So perhaps this does not merit interpretation. But the negative triangle parameter can be interpreted as providing evidence that the ties tend not to occur in triangular structures and hence will not cluster into clique-like forms. This means that the network suffer from a blockage of information during the period of disintegration, as the lack of triangular structures means that if actor A is connected to actor B and actor B is connected to actor C, actor A cannot send or receive information from actor C.

We also note that all the parameters in the (2-star, 3-star, Alternating k-stars, Alternating k-two-paths) model are substantial in magnitude in comparison with their standard errors. Interpretation is therefore relatively simple. The positive 2-star parameter indicates that there is a tendency for multiple network partners but with a ceiling on this tendency (the negative three-star parameter). So, while there is tendency for network actors to have multiple partners, there are few actors with very many partners. The negative alternating k-star parameter indicates that networks with some higher degree nodes are less probable which means there is no core-periphery structure. This example shows the importance of picking the correct parameters when attempting to fit a network. Although some authors have reported that fitting large networks with Monte Carlo Markov chain maximum (MCMC) likelihood estimation can lead to diverging parameter estimates [6], we found this not to be the case with our Enron networks.

For all the models fitted for the Enron network, there was no significant difference between the parameters of the networks around the year. But for the (2-star, 3-star, Alternating k-stars, Alternating k-two-paths) model, there was a significant difference between the Alternating k-two-paths parameter up to June 2001 (early period of disintegration) and after June 2001. A t-test on tables 2 and 3 shows this significance. The results shows that on average, the Alternating k-two-paths parameter after June (M=-6.22, SE=2.22) is more negative than the parameter up to June (M=-0.25, SE=0.92), t(9)=2.66, p<0.05. This can be clearly seen on figure 3.

The negative parameters of K-two-path indicate that the network does not tend to form cycles, and this tendency increase at the late period of disintegration. We can suggest from this that when the tendency for forming cycles decrease, the network will move into a period of disintegration. This make sense as when the network does not form cycles, the communication channels will be disconnected and as a result information can be lost in the way. We can also see that the 2-star parameter decrease to a minimum around the middle of the year and then start increasing. This indicates that the tendency for multiple network partners has increased at the last period of disintegration. We can suggest from this trend that at the last period of disintegration, only few network actors were the hub of the network and there was information load on those actors. This make sense during organizational crisis, as all actors in the network try to seek information from the hub of the network, which may increase pressure on those actors at the hub of the network. Table 4 shows the summary of our tests with all the models used in this study.

In this study, we proposed a novel approach to explore and compare organizational email networks during crisis and non-crisis period. The findings of this study provide a valuable insight into a real-world organization during its crisis and non-crisis period. These results could be practiced by managers or employees of any organization. They could monitor their organizational communication network over time and do the similar analysis as followed in this paper to have an understanding of the current state of their organizations. This will eventually help them to manage their organizations smoothly.

Previous studies on the investigation about Enron data revealed that during crisis period the network structure had become denser, more centralized and more connected [3], and more diverse with respect to established contacts and formal roles [4] compare to non-crisis period. Uddin et al. [24] demonstrated a significant difference in Enron dataset with respect to the centralization of most prominent actors between crisis and non-crisis period. In this paper, we model organizational communication network using exponential random graph to understand organizational disintegration in terms of the prevalence of micro-structures within the network.

6. CONCLUSIONS

In this study, we have introduced exponential random graph models, a family of network models and demonstrate their use in modeling the changing communication network structure at Enron Corporation during the period of its disintegration (2000-2001). We provided a new way of classifying networks and their performance based on the occurrence of their local features. We demonstrated that the local structures derived from communication networks by fitting exponential random graph models can be used to explain why the network will move into a period of disintegration.

There are a number of reasons that exponential random graph models should be considered for use in changing communication network structure. First, the statistics underlying exponential random graph models are more principled than seen in the previous network modeling efforts in networks. Previous efforts in communication network have relied on comparing networks to simulated random networks (which depend heavily on the random model) or investigating a single network feature such as degree distribution.

Second, exponential random graph models allow for much more flexibility than current communication network models. As seen in figure 1, the explanatory variables can be almost anything including shortest path lengths, node attributes and simple graph statistics. This flexibility allows researchers to ask and answer specific questions. A further reason that exponential random graph models should be considered for communication networks is that they provide an excellent framework for the comparison of networks and observing of the changes of structures in the network over time.

As an area of further research, it would be to apply the existing exponential random graph models in the context to another domain, preferably one that shares characteristics of uncertainty and unstable environments. For example, the model could be applied to other organizations in crisis to understand what factors of social network may affect their performance. It would be very interesting to see if the model is robust enough to produce similar or dissimilar results in other domains.

Table 2. Group Statistics

		N	Mean	Std. Deviation	Std. Error Mean
A2P	Up_to_june	6	-.2493	2.24393	.91608
	After_june	5	-6.2243	4.96611	2.22091

Table 3. Independent Samples Test

		Levene's Test for Equality of Variances		t-test for Equality of Means							
							Mean Difference	Std. Error Difference	95% Confidence Interval of the Difference	
		F	Sig.	t	df	Sig.(2-tailed)			Lower	Upper
A2P	Equal variances assumed	2.297	.164	2.66	9	.026	5.98	2.25	.89	11.06
	Equal variances not assumed			2.49	5.35	.052	5.98	2.40	-.08	12.03

Table 4. The summary of our tests with all the models used in this study

Model	Assumed Graph density is fixed?	Did it converge?	Are there significant difference between the parameters of the networks around the year?
edge, 2-star, 3-star, Triangle	no	no	no
2-star, 3-star, Triangle	yes	yes	no
Alternating k-stars, Alternating k-triangles, Alternating k-two-paths	yes	yes	no
2-star, 3-star, Alternating k-stars, Alternating k-two-paths	yes	yes	yes

7. REFERENCES

[1] Adamic L, Adar E. 2005. How to search a social network. *Soc Networks.*27:187-203.

[2] Ahuja MK, Carley K, Galletta DF. 1997. Individual performance in distributed design groups: an empirical study. *Proceedings of the 1997 ACM SIGCPR conference on Computer personnel research.* San Francisco, California, United States: ACM; 1997:160-170.

[3] Diesner J, Carley KM. 2005. Exploration of Communication Networks from the Enron Email Corpus. *Proceedings of Workshop on Link Analysis, Counterterrorism and Security, SIAM International Conference on Data Mining 2005.*3-14.

[4] Diesner J, Frantz T, Carley K. 2005. Communication Networks from the Enron Email Corpus "It's Always About the People. Enron is no Different". *Computational & Mathematical Organization Theory.*11:201-228.

[5] Frank O, Strauss D. 1986. *Markov graphs.* Alexandria, VA, ETATS-UNIS: American Statistical Association.

[6] Goodreau SM. 2007. Advances in exponential random graph (p*) models applied to a large social network. *Soc Networks.*29:231-248.

[7] Grimes AJ, Cornwall JR. 1987. The Disintegration of an Organization: A Dialectical Analysis. *Journal of Management.*13:69.

[8] Handcock MS, Robins G, Snijders T, Moody J, Besag J. 2003. Assessing Degeneracy in Statistical Models of Social Networks.

[9] Hanneman R, Riddle M. 2005. Introduction to Social Network Methods. In: Riverside CUoC, Riverside (published in digital form at http://faculty.ucr.edu/~hanneman/).

[10] Hunter DR, Handcock MS. 2006. Inference in Curved Exponential Family Models for Networks. *Journal of Computational and Graphical Statistics.*15:565-583.

[11] Lubbers MJ, Snijders TAB. 2007. A comparison of various approaches to the exponential random graph model: A reanalysis of 102 student networks in school classes. *Soc Networks.*29:489-507.

[12] Murshed T, Davis J, Hossain L. 2007. Social Network Analysis and Organizational Disintegration: The Case of Enron Corporation. *International Conference on Information Systems (ICIS2007).*

[13] Pattison PE, Robins GL. 2002. Neighbourhood-based models for social networks. . *Sociological Methodology* 32:301–337.

[14] Robins G, Pattison P, Kalish Y, Lusher D. 2007. An introduction to exponential random graph (p*) models for social networks. *Soc Networks.*29:173-191.

[15] Robins G, Pattison P, Woolcock J. 2004. Missing data in networks: exponential random graph (p*) models for networks with non-respondents. *Soc Networks.*26:257-283.

[16] Robins G, Snijders T, Wang P, Handcock M, Pattison P. 2007. Recent developments in exponential random graph (p*) models for social networks. *Soc Networks.*29:192-215.

[17] Saul ZM, Filkov V. 2007. Exploring biological network structure using exponential random graph models. *Bioinformatics.*23:2604-2611.

[18] Smith H, Rogers Y, Brady M. 2003. Managing one's social network: Does age make a difference? In: *Human Computer Interaction - INTERACT '03.*

[19] Snijders, T. 2002. *Markov Chain Monte Carlo Estimation of Exponential Random Graph Models.*

[20] Snijders T, Duijn MV. 2002. Conditional maximum likelihood estimation under various specifications of exponential random graph models. *Frank. University of Stockholm: Department of Statistics.*

[21] Snijders T, Pattison P, Robins G, Handcock M. 2006. New specifications for exponential random graph models. *Sociological Methodology.*36:99-153.

[22] Strauss D. 1986. On a general class of models for interaction. *SIAM Rev.*;28:513-527.

[23] Strauss D, Ikeda M. 1990. *Pseudolikelihood estimation for social networks.* Alexandria, VA, ETATS-UNIS: American Statistical Association.

[24] Uddin M, Murshed STH, Hossain L. 2010. Towards A Scale Free Network Approach to Study Organizational Communication Network. *PACIS 2010 Proceedings.*196.

[25] Wasserman S, Pattison P. 1996. Logit models and logistic regressions for social networks: I. An introduction to Markov graphs and P. *Psychometrika.*61:401-425.

[26] Wellman B. 1996. For a social network analysis of computer networks: a sociological perspective on collaborative work and virtual community. *Proceedings of the 1996 ACM SIGCPR/SIGMIS conference on Computer personnel research.* Denver, Colorado, United States: ACM; 1996:1-11.

Conceptual Aspects of IT Governance in Enterprise Environment

Sureerat Saetang
University of South Australia
School of Computer and Information Science
Mawson Lakes, Adelaide, Australia
saesy005@mymail.unisa.edu.au

Abrar Haider
University of South Australia
School of Computer and Information Science
Mawson Lakes, Adelaide, Australia
abrar.haider@unisa.edu.au

ABSTRACT

In today's business environment there are various regulations, concepts and strategies of business development that focus on how technology can support business effectively. From among these concerns, IT governance has drawn attention from corporate broads to senior management. As a result, a number of IT governance frameworks have emerged with each having its own strengths and weaknesses. These frameworks, on one hand provide multidimensional benefits to organizations to develop higher interests like competitiveness, efficiency of It infrastructure, and IT related; and on the other hand these frameworks also align IT infrastructure with strategic business agenda. Since these frameworks owe their existence to different areas of IT application, their success is also quite varied. This research is motivated by the same question, i.e. to examine what makes an IT governance frameworks work. It follows a qualitative interpretive research methodology with a case study approach. This research significantly contributes towards building theoretical base for the key issues and success factors of successful IT governance implementation processes. It also provides guidelines to executive managers about IT governance framework adoption, customization, and implementation.

Categories and Subject Descriptors

H.0 Information Systems

Keywords Corporate governance, IT governance Framework, IT infrastructure, Business / IT Alignment

General Terms

Management

1. INTRODUCTION

IT Governance is the concern that is gradually becoming the Achilles' heel of businesses in contemporary business arena [1] [2]. It is an area of corporate governance that not only enables the business through realization of automated business processes, but also enables the strategy through effective allocation of resources,

information analysis and decision support [3]. As overall corporate governance aims to enhance internal progress and mitigate risks, IT provides it with the bonding glue to bring together different organizational resources and allows for planning and execution of straggles to achieve business goals. However, managing IT infrastructure and its effectiveness has been far from simple. With the increasing advancements in technology, its governance is becoming even more complex. Realizing an IT governance framework as the foundation to support business in terms allocating, maintaining, and processing information and information related resources is a major concern [4]. The dynamic organizational tension between various stakeholders, areas, and aspects of business makes it difficult for any organization to fully grasp the scope of business and to map it with technology [5]. This why governance frameworks like COBIT and COSO are geared at different aspects/areas of the business, have narrow focus, and do not provide an all-encompassing level of strategic guidance to run and sustain IT infrastructure. On the other hand, although more accomplished frameworks like ITIL, provide a much more accomplished set of guidelines, yet they do not yield consistent level of service across all areas of business. Where is the problem? Of course it lies in the way these frameworks are applied across the organization. Organizations need to take stock of their resources, competencies, and capabilities before attempting to implement an IT governance framework. Implementation of an IT governance framework is not a one off activity, it is actually an ongoing process that maps IT to the business such that the IT infrastructure evolves and matures with the organizational capabilities. This is research in progress paper that sets the agenda for implementation of IT governance frameworks. It starts with a discussion of corporate governance, followed by the role of IT in contemporary business arena, and ends with a discussion that this research will take to address the research issue at hand.

2. LITERTURE REVIEW

2.1 Corporate Governance

Corporate governance is concerned managing performance of business through dynamic interaction of CEO, board room, and senior managers [6] [7] [8] [9] [10]. This performance evaluation is productivity based and includes financial as well as non-financial measurement criteria. [11] [12] [10]. This why CEOs and senior management rely on the concept of corporate governance to keep their businesses like a well-oiled machine to respond to internal as well as external pressures. The concept of corporate governance is multifaceted and defines guidelines on roles and responsibilities as well as interaction of people with various systems in the organizations [13]. Corporate governance is created from the methodical process of evaluation and is shaped to the systems of decision making eventually [14] [15]. Corporate governance has varied definitions which depend on different views of various authors. Corporate governance is the direction of corporate partnerships to pledge as commitment of getting benefits [16], the structure of regulations, compliance and aspects which run the functions of organizations [17], the complex system which combine two sets together by joining internal and external organizations simultaneously [18]. Corporate governance methods are dependent and governed by power to increase organizational performance that affect to profits and expenditures of headships and shareholders [19]. Corporate governance is a helpful system to enhance the behaviors of management to develop quality of organizations and maximize business value [20] [21] [22] [10]. Thus, it is important to establish corporate governance in the organizations which is the arrangement of control, authorities and limitation of executives, headships and shareholders to run the organizations by starting from different objectives of varied stakeholders to develop high value and future expectation of organizations, covering the scope of the board's authority, management's responsibility for governance and the relationship between shareholders' trading activities, voting decisions and governance along with sharing power for decision making to various authorized persons as range of constraints on board independence [21, 23-25], chairman and CEO [26] [21] to improve the business performance and gain higher profits as value of organizations [27] [28]. Corporate board attributes are vital factors which lead to influence corporate governance as shown in table 1. Moreover, corporate governance supports organization by improving itself to gain higher interests and competitive advantage to beat others and raise better image of organization to

Determinants of Corporate Governance	Author(s) and Year (s)
Board Independence	[23] [25] [24] [21]
Rights of Board Members	[30] [21]
Chairman and CEO	[26] [21]
Incentive Compensation	[19]
Funds VS Debt	[19]

be outstanding firm in the industry rather than competitors which are still in imperfect competitive situation with poor corporate governance [29] [15].

Table 1. Determinants of Corporate Governance

Board members have rights to approve and consent all essential decision makings in all main areas such as, investment plan, payment procedures and board governance [30] [21]. Therefore, they can invest in IT infrastructure and resources to develop organization for supporting business environment. They also have rights to monitor and check the errors which are vital to corporate decisions that could affect to business and lead to gain good alternative of entire good governance [21].

2.2 IT Governance

IT governance is about the responsibilities of board of directors and executive management which assesses and conducts corporate strategy, examines management performance objectives and ensures the reliability of corporate mechanisms which have reformed and developed significantly [31]. IT governance defines as the collection and employment of corporation procedures for decision makings due to adopt and implement IT resources and capabilities [32] [33]. IT governance discusses about the organizational characteristics of decision making in terms of the role of duty (authorized person, reason of decisions and method of decisions are determined) [34] [35]. Basically, IT governance was concerned in computer regulations and processes and has been adapted to business segment at the current age which includes shareholder value, policy compliance and risk mitigation along with aligning with the stakeholders and high executive management. Therefore, the board of directors take high responsibility and load of all decision makings for the entire of IT business governance [36]. IT governance agreements cover systems that allow business and IT executives to create plans and processes, deploy IT infrastructures and examine results [37] [38]. Successful IT governance produces high profits and builds reputation as good image to investors and customers including gaining high trust, leadership and decreasing costs [38], using common language with participated commitment to IT compliances and procedures [39], raising effective communication between all groups of productive associations [40]. IT governance employs considerable input about business and IT strategies from stakeholders to create an understanding of the organizations and form connections between business and IT [41] [38]. Consideration and suggestions from stakeholders regarding strategies are vital to the organization as they address core business fundamentals for operational business activities such as, IT assets. Board of director's responsibility, top managements and leaderships, all main aspects of business governance, along with policies and organizational structure are the core components of governance to build and demonstrate the organization's strategy and business objectives [42] [43].

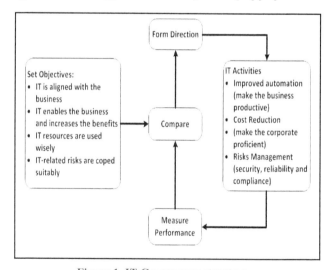

Figure 1. IT Governance structure.

Figure 1 presents IT governance comprises with management and organizational compositions and procedures which IT maintains and broadens the business strategies and goals by communicating all parties with participated commitment successfully. The responsibilities of board must be cleared and effective on management which related to IT management including business risks and value delivery to align IT and operate within and across organizations in all processes. According to this figure, it presents the model of the relations of IT governance by forming business-IT objectives as the first process to provide direction through IT activities, measuring performance, comparing objectives, and getting outcome in the re-direction processes which require changing in proper time to adjust and signify the objectives acceptably. Due to establishing direction, IT module must concern benefits by developing automation, cutting costs and controlling risks.

Developing Approach	Function	Description
Security	Business Operations	Business Risks
Policies and Controls	Responsibilities of Executive	Roles of Executives
Agreement	Procedures & Accountabilities	Authority of Leaderships
Organisational Structure	Business Administration	Methods of Customisation
Investigate, Monitor, Audit, Measure	Board of Directors	Knowledge of Leaderships

Table 2. Read's Business - IT governance perspective

Table 2 shows how IT supports business by directing different processes to drive and operate on various business functions in organizations. In order to maximizing business development, the relationships of different work operations and business roles must link together closely, as they must respond to their accountabilities firmly and powerfully. These responses may affect all departments in the organizations and also impact customers, investors, partnerships, shareholders and stakeholders as well as societies. Therefore, the executive management must be aware and alert to these concerns, such as different levels of risks, new and existing factors, knowledge based, agreement, organizational structure, compliance and regulations along with ongoing improve IT infrastructure enabling business processes by aligning business and IT with different approaches, assessing the results and business performance. Eventually, they will gain effective results which gain better knowledge, skill and stronger relationship of people within organization and external parties such as the community and environment.

3. RESEARCH METHODOLOGY

This research will utilize an interpretive qualitative approach with data collection from participated organizations through qualitative method by interviewing and personal observation with qualitative surveys to study and examine IT governance which comprises with business and information strategies along with the responsibility of various management people to achieve better business performance and outstanding results by discovering from existing conditions and latest concerns as well as developing current working processes to gain higher solutions. The goal is to indicate the implementation of IT governance initiatives in organization which align with the business objectives and requirements of organizations as well as robustly emphasized the alignment of IT with business arrangement and execution by studying the interconnection of IT governance and embedding mechanisms for risk management, decision support, responsibility and recourse participation between different functions of the business along with investigating framework for IT governance as a core component of corporate governance. This research has the main question which creates for trying to resolve problem which is 'how does implementation of an IT governance framework contribute to value profile of IT infrastructure in achieving business objectives and meeting its needs?'

4. CONCLUSION

This proposal sums up the outline of IT governance which joins a business and IT successfully to sustain organizational works. It is essential to focus on business objectives which direct organizations to carry out powerfully in the industry by adopting technology along to the business and gaining high competitive advantage. This research also identifies guideline to support senior executives and leaderships in terms of management in IT governance by having knowledge of IT as essential area to develop the business and IT using. Furthermore, senior management and managers can use their knowledge and understanding of IT to make decision on numerous projects in the organization to protect severe results which lead organization fail and unsuccessful as well as they can guide medium management to work on the right platform. However, they must monitor all projects closely before making full implementation to avoid disaster and waste more assets, longer time and surplus expenditures. This research concludes a summary of research to carry out in aspects that allocate to the effectiveness of IT governance frameworks. It demonstrates to assist board of directors, senior managements, leaderships, stakeholders and shareholders to understand and acknowledge the significance of IT governance and also guide the directions and processes by informing them to consider the impacts which can affect to organizations. IT decision in organizations is highly important to top management for their decision makings. Essentially, senior management always make improvement during the middle phase by checking and monitoring the erroneous of internal organizational processes as well as assessing and measuring the usability and credibility metrics through users to gain higher competitive position in the market.

5. REFERENCES

1. Brown, C.V. and Sambamurthy, V. 1999. *Repositioning the IT Organization to Enable Business Transformation.* Cincinnati, OH. Pinnaflex Educational Resources.
2. Weill, P. and Broadbent, M. 2000. *Managing IT infrastructure: a strategic choice. In: Zmud, R., (Ed.), Framing the Domains of IT Management: Projecting the Future Through the Past.* Cincinnati, OH. Pinnaflex Educational Resources.
3. Luo, Y., 2005. *Corporate governance and accountability in multinational enterprises: Concepts and agenda.* Journal of International Management. 11 (1), 1-18.

4. Posthumus, S. and von Solms, R. 2004. *A framework for the governance of information security.* Computers & Security. 23 (8), 638-646.

5. Schwarz, A. and Hirschheim, R. 2003. *An extended platform logic perspective of IT governance: managing perceptions and activities of IT.* The Journal of Strategic Information Systems. 12 (2), 129-166.

6. Denis, D.J., Denis, D.K. and Sarin, A. 1997. *Agency problems, equity ownership, and corporate diversification..* Journal of Finance. 52, 135-160.

7. Ahn, S. and Walker, M. 2007. *Corporate governance and the spinoff decision.* Journal of Corporate Finance. 13, 76-93.

8. Bauguess, S., Moeller, S., Schlingemann, F. and Zutter, C. 2009. *Ownership structure and target returns.* Journal of Corporate Finance, 15, 48-65.

9. Netter, J., Poulsen, A. and Stegmoller, M. 2009. *The rise of corporate governance in corporate control research.* Journal of Corporate Finance. 15, 1-9.

10. Lo, A.W.Y., Wong, R.M.K. and Firth, M. 2010. *Can corporate governance deter management from manipulating earnings? Evidence from related-party sales transactions in China.* Journal of Corporate Finance. 16 (2), 225-235.

11. Chung, R., Firth, M. and Kim, J.B. 2002. *Institutional monitoring and opportunistic earnings management.* Journal of Corporate Finance, 8, 29-48.

12. Park, Y. and Shin, H. 2004. *Board composition and earnings management in Canada.* Journal of Corporate Finance. 10, 431-457.

13. Zingales, L. 1998. *Corporate governance. In: Newman, P. (Ed.).* The New Palgrave Dictionary of Economics and the Law.

14. Alexander, L. 2000. *Corporate governance and cross-border mergers,* in *Conference Board Research Report.*

15. Bris, A., Brisley, N. and Cabolis, C. 2008. *Adopting better corporate governance: Evidence from cross-border mergers.* Journal of Corporate Finance. 14 (3), 224-240.

16. Shleifer, A. and Vishny, R. 1997. *A survey of corporate governance.* Journal of Finance. 52, 737-775.

17. Gillan, S.L. and L.T. Starks, 1998. *A survey of shareholder activism: motivation and empirical evidence.* Contemporary Finance Digest. 2 (3),. 10-34.

18. Gillan, S.L. 2006. *Recent Developments in Corporate Governance: An Overview.* Journal of Corporate Finance. 12 (3), 381-402.

19. Cornett, M.M., McNutt, J.J. and Tehranian, H. 2009. *Corporate governance and earnings management at large U.S. bank holding companies.* Journal of Corporate Finance. 15 (4), 412-430.

20. Denis, D. and McConnell, J.J. 2003. *International corporate governance.* Journal of Financial and Quantitative Analysis. 38, 1-36.

21. Bhagat, S. and Bolton, B. 2008. *Corporate governance and firm performance.* Journal of Corporate Finance. 14 (3), 257-273.

22. Chen, K.C.W., Chen, Z. and Wei, K.C.J. 2009. *Legal protection of investors, corporate governance, and the cost of equity capital.* Journal of Corporate Finance. 15 (3), 273-289.

23. Hermalin, B. and Weisbach, M. 1988. *The determinants of board composition.* Rand Journal of Economics. 19 (4), 589-606.

24. Hermalin, B. and Weisbach, M. 2003. *Boards of directors as an endogenously determined institution: a survey of the economic literature.* Economic Policy Review, 9, 7 - 26.

25. Bhagat, S. and Black, B. 2002. *The non-correlation between board independence and long term firm performance.* Journal of Corporation Law. 27, 231-274.

26. Brickley, J.A., Coles, J.L. and Jarrell, G. 1997. *Leadership structure: separating the CEO and chairman of the board.* Journal of Corporate Finance. 3, 189-220.

27. Zingales, L. 1997. *Corporate Governance.* National Bureau of Economic Research Working Paper.

28. Nelson, J. 2005. *Corporate governance practices, CEO characteristics and firm performance.* Journal of Corporate Finance. 11 (1-2), 197-228.

29. Bris, A. and Brisley, N. 2007. *A Theory of Optimal Expropriation, Mergers, and Industry Competition.*

30. Bhagat, S., Carey, D. and Elson, C. 1999. *Director ownership, corporate performance, and management turnover.* The Business Lawyer, 54.

31. Hardy, G. 2006. *Using IT governance and COBIT to deliver value with IT and respond to legal, regulatory and compliance challenges.* Information Security Technical Report. 11 (1), 55-61.

32. Henderson, J.C. and Venkatraman, N. 1993. *Strategic alignment: leveraging information technology for transforming organizations.* IBM Systems Journal. 32 (1).

33. William, B., Mezbahur, R. and Travis, H. 2006. *Home page usability and credibility: A comparison of the fastest growing companies to the Fortune 30 and the implications to IT governance.* Information Management & Computer Security. 14(3), 252-269.

34. Nielsen, J. and Tahir. 2001. *Homepage Usability: 50 Websites Deconstructed.* Indianapolis. IN.: New Riders Press.

35. Luftman, J., Bullen, C., Liao, D., Nash, E. and Neumann, C. 2004. *Managing the Information Technology Resource.* Upper Saddle River, NJ.: Pearson Prentice Hall.

36. Read, T. 2004. *Discussion of director responsibility for IT governance.* International Journal of Accounting Information Systems. 5(2), 105 - 107.

37. Weill, P. and Broadbent, M. 1998. *Leveraging the new infrastructure: how market leaders capitalize on information technology.* Boston, MA. Harvard Business School Press.

38. Bowen, P.L., Cheung, M. and Rohde, F.H. 2007. *Enhancing IT governance practices: A model and case study of an organization's efforts.* International Journal of Accounting Information Systems. 8 (3), 191-221.

39. ITGI. 2002. *IT governance executive summary.* http://www.itgi.org/2002.

40. Johnson, A.M. and Lederer, A.L. 2005. *The effect of communication frequency and channel richness on the convergence between chief executive and chief information officers.* J Manage Inf Syst. 22(2), 227-252.

41. Zee van der, H. 2002. *Measuring the value of information technology.* Hershey: Idea Publishing.

42. ITGI. 2005. *IT Governance Domain Practices and Competencies: Optimising Value Creation-From IT investments.* http://www.isaca.org/ContentManagement/ContentDisplay.cfm?ContentID=33923.

43. Brown, W. 2006. *IT governance, architectural competency, and the Vasa. Information Management & Computer Security.* 14(2), 140 - 154.

DSS Development and Implementation Within the Services Industry: A User Based Design Science Approach

Matthew D. Gonzalez, Ph.D.
Assistant Professor of Business Administration,
University of Incarnate Word
San Antonio, TX. USA
mdgonzal@uiwtx.edu

Abstract

While there is no universally accepted definition of a Decision Support System (DSS), this study will focus on the characteristics of a DSS with particular emphasis on the DSS Development and Implementation process within service industries. An analysis of traditional, DSS Development Life Cycle, and User Development within Service Industries are synthesized based on an analysis of 30 sources spanning the past 40 years. User involvement throughout the development and implementation phases is further discussed as an information systems subspecialty, in relation to the user's satisfaction level. This study contributes to the information and computing industry by recommending a Value Based DSS Methodology for developing and implementing decision support systems as a means of suggesting a user based design science approach. Four case studies within differing service industries are presented, with two illustrated as success case studies and two illustrated as unsuccessful case studies based on traditional DSS development and implementation methodologies.

Categories and Subject Descriptors: H.0. Information Systems

General Terms: Design, Human Factors, Management

Author Keywords: Decision Support Systems, Development, Implementation, Traditional DSS Methodology, Value Based DSS Methodology

Poster

The IT Professional as Stakeholder

Norah Power
Department of Computer Science and
Information Systems
University of Limerick
Ireland
+ 353 61 202769
norah.power at ul.ie

ABSTRACT

The concept of stakeholder is well established in the field of IS, yet the IT person's role as a stakeholder is often ignored because stakeholders on the customer side are, appropriately, regarded as more important than stakeholders on the supplier side. Focusing on various IT stakeholders can give us a fresh perspective on many issues of concern. Tools and techniques for stakeholder analysis, currently trained exclusively on customer-side stakeholders, can possibly lead to useful approaches for analyzing IT roles, including: understanding the skills and abilities needed to succeed in the IT profession, analyzing role profiles, supporting work satisfaction and staff retention, improving individual and team performance, facilitating group-work, particularly (globally) distributed teams. In particular, an analysis of stakeholder relationships can lead to a conceptual framework that will help researchers and educators to understand and communicate the ways IT professionals work with other categories of stakeholders in different development contexts.

Categories and Subject Descriptors

K.7.1 [Occupations]

General Terms

Human Factors, Theory.

Keywords

Stakeholders, Onion Model

1. OVERVIEW

The term stakeholder originated in the strategic management literature but is widely used in the theory and practice of IS and related disciplines. Stakeholder types include different types of users, including beneficiaries of the system, their managers and business owners, but also a variety of regulators, standards bodies, and other external parties. One major category in Alexander's taxonomy of stakeholder roles [1] is the Developer category, which covers such roles as Analyst, Designer, Programmer, Tester, Safety Engineer, Security Engineer and Project Manager. Another category is Consultant, such as legal and human factors specialists who are consulted at various stages of a project. The Operator category covers Normal Operator, Maintenance Operator and Operational Support [1].

In any project, the Client or the Customer stakeholders are most significant as are the user stakeholders (Normal Operators). Most authors focus on the need to involve such stakeholders in project planning, development, testing, and evaluation. Supplier-side (Developer) stakeholders typically do more work in a project than customer-side stakeholders, so it is interesting that their roles as stakeholders are generally overlooked in favor of the other types of stakeholders and not typically analyzed from this point of view. The purpose of this research is to focus on supplier-side stakeholders from these two perspectives. It will explore the implications of the stakeholder concept for issues such as skills and abilities, role profiles, work satisfaction and teamwork. It will also look at how stakeholder analysis tools can help us to understand the different types of situations in which supplier-side stakeholders exercise these skills.

The graphical Onion Model [1] is often used to analyze the relationships among stakeholders. The model provides a systems view, with the product core at the centre, typically surrounded by three enclosing layers: the System, the Containing System and the Wider Environment. Stakeholders occupy different slots in the Onion Model depending on how directly or indirectly they will interact with the finished core system. Developer and Consultant category (or slot) stakeholders are placed in the outmost layer, while Operational stakeholders are in the inner-most layer. Functional beneficiaries (a type of user) are positioned in the intermediate layer; they don't operate the product but receive outputs from it. Stakeholders in the Operational category are not just users, but include Operational support (e.g. helpdesk personnel) and Maintenance operators. There is scope to refine this model, differentiating the roles of IT personnel in system development, operation and maintenance, adding more layers to the model, perhaps, and positioning the roles in different layers.

RQ1: How can the Onion Model be extended and/or refined to encompass the differences among the roles of supplier-side stakeholders?

RQ2: How can the configuration of stakeholder relationships be refined to explain/depict the variety of ways that IT people work in different development contexts?

2. REFERENCE

[1] Alexander, I., 2005. "A Taxonomy of Stakeholders: Human Roles in System Development" International Journal of Technology and Human Interaction, (1:1), pp 23-59

Poster

Cloud Computing for Enterprises One Size Does Not Fit All

Janet L Bailey, PhD
University of Arkansas at Little Rock
2801 S. University Ave
Little Rock, AR 72204
(501) 569-8851

jlbailey@ualr.edu

Steven Lamey
Walmart Corporation
2001 SE 10th Street
Bentonville, AR 72716
479-204-6539

Steven.Lamey@Wal-mart.com

Bradley K Jensen, PhD
Microsoft Corporation
1950 N Stemmons Fwy Ste 5010
Dallas, TX 75207
(214) 674-3630

bjensen@microsoft.com

POSTER SUMMARY OR OVERVIEW

This paper presents research in progress precipitated by a proof-of-concept project on Microsoft Azure requested by Walmart Corporation.

Categories and Subject Descriptors

K.6.2 [**Management of Computing and Information Systems**]: Installation Management – *selection criteria, implementation considerations*

General Terms

Economics, Management, Measurement, Performance, Reliability, Security

Keywords

Cloud computing, enterprise-level cloud requirements, system needs, PaaS, IaaS, SaaS

1. INTRODUCTION

According to the Cloud Computing Journal there were 150 players in cloud computing by October of 2009 (Geelan, 2009). As with emerging technologies from the past including the PC and the early World Wide Web, a number of these providers will predictably fail or be too small to provide adequate provide the "massively scalable, IT-enabled capabilities (Gartner Newsroom, 2009)" required by large enterprises. The sheer number of players and the variety of their offerings contributes greatly to the confusion surrounding the cloud. Enterprise-level managers are much clearer on what they need than they are on the capabilities offered by various cloud providers. When discussing enterprise-level cloud computing needs, one size does not fit all.

2. METHODOLOGY

The study entailed conducting a meta-analysis of considerations regarding cloud adoption, interviews with management and senior executives at Walmart, and a UALR student-conducted project for Walmart where numerous discussions with front-line personnel regarding enterprise cloud requirements were conducted.

3. RESULTS

A meta-analysis of issues and concerns presented in the academic literature produced the following list of considerations.

- Security
- Performance
- Services provided – IaaS, SaaS, PaaS, managed
- Storage
- Availability/continuity
- Vendor lock-in
- Scalability
- Virtual environments
- Hybrid environments
- Cost

A 9-month project with Walmart revealed the following enterprise-level requirements. Items that differed from meta-analysis results appear in italics.

- *Ability to provide capacity required by a corporation the size of Walmart*
- *Flexibility in application development*
- *Vendor willingness to provide information on their cloud architecture*
- Capability for providing a 99% or better system uptime
- Fast and easy scalability
- *Environment-supported rapid application deployment*
- Rapid application response times
- *Environment that supports data quality and integrity*
- *Environment that places control in the hands of trained it professionals*
- Secure deployment and operational environment
- Accessibility and integration of in-house based applications and data
- Cost-effective for Walmart and their vendors
- *Business intelligence capabilities*
- *Suited to mobile applications and accessibility*

4. REFERENCES

[1] Gartner Newsroom. 2010. Retrieved 10 19, 2010, from Gartner.com: http://www.gartner.com/it/page.jsp?id=1454221

[2] Geelan, J. 2009. Cloud Computing Journal. Retrieved Oct 20, 2010, from Cloud Computing Journal: http://cloudcomputing.sys-con.com/node/77017

Explaining the Influence of User Personality on the Evaluation of IT Usage Drivers and IT Usage Consequences

Christian Maier
Centre of Human Resources
Information Systems
University of Bamberg
+49 951 863 2873

christian.maier@uni-bamberg.de

ABSTRACT

This proposal pursues the goal to combine personality and IT usage behavior. Therefore, a psychological theory - which is named Five-Factor Theory of Personality - is applied to offer a theoretical framework for the interaction between personality and typical adoption theories or models (as TAM, UTAUT, etc.).

The insights should help to gain insights of the impact of personality on IT usage, IT usage drivers and IT usage consequences in different IS research fields. The proposal focuses on IT (non-)usage behavior and IT diffusion, but should also offer valuable insights for IT management research as IT outsourcing decisions or how to handle employees.

Categories and Subject Descriptors

J.4 [SOCIAL AND BEHAVIORAL SCIENCES] Psychology

General Terms: Management, Human Factors, Theory

Keywords: Personality Traits, Five-Factor Theory of Personality, Diffusion of Innovations, Transtheoretical Model of Behavior Change, Big Five, Major Life Goals, Subjective Well-Being.

1. INTRODUCTION

Although, thanks to modern information technologies, new applications constantly appear and simplify individuals and organizations daily work, an astonishing number of individuals and organizations do not use these technologies or do not take the full advantage of capabilities offered by innovative technologies ([12]; [21]; [24]; [32]). In the context of organizations – if employees did not use an introduced technology as planned – an organization will not be able to reduce process costs, process time or increase output. In the context of households – if individuals do not use innovative technologies as social networks – social phenomena as the Digital Divide will become noticeable. Consequently, such an apparently paradoxical behavior is discussed both, as an essential practical problem for organizations [14] and households [9] as well as a meaningful theoretical issue within information systems (IS) research ([29]; [30]).

Mostly, the focus in analyzing IS usage behavior is set on characteristic adaptations ([18]; [19]) or perceptual beliefs and therefore investigate individuals' habits, preferences, skills and attitudes towards an IS. Although these technology perceptions and habits are of central importance for understanding IS usage behavior they are a result of the interaction between basic tendencies like biological based personality traits and one's environment or external influence ([18]; [19]). As a consequence, characteristic adaptations vary over time when the external influence changes. There again, basic tendencies as personality traits are cross-situational and temporally stable ([4], [17]) as well as detached from technologies [31]. Such traits are the basis for one's affective, behavioral and cognitive style [23], indicate attitudinal patterns and are responsible for one's behavior and extent of IS usage ([4], [17]).

By following the advice of Devaraj and his colleagues, who pointed out that "*several research streams of IS research may benefit by incorporating personality into theoretical models*" [8], it should be investigated how IS usage behavior is influenced by personality traits and other basic tendencies. Therefore, different IS research areas will be considered and analyzed. As illustrated in the first subsection, personality will be analyzed to create an understanding why people do (not) adopt IS. Besides, it will be investigated within IT management to reveal the correlation between personality traits and turnover rate. Furthermore, it will be analyzed if personality has an impact on outsourcing decisions or if decision makers' personality is of less importance. Finally, the link between individuals' personality and the diffusion of innovations will be regarded. Here, the personality of key users should be unfolded. In the following, the focus is – because of the limited space – on technology diffusion and the role of personality within individual technology (non-) adoption.

Therefore, the main research question – how do personality traits influence an individual's life in the IS context? – will be decomposed to analyze the question in more detail:

1) Which personality traits are responsible for different IS usage behavior patterns (e.g. usage and non-usage; extent of usage)?

2) How to explain – or if possible how to generalize – IS usage behavior with the help of basic tendencies (as personality traits) and antecedents of IS usage behavior (as attitude, social influence, perceived behavior control etc.)?

3) What are the differences in the influence of personality traits on IS usage behavior in households compared to organizations?

4) How does basic tendencies influence IS usage behavior (direct, indirect or as moderator variable)?

To scrutinize this proposal the reminder is as follows. First of all an introduction to the knowledge required for an understanding of the themes of personality and IS usage research is presented in section 2. In section 3 and 4, the research model and the research design will be visualized and explained. In the end, section 5 contains first research results.

2. RESEARCH BACKGROUND

After these introductory remarks, this section contains theories and topics which are relevant to this research endeavor as personality, the Five-Factor Model (FFM), the Five-Factor Theory of Personality (FFT) and cognitions of research in IS usage behavior.

2.1 Personality Traits, FFM & FFT

Robert R. McCrae stressed out that personality traits – which can be defined as *"basic, endogenous, stable, hierarchically structured basic dispositions governed by biological factors such as genes and brain structures"* [28] – and the associated research stream is *"so successful that it threatens to overwhelm the whole field of personality psychology"* [16]. Although it is regarded skeptically if personality is stable over time several points as the heritability, studies of parental influences, comparative studies, cross-cultural and temporal stability of personality and its structure, confirms the non-influenceable characteristic of individuals personality. As a result *"personality traits are more expressions of human biology than products of life experience"* [20].

To systemize personality, researchers tried to establish a framework which explains personality from the cradle to the grave. One of these endeavors results in a three-layered system developed by McAdams [15] and unites personality traits on level 1, mental concerns and strategies on level 2 and integrative narratives on level 3. Similar to this approach is the Five-Factor Theory of Personality. This theory is a more general metatheoretical framework which describes five categories of variables and their relations [19]. The mentioned categories are called basic tendencies, characteristic adaptations, self-concept, objective biography and external influences [19] and is dedicated to *"summarize the kinds of variables that all theories of personality [...] must be concerned with"* [22]. The first-mentioned, basic tendencies, comprises elementary capacities and dispositions, depicts individual interpersonal differences, is described as grounded in biology and consequently represents an endogenous variable ([19]; [22]). These potentials are captured in an abstract manner and are the basis for an individual's behavior. Next to intelligence, health, and other hereditary aspects, age, gender and traits are considered as basic tendencies. Particular attention is devoted to the field of traits which are organized hierarchically and could be described in a specific or general way. A familiar model acquiring dispositions with five dimensions on the topmost hierarchy level is the Five-Factor Model – also named Big Five [10] – and includes neuroticism (expresses one's tendency to experience negative affects and thereby an absence of emotional stability), extraversion (expresses one's tendency to be talkative, active, enthusiastic, dominant, assertive and prefer being in large groups because of their tendency to like people ([7]; [11]), openness to experience (represents one's tendency to explore new ideas, seek new experiences and have an intellectual curiosity and active imagination), agreeableness (represents one's interpersonal orientation through describing one's tendency to be cooperative, trusting and altruistic) and

conscientiousness (expresses one's tendency to be organized, reliable, determined, purposeful and the motivation in the pursuit of goal accomplishment). Each of these dimensions outlines an immense number of narrower and more specific traits, as described by several researchers ([5]; [13]). Another FFT variable is called external influences and regards developmental, macro- and micro-environmental influences. Two other variables within the FFT are characteristic adaptations and self-concept. The latter describes one's identity and is part of characteristic adaptations. Nonetheless, because of the high importance of this concept, the authors separated it to an extra variable. The other one, characteristic adaptations, unites habits, preferences, skills and attitudes which people learn when their basic tendencies interact with their environments. Thereby, they concretize abstract basic tendencies and can change over time. The last missing FFT variable is objective biography and includes overt behaviors. Nonetheless, the variables are not interconnected among each other, only characteristic adaptations which result through the interplay between basic tendencies and external influences has an impact on the objective behavior.

2.2 Stages before and after using IS

After an innovative or new technology is made public, it can theoretically be used immediately by everybody. Yet the diffusion of technologies can be described stepwise with the help of Rogers Diffusion of Innovations [27]. The DOI assumes that humans have a distinct willingness to use an innovation (innovators, early adopters, early majority, late majority, laggards) or – especially in households – are not aware of the existence of a new technology. Consequently, people have to pass through a process starting by the stage at which one does not know a technology (*unaware non-user*) through the point of time one learns the existence about the corresponding technology (through friends, acquaintances or supervisors), but still does not use it (*aware non-user*). Arrived at this point, an individual period of time elapses until one decides to – or in context of organizations has to – use it (*user*). Depending on the extent to which one uses the technology, one could be described as *high-end user* or even discontinuing one's usage again (*experienced non-user*).

Thus, individuals run through different stages which can be partially explained with the help of the transtheoretical model (TTM; Prochaska et al. 1994). This model explains individuals' readiness to perform a behavior and to facilitate behavioral changes. The five stages are precontemplation (no intention to change), contemplation (consider a change), preparation (ready to change), action (change behavior) and maintenance (change is sustained).

3. RESEARCH MODEL

According to the research questions, two approaches will be traced. First of all, each group of users will be consulted to analyze their basic tendencies and characteristic adaptations. In particular, personality traits and thus the Big Five on the topmost hierarchy level should be focused in this descriptive analysis to understand and explain individual behavior. Moreover, users of a technology should be separated additionally by means of their extent of technology usage behavior.

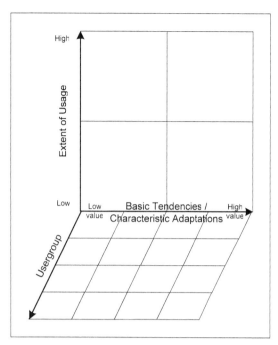

Research Model 1: Relation between basic tendencies / characteristic adaptations, usage behavior, knowledge stage

Expected outcomes of this research endeavor should be for example that unaware non-users have a low value in extraversion and openness to experience but are very neurotic. Otherwise experienced non-users stopped using a technology because of perceptions towards it but have the some personality as users. The latter could moreover, differentiate relative to their individual extent of usage, which is in particular important in organizational context. Besides, Rogers' five groups (c.f. section 2.2) and the stages of TTM should be consulted in order to illustrate that laggards are more resistance than innovators or other groups.

Build on these insights, the focus now is on the question how IS usage behavior is influenced by basic tendencies (in particular personality traits) and characteristic adaptations. Typical theoretical technology acceptance paradigms comprise attitudes and beliefs, social influence or subjective norm and perceived behavior control or situational influences ([1]; [2]; [3]). According to FFT, each of these aspects is a result of the interaction between basic tendencies and external influence. Hence it could be hypothesized that basic tendencies as personality traits have an influence on characteristic adaptations (as attitude) which influence IS usage behavior for their part.

H1: Basic Tendencies have an influence on Characteristic Adaptations.

H2: Characteristic Adaptations have an influence on IS Usage Behavior.

Moreover, it should to be investigated if basic tendencies have a direct influence on characteristic adaptations, as postulated in TPB and presented in FFT, and / or if they moderate the relation between characteristic adaptations and IS usage behavior, an effect that was identified by Devaraj et al. [8].

H1_{med}: The influence of Basic Tendencies on IS Usage Behavior is (fully or partial) mediated by Characteristic Adaptations.

H1_{mod}: Basic Tendencies moderate the relation between Characteristic Adaptations and IS Usage Behavior.

Within characteristic adaptations, several psychological constructs as major life goals [26] are included and offer valuable insights in understanding human behavior. Within IS research, these aspects were not regarded but should be analyzed within this research endeavor. It will be hypothesized that such individual differences unfold – next to the influence on IS usage behavior – also an impact on beliefs and attitudes [1] which is a central aspect within each technology acceptance paradigm.

H3: Individual Differences as Major Life Goals have an impact on antecedents of IS Usage Behavior.

Furthermore, especially within organizational context, the external influence should be regarded. It will be investigated if organizational characteristics as size or culture have an influence on characteristic adaptations and on objective biography [19].

H4: External Influence has a direct impact on Characteristic Adaptations.

H5: External Influence has a direct impact on Objective Biography.

Finally, the research model starts with constructs known from psychological research and should finish with them. The first aim is to understand IS usage behavior but within a next step the influence on post-adoption constructs as subjective well-being (context: households and technologies as SNSs) should be analyzed.

H6: The individual IS Usage Behavior has a direct impact on psychological Post-Adoption aspects.

4. HOW TO PRECEED

To increasingly deal with personality in IS research, three different IS research topics will be considered. First of all, technology diffusion will be regarded by launching an online-study. Here, the link between personality and IS usage behavior should be regarded. To analyze diffusion within a smaller group of people, a case study is planned, which investigates how Facebook marketing activities – by establishing a Facebook fan-group – affect the diffusion of the advertised product within this whole group and how the personality of (non-)users could be generalized.

Closely linked is the research stream of (non-)adoption behavior. At this, a case study will be conducted which investigates the role of personality, as resistance to change within organizational context. To unfold adoption processes in organizations, Germany's top-1,000 organizations and 1,000 SME will be also addressed and questioned with the help of a survey to topics concerning with Human Resources Information Systems as e-recruiting and applicant tracking systems. Here, it should be investigated if personality has a direct, indirect or moderating influence on intention or behavior (Research Model 2). The same will be done for households by analyzing the impact of personality on the intention to use Facebook [6] or HRIS topics as e-recruiting.

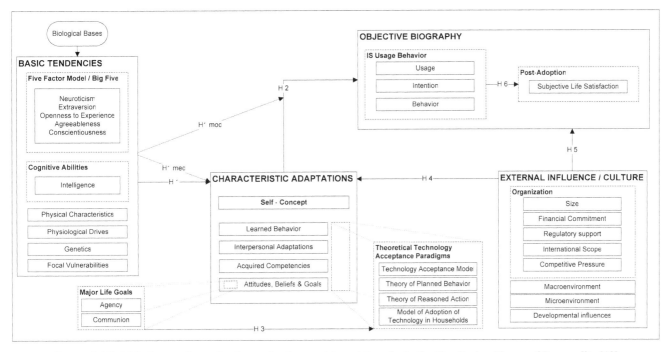

Research Model 2: Integrating technology adoption models and theories in the Five Factor Theory of Personality [19]

IT management is the last research topic which will be focused. At this, several IT recruiters and job seekers will be interviewed to identify traits of these persons to restrict staff turnover for example. Besides, these analyzes could also be done in the context of outsourcing decisions.

To analyze the survey, SPSS will be used to gain descriptive results and SmartPLS [25] to evaluate structural equation modeling and to investigate the relationships between different variables, as it could be seen in research model 2.

5. REFERENCES

[1] Agarwal, R. 2000. Individual Acceptance of Information Technologies, in *Framing the domains of IT management. Projecting the future through the past*, R. W. Zmud (ed.), Cincinnati: Pinnaflex Education Resources.

[2] Ajzen, I. 1985. From intentions to actions: A theory of planned behavior, in *Action control. From cognition to behavior*, J. Kuhl (ed.), Berlin: Springer.

[3] Ajzen, I. 1991. The theory of planned behavior, *Organizational Behavior and Human Decision Processes* (50:2), pp. 179–211.

[4] Ajzen, I. 2005. Attitudes, personality and behavior, Maidenhead: Open Univ. Press.

[5] Block, J. 1995. A contrarian view of the five-factor approach to personality description, *Psychological Bulletin* (117:2), pp. 187–215.

[6] Brown, S. A. 2008. Household Technology Adoption, Use, and Impacts: Past, Present, and Future, *Information Systems Frontiers* (10:4), pp. 397–402.

[7] Costa, P. T., and McCrae, R. R. 1992. Revised NEO personality inventory, NEO PI-R, and NEO five-factor inventory, NEO-FFI. Professional manual, Odessa, Fla.: Psycholog. Assessment Resources.

[8] Devaraj, S., Easley, R. F., and Crant, J. M. 2008. How Does Personality Matter? Relating the Five-Factor Model to Technology Acceptance and Use, *Information Systems Research* (19:1), pp. 93–105.

[9] Dewan, S., and Riggins, F. J. 2005. The Digital Divide: Current and Future Research Directions, *Journal of the Association for Information Systems* (6:13).

[10] Goldberg, L. R. 1981. Language and individual differences the search for universals in personality lexicons, in *Review of personality and social psychology*. 2, L. Wheeler (ed.), Beverly Hills, Calif.: Sage, pp. 141–165.

[11] Hogan, R. 1991. Personality and Personality Measures, in *Handbook of industrial and organizational psychology*, M. D. Dunnette (ed.), Palo Alto, CA: Consulting Psychologists Press.

[12] Johansen, R., and Swigart, R. 1996. Upsizing the individual in the downsized organization. Managing in the wake of reengineering, globalization, and overwhelming technological change, Reading, Mass: Addison-Wesley.

[13] John, O. P., and Srivastava, S. 2001. The Big 5 trait taxonomy: History, measurement, and theoretical perspectives, in *Handbook of personality. Theory and research*, L. A. Pervin (ed.), New York NY: Guilford Press.

[14] Luftman, J., Kempaiah, R., and Rigoni E. H. 2009. Key Issues for IT Executives 2008, *MIS Quarterly Executive* (8:3), pp. 151–159.

[15] McAdams, D. P. 1996. Personality, Modernity, and the Storied Self: A Contemporary Framework for Studying Persons, *Psychological Inquiry* (7:4), pp. 295–321.

[16] McCrae, R. R. 1994. New Goals for Trait Psychology, *Psychological Inquiry* (5:2), pp. 148-153s.

[17] McCrae, R. R., and Costa, P. T. 1987. Validation of the five-factor model of personality across instruments and observers, *Journal of Personality and Social Psychology* (52), pp. 81–90.

[18] McCrae, R. R., and Costa, P. T. 1996. Toward a new generation of personality theories: Theoretical contexts for the five-factor model, in *The five-factor model of personality. Theoretical perspectives*, J. S. Wiggins (ed.), New York, NYa.: Guilford Press.

[19] McCrae, R. R., and Costa, P. T. 2001. A five-factor theory of personality, in Handbook of personality. Theory and research, L. A. Pervin (ed.), New York NY u.a.: Guilford Press, pp. 139–153.

[20] McCrae, R. R., Costa, P. T., Ostendorf, F., Angleitner, A., Hrebícková, M., Avia, M. D., Sanz, J., Sánchez-Bernardos, M. L., Kusdil, M. E., Woodfield, R., Saunders, P. R., and Smith, P. B. 2000. Nature over nurture: temperament, personality, and life span development, *Journal of Personality and Social Psychology* (78:1), pp. 173–186.

[21] Moore, G. A. 1999. Crossing the chasm. Marketing and selling high-tech products to mainstream customers, New York: Harper Business.

[22] Motowildo, S. J., Borman, W. C., and Schmitt, M. J. 1997. A Theory of Individual Differences in Task and Contextual Performance, *Human Performance* (10:2), pp. 71–83.

[23] Mount, M. K., Barrick, M. R., Scullen, S. M., and Rounds, J. 2005. Higher-order dimensions of the big five personality traits and the big six vocational interest types, *Personnel Psychology* (58), pp. 447–478.

[24] Norman, D. A. 1999. Things that make us smart. Defending human attributes in the age of the machine, Reading, Mass.: Perseus Books.

[25] Ringle, C. M., Wende, S., and Will, A. 2005. SmartPLS: University of Hamburg.

[26] Roberts, B. W., and Robins, R. W. 2000. Broad dispositions, broad aspirations: The intersection of personality traits and major life goals, *Personality and Social Psychology Bulletin* (26), pp. 1284–1296.

[27] Rogers, E. M. 2003. Diffusion of innovations, New York, NY: Free Press.

[28] Romero, E., Villar, P., Luengo, M. Á., and Gómez-Fraguela, J. A. 2009. Traits, personal strivings and well-being, *Journal of Research in Personality* (43:4), pp. 535–546.

[29] Venkatesh, V., and Bala, H. 2008. Technology Acceptance Model 3 and a Research Agenda on Interventions., *Decision Sciences* (39:2), pp. 273–315.

[30] Venkatesh, V., and Brown, S. A. 2001. A Longitudinal Investigation of Personal Computers in Homes: Adoption Determinants and Emerging Challenges, *MIS Quarterly* (25:1), pp. 71–102.

[31] Venkatesh, V. 2000. Determinants of Perceived Ease of Use: Integrating Control, Intrinsic Motiva-tion, and Emotion into the TAM, *Information Systems Research* (11:4), 342-365

[32] Wiener, L. R. 1993. Digital woes. Why we should not depend on software, Reading, Mass: Addison-Wesley Pub.

[33] Prochaska, J.O.; Norcross, J.C.; DiClemente, C.C. Changing for good: the revolutionary program that explains the six stages of change and teaches you how to free yourself from bad habits. New York: W. Morrow; 1994.

Mobile IS Success in Personnel Marketing: A Consumer-based Analysis of Quality and Perceived Value

Susanne J. Niklas

RheinMain University of Applied Sciences/Saarland University; Germany
+49 611 9495 2156
susanne.niklas@hs-rm.de

ABSTRACT

The "war for talents" is getting more relevant than ever and especially the demand for qualified trainees and IT- and engineering specialists is massively increasing [18]. To meet this recruiting challenge a research project on the potentials of new innovative ways of mobile personnel recruitment, "ReMoMedia – Recruiting in the Mobile Media", was initialized at the University of RheinMain, Wiesbaden, Germany. The three-year project is funded by the German Federal Ministry of Education and Research, and investigates the practicability and feasibility of applying mobile media as an additional channel for personnel recruiting in the HR marketing mix. Accompanying the practical implementation possibilities this dissertation project aims at providing a scientific approach to the topic. To offer some guide for the organizational challenge of attracting and recruiting qualified employees the study in hand will apply theory on information system (IS) success adapted to the mobile requirements and the recruiting context. Working up on the success factors of mobile IS as an additional channel for personnel recruiting the analysis of the appropriate target group as well as the target group's expectations towards these applications will be subject of the study.

Categories and Subject Descriptors
H.4.0. [**Information System Applications**]: General; H.4.3. [**Information System Applications**]: Communication Applications – *Internet.*

General Terms
Management, Design, Human Factors, Theory.

Keywords
Mobile Information Services, IS success, Recruiting.

1. RESEARCH BACKGROUND
While e-recruiting nowadays is common practice, the mobile channel experiences a similar development as online did in the 1990s, continuously converging to a ubiquitous Internet. That way, communication patterns are successively changing as mobile technologies, systems and services becoming commonplace in our workday life in an increasingly mobile society [15]. Correspondingly, today's young generation of future employees is a continuous user of social networks: applications like Facebook,

LinkedIn or Twitter are constantly used independent of time and location and oftentimes accessed by mobile devices – and do also already play a role in job search processes [17, 27]. Therefore, IT and IS support in recruiting should not only include online channels like job portals, corporate career websites or social media applications [17] but also take account of respective mobile offers which differ from existing web services [29]. Based on the wide diffusion of high quality devices one could argue whether or to what extend mobile (recruiting) activities and applications differ from conventional web offers. The provision of Internet browsers as an almost standard feature of currently sold mobiles as well as increasing network connections already provide considerable access to online offers for the most part. That means that triggering online information by mobile devices is indeed possible but, due to the missing "fit", not providing best quality of experience [14, 29, 32]. This can be seen from two angles: firstly, mobile devices do have resource-based limitations like smaller screens and limited input options [14]. Secondly, mobiles come with features and functionalities which conventional PCs do not or not equally hold, like time and place independency and personalization [2, 14] as well as functionalities like SMS and MMS. Beyond that, differences in usage patterns necessitate content adjustments but also provide potentialities for generating added value and competitive advantage [32]. Services which are specially designed for the mobile access can take into account the limitations of the devices as well as their additional functionalities like location awareness [29]. All in all, this raises the managerial question whether or not to jump on the bandwagon: similar to the mid 90s where the question of necessity and possibility of online activities aroused, organizations currently face the question if an engagement in the field of mobile as an additional channel for business and communication is required. At this, mobile recruiting can be seen under the umbrella of mobile marketing as "a set of practices that enables organizations to communicate and engage with their audience in an interactive and relevant manner through any mobile device or network" [23]. In this respect, forms of applications and potential instruments for mobile recruiting could range from simple SMS or MMS notifier, like sending/receiving newly custom-fit vacancies, to mobile optimized job portals or corporate career websites. As for giving recommendations for managerial action for extending and optimizing the own personnel marketing mix successfully, this research will focus on mobile recruiting in terms of mobile web services as retrieving job information form a corporate career website via a mobile devices. In that, investigation will examine a consumer perspective to analyze relevant factors of success and usage acceptance.

2. RESEARCH QUESTION
Being a novel and innovative way to cater applicants, the assessment of organizational input related to prospective outcomes and thus, the decision on implementing a mobile recruiting campaign, cannot be made on existing experiences or

funded strategies. On the part of organizations the relevant questions arise of which target groups could best be reached within the innovative engagement (according to sociodemographics, educational background, profession or work experience), and which factors would affect their usage acceptance and satisfaction of the services offered, in terms of how doe these services have to look like to meet the user's expectations (e.g. function, design, content etc.). That way, the consideration and decision for or against an engagement in mobile recruiting have to be made on preliminary assumptions on the potential success of the new IS implemented. Building on theoretical findings considerable contributions on IS acceptance and success have been made for both, mobile IS as well as e-recruiting but investigations have not integrated both areas yet. Thus, tying up this gap the proposed thesis will focus on a consumer-based view of mobile IS success in recruiting. At this, research subjects can not merely be seen as technology users but also as consumers of information and services. At this juncture, individual quality perception and resulting evaluations of mobile recruiting services have to be analyzed as well as their influencing relationship usage intention, satisfaction of usage and continued use. To investigate user perception of innovative IT and IS as well as its consequences and impacts of use, primary two research orientation have been employed: behavioral oriented research on user acceptance and satisfaction oriented research on IS success [37]. While behavioral acceptance theories provide sound theory for explaining and predicting system usage by means of linking perceptions and beliefs about system use to attitudes, these approaches only provide limited guidance for well-suited system design and implementation [35, 37]. On the other hand, satisfaction oriented research studies focusing on design characteristics and IT artifacts resulting in (quality) perceptions and user satisfaction are considered as poor predictors of acceptance and behavioral *intentions* to use by disregarding motivational aspects and thus, missing behavioral relevance [37].

In order to investigate the above posed practitioner-oriented questions, the beforehand question concerns the adequate theoretical approach for explaining user acceptance as well as giving design and implementation guidelines as managerial intervention for positively enhancing user acceptance and use and finally success of the offered mobile information services. Considering the hitherto unexplored field of mobile recruiting in particular as a part of mobile information services in general, theories commonly used in IS research will have to be modified to the context at hand, as it has been shown that next to individual characteristics, IS and IT context as well as situational context do play a significant role in consumer-based IS research and context definition also defines research model granularity and adjustment [7, 8]. Thus, on the part of theoretical approach and scientific IS research regarding mobile recruiting IS the following academic research questions arise:

- How can predications about user acceptance and propositions about design and implementation be brought together theoretically?
- To what extend do universalistic theories on IS success research have to be modified for a) mobile IS in general and b) mobile recruiting IS in particular?
- How/to what extend has research on e-recruiting success to be modified for research on m-recruiting?
  Which factors determine mobile recruiting IS success considering the user's point of view? *With respect of:*

· From which mobile IS characteristics do users benefit generally and with regard to mobile recruiting particularly?
· Which mobile recruiting IS design characteristics regarding finer grained attributes constitute quality perceptions of mobile recruiting IS relevant to the specific benefits?

To answer the posed questions the following literature review will examine some core contributions of IS research building a theoretical basis for the further analysis for mobile IS success in the context of HR marketing communication.

3. THEORETICAL FOUNDATION

Dealing with the explanation and prediction of human behavior in terms of general diffusion of innovations as well as their individual adoption decision and behavior, the behavior oriented approaches to the diffusion, adoption and acceptance theory gained important interest. Regarding mobile (web) services and mobile recruiting in terms of technology, in Europe and the United States one can act on the assumption of an ample diffusion of required hardware: the estimated number of UMTS capable phone accounts in 2009 was about 108 million for the United States and around 172 million for Europe [10]. Thus, besides diffusion, a more relevant question concerns their usage in terms of adopting the applications and services available into behavioral patterns. Concepts of innovation acceptance and adoption lack a standardized definition and understanding and publications on this topic refer to e.g. approval, attitude resistance, rejection, trial, or postponement [26]. Commonly, adoption is seen as a process of assumption and Rogers [2003] probably most cited adoption definition describes adoption as "a decision to make full use of an innovation as the best course of action available" (p. 177). Using term of "decision" definition may led to the widely held notion, that adoption is merely seen as a mere intention [26] and ends with purchase or, at least, initial trial [20]. However, Rogers Diffusion of Innovation Theory (DOI) in the temporal dimension presents a complex process model, which implies an awareness-interest-evaluation/decision-trial-adoption sequence [1, 26], and thus, including use (trial) as well as its confirmation (continued usage). Tending to enlarge the understanding of the determinants of initial use and continued usage, the acceptance research stream is mostly seen as an enhancement of adoption theory considering acceptance as post-adoption usage behavior [20]. But, not wanting to digress, it should be noted that the full adoption process includes a stage of acceptance (as e.g. shown in DOI), assuming acceptance as a "psychological stage […] before entering the trial stage" [26], and thus, located at the preceding evaluation and intention level as a precursor of adoption. As an attitude-shaping process, acceptance can therefore be classified as a behavioral-anteceding construct within the adoption process [3, 26].

In order to explain and predict human adoption and usage behavior the Technology Acceptance Model (TAM) [6] became the most common model for understanding individual attitude and behavioral intention towards novel IT. Originating from an organizational context TAM was criticized for not reflecting the variety of user task environments, missing out on considering non-work related behavioral intentions and value adding expectations of personal usage [19, 20, 24]. Expecting that individual influences on adoption and use are different within a free adoption choice [20], it can be also assumed that further influences, do not only antecede perceived usefulness and ease of use but also determine consumer perception, attitude forming and decision itself. Accordingly, the focus on instrumental values regarding useful and usable systems should be enhanced to a comprehensive observation of human experiences satisfying personal goals. Thus, despite the consideration of relevant non-technological determinants like computer playfulness or perceived enjoyment these factors are merely considered in relation to the system's usefulness and ease of use as technology-based factors. Realizing the inherent relevance of aspects of fun and enjoyment in mobile interaction several studies modified the TAM by verifying a direct casual relationship between enjoyment and intention to use in mobile contexts 21.

Recognizing that adopter-related personality as well as sociodemographic influences play an important role in individual adoption decision, from an organizational point of view these factors play a more important role in decision on IS implementation planning itself rather than providing a framework for active interventions on mobile IS deployment. According to the present study, it appears like these demographic aspects could act as an indicator for targeting activities like appealing to a specific target group. Recommendations for interaction regarding mobile IS application for recruiting and personnel marketing however would need a more system-based understanding of characteristics and design, being valuable to its users and satisfying in use. Though, TAM merely treats technology as a black box, missing out on focusing system design characteristics that exactly determine its inherent usefulness answering the question of "what actually makes a system useful" [4]. A closer examination of the system design characteristics is a main focus in design oriented research on IS satisfaction and success. Here, system and service attributes like system reliability or information accuracy are enumerated to analyze overall system quality, satisfaction and thereof belief and attitude towards the IS [13, 37]. A common model to measure IS success is the DeLone & McLean IS success model (ISSM) [9]. By differentiating IS success into quality-based system characteristics ISSM explicitly enumerates design attributes like information accuracy or system response time, providing design and implementation guidelines [37]. Since TAM does not really shed light on IS design characteristics and their evaluation explaining what exactly makes a system useful regarding the usefulness antecedents [4], the questions of how to best implement mobile recruiting services to elevate usage acceptance could not be sufficiently answered and ISSM seems to be a more appropriate approach. However, ISSM is said to make a poor contribution to the technology acceptance in terms of behavioral *intention* to use [36, 37]. For a belief—like the object-based quality belief in ISSM— to be predictive of behavior and to conduct explanations and predictions on usage behavior, it has to be consistent with the particular target and context of behavior [37]. Such individual target-orientation in object perception and evaluation is said to be missing in ISSM. Accordingly, object-based belief like satisfaction on system reliability do not directly impact system use like the behavioral beliefs of perceived ease of use or usefulness do in TAM [37]. That way, a system could be perceived as highly qualitative and satisfactory but, not leading to further use as long as there is no relevance according to a targeted goal or objective. Anyhow, Net Benefits of ISSM constitute added values, determined by context, and dimensions of benefit depend on the individual objectives of the subject under investigation [8]. Additionally, casual relations between system quality, use, user satisfaction and individual benefit have been empirically validated and DeLone and McLean [7] state that expected benefits "are unlikely to be realized when system quality is unsatisfactory" (p. 35-37) and "cannot be fully understood without an [*quality*] evaluation […] and the [*objective*] relevance" (p.35). Though, as criticized, and contrary to the explicitly context- and objective based determination of the Net Benefits, dimensions of quality as well as their evaluation are more considered as (generally) "desirable characteristics" ([7] p. 34). But, under the overall advice that "success dimensions and measures should be contingent on the objectives and context of the empirical investigation (p.11).

In order to specify and analyze not just contingent qualities but also targeted quality expectations and evaluations, a definite conception of the users' underlying value systems in terms of needs, goals and objectives, and thus, inherent expectations is of importance for evaluating quality and IS success. In the actual context this would concern consumer expectations of mobile recruiting IS, regarding mobile system as well as anticipated extend and quality of service and (job-related) information. Investigations on underlying value systems triggering expectations originate from common consumer behavior research [33] based on the assumption that consumer's product choice follows a means-end chain. Thus, underlying an individual value system, products in terms of attribute bundles (means) are acquired/used to satisfy desirable consequences (ends) [38]. In this, not only the actual product attributes are considered but also their usage characteristics for reaching a higher ranked value concept. Relating this to the context of mobile recruiting, a consumer's goal could be the retrieval of information on a specific job offer. Surfing a company's career website would serve to achieve that goal. Doing this via a mobile device could additionally meet desires like time and place independency, temporary entertainment or even social recognition. In understanding the multiplicity of consumption related values Sheth et al. [1991] categorized five value dimensions to explain utilitarian as well as hedonic consumption needs. According to the value hierarchy model, consumers conceive value claims by learning [38]. Related to the topic in hand this would concern conceivabilities and prospects on the usage of mobile applications and services as well as on potential "job products" like modality of offered information etc. In the context of e-recruiting it e.g. has been shown, that prior knowledge influences applicant's information processing of the "job product" [22]. Given that products are not only for delivering a bundle of functional attributes but for providing capacious experience including hedonic needs, also non-functional attributes should be considered. Based on these findings, it appears appropriate to draw on a ISSM based model that allows for a deeper consideration of relevant design characteristics influencing individual intention to use mobile IS in a job-related context. Along with the demand for appropriate adaption and extension contingent to the specific field of research [7, 8] and the given relevance of behavioral motivation as well as emotional values and perceived enjoyment in mobile service usage [25, 33] these aspect should be incorporate into the analysis.

4. COURSE OF ACTION

Relating to the outlined theory above, the first objective of the study will be a comprehensive literature review on IS success and acceptance with special regard to mobile technology as well as e-recruiting/personnel marketing. Focusing on consumer-based research studies applying ISSM taking into account consumer value and mobile usage (e.g. [25, 36, 37]) will provide a basis for relevant success dimensions and characteristics. Additionally, analysis of acceptance research on mobile information services as well as on IS in the context of e-recruiting will reveal further consumer-based objectives. That way, success dimensions will be directed to the study objective of mobile recruiting IS success. For example, Net Benefits in ISSM capture the balance of the positive and negative impacts of IS on organizational as well as on consumer level [7, 8]. Taking into account the consumer-based view the construct of Net Benefits is closely related to the value-term in consumer behavior research, like Zeithamls well-known definition of perceived value as the perception of give an get components in terms of "what I get for what I give" [39]. Relating to Net Benefits of mobile IS, typically referenced mobile values like ubiquity, time-criticality, accessibility, localization, convenience or personalization [2, 15, 16] would be relevant objectives of investigation. Working out context-specific objectives and integrating them into the quality evaluation process will provide the opportunity to draw on the attitude-intention-behavior chain as quality evaluations in terms of object-based attitudes then will be consistent in time, target and context with the behavior of interest [37]. That way, quality evaluations comprise an individual assessment of the system regarding its potential to further desired objectives in terms of Net Benefits [7]. Specifying this, integrating a construct of Expected Net Benefits would enable linking quality evaluations to behavioral intentions.

Drawing on the attitude concept of consumer behavior, attitudes constitute both cognitive beliefs and affective impressions [31]. In that, quality evaluations with regard to expected benefit represent cognitive beliefs mostly missing out non-instrumental aspects of intrinsic motivation [34]. In acceptance research intrinsic motivations were analyzed in the context of hedonic systems, where system interaction is seen as an end in itself and as non-instrumental as there is no objective external to system usage as such [12]. Along with that, prior research generally distinguishes between hedonic and utilitarian consumer values [34]. This differentiation has also been made in information seeking processes in being either subject to utilitarian purpose, when assessing information for solving problems, or to non-instrumental hedonic purpose, when message and content consumption is just for the entertaining and pleasurable sensation per se. However, it certainly can be questioned if achieving enjoyment out of pure system interaction lives up not being considered as useful in that usefulness and enjoyment are seen as either or aspects of technology with usefulness not being prevalent in hedonic purposes [5, 12, 34]. Broadening IT acceptance research onto non-working settings and hedonic contexts, usefulness now just ought to lose its solely productivity-oriented meaning [34]. However, Davis et al. [5] also found significant effects of enjoyment on intention to use computers in the workplace additive to primarily extrinsic motivation. This multiplicity of value adding dimensions throughout technology use bear out in the context of new and multi-purpose IS which are universally accessible and also used beyond work settings like mobile services [34]. In the present context it seems obvious that searching for a job makes up a task-related manner with functional system usage and extrinsic goals. In that, instrumental aspects would be of interest. But, building on the multiplicity of consumption values [30] affective, emotional aspects of pleasure and enjoyment would additionally play a role as they also have been related to perceived consumer value as an overall assessment of utility [34]. Accordingly, the information construct, as a part of the quality assessment in ISSM, is also to be considered more as a construct of content as e.g. in the context of e-commerce [7] as well as in the context of mobile IS by also covering sound and image as important aspects of (intrinsic) behavioral intention to use [25]. At this, visual and musical appeal has been identified as non-functional value components for example [34]. Depicting those hedonic aspects and in line with the multimedia-based

design of content, it can be presumed that enjoyable aspects in system interaction should also play a role in the current context and thus, should also be considered in the value assessment and consequential Perceived Net Benefits and following influences. A further focus in the literature review will compose research on hedonic usage motivations in relation to value assessment and mobile IS usage intention. All in all, the analysis of prior research will provide a framework for the integration and specification of functional as well as non-functional aspects for setting up a respective research model for mobile recruiting IS success. Figure 1 displays a possible research model, where quality aspects comprise mobile recruiting specific characteristics also including mobile specific restrictions as depicted above and expected Net Benefits constitutes the cognitive trade-off of mobile recruiting IS quality assessments according to an individual's overall objective.

Main focus of investigation

Figure 1. Proposed Research Model

In a second stage, qualitative methods will be conducted to complement and extend the findings from the literature review. At this, design-oriented aspects in terms of quality characteristics as well as behavioral-oriented aspects in terms of pursued goals and targets within IS usage can be revealed [11]. A qualitative evaluation within a smaller subsample could be deployed to evaluate user requirements and needs before and after mobile recruiting specific system interaction. This would allow deriving implications for experience effects which have found to be important moderating variables within the evaluation of quality assessment and behavioral intention [35] and being relevant factors of user satisfaction [9]. Hereafter, the research model will be drawn up, meeting the demand for being contingent on the objective and context of the empirical investigation [8]. Applying the compiled model, a quantitative analysis will give deeper insight into the valuation of the relevant quality dimensions, user requirements and perceptions via structural analysis. Here, besides the revealed casual relationships the existence and influence of moderating factors is of interest as well which will be discussed in the SIGMIS CPR Consortium due to page limitations.

Overall, the proposed research study will provide a foundation for illustrating and evaluating success factors on the deployment of mobile IS in the context of HR communication. At this, the hitherto unexplored analysis and specification of success potentials of mobile recruiting measures as an additional communication channel in HRM, this study will contribute to a deeper understanding of relevant factors and IS design characteristics for the incessant upswing realm of mobile media and its application prospects. Compiling and validating an adjusted ISSM will extend the theoretical understanding of mobile IS success research in general and mobile IS in the context of mobile personnel marketing and corporate career websites in particular. Finally, findings and implications will be consulted for deriving concrete managerial recommendations in order to design and implement mobile recruiting IS.

5. REFERENCES

[1] Agarwal, R. (2000): Individual Acceptance of Information Technology, Framing the domains of IT Managmenet.

[2] Anckar, B. and D'Incau, D. (2002): Value-Added Services in Mobile Commerce, *Proceedings of the 35th Hawaii International Conference on System Sciences*, 1444–53.

[3] Bagozzi, R. P. and Lee, K.-H. (1999): Consumer Resistance to, and Acceptance of, Innovations, *Advances in Consumer Research*, 16/26, 218–225.

[4] Benbasat, I. and Barki, H. (2007): Quo Vadis, TAM? *Journal of the Association for Information Systems*, 8/4, 211–218.

[5] Davis, F. D., Bagozzi, R., and Warshaw, P. (1992): Extrinsic and Intrinsic Motivation to Use Computers in the Workplace, *Journal of Applied Social Psychology*, 22/14, 1111–1132.

[6] Davis, F. D., Bagozzi, R. P., and Warshaw, P. R. (1989): User Acceptance of Computer Technology: A Comparison of Two Theoretical Models, *Management Science*, 35/8, 982–1003.

[7] DeLone, W. H. and McLean, E. R. (2004): Measuring e-Commerce Success: Applying the DeLone & McLean Information Systems Success Model, *International Journal of Electronic Commerce*, 9/1, 31–47.

[8] DeLone, W. H. and McLean, E. R. (2003): The DeLone and McLean Model of Information Systems Success: A Ten-Year Update, *Journal of Management Information Systems*, 19/4, 9–30.

[9] DeLone, W. H. and McLean, E. R. (1992): Informations System Success: The Quest for the Dependent Variable, *Information Systems Research*, 3/1, 60–95.

[10] EITO (2009), *More than four billion mobile phone users worldwide*. Berlin, Germany.

[11] Gebauer, J. (2009): User requirements of mobile technology, *Information Systems Management*, 7, 101–119.

[12] Heijden, H. van der (2004): User Acceptance of Hedonic Information Systems, *MIS Quarterly*, 28/4, 695–704.

[13] Hevner, A. R., March, S. T., and Park, J. (2004): Design Science in Information Systems Research, *MIS Quarterly*, 28/1, 75–105.

[14] Kaasinen, E. (2005), *User acceptance of mobile services: Value, ease of use, trust and ease of adoption*, Espoo: VTT.

[15] Kim, D., Hwang, Y. (2010): A study of mobile internet user's service quality perceptions from a user's utilitarian & hedonic value tendency perspectives, *Information Systems Frontiers*.

[16] Landor, P. (2003): Understanding the Foundation of Mobile Content Quality, *Proceedings of the 36th Hawaii International Conference on System Sciences*.

[17] Laumer, S., Eckhardt, A., and Weitzel, T. (2010): Electronic HRM in an E-Business Environment, *Journal of Electronic Commerce Research*, 11/4.

[18] Lee, I. (2007): An Architecture for a Next-Generation Holistic E-Recruiting System, *Communications of the Association for Information Systems*, 50/7, 81–85.

[19] Lee, Y, Kozar, K. and Larsen Kai R. (2003): The Technology Acceptance Model: Past, Present, & Future, *Communications of the Association for Information Systems*, 12, 752–780.

[20] Lu, J., Yao, J. E., and Yu, C.-S. (2005): Personal innovativeness, social influences and adoption of wireless Internet services via mobile technology, *Journal of Strategic Information Systems*, 14/3, 245–268.

[21] Lu, Y., Deng, Z., and Wang, B. (2010): Exploring factors affecting Chinese consumers' usage of Short Message Service for personal Communication, *Information Systems Journal*, 20/2, 183–208.

[22] Maurer, S. D. and Liu, Y. (2007): Developing effective e-recruiting websites: Insights for managers from marketers, *Business Horizons*, 50/4, 305–314.

[23] MMA (2009), MMA Updates Definition of Mobile Marketing: http://mmaglobal.com/news/mma-updates-definition-mobile-marketing.

[24] Moon, J.,Kim, Y. (2001): Extending the TAM for a World-Wide-Web context, *Information & Management*, 38, 217-230.

[25] Mun, H. J., Yun, H., Kim, E. A., Hong, J. Y., and Lee, C. C. (2010): Research on factors influencing intention to use DMB using extended IS success model, *Information Technology and Management*, 11/3, 143–155.

[26] Nabih, M. I., Bloem, S. G., and Poiesz, T. B. C. (1997): Conceptual Issues in the Study of Innovation Adoption Behavior, *Advances in Consumer Research*, 24/1, 190–196.

[27] NACE (2010), *Social Networking Accounts for Little Job-Search Activity*.

[28] Rogers, E. M. (2003), *Diffusion of innovations*, 5. ed.

[29] Roto, V. and Kaasinen, E. (2008): The second international workshop on mobile internet user experience, *Proceedings of the 10th International Conference on HCI with Mobile Devices*, 571–73. New York, New York, USA.

[30] Sheth, J. N., Newman, B. I., and Gross, B. L. (1991), *Consumption values and market choices: Theory and applications*. Cincinnati, Ohio: South-Western Publ.

[31] Solomon, M. R. (2010), *Consumer behaviour*, 4th ed. Harlow (England), New York: Prentice Hall/Financial Times.

[32] Tanner, J. C. (2010): Optimized mobile content for everyone, *Telecom Asia*, 21/7, 33-33.

[33] Turel, O., Serenko, A., Bontis, N. (2007): User acceptance of wireless short messaging services: Deconstructing perceived value, *Information & Management*, 44/1, 63–73.

[34] Turel, O., Serenko, A., Bontis, N. (2010): User acceptance of hedonic digital aritfacts: A theory of consumption values perspective, *Information & Management*, 47, 53–59.

[35] Venkatesh, V., Morris, M. G., Davis, G. B., and Davis, F. D. (2003): User Acceptance of Information Technology: Toward a Unified View, *MIS Quarterly*, 27/3, 425–478.

[36] Wang, Y.-S. (2008): Assessing e-commerce systems succes: a respecification and validation of the DeLone and McLean model of IS success, *Information Systems Journal*, 18/5, 529–557.

[37] Wixom, B. H. and Todd, P. A. (2005): A Theoretical Integration of User Satisfaction and Technology Acceptance, *Information Systems Research*, 16/1, 85–102.

[38] Woodruff, R. B. (1997): Customer Value: The Next Source for Competitive Advantage, *Journal of the Academy of Marketing Science*, 25/2, 139–153.

[39] Zeithaml, V. A. (1988): Consumer Perceptions of Price, Quality, and Value: A Means-End Model and Synthesis of Evidence, *Journal of Marketing*, 52/3, 2–22.

SIGMIS-CPR'11 Tutorial - Developing a Digital Persona

Barbara L. Ciaramitaro, Ph.D.
Ferris State University
Big Rapids, Michigan, United States
(231) 591-3199
ciaramb@ferris.edu

ABSTRACT

The standard resume is all but extinct, replaced by the Digital Persona. Unfortunately, IT students and professionals are generally careless about their digital footprint. They drop digital bread crumbs at random spots through the Internet primarily in social media sites such as Facebook, Twitter or LinkedIn remarking on personal events, but failing to use a comprehensive strategy to create, maintain and present their Digital Persona. In order to compete effectively for employment positions in today's environment, IT professionals must learn how to present their knowledge, skills, and expertise through their digital reputation – their Digital Persona.

Categories and Subject Descriptors

H.m [**Information Systems**]: Miscellaneous.

General Terms

Human Factors.

Keywords

Digital Persona; Reputation; Social Media.

1. INTRODUCTION

The recent book, The 2020 Workplace (Meister & Willyerd, 2010), states that your social media competence and reputation is becoming a required component for future employment. Common questions by future employers now include:

- How many Twitter followers do you have? Who do you follow?
- How do you represent yourself on Facebook?
- Who are you connected with on LinkedIn?
- What expertise do you display in your Blog or in responding to other blogs?
- What groups are you a member of in social media and what knowledge do you demonstrate in answering or posting questions?
- What kinds of videos or podcasts have you posted?

In fact, the standard resume is all but extinct, replaced by the Digital Persona. Unfortunately, IT students and professionals are generally careless about their digital footprint. They drop digital bread crumbs at random spots through the Internet primarily in social media sites such as Facebook, Twitter or LinkedIn remarking on personal events, but failing to use a comprehensive strategy to create, maintain and present their Digital Persona. In order to compete effectively for employment positions in today's environment, IT professionals must learn how to present their knowledge, skills, and expertise through their digital reputation – their Digital Persona.

The creation and maintenance of a Digital Persona is not a haphazard event. An effective and comprehensive Digital Persona is the result of developing a personal strategy and plan. IT students and professional must begin with an examination of their current strengths, weaknesses, skills and expertise. This will also assist in identifying areas requiring further development. Some of the questions to be asked include:

- What are your strengths?
- Do you communicate well?
- What are you passions and interests? Are you a musician, a scientist, an athlete, a serious gamer, a thought leader?
- What kinds of careers are you considering?
- What do you know well and what would you like to learn?
- Do you collaborate with others virtually?
- Do you appear arrogant or confident? Obnoxious or courteous? Lazy or productive? Dominant or collaborator? Dependable or distracted?

Once you answer these initial questions, you can identify the gap between how you are now perceived, and how you would like to be perceived. It is important to remember that perception is reality to those seeing you through the eyes of the Web. Closing the gap between the current and desired future state of a Digital Persona requires a comprehensive strategy using a variety of social media and other tools, consistently implemented over time. It is also essential to remember that your Digital Personal is dynamic. It should continue to develop throughout one's professional career.

This tutorial is focused on presenting a guide for IT students and professionals on creating an effective Digital Persona Strategy and Plan. This tutorial is of value to IT faculty and students, as well as IT professionals and recruiters. The proposed structure of the tutorial is as follows:

- Introduction to the Digital Persona Plan
- Assessing your current Digital Persona
- Developing a personal inventory of strengths, weaknesses and areas of expertise
- Conducting a gap analysis between current and future (desired) digital reputation.
- Examination of Social Media tools and their benefits and weaknesses in building a Digital Persona including social networking, blogs, micro-blogs, web publishing, audio and video publishing, web sites, forums, conferences, etc.
- Developing of a personal Digital Persona Strategy and Plan

REFERENCES

[1] Meister, J & Willyerd, K, 2010. The 2020 Workplace: How Innovative Companies Attract, Develop and Keep Tomorrow's Employees Today. HarperCollins.

Stay or Quit: IT Personnel Turnover in Botswana

F.M.E. Uzoka
Department of Computer
Science and Information
Systems, Mount Royal
University, Calgary, Canada.
uzokafm@yahoo.com

K.V. Mgaya, A.P. Shemi,
Information Systems Group,
Department of Accounting and
Finance, University of
Botswana.
mgayakv@mopipi.ub.bw,
shemiap@mopipi.ub.bw

B.A. Akinnuwesi
Department of Information
Technology, Bells University of
Technology, Ota, Nigeria.
akinboluade@yahoo.com

Kitindi E.G.
Department of Accounting,
University of Dar es Salaam.
ekitindi@udbs.udsm.ac.tz

ABSTRACT
Information Technology (IT) has become a major driver of business functions of organizations. Recruiting and retaining competent IT personnel has become a key managerial function. A number of studies (especially in the developed world) have focused on IT personnel issues such as career orientations, recruitment, and turnover. This study contributes to the literature on IT personnel turnover intentions from a developing country perspective. The results of the study indicate that majority of the IT personnel either intend to leave their jobs for another or uncertain about whether or not to leave their jobs. Job satisfaction and growth opportunities are key influences on turnover intention. Career satisfaction, supervisor support, organization commitment, length of service, and age did not contribute significantly to turnover intention.

Categories and Subject Descriptors:
K.7 [**The Computing Profession**];
K.7.1 [**Occupations**]

General Terms
Human Factors

Keywords
Information systems personnel, Botswana, organizational commitment, supervisor support, job satisfaction, turnover intention.

1. INTRODUCTION
Nearly all organisations in the world use information and communications technologies (ICTs) to capture, process, store, and transmit information. This has made information technology/information systems personnel ubiquitous in our society and more are still needed. The most important challenge facing many organisations is the recruitment and retention of highly skilled information systems personnel [6, 15].

Even when there is an apparent lack of job opportunities, the highly skilled information systems personnel are still in great demand because of the continued sophistication of information and communication technologies and the ever increasing appetite by organisations to use ICTs to gain or sustain competitive advantage.

Information systems personnel turnover is a chronic problem [3, 16]. Organisations use a variety of incentives in trying to recruit and retain information systems personnel. The most basic one is a good salary. The role played by monetary compensation in reducing employee turnover is somehow inconsistent. Some studies have shown that salary is not the only incentive needed by employees, although employees with high need for achievement see monetary earnings as an indicator of their achievements [3]. Other studies have shown that higher remuneration offered by other employers is one of the major factors which make information systems personnel leave their jobs [34, 35].

In this study, we examine the turnover intentions of IS personnel in Botswana in the light of Igbaria's model of IS employee turnover intentions [11]. For some time in the 1980s and 1990s Botswana's economy grew at the fastest rate in the world (US Department of Commerce, 2000) and its GDP per capita is ranked fifth highest in Africa [38]. Botswana's population is only 1.84 million people [13]. The country's economy is very well managed although it is mainly dependent on the export of diamonds. Other significant sources of foreign exchange include tourism and beef exports.

The economic achievements of Botswana have trickled to many sectors of the economy. The IT industry has helped in bringing about a lot of changes in all the economic and social sectors of Botswana. Computers are used to process information in the public as well as the private sector. With the networking of all government schools the government is now putting more efforts in getting ICTs to almost all rural communities. The rate at which computers, software and networks have been adopted has resulted in a very high-tech, complex infrastructure that needs to be supported. Just as it is elsewhere in the world, Botswana is going to find it difficult to recruit and retain highly skilled IT and IS personnel.

Understanding the turnover intentions of IS personnel is critical to the retention of qualified staff that would support the IS activities of organizations in the drive towards achieving the developmental visions of the country. The rest of the paper is organised as follows: Section 2 examines existing literature in the area of IS personnel turnover intentions. Section 3 outlines the methodology of the study. The results of the data analyses are presented in Section 4, and discussed in Section 5, while some conclusions are drawn in Section 6.

2. REVIEW OF THE RELEVANT LITERATURE

Today the use of IT has permeated almost all nations and all organizations, profit-making and non-profit-making. In most organisations IT is used to support business processes. When used innovatively IT can deliver strategic and competitive advantage by allowing an organization to become more efficient, to reduce the time spent in bringing new products to market, to improve the speed and quality of production, to facilitate sales and consumer service or streamline infrastructure activities such as financial operations and billing systems [7, 23]. Information technology has become more and more integral to the success and profitability of organizations. Research has further shown that information technology plays a major role in raising national productivity [12]. Of the major resources of IS that include data, hardware, software, telecommunication facilities and personnel, the most important of them is personnel. The human being makes all the other components work properly. The widespread use of IT has meant that IS personnel are found in almost every organization.

The rate of change of IT is phenomenal. The rate of change has brought two major impacts on the IS personnel. Firstly, it is putting a substantial pressure on them to constantly update their knowledge at the same pace as the change of technology [7]. For various reasons not all personnel can cope with the pace. Secondly, because of high demand of IS personnel, there is a worldwide scarcity of qualified and well trained IS personnel. Research done in developed countries has shown that use of monetary incentives alone does not bring the desired effect of stemming the rate of IS employees turnover [15]. Monetary incentives tend to work during the early years of the career after which employees tend to strive for achievement and authority.

2.1 Information Systems Employees Turnover Intentions

The IS profession is facing a big problem of personnel turnover. This problem has been reported from many countries and for a long time. Rouse in [30] hinted that "voluntary turnover in many fields, especially in information technology is reaching epidemic proportions". The information technology trade magazines such as Computerworld and PC Computing, have been indicating that money was the main reason for IS employees to move into new position. Jiang and Klein in [16] reported that the "continuing challenge in information systems (IS) personnel is the high turnover rate in the profession. Ever since statistics have been kept, IS turnover has been a problem." Joseph et al in [18] noted that the problem of IS personnel turnover has continued to persist notwithstanding the recent trend by companies to relocate IT jobs offshore.

Several factors contribute to turnover intentions of IS employees. Age, education, pay and promotion have been some of the factors which influence intention to leave. Research by Rouse in [32] showed that young, entry level IS employees, who were 25 years old and under were the most dissatisfied:

The perception of this young crowd is that they are not being fairly compensated for the levels of performance that they are producing. Many of the high tech trades are grappling with the fact that newly trained members may provide organizations with equal or even greater skills than the seasoned veterans who are receiving larger salaries, more vacation, better offices, etc. Many believe that these scenarios lead to job dissatisfaction and eventually to voluntary turnover (p.281-2)

Earlier studies have established that job satisfaction and commitment to the organizational characteristics are the most substantial and the most direct influences on the turnover intentions even among IS personnel [11], which is similar to other findings concerning other professions in organizations except that job satisfaction would have more influence on turnover than organization commitment [29, 30]. Muliawan *et al.* in [29] observed that factors affecting IS auditors' turnover intentions are role conflict, satisfaction with pay, and fulfilment of growth needs which are moderated by organizational commitment and job satisfaction as expected, and argue that the need to satisfy personal and professional growth exerts a particularly strong influence on IS auditors' turnover intentions. They also found that IS auditors share similar characteristics to other IS professionals rather than with general accountants and auditors.

Pay and promotion is part of distributive justice [4]. Distributive justice relates to the perceived fairness of reward allocation and has been mentioned as the beginning of organizational justice which is the employees' perceived fairness in the workplace. According to DeConinck and Johnson in [8] an employee's perceptions of equity or inequity are based on a social comparison with a reference person or group such that the "employee expects to receive similar outcomes (e.g. pay and promotion) as another person with whom he or she believes has equal inputs (e.g. the same level of education and seniority)". Igbaria and Greenhaus in [11] found that young and highly educated employees tended to hold low levels of satisfaction with their jobs and careers and tend to experience low levels of commitment to their organizations with concomitant intentions to leave.

Several researchers have underscored the contribution of role stressors (role conflict and role ambiguity) on work-related attributes (job satisfaction, career satisfaction, organizational commitment; and intention to leave) [1, 11, 9, 14, 37]. Role ambiguity may be caused by insufficient information on how to perform a job or conflicting expectations from peers while role conflict may be caused by ambiguity of performance evaluation methods [11]. Recently, Rutner et al in [33] introduced another factor called emotional dissonance, which works better than perceived workload, role conflict or role ambiguity. Emotional dissonance is defined as the "conflict between the way one feels toward interaction partners and the emotion one feels compelled to display toward those individuals" [33]. Many organizations may explicitly stipulate what type of emotional demeanour employees are supposed to maintain even under the strangest of the circumstances in order to maintain good customer relations. A dissonance occurs when an employee's deep felt emotions are suppressed in order to display the desirable emotions. Research by Rutner et al in [33] found that emotional dissonance significantly contributes to work exhaustion and job dissatisfaction.

Work related attitudes which include career satisfaction, job satisfaction and organizational commitment play a major role in the intention to leave by IS personnel [11].The components of job satisfaction include satisfaction with work, satisfaction with supervisor, satisfaction with co-workers, satisfaction with pay and satisfaction with promotion, while organizational commitment is the employee's identification with a particular organization and the desire to maintain the membership [11].

3. RESEARCH FRAMEWORK

There are several theories which have been put forward to try to explain why employees leave their organizations. Joseph et al in [18] discuss five of them: the theory of organizational equilibrium put forward by March and Simon in [24]; the met expectations model by Porter and Steers in [31]; the linkage model by Mobley in [27] and Mobley et al. in [28]; the unfolding model of turnover by Lee and Mitchell in [19], Lee et al. in [20], Lee et al. in [21]; and the job embeddedness theory propounded by Mitchell and Lee in [26]. In addition we can add the discrepancy theory as propounded by Jiang and Klein in [17].

All traditional turnover theories can be traced to the theory of organizational equilibrium as propounded by March and Simon in [24]. According to March and Simon's motivation theory which explains the decisions of people to participate in and remain in organizations [25] "it is postulated that the motives of each group of participants can be divided into inducements (aspects of participation that are desired by the participants) and contributions (aspects of participation that are inputs to the organization's production function but that generally have negative utility to participants)". Individuals, therefore, sustain their participation in an organization as long as the inducements to stay (i.e. the rewards they get from the organization) match or exceed their contributions (e.g. effort).

The major factors that impact this equilibrium are job satisfaction and perceived job alternatives [26]. Employees' turnover occurs when employees perceive that they do not get inducements which are comparable to the contributions they make to an organization. The inducement-contribution balance is influenced by one's desire to move which is a function of one's satisfaction with the work environment and one's ease of movement which is influenced by macro- and individual-level factors that determine employability [18].

The turnover models posit that job and organizational characteristics determine job satisfaction, which in turn, determines turnover intention. Our study is based on a modified IS employee turnover model by Igbaria and Greenhaus in [11]. The Igbaria and Greenhaus turnover model considers demographic variables, role stressors, and career experiences to affect work related attitudes and turnover intention. The model takes a comprehensive look at the direct and indirect effects of these variables on turnover intention. Our study replaces organizational tenure with length of employment in the present organization. This is because in Botswana, the concept of job tenure is not common. We also recognize growth opportunity and supervisor support as key internal career related variables [25]. Our research model is presented in Figure 1.

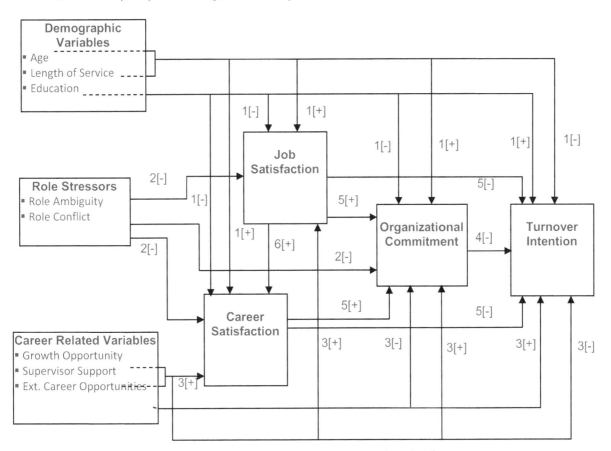

Figure 1: Employee Turnover Intention Model

The model predicts direct effects of demographic variables (age, length of service, and level of education), role stressors (role ambiguity, and role conflict), and career related variables (growth opportunity, supervisor support, and external career opportunities) on work related attitudes (job satisfaction and career satisfaction), as well as direct effect of the demographic, role stressors and career related variables on turnover intention. The model also suggests a direct relationship of job satisfaction on career satisfaction, job and career satisfaction on organizational commitment and direct effect of organizational commitment on turnover intention. The following hypotheses/sub-hypotheses are tested based on the results obtained by Igbaria and Greenhaus in [11]. The signs (+ or -) indicate the direction of effect of each independent variable(s) on the corresponding dependent variable.

Table 1: Research Hypotheses

Hypotheses	Independent Variables	Sub-hypotheses	Dependent Variables	Effect [+/-]
1	Age	$H_{1.1.1}$	Career satisfaction	+
		$H_{1.1.2}$	Job satisfaction	+
		$H_{1.1.3}$	Org. Commitment	+
		$H_{1.1.4}$	Turnover Intention	-
	Education	$H_{1.2.1}$	Career satisfaction	+
		$H_{1.2.2}$	Job satisfaction	-
		$H_{1.2.3}$	Org. Commitment	+
		$H_{1.2.4}$	Turnover Intention	-
	Length of Service	$H_{1.3.1}$	Career satisfaction	-
		$H_{1.3.2}$	Job satisfaction	-
		$H_{1.3.3}$	Org. Commitment	-
		$H_{1.3.4}$	Turnover Intention	+
2	Role Ambiguity	$H_{2.1.1}$	Career satisfaction	-
		$H_{2.1.2}$	Job satisfaction	-
		$H_{2.1.3}$	Org. Commitment	-
	Role Conflict	$H_{2.2.1}$	Career satisfaction	-
		$H_{2.2.2}$	Job satisfaction	-
		$H_{2.2.3}$	Org. Commitment	-
3	Growth Opportunity	$H_{3.1.1}$	Job satisfaction	+
		$H_{3.1.2}$	Org. Commitment	+
		$H_{3.1.3}$	Turnover Intention	-
	Supervisor support	$H_{3.2.1}$	Job satisfaction	+
		$H_{3.2.2}$	Org. Commitment	+
		$H_{3.2.3}$	Turnover Intention	-
	External Career opportunity	$H_{3.3.1}$	Org. Commitment	-
		$H_{3.3.2}$	Turnover Intention	+
4	Org. Commitment	H_4	Turnover Intention	-
5	Career satisfaction	$H_{5.1}$	Org. Commitment	+
	Job satisfaction	$H_{5.2}$		+
	Career satisfaction	$H_{5.3}$	Turnover Intention	-
	Job Satisfaction	$H_{5.4}$		-
6	Job satisfaction	H_6	Career satisfaction	+

4. METHODOLOGY

4.1 Sampling

The study population was all IS employees in Botswana who are employed as computer programmers and above, excluding all support staff such as technicians and computer operators. A list of employers was obtained from the Botswana Chamber of Commerce Industry and Manpower (BOCCIM). Data was also collected from government employees through the Government Computer Bureau. There are a few parastatal organizations in Botswana. Most of them are heavy users of IT. The research tried to cover all parastatal organizations that employ IS personnel. The researchers identified 48 organizations that employ IS personnel. The research therefore concentrated on the 48 organizations. Two hundred and forty three questionnaires were administered to IS employees in 48 organizations. One hundred and four employees from 29 organizations completed and returned the questionnaires, giving a 42.8% response rate.

4.2 Measures

This questionnaire consisted of seven parts. The first part was used to collect demographic data of the respondents. The second part of the questionnaire had seven statements on supervisory support that employees get from their organizations, designed using a five point Likert-type scale. The third part of the questionnaire had five statements on career satisfaction. Part four of the questionnaire collected data for determining the career orientations of IS personnel in Botswana.

The fifth section of the questionnaire dealt on external career opportunities and factors that may influence IS employees to leave their current jobs. The sixth part of the questionnaire had ten items on work environment, while the seventh part focused on gender issues and was to be answered by female employees only. In this paper, we present the results of the analysis of the components that deal with the turnover intentions.

4.3 Analysis Procedure

SPSS package was utilized in the analysis of data. The first part involved the use of descriptive statistics to present the data obtained in terms of the demographics of the respondents. The turnover factors identified in the model were extracted using the mean score of the variables identified in each factor. The reliabilities of the factors were measured using the Cronbach's alpha, which is based on the average correlation of items within an instrument or scale; and is regarded as an indication of internal consistency. Multivariate regression analyses were carried out in order to test the hypotheses relating to employee turnover.

5. ANALYSES AND RESULTS

Table 2 shows the various test constructs and the questionnaire variables that measured the constructs, while Table 3 shows a summary of the demographic characteristics of IS employees in Botswana. Out of 104 respondents 83 (79.8%) were Botswana citizens and 21 (20.2%) expatriates, 26 (25%) were females and 78 (75%) males. It can be seen that the proportion of female employees in the IS profession

in Botswana is still very low. Age-wise, IS employees in Botswana are very young. None of the respondents was aged more than 50 years and the highest percentage of respondents came from those aged between 20 and 30 years (57%). This shows that the profession is relatively new to Botswana. This is also supported by statistics which show that 51% of the respondents have less than five years in the IS field while only 11% have worked for more than 15 years in the IS field.

In the area of education, 9.6% of the respondents had attained a maximum of high school education, 35.6 % had a diploma and the rest had a first degree (40.4%) or second degree (14.4%). Most of the respondents are still in the low salary bands. About 25% of the respondents earn an annual salary of between P50,000 and P99,999; 60% earn below P150,000 per annum. Only 10.5% of IS employees earn P249,999 and above per annum. One of the reasons for the large number of employees in the low salary scales could be the fact that the IS profession is still very young in Botswana. The results show that only 29% had worked for 10 or more years in the IS field

Table 2: Test Constructs

Constructs	Variables	Reliability
Age [AGE]	Age	1.000
Education [EDUCATN]	Education	1.000
Length of service [LENTSERV]	Length of Service	1.000
Role ambiguity [ROLEAMB]	Duties-qualifications mismatch [dutqualmismatch]	1.000
Role conflict [ROLCNFLT]	Non- core IT duties [noncoreduties]	1.000
Growth Opportunity [GRWTOPPT]	Opportunity for promotion [promotion]	0.739
	Career development support [cardevtsppt]	
	Training opportunities [trainingoppt]	
	Fairness of annual assessment [annualass]	
Supervisor Support [SUPSUPPT]	Supervisor learns employee careers goals [suplearngoals]	0.889
	Supervisor cares about goal achievement [supcargoalach]	
	Supervisor Informs employee about career opportunities [supinfomcaropp]	
	Supervisor gives credit for on the job task accomplishment [supgivescredt]	
	Supervisor gives helpful performance feedback [supprffeedback]	
	Supervisor gives helpful performance advice [supgivesadvice]	
External Career Opportunities [EXTCAROPP]	External offer of better salary and benefits for same job [salary]	0.631
	External offer of higher position but about same benefits [higherposit]	
	External offer of tenured position but same salary [tenure]	
	External offer of more challenging job but same salary [jobchallenge]	
Organizational Commitment [ORGCMIT]	How loyal the individual is to the present organization [loyalty]	1.00
Career Satisfaction [CARRSAT]	Satisfaction with achieved career success [satcarsucess]	0.808
	Satisfaction with progress towards career goals [satcargoalprgrss]	
	Satisfaction with progress towards advancement goals [satadvcmtglprgrs]	
	Satisfaction with progress towards income goals [satincmeglprgrss]	
	Satisfaction with skills development goals [satskldvtglprgrs]	
	Integration	
	No difficulty in being accepted [acceptnotdiff]	
	Contributions valued [contrvalued]	
	Interaction with internal peers [peerinteraction]	
	Interaction with eternal peers [peerinteractout]	
	Pre-Employment Expectations	
	Meeting of pre-employment expectations [jobexpect]	
	Job Characteristics	
	How much variety is in the job [jobvariety]	
	How much organizational stability is in the job [orgstability]	
	How much identity the job provides [jobidentity]	
	How much geographic security the job has [geosecurity]	
	How much technical competence does the job require [tchcmptence]	
	How much managerial competence does the job require [mgrcmptence]	
	How much autonomy is in the job [autonomy]	
	How much skill and talent related service is in the job [service]	

Majority of IS employees in Botswana are of a young age. The average age of female employees is 27.1 years while that of male employees is 28.3 years. None of the respondents was more than 50 years old and more than half of the respondents were below 30 years old. More than half of the respondents have worked for less than 4 years in the IS field. The young working population is putting a lot of pressure on the organizations in which they work because, compared to their mature colleagues, they are the least stable in employment. There are a number of reasons as to why this is the case. Young employees generally tend to earn less than older employees because they have worked for a relatively shorter period of time and are therefore not as experienced as their older colleagues. They are thus more inclined to quit their current jobs in search of better remuneration elsewhere. Secondly, most of the young employees, being in the early phases of their careers, are in need of career development support, including training, from their employers. In order to ensure that these young employees are satisfied to remain in

their employment, employers should strive to put forth training programmes which would provide the young employees with both theoretical and hands on training in aspects related to their work. On its part, government should create an environment that is conducive for employers to be able to provide this training to its young recruits.

About 50% of the IS employees have at least a Bachelor's degree. On the face of it, this is an encouraging situation. However, the findings show also that there are a sizable number of expatriates in the profession. Although the percentage of expatriates is not too high (20.2%) it is worth considering the possibility that these could be occupying relatively senior positions in the profession. There is need to explore the necessity for training citizens for higher qualifications so that they are prepared to occupy senior positions that may fall vacant in future. This will also be good for morale and long term stability in the profession.

Table 3: Demographic Characteristics of the IS Employees

Variable		Number of Respondents	Percent
1. Age	20 – 30 Years	56	57
	31 - 35 Years	20	20
	36 – 40 Years	10	10
	41 - 50 Years	13	13
2. Citizenship	Expatriates	21	20.2
	Batswana	83	79.8
3. Gender	Females	26	25
	Males	78	75
4. Education	High School or less	10	9.6
	Diploma	37	35.6
	First Degree	42	40.4
	Masters Degree and above	15	14.4
5. Annual Basic Salary [in Botswana Pula (P)]	Below 50 000	8	8
	50 000-99, 999	25	25
	100, 000-149, 999	28	27
	150, 000-199, 999	19	19
	200, 000-249, 999	11	10.5
	Above 249,999	11	10.5
6. Years in IS field	0 – 5 Years	48	51
	6 – 10 Years	19	20
	10 – 15 years	17	18
	More than 15 Years	11	11
7. Years in Current Organization	0 – 3 years	68	66
	4 – 5 Years	10	9.7
	6 – 10 Years	14	13.6
	Above 10 Years	11	10.7

5.1 Turnover Intentions

The results of the study also indicate that the percentage of IS personnel who intend leaving their jobs is the same with the percentage who are uncertain about whether to stay on their jobs or not. 36.2% of the IS personnel would leave their jobs if there is an opportunity to do so (22.5% strongly agree, 13.7% agree), while 36.3% were uncertain about their turnover intentions.

We can divide the IT employers in Botswana into three major groups. The private sector, the government sector and the semi-government sector (parastatals) in which we find some big corporations such as the utility companies and government-owned banks. The study found that 41.6% of the IT employees employed in the government sector would like to leave, followed by 38.5 % of those employed in the private sector while only 32.7% of those employed by parastatals indicated that they would like to leave at the earliest available opportunity. The resolve by government sector employees to leave their current jobs is resolute given that only 8.3 % of them indicated that they don't intend to leave their current jobs. The corresponding figures for the private sector and parastatals were 28.2% and 30.6% respectively. Further analysis shows that although it is known that government employees generally earn less compared to the other two types of employers, it is not pay which is making them unhappy as they expressed more satisfaction with pay compared to the other two groups. Government employees expressed huge satisfaction (75.1%) with the career development support that they get from their employer with only 8.3% of them showing dissatisfaction. Employees who work in the parastatal organisations showed the least satisfaction (38.8%) with the career development support given by their employers. Government employees, however, expressed deep dissatisfaction with all aspects of supervisory support. This, it

seems, is the major factor that makes government IS employees want to quit their current jobs.

The results of the hypotheses tests (using multivariate regression analysis) are presented in Table 4. The results show that demographic variables do not have a significant effect on job satisfaction, career satisfaction, organizational commitment or turnover intention. However, the effects of age on job satisfaction ($t= -1.679$) and career satisfaction ($t= 1.615$) are quite sizable, even when they are not statistically significant. The older people tend to be more satisfied with their jobs and careers than young people. Also, the effects of length of service on career satisfaction ($t= 1.870$) and turnover intentions ($t= -1.624$) are quite reasonable. The longer a person stays on the job, the more his career satisfaction and the less likely the tendency to leave the job. Growth opportunity has a reasonable (not significant) effect ($t=1.947$) on organizational commitment, and the same can be said of job satisfaction and career satisfaction ($t=1.736$).

Table 4: Results of Hypotheses Tests

Hypotheses	Independent Variables	Sub-hypotheses	Dependent Variables	Effect [+/-]	β	t	Sig	Conclusion
1	Age	$H_{1.1.1}$	Career satisfaction	+	-.189	-1.615	.109	Not supported
		$H_{1.1.2}$	Job satisfaction	+	-.197	-1.679	.096	Not supported
		$H_{1.1.3}$	Org. Commitment	+	-.032	-.267	.790	Not supported
		$H_{1.1.4}$	Turnover Intention	-	.101	.866	.389	Not supported
	Education	$H_{1.2.1}$	Career satisfaction	+	-.117	-1.153	.252	Not supported
		$H_{1.2.2}$	Job satisfaction		-.109	-1.071	.287	Not supported
		$H_{1.2.3}$	Org. Commitment		-.012	-.112	.911	Not supported
		$H_{1.2.4}$	Turnover Intention	-	.164	1.612	.110	Not supported
	Length of Service	$H_{1.3.1}$	Career satisfaction	-	.211	1.870	.064	Not supported
		$H_{1.3.2}$	Job satisfaction	-	.100	.878	.382	Not supported
		$H_{1.3.3}$	Org. Commitment	-	-.030	-.256	.798	Not supported
		$H_{1.3.4}$	Turnover Intention	+	-.183	-1.624	.108	Not supported
2	Role Ambiguity	$H_{2.1.1}$	Career satisfaction	-	-.225	-2.333	.022	Supported
		$H_{2.1.2}$	Job satisfaction	-	-.120	-1.216	.227	Not supported
		$H_{2.1.3}$	Org. Commitment	-	.095	.957	.341	Not supported
	Role Conflict	$H_{2.2.1}$	Career satisfaction	-	-.017	-.173	.863	Not supported
		$H_{2.2.2}$	Job satisfaction	-	-.079	-.798	.427	Not supported
		$H_{2.2.3}$	Org. Commitment	-	-.013	-.126	.900	Not supported
3	Growth Opportunity	$H_{3.1.1}$	Job satisfaction	+	.624	8.015	.000	Supported
		$H_{3.1.2}$	Org. Commitment	+	.190	1.947	.054	Not supported
		$H_{3.1.3}$	Turnover Intention	-	-.430	-4.785	.000	Supported
	Supervisor support	$H_{3.2.1}$	Job satisfaction	+	.435	4.884	.000	Supported
		$H_{3.2.2}$	Org. Commitment	+	.001	.011	.991	Not supported
		$H_{3.2.3}$	Turnover Intention	-	-.349	-3.757	.000	Supported
	External Career opportunity	$H_{3.3.1}$	Org. Commitment	-	-.086	-.868	.387	Not supported
		$H_{3.3.2}$	Turnover Intention	+	.321	3.407	.001	Supported
4	Org. Commitment	H_4	Turnover Intention	-	-.061	-.615	.540	Not supported
5	Career satisfaction	$H_{5.1}$	Org. Commitment	+	.049	.498	.620	Not supported
	Job satisfaction	$H_{5.2}$		+	.092	.932	.354	Not supported
	Career satisfaction	$H_{5.3}$	Turnover Intention	-	-.139	-1.417	.159	Not supported
	Job Satisfaction	$H_{5.4}$		-	-.466	-5.296	.000	Supported
6	Job satisfaction	H_6	Career satisfaction	+	.169	1.736	.085	Not supported

From Table 4, it is evident that role ambiguity has a statistically significant negative effect on career satisfaction ($t= -2.333$, $p = 0.022$); thus $H_{2.1.1}$ is supported. Most of the hypotheses relating to career variables are strongly supported ($H_{3.1.1}$, $H_{3.1.3}$, $H_{3.2.1}$, $H_{3.2.3}$, $H_{3.3.2}$). The effect of job satisfaction on turnover intention is equally very significant. A high level of job satisfaction leads to less tendency to leave the job ($t=-5.296$, $p= 0.000$).

The results of the study indicate that majority of the IT personnel either intend to leave their jobs for another or uncertain about whether or not to leave their jobs. Job satisfaction and growth opportunities are key influences on turnover intention. Career satisfaction, supervisor support, organization commitment, length of service, and age did not contribute significantly to turnover intention.

5.2 DISCUSSION OF RESULTS

According to the results, the major contributors to the turnover intentions of IS personnel in Botswana are job satisfaction and growth opportunities. In this study, the majority of the IT personnel either intend to leave their jobs for another or uncertain about whether or not to leave their jobs. This is contrary to research findings by Igbaria and Greenhaus in [11] who found that the immediate determinants of turnover intentions were job satisfaction and organizational commitment.

The question of growth opportunities covers issues such as opportunity for promotion, career development, training opportunities and annual assessments. Apart from contributing significantly to turnover intentions, growth opportunity has got a direct positive impact on job satisfaction and career satisfaction. It was observed from the study that young employees have got the highest propensity to turnover. Most of the young employees are in the lower salary bands, have got one degree, and do not have enough working experience. For a long time it has been like a culture in Botswana that most employees get sponsored for further education by their employers, especially for second degrees and short courses. The sponsorship could cover all costs such as tuition and paid leave. Those employers who cannot afford to release their employees and or pay them while they are pursuing further studies would at least make certain concessions which will allow their employees to smoothly carry on with their studies. This is engrained in the minds of employees, especially the young ones. As a result, employees jump from one job to another trying to find an employer who would be willing to meet their training needs. Indeed, 46.25 percent of all the employees indicated that one of the factors that would make them leave their current jobs would be if the employer does not like to sponsor them for further education or new skills development. It is further observed that employees who fail to find any growth opportunities at their places of work indicate that their careers have been a failure which in turn contributes to turnover intentions.

Another issue that relates to growth opportunities in the Botswana context is the characteristic of the IT job market that is mainly centred on government and government related institutions. As the largest employers of most IT professionals, there is little job diversity for young citizens who may prefer to work locally, at least for now. The cultural inclination of most citizens who want to maintain close family ties still causes them to prefer to work at home and not venture outside the country. This contrasts with the IT professionals in the Igbaria and Greenhaus study in [11] who were drawn from a diverse background and worked for many organisations in the US job market. This study was undertaken prior to the 2008 recession. The 2008 recession brought a general freeze of resources and fringe benefits that affected all IT employees in the local market but we are of the opinion that the results could still hold in recession times as Laumer and Eckhardt [21] found that IT employees' thoughts about quitting their current job remained unchanged even during tough economic times.

Benson in [2] researched on two types of employee development which can be provided to employees: on-the-job training and tuition-reimbursement which provides general or marketable skills. It was observed that on-the-job training was positively related to organizational commitment and negatively related to intention to turnover. Participation in tuition-reimbursement was positively related to intention to turnover, although the intention to turnover seemed to be reduced if after earning a degree (through tuition-reimbursement) the employees were subsequently promoted.

According to Benson in [2], therefore, employees who participate in on-the-job training and gain specific skills which are relevant to their current jobs "are more committed and less likely to intend to leave the firm, while employees who participate in tuition-reimbursement express higher intention to leave the firm".

According to the results growth opportunities have got a major impact on job satisfaction. Items under job satisfaction cover issues such as pre-employment expectations, the easiness with which a new employee gets integrated at place of work, and job characteristics. Job satisfaction is negatively correlated with intentions to turnover. This means that employers can try to reduce their employees' intentions to turnover by ensuring that the above factors are taken care of.

Sector-wise comparisons in this study show clearly that employees who work in the government sector are very happy with the career advancement support which they get from their employer but they are the most disgruntled and would like to leave their jobs. Government employees are very unhappy with all aspects of supervisory support that they get from their employer. The inadequacy of supervisory support in the government sector can be pointing to a much complex problem. Does a government supervisor possess enough discretionary powers for motivating his/her subordinates? What is the impact of the government's bureaucratic system on the supervisory support given to its employees?

6. CONCLUSION

The study examined the factors that affect the IS employees' intention to leave their current jobs using the Igbaria and Greenhaus model in [11]. The results of the study show that role ambiguity has a negative effect on career satisfaction, while supervisor support and growth opportunity have positive effects on job satisfaction. Turnover intention is influenced negatively by internal growth opportunity, supervisor support, and job satisfaction. External career opportunity tends to have a positive significant effect on the employee's intention to quit. Most of the results obtained in this study are not in consonance with the results obtained by Igbaria and Greenhaus in [11] upon which the turnover intentions study was based. For example, Igbaria and Greenhaus found strong negative relationship between organizational commitment and turnover intention, but our study found a very non significant negative relationship between the two. Some of our results have partially corroborated the Igbaria and Greenhaus results. For example, Igbaria and Greenhaus identified that role stressors affect turnover intentions indirectly through job satisfaction. Our study found that role stressors (role ambiguity and role conflict) have non- significant negative effects on job satisfaction, whereas, job satisfaction had significant negative effect on turnover intention.

It is expected that employers in Botswana would realise the unique career needs of IS personnel in the country and emphasize growth opportunities and supervisor support as instruments for increasing the levels of job and career satisfaction of IS employees in order to reduce the rate of turnover of IS employees. High employee turnover can be a serious obstacle to productivity, quality, and profitability to firms of all sizes [10, 5]. Analysis of employee responses from the three major types of employers in Botswana shows that the government sector employees have the highest propensity to turnover because of poor supervisory support although they are happy with pay and the career development support that their employer provides. As the government continues to lay more emphasis on the use of information and telecommunications technologies in its operations it is expected that the government will continue being an important employer of IS personnel in the country. More attention should therefore be paid into ways of improving the supervisory support that is given to its employees.

This study is one of the few additions to the literature on information systems personnel turnover in developing countries. It examines turnover intentions and offers organizations the basis of focusing on ways of reducing IS employee turnover, which could be costly to organizations. Igbaria and Greenhaus in [11] suggested that further studies be conducted in different contexts. In their study, ACM members in some states in the USA were surveyed. This presents some level of professional homogeneity, which could bias the results. Our study utilized the same model, while surveying a more heterogeneous IS personnel sample in a small developing economy. The key limitation of this study is the small sample size. The utilization of regression for small sample sizes tends to produce low model power, which implies that some of the non-significant findings identified in this study could become significant with a larger sample size. Another limitation is the instrument design, which produced single-variable factors with reliability values of 1.000. It could be argued that such factors might increase the level of bias in the regression analysis. This study focuses on Botswana, which is a relatively small economy, with peculiar characteristics. A future study could consider a larger developing economy in order to provide a basis of result generalization.

REFERENCES

[1] Baroudi, J.J. 1985. The impact of role variables on IS personnel work attitudes and intentions. *MIS Quarterly*, Vol. 9, Issue 4, pp. 341-356.

[2] Benson G.S. 2006. Employee development, commitment and intention to turnover: a test of 'employability' policies in action, *Human Resource Management Journal*, Volume 16, Issue 2, (April 2006), pp. 173–192.

[3] Bartol, M. and Martin, D. 1982. Managing information systems personnel: a review of the literature and managerial implications, *MIS Quarterly*, Vol. 6, No.1, pp. 49-70.

[4] Byrne, Z. S., and Cropanzano, R. 2001. The history of organizational justice: The founders speak. In R. Cropanzano (Ed.), Justice in the workplace: From theory to practice (Vol. 2). Mahwah, NJ: Lawrence Erlbaum Associates, Inc.

[5] Catherine M G. 2002. Staff turnover: Retention. *International Journal of Contemporary Hospitality Management*. Vol. 14, No. 3, pp. 106-110.

[6] Cone, E. 1998. Managing that churning sensation, *InformationWeek*, 05/04/1998 Issue 680, pp. 50.

[7] Cremer, C. 1993. Information systems people: A valuable resource, *Business Quarterly*, Spring, Vol. 57 Issue 3 [sic], pp.121-125.

[8] DeConinck J.B. and Johnson J.T. 2009. The Effects of Perceived Supervisor Support, Perceived Organizational Support, and Organizational Justice on Turnover Among Salespeople. *Journal of Personal Selling and Sales Management*, Vol. 29, No. 4 (Fall 2009), pp. 333 - 351

[9] Goldstein, D.K. and Rockart J.F. 1984. An Examination of Work-Related Correlates of Job Satisfaction in Programmer/Analysts. *MIS Quarterly* **8**(2), pp. 103-115.

[10] Hogan J.J. 1992. Turnover and what to do about it, *The Cornell HRA Quarterly*. Vol. 33, No. 1, pp. 40-45.

[11] Igbaria, M. and Greenhaus, J.H. 1992. Determinants of MIS Employees' turnover intentions: A Structural Equation Model, *Communications of the ACM*, Vol. 35, No. 2, pp. 34-49.

[12] Inklaar, R. O., M., Timmer, M. 2005. ICT And Europe's Productivity Performance: Industry-Level Growth Account Comparisons With The United States, *Review of Income and Wealth*, v. 51, issue 4, pp. 505-36

[13] Internet World Stats, Botswana Internet Usage and Marketing Report. Retrieved October 23, 2008

URL: http://www.internetworldstats.com/af/bw.htm.

[14] Jackson, S.E., and Schuler, R.S. 1985. A meta-analysis and conceptual critique of research on role ambiguity and role conflict in work settings. *Organizational Behaviour and Human Decision Processes* 36, pp. 16-78.

[15] Jiang, J.J. 2000. Supervisor Support and Career Anchor Impact on the Career Satisfaction of the Entry-Level Information Systems Professional, *Journal of Management Information Systems*, Winter, Vol. 16 Issue 3, pp. 219-241.

[16] Jiang, J.J. and Klein, G.A. 2002. Discrepancy model of information system personnel turnover. *Journal of Management Information Systems*, *19*(2), pp. 249-272.

[17] Jiang, J.J., and Klein, G. 2003. A Discrepancy Model of IS Personnel Turnover. Journal of Management Information Systems (JMIS), 19 (2), pp. 251-274 (SSCI, IF 1.818)

[18] Joseph, D., Ng, K., Koh, C. 2007. Turnover of Information technology Professionals: A narrative review, meta-analytic structural equation modelling, and Model development, *MIS Quarterly*, Vol. 31, No. 3, pp. 547-577

[19] Lee, T.W. & Mitchell, T.R. 1994. An alternative approach: The unfolding model of voluntary employee turnover. *Academy of Management Review*, 19, pp. 51-89.

[20] Jung-Chul L., Youngjik L., Sang-Hun K., and Minsoo H. 1996. Intonation processing for TTS using stylization and neural network learning method. In 4th International Conference on Spoken Language Processing (*ICSLP-1996)*, pp. 1381-1384.

[21] Laumer, S and Eckhardt, A. 2010. Analyzing IT Personnel's Perception of Job-related Factors in Good and Bad Times In: Proceedings of the 2010 ACM SIGMIS CPR Conference; Vancouver, BC, Canada

[22] Lee, T.W., Mitchell, T.R., Holtom, B.C., McDaniel, L. S., and Hill, J.W. 1999. The unfolding model of voluntary turnover: A replication and extension. Academy of Management Journal, *42*(4), pp. 450-462.

[23] Love, P.E.D., Irani, Z. and Edwards, D.J. 2004. Industry-centric benchmarking of information technology benefits, costs and risks for small-to-medium sized enterprises in construction, Automation in Construction Vol. 13, No 4, pp. 507-524

[24] March, J., and Simon, H. 1958. A *Organizations*, Wiley, New York.

[25] Michaels C.E and Spector P.E. 1982. Causes of employee turnover: A test of the Mobley, Griffeth, Hand, and Meglino Model, Journal of Applied Psychology, Vol. 67, No. 1, pp. 53-59.

[26] Mitchell, T.R., and Lee, T.W. 2001. The unfolding model of voluntary turnover and job embeddedness: Foundations for a comprehensive theory of attachment. In B. M. Staw & R. I. Sutton (Eds.), Research in Organizational Behavior, Vol. 23,   pp 189-246). New York: JAI.

[27] Mobley, W.H. 1977. Intermediate Linkages in the Relationship between Job Satisfaction and Employee Turnover, Journal of Applied Psychology, vol.62, No.2, pp. 237-240.

[28] Mobley W, Horner S, and Hollingsworth, A. 1978. An evaluation of precursors of hospital employee turnover, Journal of Applied Psychology, Vol. 63, pp. 408-424.

[29] Muliawan A.D., Green P.F., and Robb D.A. 2009. The Turnover Intentions of Information Systems Auditors. International Journal of Accounting Information Systems. Volume 10, Vol. 3, (September 2009), pp. 117-136.

[30] Niederman, F., Sumner, M. and Maertz, C.P. 2006. An analysis and synthesis of research related to turnover among IT personnel', *Proceedings of ACM SIGMIS-CPR*, Claremont, CA, pp.130–136.

[31] Porter, L. W., and Steers, R. M. 1973, Organizational Work and Personal Factors in Employee Turnover and Absenteeism, Psychological Bulletin [80:2], pp. 151-176.

[32] Rouse, P. 2001. Voluntary turnover related to information technology professionals: A review of rational and instinctual models. International Journal of Organizational Analysis (9:3), pp. 281-291.

[33] Rutner, P.S., Hardgrave B.C., and McKnight D.H. 2008. Emotional Dissonance and the Information Technology Professional, *MIS Quarterly* 32(3), pp. 635-652.

[34] Tan, M. and Igbaria, M. 1993. Exploring the status of the turnover and salary of information technology professionals in Singapore, SIGCPR '93 Proceedings of the 1993 conference on Computer personnel research

[35] Termsnguanwong, S. 2009. Influence of viewpoints, job satisfaction on it workers Turnover: a study of northern region of Thailand, International Conference on the Role of Universities in Hands-On Education Rajamangala University of Technology, Lanna, Chiang-Mai, Thailand 23-29 August 2009

[36] Tiedemann, J., Taylor S., Fiorile R. and Sciarappa W. 2006. Vulnerable Wetlands and Associated Riparian Areas in the Shark River Estuary Watershed. US EPA Wetlands Protection Project Grant Final Report Monmouth University Centre for Coastal Watershed Management. W. Long Branch, N.J.

[37] Van Sell, M., Brief, A.P. and Schuler, R.S. 1981. Role Conflict and Role Ambiguity: Integration of the Literature and Directions for Future Research. Human Relations, Vol. 34 No. 1, pp. 43-71.

[38] World Bank; World Development Report Washington DC, 2009.

Challenges and Barriers Facing Women in the IS Workforce: How Far Have We Come?

Deborah J. Armstrong
Florida State University
djarmstrong@cob.fsu.edu

Cynthia K. Riemenschneider
Baylor University
c_riemenschneider@baylor.edu

Margaret F. Reid
University of Arkansas
mreid@uark.edu

Jason E. Nelms
Florida State University
jen10@fsu.edu

ABSTRACT

In 2006, Riemenschneider et al. asked women working in the IS department at a Fortune 500 company what workplace barriers they faced that had influenced their voluntary turnover decisions that men did not. The current investigation offers a replication and extension of the Riemenschneider et al. (2006) study. Specifically, this research begins to examine what changes have (or have not) taken place in the IS workplace regarding the challenges and barriers facing women in the IS field. Preliminary findings indicate that while *Barriers: Promotion, Managing Family Responsibilities, Work Schedule Flexibility, Work Stress* and *Turnover* were the key concepts identified by Riemenschneider et al. (2006), *Work Stress* is one of the few key issues that remains salient. What seems to be more salient for the current participants are issues related to the work environment, such as politics and bureaucracy (e.g., *Barriers: Politics*).

Categories and Subject Descriptors

K.7.1 Occupations; K.6.1 Project and People Management: Staffing; K.4.2 Social Issues: Employment

General Terms

Management

Keywords

IS Workforce, Gender, Barriers, Qualitative

1. INTRODUCTION

In December 2009, The Economist reported that women not only make up the majority of the professional workforce in many countries, but also that they earn nearly 60 percent of university degrees in America and Europe (Women in the Workforce: Female Power, 2009). Unfortunately, the statistics for women in the IS field are not so glowing. Only 18% of computer and information science degrees awarded in 2008 went to women, down from 37% in 1985, according to a study by the National

Center for Women & Information Technology, and about 56% of women in technical fields leave their jobs at the midlevel point, which is more than double the rate of men (Collett, 2010).

For almost a decade, researchers have sought to identify barriers to the retention of female IS employees (e.g., Ahuja, 2002; Trauth and Howcroft, 2006). Riemenschneider et al. (2006) studied female IS employees and identified key workplace barriers that often lead to voluntary turnover decisions (e.g., managing family responsibilities, stress, work schedule flexibility, job qualities, promotion barriers, discrimination and a lack of consistency on the part of management). The current investigation examines what changes have taken place regarding the barriers identified for women in the IS workplace four years later. Have the barriers facing women been removed? If so, why are women still underrepresented in the IS field and continue to leave the profession?

Both the 2006 study and the current research use the same qualitative methodological tool and an interpretivist perspective to identify respondents' cognitions regarding the perceived barriers. Consistent with the Riemenschneider et al. (2006) study, we asked women in the in-house IS department of one of the organizations used in the 2006 study to discuss what challenges they face that their male colleagues might not. What is reported here is the initial causal map evoked from the current respondents and a preliminary comparison to the previous work. A literature review is followed by a discussion of the method and then we conclude with our initial findings and an outline of the next steps.

2. LITERATURE REVIEW

In the first part of this longitudinal study, Riemenschneider et al. (2006) conducted a series of interviews aimed at uncovering women's perceptions of barriers they face in the IT field. The current study is a follow-up study to Riemenschneider et al. (2006) that aims to investigate perceptual changes, if any, which have occurred among women in the IT workforce.

In their initial literature review, Riemenschneider et al. (2006) focused on voluntary IT employee turnover, barriers in within the workplace, work-family conflict, and work stress. Since the original publishing, research on the topic of the barriers faced by women in IS has been limited. What has been published on the topic of gender and barriers/turnover in IS ranges from a discussion of parity in academia (Johnson et al., 2008; Lamp, 2007) to critical theory (Reid et al., 2010) to gender identity in the IS field (Adam et al., 2006; Woszczynski and Shade, 2010). With regard to retention and turnover scholars have utilized the individual differences theory of gender to explore retention (Trauth et al., 2009), and have examined differences in stress-related effects on turnover within the IS workforce such as burnout (Chilton et al., 2010; Chilton et al., 2005; Pawloski et al., 2007) and work overload (Ahuja et al., 2007) while addressing coping and adjustment among personnel in the ever-changing field of IS (Love and Irani, 2007).

Based on our review of the literature, it seems clear that the challenges facing women in the IS workforce is still a topic worthy of exploration. Women in IS continue to face glass ceilings and there is still no definitive explanation for the high levels of voluntary turnover. This research attempts to further clarify these issues by: 1) identifying the perceived workplace barriers women in IS experience; 2) identifying which barriers are related to turnover; and 3) determining the status of the barriers facing women in IS since first studied in 2006. The next section addresses the methodology we employed to explore the phenomenon.

3. METHOD

Using a social constructionist perspective (e.g., Berger and Luckmann, 1966; Dick and Nadin, 2006) and a qualitative data analysis method we seek to elucidate and graphically represent the emergent cognitions evoked from group interaction. From the cognitive representations we identify the unique challenges facing women in IS (content) and the organization of these challenges (structure) within the participants' mental models (Nadkarni and Narayanan, 2005).

What is presented here is part of a larger project that looks at IS workers' perceptions of challenges faced in the IS workplace. The researchers started investigating similar issues in 2002, and this study follows previous studies on similar topics. We conducted five focus groups with women working in the IS department at the headquarters of the same organization as previously explored. Participants were identified by the CIO and recruited via email invitation and the contact person within the organization handled the room scheduling and invitation process. The focus groups were held during working hours in on-site conference rooms. The organization, FoodCo (a pseudonym), is one of the world's largest processors and marketers of protein, and the second-largest food production company in the Fortune 500. The company has approximately 117,000 team members at more than 400 facilities and offices in the United States and around the world.

Our participants were 15 female IS workers, which, while small, is consistent with sample sizes in other qualitative studies (e.g., Gershon et al. 2004). Job titles of the participants included Business Analyst, Database Administrator, Organizational Change Specialist and Director of Business Process Change, to name a few. Due to the nature of some topics discussed in the larger study, and to increase interviewee trust in the researchers, a decision was made to gather limited demographic information from the participants.

The focus group interviews, which ranged from 45 to 65 minutes, were tape recorded and then transcribed verbatim. The responses to the question, "Do you think women in the IS workplace face different challenges than men? Please explain." provided the data for this study. To ensure confidentiality each participant was given a number, and asked to use those numbers instead of each other's names in the conversation. Two researchers were present for each focus group. The researchers were trained in group

interview techniques to promote consistency and reduce interviewer variance. While differences in the evoked mental models could be attributed to the different researchers, we do not believe this to be the case. The interview guide was strictly adhered to by the researchers as confirmed in the verbatim transcriptions. While steps were taken to mitigate researcher bias in the data collection and analysis processes, the researchers acknowledge that they are representing the concepts identified by the participants as experienced through their own subjectivity.

3.1 Data Analysis

In the data analysis phase our task was to elicit the relevant concepts from what participants said regarding the unique challenges women in IS profession face and map these concepts into a structural representation. We used revealed causal mapping (RCM), a multi-step process previously described in the literature (e.g., Narayanan and Armstrong, 2005; Riemenschneider et al., 2006) to access the salient concepts and cognitive connections between the concepts. This analytical technique has been applied in a wide variety of disciplines and has been applied in various ways to the IS discipline (e.g., Lee and Kwon, 2008; Nelson et al., 2000; Siau and Tan, 2005; Tegarden and Sheetz, 2003). Due to space limitations, much of the detail regarding the method has been omitted. Interested readers should refer to Riemenschneider et al. (2006), or Narayanan and Armstrong (2005) for details of the revealed causal mapping method. We provide an abbreviated description of the method here.

The four major steps in RCM are gathering the narratives from the focus groups, identifying the causal statements through the use of keywords (e.g., because, so, if-then) (Axelrod, 1976), separating the statements into the 'effect' and 'cause', and developing a coding scheme. A total of 132 causal statements were identified in the transcripts. In the coding process, frequently mentioned words in the statements are grouped together (Narayanan and Fahey, 1990), and a word or word group (i.e., concept label) summarizes the statements. The researchers assign the concept labels; however the concepts themselves emerge from the participants through the phrases captured in the language of the participants. As this study is a comparison to a previous study, the coding scheme developed in the first study was used. Any disagreements among the researchers regarding identification of a statement or the coding of those statements are resolved through discussion leading to a 100% level of agreement. The maps are drawn by replacing the participants' phrases with the concept labels.

Once the maps are drawn, measures for the analysis and comparison of the maps are developed: adjacency, which represents the strength of the direct linkage (relationship) between two concepts and contained values between 0 and 10, indicating the frequency (number) of mentions of this relationship; reachability, which includes both the direct and indirect effects of one concept on another; and centrality, which is the ratio of the direct linkages involving the concept divided by the total number of linkages in the map (Knoke and Kuklinski, 1982). While the adjacency matrix provides the foundation, the reachability matrix allows a more holistic picture of the causal relationships and thus the reachability numbers are reported on the line between the concepts on the causal map. Centrality measures how central or involved the concept is in the map, and is calculated as the ratio of the direct linkages involving the concept divided by the total number linkages in the map.

4. PRELIMINARY RESULTS

Per the social constructionist perspective, we do not claim to have *the* interpretation of the data, but *an* interpretation grounded in our understanding of the literature and the data. Descriptions of the key concepts that emerged are included in the Appendix.

4.1 Map Content and Structure

Figure 1a shows the aggregate map that reveals 31 concepts that the participants in the focus groups identified as the unique challenges facing women in the IS profession. Of the 31 concepts, the participants identified eight concepts specifically as barriers, and five concepts directly related to turnover. The remaining concepts identified were focused around the workplace environment and work-family balance issues. Recall that reachability is a measure of the strength of connection between two concepts, and the concepts shown on the map in Figure 1a are a result of using a reachability cutoff of >0.100. This cutoff value allows a maximum inclusiveness of concepts within the constraint of map readability. The reachability is indicated by the number next to the arrow on the map, and takes into account all paths (both direct and indirect) from one concept to another. The concepts with the highest reachability (i.e., strongest relationship) are between the *Positive Comments* concept and the *Opportunities* concept (1.000), followed by *Negative Comments* and *Stress* (.405), *Work Stress* and *Negative Comments* (.401), and *Barriers: Women's Characteristics* and *Barriers: Politics* (.400) and *Barriers: Women's Characteristics* and *Barriers: Respect* (.400).

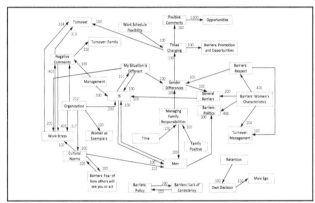

Figure 1a. Current Revealed Causal Map

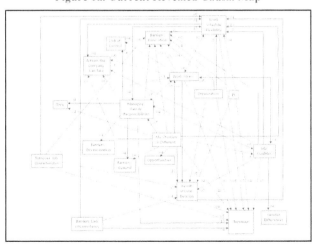

Figure 1b. Previous Revealed Causal Map

Some of the concepts are more central than others. Recall that a high centrality measure means that the concept is at the core of the mental model. The concepts possessing the highest centrality are *IS* (.778), then *Negative Comments* and *Work Stress* (.667), followed by *Cultural Norms, Men, Organization, Times Changing, and Gender Differences* (.556). The centrality data are presented in Table 1.

Table 1. Map Comparison Data

Measure	Previous Map	(a)	Current Map	(b)
Reachability	MFR → Turnover	.100	PC → Opportunities	1.000
	MSD → Turnover	.100	NC → Work Stress	.405
	MSD → ROD	.100	Work Stress → NC	.401
	MSD → WSF	.100	WC → Barriers: Politics	.400
	MFR → WSF	.100	WC → Barriers: Respect	.400
Centrality	Barriers: Promotion	.999	IS	.078
	Turnover	.940	Work Stress	.067
	Work Stress	.789	NC	.067
	MFR	.789	Cultural Norms	.056
	WSF	.752	Organization	.056
	Job Qualities	.752	Men	.056

MFR = Managing Family Responsibilities; MSD = My Situation is Different; ROD = Result of Own Decision; WSF = Work Schedule Flexibility; PC = Positive Comments; NC = Negative Comments; WC = Women's Characteristics

4.2 Initial Comparison & Next Steps

The map developed by Riemenschneider et al. (2006) is included as Figure 1b. There are 14 concepts in common for the two maps, 17 concepts appearing on the current map that did not appear previously, and there are five concepts on the previous map that were not articulated by the current respondents. Of the new concepts, five are focused on barriers faced by the women. There are only three relationships in common: between *Work Stress* and *Turnover*, between *Time and Managing Family Responsibilities*, and between *My Situation is Different* and *Work Stress*.

The reachability and centrality numbers are map/sample specific and cannot be directly compared. For example, centrality is the ratio of the concept linkages divided by the total linkages in the map. As the total number of linkages in the previous map was different than the number in the current map, the scale is different. The key to comparing the numbers is the relative order. Interestingly, when comparing the centrality numbers for the two groups, there is very little overlap. For example, *IS* was not mentioned on the previous map, and yet it is the most central concept in the new map. In contrast, *Work Stress* was in the second tier of centrality in the previous map, and remains in the second tier in the current map. Thus, it seems clear that *Work Stress* is the one constant across time.

When we combine the reachability and centrality measures we see that *Barriers: Promotion, Managing Family Responsibilities,*

Work Schedule Flexibility, Work Stress and *Turnover* were the key concepts identified by Riemenschneider et al. (2006). In contrast, while *Work Stress* remains a key issue, what seems to be more salient for the current participants are issues related to the organization, such as politics and bureaucracy (e.g., *Barriers: Politics*).

It is important to note that at the time of the data collection, FoodCo was engaged in a multi-pronged change process with initiatives ranging from expansions in production capacity to turnover within the Board of Directors and executive personnel. Also, during the time of data collection, FoodCo worked extensively on its Team Member Bill of Rights (TMBR) and statement of core values. Several aspects of FoodCo's TMBR that are relevant to our topic of study include the right to be free from discrimination, the right to compensation for work performed, and the right to continued training including supervisory training.

The authors are in the process of further analyzing and interpreting the current data collection, comparing the current findings to the previous findings, and exploring theories within which to frame the findings. We hope to further refine the initial model developed by Riemenschneider et al. (2006) and contribute to the practice of managing IS personnel.

5. ADDRESS INFORMATION

Florida State University, College of Business, Management Department, PO Box 3061110, Tallahassee, FL, USA, 32306-1110, 01 850 644 8228; Baylor University, Hankamer School of Business, Information Systems Department, Waco, TX, USA, 76798, 01 254 710 4061; University of Arkansas, Department of Political Science, Fulbright College of Arts and Sciences, Fayetteville, AR, USA, 72701, 01 479 575 3356.

6. REFERENCES

[1] Adam, A., Griffith, M., Keogh, C., and Moore, K. 2006. Being an 'it' in IT: Gendered identities in IT work. *European Journal of Information Systems* 15, 4 (August, 2006), 368-378.

[2] Ahuja, M. 2002. Women in the information technology profession: A literature review, synthesis, and research agenda. *European Journal of Information Systems* 11, 1 (March, 2002), 20–34.

[3] Ahuja, M. K., Chudoba, K. M., Kacmar, C. J., McKnight, D. H., and George, J. F. 2007. IT road warriors: Balancing work-family conflict, job autonomy, and work overload to mitigate turnover intentions. *MIS Quarterly* 31, 1 (March, 2007), 1-17.

[4] Axelrod, R. 1976. *The Structure of Decisions*. Princeton University Press, Princeton, NJ.

[5] Berger, P. L., and Luckmann, T. 1966. *The Social Construction of Reality: A Treatise in the Sociology of Knowledge*. Doubleday, New York, NY.

[6] Chilton, M. A., Hardgrave, B. and Armstrong, D. J. 2005. Person-job cognitive style fit for software developers: The effect on strain and performance. *Journal of Management Information Systems* 22, 2 (September, 2005), 193-226.

[7] Chilton, M. A., Hardgrave, B. C. and Armstrong, D. J. 2010. Performance and strain levels of IT workers engaged in rapidly changing environments: A person-job fit perspective.

Database for Advances in Information Systems 41, 1 (February, 2010), 8-35.

[8] Collett, S. 2010. The shrinking female IT workforce. *Computerworld*, April 5, 2010. Retrieved 10/19/2010 from: http://www.reuters.com/article/idUS369938076220100405.

[9] Dick, P., and Nadin, S. 2006. Reproducing gender inequalities? A critique of realist assumptions underpinning personnel selection research and practice. *Journal of Occupational and Organizational Psychology* 79, 3 (September, 2006), 481-498.

[10] Gershon, A., Gowen, L. K., Compian, L., and Hayward, C. 2004. Gender-stereotyped imagined dates and weight concerns in sixth-grade girls. *Sex Roles: A Journal of Research* 50, 7-8 (April, 2004), 515-523.

[11] Johnson, R. D., Veltri, N. F., and Hornik, S. 2008. Attributions of responsibility toward computing technology: The role of interface social cues and user gender. *International Journal of Human-Computer Interaction* 24, 6 (August, 2008), 595 – 612.

[12] Knoke, K., and Kuklinski, J.H. 1982. *Network Analysis: Quantitative Applications in the Social Sciences*. Sage University Paper Series 07-028. Sage Publications, Beverly Hills, CA.

[13] Lamp, J. W. 2007. Perceptions of gender balance of IS journal editorial positions. *Communications of the Association for Information Systems* 20, 1 (November, 2007), 124-133.

[14] Lee, K. and Kwon, S. 2008. Online shopping recommendation mechanism and its influence on consumer decisions and behaviors: A causal map approach. *Expert Systems with Applications* 35, 4 (November, 2008), 1567-1574.

[15] Love, P. E. and Irani, Z. 2007. Coping and psychological adjustment among information technology personnel. *Industrial Management and Data Systems* 107, 6, (2007), 824-844.

[16] Nadkarni, S. and Narayanan, V. K. 2005. Validity of the structural properties of text-based causal maps: An empirical assessment. Organizational Research Methods 8, 1 (January, 2005), 9-40.

[17] Narayanan, V. K. and Armstrong, D. J. 2005. *Causal Mapping for Research in Information Technology*. Idea Group Publishing, Hershey, PA.

[18] Nelson, K. M., Nadkarni, S., Narayanan, V. K., and Ghods, M. 2000. Understanding software operations support expertise: A causal mapping approach. *MIS Quarterly* 24, 3 (September, 2000), 475-507.

[19] Pawlowski, S. D., Kaganer, E. A. and Cater III, J. J. 2007. Focusing the research agenda on burnout in IT: Social representations of burnout in the profession. *European Journal of Information Systems* 16, 5 (October, 2007), 612-627.

[20] Reid, M. F., Allen, M. W., Armstrong, D. J., and Riemenschneider, C. K. 2010. Perspectives on challenges facing women in IS: The cognitive gender gap. *European Journal of Information Systems* 19, 5 (October, 2010), 526-539.

[21] Riemenschneider, C. K., Armstrong, D. J., Allen, M. W., and Reid, M. F. 2006. Barriers facing women in the IT work force. *Database for Advances in Information Systems* 37, 4 (October, 2006), 58-79.

[22] Siau, K. and Tan, X. 2005. Technical communication in IS development: The use of cognitive mapping. *IEEE Transactions on Profession Communication* 48, 3 (September, (2005), 269-284.

[23] Tegarden, D. P. and Sheetz, S. D. 2003. Group cognitive mapping: A methodology and system for capturing and evaluating managerial and organizational cognition. *Omega* 31, 2 (April, 2003), 113-125.

[24] Trauth, E. M. and Howcroft, D. 2006. Critical empirical research in IS: An example of gender and the IT workforce. *Information, Technology & People* 19, 3 (2006) 272-292.

[25] Trauth, E. M., Quesenberry, J. L., and Huang, H. 2009. Retaining women in the U.S. IT workforce: Theorizing the influence of organizational factors. *European Journal of Information Systems* 18, 5 (October, 2009), 476-497.

[26] Woszczynski, A. B. and Shade, S. 2010. A call to IS educators to respond to the voices of women in information security. *Journal of Information Systems Education* 21, 2 (June, 2010), 223-231.

[27] Women in the workforce: Female power. *The Economist*, December 30, 2009. Retrieved November 1, 2010, from http://www.economist.com/node/15174418.

7. APPENDIX

Brief descriptions of the core concepts that emerged from the participants with sample phrases captured in the language of the respondents are included here. The concept labels listed below were developed to capture the essence of the participants' phrases.

Actions the Company Can Take
Description: Actions the company can take to solve problems, increase performance, bring in new blood. Examples: "Your computer hook up from home to the mainframe," "Stagnant management holders are moved out"

Barriers: Discrimination
Description: Examples of people not being treated equally; statements about how things are not fair; discrimination in terms of the money they receive. Examples: "They don't see that we need to be paid for what we do for our position," "My increases stopped when I moved into IT"

Barriers: General
Description: Barriers they are experiencing in the workplace that do not fit into any of the more specific barriers. Examples: "You have more people in your group," "I don't live really close"

Barriers: Lack of Consistency
Description: Comments about a lack of consistency at the organizational level, a lack of consistency on the part of the supervisor in how treats employees, how some people in the department get treated a certain way and not others, how different supervisors do different things. Examples: "Each manager feels a totally separate way," "it depends on the manager"

Barriers: Management
Description: Deals with upper management's attitudes, beliefs and actions which seem problematic for women; ineffective management. Examples: "Then there's also management, higher up that I deal with" "They're the ones that are approving the projects"

Barriers: Policy
Description: Lack of policies, or policies not followed. Examples: "There is no overarching policy" "Some people want to work part-time, but aren't allowed to cause it depends on your job"

Barriers: Politics
Description: Informal interaction with management; schmoozing; need to be political. Examples: "I wouldn't be able to go out to lunch with my team" "you're not going to cut it on the team"

Barriers: Promotion
Description: Problems being promoted; lack of criteria for promotion; arbitrary promotion decisions; anything that casts problems with promotion as a potential barrier. References to glass ceiling go here. Examples: "When I look up there are just not that many spots," "How they decide who gets promoted isn't really clear to everyone"

Barriers: Respect/Men Taking Control
Description: Feeling not listened to or not treated with consideration or respect. Also includes the desire for more autonomy (e.g., signing yourself in or out of work, setting own schedule, as long as it is identified as a problem). Examples: "Some of the men overpower and step in and compensate," "I had enough of not being recognized."

Barriers: Women's Characteristics
Description: Failure to communicate effectively; personality traits; anything that puts blame on women; self-doubt. Examples: "If I liked girly girl stuff" "If they may be teary-eyed, then its frowned upon by the male peers"

Cultural Norms
Description: Informal knowledge that shapes the employees behavior; how things are done. Examples: "you're just gonna put in 45 hours" "IS gets paid at that rate"

Gender Differences
Description: Express discussion of there being a gender difference - maybe in how they are treated, interest areas they like, different emotions, and the way they deal with stress. Direct comparisons of men and women. Examples: "This girl came to my department. The guy in front of her was salaried. She was hourly," "Women kind of have a different mindset than men do"

Information Systems (IS)
Description: Reference to job, getting job done, special programs, projects, job duties; characteristic of IT; move into IT. Examples: "If you are developing systems," "We are in the middle of a networking project"

Job Qualities
Description: Positive job-related qualities, positively viewed actions, qualities needed, skill sets, positive qualities in someone; relationship with someone where feel comfortable or positive. Examples: "I can say a lot of good things for the people who are willing to go those extra hours to meet that customer demand," "I learned the system and hit the ground running"

Lack of Control
Description: This is how things are, this is what I have seen, cannot change it, take what you can get; situation described as out of control, just coincidence; denials and disclaimers. Examples: "I don't know who is getting paid what," "You can't change it."

Managing Family Responsibilities
Description: Women do the most of the child rearing. Include here unless identified as why a woman left a job or if talk about the choice to have a family being a decision they had made. Examples: "It's kind of expected that the Mom will take care of things," "If the family is more important, which it should be"

Men
Description: Male activities and interests; things men can do that married women or mothers cannot. Examples: "They tend to play golf and baseball together" "It's easy for them to work 'til 7:00 every night"

My Situation is Different
Description: Says their situation is different or that they cannot relate to what is being discussed. Generally they will say "my situation is different". Also, this includes when they mention a situation facing a specific individual or mention specific people when the comment can't be coded any other way. Examples: "She had different circumstances," "My users don't tend to, they may try, but they don't push me around that much"

Negative Comments
Description: Statements regarding negative emotions such as: beat down, irritated; negative situations, dilemma. Examples: "turmoil creates demoralization" "we weren't happy"

Opportunities
Description: New, growth or promotion opportunities; broaden horizons; challenging job. Examples: "Our job is very challenging," "We don't do the same thing two days in a row"

Organization
Description: References to company size, changes, number of buildings, or other companies / comparisons. Examples: "the whole matrix organization" "a lot of change in the organization"

Positive Comments
Description: Statements regarding positive emotions such as: happy, love, interesting, like what I do; feel better. Examples: "getting it done," "we were successful," "they were a lot happier."

Result of Own Decision
Description: Make decisions that move their career from being their primary interest; people are responsible for their own decisions; people show different levels of initiative; includes statements of decision to remain in organization / position; statements indicating they take control of their career. Examples: "I think everybody who has children makes that decision," "I personally have made that decision [to put family first]"

Time
Description: Mentions of time either as problems or simply hours worked. Examples: "Now you have to work just 6:30am until 3:30pm or 7:00am to 4:00pm"

Turnover
Description: Statements about leaving an organization. Examples: "A very good employee that was going to leave the company," "Otherwise they just come in, get the training, and go"

Turnover: Family
Description: Left organization or IS due to family considerations like change in family status or family pressure. Examples: "A few women have left when they've had their second child"

Turnover: Job Characteristics
Description: Comments indicating an employee left a job because she was either bored, stressed out, overloaded, not acquiring needed new skills, job or projects were unclear, worked long hours, or had too much challenge on the job. Examples: "If you are stuck in old technology," "I was on call 24 hours a day 7 days a week"

Turnover: Management
Description: Left organization or IS group because management was inattentive, unfair, ineffective or inappropriate. Examples: "The good ol' boys thing kind of shoved her out of IT," "I was tired of working for people who were sitting around waiting to retire."

Work Schedule Flexibility
Description: Positive ability to have flexible work schedules. Positive statements regarding breaking rules, asking for flexibility, flexibility exists, autonomy, personal business, part of give and take, or choice. Examples: "If they have personal things that they need to leave and do, then they go do it," "I wanted to work part-time and still get some pay during that time"

Work Stress
Description: Direct statements regarding stress or descriptions of elements within the working environment that are stressful. May include long work hours, problems with competing demands, things moving at Internet speed or competition. Examples: "I'm definitely over committed," "I couldn't take any more change right now," "It's a competition to move up."

Researching the Older IT Professional: Methodological Challenges and Opportunities

Michelle L. Kaarst-Brown
School of Information Studies
Syracuse University
Syracuse, NY 13244, USA
mlbrow03@syr.edu

Johanna L.H. Birkland
School of Information Studies
Syracuse University
Syracuse, NY 13244, USA
jlbirkla@syr.edu

ABSTRACT
Many developed nations' populations are aging. For workplaces, this has two important implications: organizations face an increasingly older workforce, at the same time that they experience a higher level of retirements. Both of these factors suggest some dramatic implications for those studying the workplace that must be considered. Regrettably, findings show that age-based research on older adults' experiences with technology is severely lacking (Birkland & Kaarst-Brown, 2007). To help address this gap, this paper reviews the sampling, ethical, and methodological implications for those who seek to study IT professionals and IT use in the aging workplace.

Categories and Subject Descriptors
K.7.1 The Computing Profession: Occupations

General Terms: Human Factors, Measurement.

Keywords: IT Workforce, IS/IT Professionals, Older Adults, Careers, Research, Sampling, Methodology.

1. INTRODUCTION

Most developed societies around the world are aging rapidly. In the U.S., it is estimated that the population age 65 and older is expected to grow from 12.97% of the population to 20.17% of the population by 2050 (U.S. Census Bureau, 2008). As the population ages, our workforce ages as well, and there is increased pressure to maintain employees beyond the traditional age of retirement. Many employers in the U.S. are just starting to realize the importance of older employees (Hedge, Borman, & Lammlein, 2006). In Europe, increased awareness of aging issues has included a raising of the retirement age in many countries, as well as goals of increasing the percentage of older adults in the workplace (European Foundation for the Improvement of Living and Working Conditions, 2007).

It is increasingly acknowledged by many practitioners that the looming changes their organizations face due to boomer retirement (those born between 1946 and 1964, Carlson, 2009)

will also result in problems in knowledge management and retention (DeLong, 2004). Additionally, as more boomers intend to work longer, issues regarding technological retraining will arise. Organizations will have to determine how they can use information technology to facilitate knowledge retention, mentoring between older and younger workers, and accommodate older workers who choose to remain in a position beyond the traditional age of retirement. We argue that as the workforce ages, it will become even more important to maintain older IT workers, particularly as fewer younger workers become available due to population aging and ongoing shortages of skilled IT professionals.

Although the focus of the Special Interest Group on Computer Personnel Research (SIG-MIS-CPR) is typically on recruiting and maintaining younger workers, in this changing environment it will become even more important for organizations to maintain the workforce they currently have in this aging society. Beyond a generic focus on "retention" is the issue of how to sustain and motivate a productive IT workforce as it ages or becomes increasingly multi-generational. Maintaining older workers becomes especially important considering that these individuals have valuable knowledge and expertise that often leaves the organization when they retire (Hedge et al., 2006). Organizations will also seek to continue to develop these employee's skills and knowledge, understanding that their valuable contributions to the workplace will continue even beyond current knowledge and skills (Salkowitz, 2008).

With a higher portion of older workers remaining in the workforce, workforces will also become more generationally diverse. Workplaces will no longer be made up of just three generations (with the eldest generation leaving the workforce at the same time the youngest enters), but instead could contain as many as four or five actively working generations at once. Generational perspectives and issues surrounding technology use will be important to understand in this age-diversified environment.

Beyond design issues found in traditional organizational IT workforce research, there are several specific methodological challenges associated with the study of aging and older IT professionals that information systems researchers need to consider (Birkland & Kaarst-Brown, 2010). This paper reviews some of the particular research issues surrounding studying older workers in the IT environment, including some unique sampling and methodological concerns. We argue that further research must be done not only on older workers, but also that researchers who study the workforce (including IT professionals) must ensure that older workers (an increasingly important part of the workplace) are captured in their studies.

Throughout this paper, a discussion of the issues regarding studying older adults in the workplace draws heavily upon a multi-disciplinary meta-analysis of 622 published journal articles from the past 20 years. The goal of this previous study was to identify the breadth and depth of the literature on older adults and ICTs, including the topics researched, methods used, theoretical backgrounds, and the ICTs studied. Papers for this meta-analysis were gathered from an extensive search of 10 databases using combinations of terms for "ICTs" (information technology, computer, pc, email, etc.) and "older adults" (such as senior, elderly, older adult, etc.). The top IS journals (according the Association of Information Systems (AIS)) were also independently searched for relevant articles using the same search terms. Only research, literature review, and conceptual articles are included in this analysis (popular literature is not included).

2. THE WORK ENVIRONMENT: SAMPLING ISSUES

There are several unique sampling issues that must be considered when a researcher is studying older adult workers. This includes issues surrounding having older adults as a sample (or as part of a sample of workers in general), stereotypes, and fears of retribution associated with participation in the study.

2.1 Older Adults as a Sample

Older adults have some unique features as a sample that become especially important in the organizational context. Older adults in the United States, as a group, are extremely diverse in terms of ethnicity (Hayes-Bautista, Hsu, Perez, & Gamboa, 2002) and cognitive abilities due to differing changes in cognitive abilities as we age (Finkel, Reynolds, McArdle, & Pedersen, 2007; Reynolds, Finkel, Gatz, & Pedersen, 2002). Since an age definition is often used as the cutoff for an older adult sample (typically age 65 and older in many studies), this means that several different birth cohorts (commonly referred to as generations) can be "older adults" at any given time. These generations may have had very different experiences with technology, initial training for their fields, knowledge, and vested experiences with various organizational systems.

Older adults in any workplace will similarly be a very diverse group due to different work-life trajectories, even when a younger age cutoff is used. These life trajectories include different roles in the workplace, which tend to be particularly prominent for individuals once they are past the traditional age of retirement. While one would expect younger or middle aged individuals to be working full time, older adults in the workplace may be working full-time, part-time, or in other roles such as part-time consultants. Some of these choices are due to financial needs (the necessity to keep working), health requirements (working to maintain health coverage or working only part time because of health issues), and/or due to personal desires (to keep working for social interaction or to have time to follow other interests) (Hedge et al., 2006).

Another consideration in studying older adults as a group is that as a sample, *the older adult population changes over time as birth cohorts/generations age*. Therefore, the older adult population changes as younger generations age into "elderhood". Cultural values and perceptions about ICT's change over time as individuals are exposed to different

knowledge and experiences (Martin, 1995; Sackmann 1992; Kaarst-Brown 1995). As an example, current IT professionals over the age of 50 were not born into the microprocessor or Internet era – in fact color televisions were not the norm in many childhood homes. Conversely, in twenty years, those IT workers 50 years of age and older will never remember a time when they could not access information through a computer. From a generational perspective, most IT workers *currently 30 years of age and younger* cannot remember such a time! We rarely consider that repeated sampling of "older adults" may yield quite different "samples", but *comparatively* valuable information.

2.2 Stereotypes of Older Workers

As researchers, we work to reduce bias in our studies. In IT workforce studies of older workers, the bias from stereotypes is a very real challenge. Until one has actually reached a certain age, it is often difficult to understand the many stereotypes that come into play as we become "older". Stereotypes of older individuals regrettably abound, and have been found to be particularly prevalent in the workplace environment. Stereotypes about older workers have included that they are incapable of using new technologies (Larwood, Rodkin, & Judson, 2001; Larwood, Ruben, Popoff, & Judson, 1997), are unwilling or unable to adapt to changes in the workplace (Rix, 2001), and cannot learn new procedures or new technologies (Larwood et al., 2001; Larwood et al., 1997; Rosow & Zager, 1980; Simon, 1996).

Research has even shown that managers believe older workers are less efficient than their peers (Rosen & Jerdee, 1985). All of these stereotypes *have been proven untrue*, but despite this evidence, they are still pervasive in our work environments and greater society (Hedge et al., 2006). While we may think that some of these stereotypes could not possibly apply to the IT worker, the sad reality is that many older employees are viewed differently once they reach a certain age or if there is significant age disparity with other groups of workers, regardless of their department, skill, set or prior contributions to the organization.

These stereotypes of older adults can be seen to have three potential impacts on our research on older IT workers: access issues, validity of our results due to internalization of these stereotypes, and the introduction of our own bias into our research.

2.2.1 *Stereotypes and Access Issues*

First, as a result of these stereotypes about older workers, it is quite possible that managers may resist (either consciously or unconsciously) introducing older adults as possible research participants in studies. Therefore, older IT workers who might have important insights into research questions associated with IT workforce development, motivation, retention and other issues may be left out of the study because managers believe they would be less unimportant or valuable based on their interpretation of the researcher goals (or their own objectives).

Similarly, despite knowing and working with older workers and IT professionals, younger managers in particular (or managers from a different generational cohort) may unconsciously hold stereotypes about their older workers, and therefore not suggest including any individuals they believe to be resistant to changing technology, incapable of learning new systems, or those soon-to-retire. Stereotypes can be very deeply ingrained, and managers (and researchers) may not even realize that they are making these assumptions. Researchers should detail the sample they are seeking to important persons providing access to the organization, and emphasize that they are also very interested in including older workers, particularly if they are interested in older adults or in generational issues associated with attracting, developing and retaining quality IT professionals.

For example, although she did so anyway, one of the authors was discouraged from talking to an older woman in her early 60's because this employee was well known to express her personal dislike of computers and criticism of a highly touted and very expensive new personnel system. Several management and junior personnel explained that they "did not want the researcher to waste her time" (Kaarst-Brown, 1995).

Older adult employees also face some unique issues. As people delay childbirth and live longer, more individuals are finding themselves involved in multi-generational living environments where they are caring for their children and their parents at the same time (Spillman & Pezzin, 2000). Many older individuals may find themselves working, while caring for other family members. These individuals may have additional stresses outside of their work lives, which impact their abilities (or perceived ability) to participate in studies within the workplace. Conversely, co-workers aware of these situations may similarly steer researchers away from these individuals.

Given that management support in organizations is important for researchers, we need to be aware that there may be some bias in the actual selection of individuals for the research projects, or implicit bias in those selected for training for a device or system due to stereotypes in the workplace regarding older adults and their inability to use or learn new technology.

2.2.2 Stereotypes and Validity Issues

A second way in which these stereotypes can impact our studies is in the validity of our findings. Studies have found that stereotypes regarding older adults' ability to learn or use technologies is often internalized by older adults (Maurer, Wrenn, & Weiss, 2003). Therefore, older adults tend to understate their technological skills and knowledge, especially when compared to younger individuals (Marquié, Jourdan-Boddaert, & Huet, 2002). If a researcher is relying on self-report methods, they may find that older adults are underrating their skills compared to younger individuals. As a result of these biased reports, researchers may find it difficult to reliably determine technological usage, skills, or efficacy. By extension, older adults may be more hesitant to participate in research where they know technological topics will be discussed because they have internalized negative stereotypes. Ideally, researchers in these situations should rely on other sources of data beyond self-reports to access skills and use, such as observation, testing, and reviewing log files. With the older IT professional, these issues translate to potential concerns that they may not be as skilled with new technologies and would compare less favorably with younger IT workers.

2.2.3 Stereotypes and Researcher Bias

Finally, it is important to recognize that these pervasive stereotypes also impact our role as a researcher. Our own stereotypes about older workers may interfere with our data collection and analysis. Researchers will need to examine their own biases and stereotypes about this population throughout all phases of the study and determine how it might be impacting

their conclusions. Kaarst-Brown and Guzman (2010) argued that attributing *"different cultural attitudes toward ICT's as being 'generational differences' is a 'broad brush' explanation that overlooks many important multi-level cultural differences* within *generational groups".*

Even if researchers are *not* specifically focused on age or generational factors, we strongly encourage checking samples and comparing the ages of participants against other information that the organization provides about the age makeup of their IT and overall workforce. Researchers may need to actively seek individuals based upon this information, rather than relying on managers to recommend individuals or assuming a representative sample based on random responses. In our aging society, we do ourselves, our participants, and the users of our research a major disservice if we ignore *the age diversity* in the IT workforce of any organization we study.

2.3 Fears of Retribution in the Workplace Environment

Older adults are more likely to be laid off than younger workers during economic downturns. Once an older IT worker is laid off, it is a sad fact that they are less successful in finding work, particularly work in a similar position to the one they left (AARP, 2010). Many older adults may be afraid that their inclusion in research – particularly if they are selected as the sole population or a target group of the study – is an attempt by management to identify individuals for justification of layoffs or firings. Older workers may actively avoid contact with the researcher, limiting a researchers' access to this important part of the population.

Conversely, older workers, including IT professionals, may feel that they *must* participate in research because of fear and concerns about the consequences if they do not participate, even if they are uncomfortable with the study due to perceived or actual pressure from their supervisors. These participants may not be forthcoming or honest in their answers, again for fear of retribution by their employers. Given the fact that the older worker population is disproportionally impacted by layoffs, these concerns are valid, even if they are not justified based upon the subject of the researchers' project.

A significant part of the researchers' work in these types of environments should be focused on educating individuals about the goals of the research and reassuring employees that the researcher is not providing information that could be used in potential layoffs. Additionally, a researcher should be cautious in these environments to ensure that their research presence is not being unfairly used to stereotype older IT workers or used to facilitate or justify disproportional layoffs of older IT workers.

3. METHODOLOGICAL ISSUES

Normally, we would include the broader issue of research design before a discussion of sampling; however, given the specific focus on the older spectrum of workers and IT professionals as a sample, we see fit to discuss the other methodological challenges and opportunities after the sampling discussion. This is also consistent with our previous assertions that we not only need studies that specifically examine older workers, but also to be mindful to ensure that older workers are not excluded from our work because of some of the issues raised above. We need to ensure that we are using methods that are equally assessable and reliable for the entire workplace, rather than favoring younger workers (and therefore biasing our results).

As noted above, older adults may be different in many ways beyond the cultural variations among generational cohorts – their breadth and depth of training with many generations of ICT's, lived experience over decades of change in one or more organizational settings, as well as real differences in physiological and cognitive styles.

As one example, research has shown that older and younger adults differ in their cognitive skills, with older adults often being characterized as having *more crystallized intelligence* (including knowledge about relationships, practices, and networks), and younger individuals having *more fluid intelligence* (such as problem solving skills) (Cattell, 1971; Cavanaugh & Blanchard-Fields, 2006). This, among other things, has implications for the design and focus of many types of organizational studies, not just those that include multi-generational samples. (Ironically, as noted in table 1 below, many of the designs and data collection methods used in studies of older adults may actually be better suited to younger persons.)

For IT researchers interested in attraction, retention, and development of the IT workforce, perhaps one of the biggest challenges and opportunities in studying the older IT worker is that there are few studies and limited prior "maps" to follow in how to design studies of older adults. As a result, there are very few studies in organizational settings to which to compare, analyze for gaps, or draw upon for theories. Again, this presents both a challenge *and* an opportunity as there is much research still to be done.

3.1   Lack of Research on Organizational Issues

As noted earlier, findings show that age-based research on older adults' experiences with technology is severely lacking (Birkland & Kaarst-Brown, 2007). Recent bibliographic work indicates that less than 0.01% of literature in the top information systems journals (7:75,860 articles) addresses older users (or non-users) of ICTs[1]. This gap highlights not only a lack of multi-generational studies, but a lack of attention to aging and older adult users or IT professionals. This same study highlights that while there is methodological diversity, there are very few studies that IS researchers can draw upon to study the older IT workforce. Research on older adults and ICT's includes a wide range of design and methods, with the vast majority of them quantitative. As commented above, however, this again presents numerous opportunities for researchers to add to this small body of research.

Based on our meta-analysis of 622 journal articles across multiple academic disciplines, the study of older adults and ICT's shows that humanistic issues (social and physical/cognitive concerns) remain more fully researched than economic issues (financial and organizational issues). Of 622 papers used for a larger meta-analysis, only 73 papers (11.7 %) were

classified as "organizationally focused". (Organizationally focused includes any articles that examined workplace issues, such as knowledge management systems and retiring workers, retraining or training issues surrounding older workers, the impacts of an aging population on a workplace or industry, etc..) Of these 73 organizationally focused papers, 46 (63.1 %) or slightly less than two thirds addressed some type of health care issue (using ICT's to train healthcare workers or using ICT's to reducing healthcare costs in light of the demands of an aging population on the industry). The remaining 27 (36.9 %) papers focused on issues associated with the aging of the workforce – a shockingly small number given the magnitude of the issues.

Given that we know that there will be greater generational diversity in the IT workforce, there are not only opportunities for new questions, but the design must also consider the unique qualities and issues for this group. The sampling discussion above raised two design issues that this lack of empirical research highlights: Lack of Researcher Experience and Institutional Review Board Approval.

3.1.1   *Lack of Researcher Experience*
As researchers, any new study is often an exploration into unknown territory – be it the use of new theory, new design and methods, or new sample. Studying older adults and ICT's is currently conducted in nearly every discipline, from psychology and sociology to healthcare and law, and more recently in gerontology. We actually see the emergence of a new field called "Gerontechnology" to study older adults and a wide range of computerized and non-computerized "assistive technologies" and services.

Who is the best qualified to study the older IT worker: those who understand aging, those who understand human resource issues associated with IT workers, or IS researchers who understand organizational technologies and practices?

If we wish to begin exploring issues associated with aging and older IT professionals, we may wish to approach these new research studies much as doctoral students approach their first studies – with colleagues who have diverse experience and with exploratory studies. Studies of the older adult may benefit from pilot tests, as well as mixed-method studies that allow us to develop both rich understanding of the sample, and breadth of coverage. They may also benefit from multi-disciplinary teams who bring diverse perspectives to the exploration.

3.1.2   *Institutional Review Board Approval*
As noted above, there are some very real potential risks to the older IT professional or IT worker who participates in research studies. Some seemingly ideal organizational settings where an aging IT and other professional workforce may be a growing concern may have their own institutional review process that researchers must additionally obtain approval through. This includes many government or public sector firms, the military and educational settings. It may be necessary to allow additional time for this process, but the sampling issues mentioned above also highlight other important issues that IS researchers must consider in all organizational settings. For example, identifying an age-representative sample, avoiding unintended harm due to focusing attention on older workers, care in interpretation of results to avoid biased analysis of multi-generational samples, and acknowledgement that older workers may have cognitive advantages and disadvantages depending on the design and methods used.

---

[1] Birkland & Kaarst-Brown (2007). This study identified journals based on standings reported by the Association of Information Systems, as well as a broader search for any journal including an article on older users. For additional details on methods used in this meta-analysis or other findings, please contact these authors.

3.2 Diversity of Methods

While our research questions in turn shape our design and methods, we also often turn to existing research for ideas. As noted above, there are relatively few organizational studies that consider older users of ICT's, and even fewer that consider the older IT professionals or IT workers.

In terms of research design, 52 (or 71.2%) of the 73 organizationally classified papers were empirical, with the remainder being review, conceptual or discussion papers. As noted in Table 1, *only five* (29.4%) of the 17 empirical papers focused on issues associated with the aging workforce were *qualitative designs or case studies*, with the remaining 12 (70.6 %) papers representing *quantitative designs* such as experiments, quasi-experiments, or surveys. None of the workplace studies used a mixed-method design.

While this is a very small number of articles to draw conclusions from, it is not unlike the results using the larger sample of over six hundred articles which focused on older adults and information and communication technologies (Author Concealed). This larger study found that *"over one quarter of articles (25.72%) were conceptual, lacking empirical data. Sixty-nine percent of the empirical studies used predominately quantitative methods (318 or 51.12%; or 69% of the 462 empirical studies). Only 10.8% of the empirical papers used a qualitative design and only 7.6% of empirical studies used a mixed-method design (p. 246)."*

While there is ample room for additional qualitative studies that seek a deeper understanding of the needs and motivations of the older IT worker, is it obvious that there is a need for studies of all types that consider the unique retention, motivation, and development concerns of the older IT professional.

4. SUMMARY: THE PATH LESS TRAVELLED

Various studies suggest that over seventy percent of baby boomers intend to continue working in some form beyond retirement, placing pressure upon organizations, educational institutions, and libraries to adapt practices, culture, physical space, and technological devices to meet their learning and work needs (Birkland & Kaarst-Brown, 2007; Korczyk and Rix 2004). While these findings support inclusion of generational factors in a wide range of organizational studies, it is critical that we begin to consider the impact of aging on the IT workforce. A multi-generational IT workforce will require different strategies for retention and motivation, but also challenges the IS researcher to come up with insightful, sensitive and creative research studies.

We hope that his paper has detail some of the methodological challenges, but also provided insights on some of the opportunities available to IS researchers who seek to understand the older IT worker.

5. ACKNOWLEDGMENTS

Our sincere thanks to reviewers who provided their insights and helpful feedback on earlier work. We are also indebted to the many participants in the foundation studies used for this paper.

Organizational Concerns Domain Issues and Methods (73 of 622 papers)			Growing % of Older Adults in Workplace	Training Healthcare Workers	Reducing Healthcare Admin. Costs
Methodology		**Issues**			
Quantitative	Experiment		3	3	-
	Quasi-experiment		5	-	1
	Survey		4	3	-
	Prototype Test	Descrip.	-	3	3
		Eval.	-	-	5
Qualitative	Structured Interview		-	-	-
	Semi-Structured Interview		1	-	2
	Focus Groups		1	1	-
	Observation		-	-	-
	Ethnography		-	-	-
Case Study			3	2	3
Longitudinal			-	-	-
Mixed Methods			-	-	4
Extant/ Secondary Data			-	-	2
Class or Center Evaluation			-	3	-
Total Empirical Studies (N=52)			17	15	20
Total Non-Empirical: Review, Conceptual, or Discussion (N=21)			10	6	5
TOTAL Studies (N=73)			27	21	25

Table 1: Organizational Concerns Domain Issues and Methods: Total Number of Articles

6. REFERENCES

[1] AARP. (2010). *The Employment Situation, September 2010: Older Workers Have Little to Cheer About Once Again.* Retrieved November 1, 2010

[2] Birkland, J. L. H. (2007). Myths of the Older Adult User and ICTs: What We Know and Don't Know and How We Know It. Working Paper - School of Information Studies. Syracuse, University: 1-65.

[3] Birkland, J. L. H., & Kaarst-Brown, M. L. (2010). 'What's so special about studying old people?': The ethical, methodological, and sampling issues surrounding the study of older adults and ICTs. In F. Sudweeks, H. Hrachovec & C. Ess (Eds.), *Proceedings of the seventh international conference on Cultural Attitudes Towards Technology and Communication* (pp. 341-356). Vancouver, B.C., Canada.

[4] Carlson, E. (2009). *20th-Century: U.S. Generations.* Population Reference Bureau, 64(1).

[5] Cattell, R. B. (1971). *Abilities: Their structure, growth, and action.* New York: Houghton Mifflin.

[6] Cavanaugh, J. C., & Blanchard-Fields, F. (2006). *Adult development and aging* (5th Ed.). Belmont, CA: Wadsworth Publishing/Thomson Learning.

[7] DeLong, D. W. (2004). *Lost knowledge: Confronting the threat of an aging workforce.* New York: Oxford University Press.

[8] European Foundation for the Improvement of Living and Working Conditions. (2007). *Ageing and work in Europe.* Retrieved November 1, 2010, from http://www.eurofound.europa.eu/ewco/reports/TN0407TR01/TN0407TR01.pdf

[9] Finkel, D., Reynolds, C. A., McArdle, J. J., & Pedersen, N. L. (2007). Cohort differences in trajectories of cognitive aging. *Journal of Gerontology: Psychological Sciences, 62*(5), 286-294.

[10] Hayes-Bautista, D. E., Hsu, P., Perez, A., & Gamboa, C. (2002). The 'browning' of the graying of America: Diversity in the elderly population and policy implications. *Generations 26*(3), 15-24.

[11] Hedge, J. W., Borman, W. C., & Lammlein, S. E. (2006). *The aging workforce: Realities, myths, and implications for organizations.* Washington, D.C.: American Psychological Association (APA).

[12] Kaarst-Brown, M. L. (1995). A Theory of Information Technology Cultures: Magic Dragons, Wizards and Archetypal Patterns. Schulich School of Business. Toronto, ON Canada, York University: 700.

[13] Kaarst-Brown, M.L. & Guzman, I.R. (2010) "A Cultural Perspective on Individual Choices of STEM Education and Subsequent Occupations". SIGMIS CPR'10 Proceedings of the 2010 ACM SIGMIS Computer Personnel Research Conference. May 20-22, 2010. Vancouver, BC, Canada. 55-65.

[14] Korczyk, S. and S. A. Rix (2004). Is early retirement ending? Washington, D.C., AARP Public Policy Institute.

[15] Larwood, L., Rodkin, S., & Judson, D. (2001). Retraining and the technological productivity paradox. *International Journal of Organizational Theory and Behavior, 4*(3&4), 201-224.

[16] Larwood, L., Ruben, K., Popoff, C., & Judson, D. H. (1997). Aging, retirement, and interest in technological retraining: predicting personal investment and withdrawal. *The Journal of High Technology Management Research, 8*(2), 277-300.

[17] Martin, J. (1995). "The Style and Structure of Cultures in Organizations - 3 Perspectives". Organization Science 6(2): 230-232.

[18] Marquié, J. C., Jourdan-Boddaert, L., & Huet, N. (2002). Do older adults underestimate their actual computer knowledge? *Behaviour & Information Technology, 21*(4), 273-280.

[19] Maurer, T. J., Wrenn, K. A., & Weiss, E. M. (2003). Toward understanding and managing stereotypical beliefs about older workers' ability and desire for learning and development. In J. J. Martocchio & G. R. Ferris (Eds.), *Research in personnel and human resources management* (Vol. 22, pp. 253-285). Stamford, CT: JAI Press.

[20] Reynolds, C. A., Finkel, D., Gatz, M., & Pedersen, N. L. (2002). Sources of influence on rate of cognitive change over time in Swedish twins: An application of latent growth models. *Experimental Aging Research, 28*, 407-433.

[21] Rix, S. E. (2001). *Toward active aging in the 21st century: Working longer in the United States.* Paper presented at the Japanese Institute of Labour Millennium Project. from http://www.jil.go.jp/jil/seika/us2.pdf.

[22] Rosen, B., & Jerdee, T. H. (1985). *Older employees: New roles for valued resources.* Homewood, IL: Dow Jones-Irwin.

[23] Rosow, J. M., & Zager, R. (1980). *The future of older workers in America: New perspectives for an extended work life.* Scarsdale, NY: Work in America Institute.

[24] Sackmann, S. A. (1992). "Culture and Subcultures: An Analysis of Organizational Knowledge". Administrative Science Quarterly 37(1): 140.

[25] Salkowitz, R. (2008). Generation Blend: Managing Across the Technology Age Gap. NY, John Wiley & Sons.

[26] Simon, R. (1996). Too damn old. *Money, 25*(7), 118-126.

[27] Spillman, B., & Pezzin, L. (2000). Potential and Active Family Caregivers: Changing Networks and the 'Sandwich Generation'. *The Milbank Quarterly, 78*(3), 347-374.

[28] U.S. Census Bureau. (2008). *Table 3. Percent Distribution of the Projected Population by Selected Age Groups and Sex for the United States: 2010 to 2050 (NP2008-T3).* Retrieved from http://www.census.gov/population/www/projections/summarytables.html.

A Review of Difference Score Research in the IS Discipline with an Application to Understanding the Expectations and Job Experiences of IT Professionals

Hyung Koo Lee
Georgia State University
Robinson College of Business
CIS Department, Atlanta, USA
1 404 413-7390

hklee@cis.gsu.edu

Mike Gallivan
Georgia State University
Robinson College of Business
CIS Department, Atlanta, USA
1 404 413-7363

mgallivan@gsu.edu

ABSTRACT

In recent decades, IS researchers have collected and analyzed difference score data with regard to IS service quality research, system functionality and user interface features, as well as job- and career-related expectations of IT personnel. Despite the prevalence of difference scores in IS research, these methods have been criticized due to various theoretical and statistical anomalies. In this research in progress study, we identify some problems that have been identified in the organizational behavior literature. We review various research streams that employ difference scores, focusing in depth on one popular stream of "difference score" research: work on person-environment fit or person-job fit in shaping IT employees' job satisfaction, performance and turnover intentions. We analyze a dataset containing difference score data for 120 software developers with regard to their preferences for specific job attributes, along with their self-reports regarding how well their current job matches these preferences. We analyze our data using both conventional difference score methods, as well as using new techniques suggested in the OB and IS literature.

Categories and Subject Descriptors

K.6.1 [Management of Computing and Information Systems]: Project and People Management – Staffing

General Terms

Management, Human Factors

Keywords

Difference scores; service quality, person-job fit; IT professionals, polynomial regression; response surface methodology

1. INTRODUCTION

Information systems research has long sought improvements to theoretical perspectives and analytic methods for conducting research. In this paper, we focus on a broad genre of research that uses "difference scores" to analyze analogous pairs of constructs. Difference scores have long been a mainstay of research in marketing and organizational behavior (OB), as well as in IS. For instance, in a "difference score" study, a respondent may be asked to state her expectations for several perceived quality aspects for IT systems and services that they expect to receive, and later be asked to rate the perceived level of service they received on a set of analogous items. For each pair of matching items, a difference score is then computed by subtracting the respondent's self-report for perceived service quality from her original service expectation.

In recent decades, IS scholars have collected and analyzed difference score data with regard to IS service quality research [16], system functionality and user interface features [25], and the job or career expectations of IT personnel [15]. Despite the prevalence of difference scores data in IS research, these methods are often subject to criticism due to various statistical anomalies that they raise [13, 16]. In this research in progress study, we start with an overview of difference score research in IS, then we identify controversies that have appeared in the OB and marketing literatures. Finally, we describe a study that addresses the methodological concerns and suggestions raised by leading OB scholars. Specifically, we analyze a dataset of 120 IT employees regarding their preferences for specific job attributes (which we label as "P" or person attributes), along with their self-reports of the degree to which their job fulfills such preferences ("J" or job-related data). To demonstrate the problems that have been claimed for traditional methods for analyzing difference score data, we analyze our dataset according to traditional methods (P–J difference scores), as well as using the newer techniques that have been proposed in the OB [7] and IS literatures [6].

2. LITERATURE REVIEW

Many studies of person-environment fit (P-E fit) and person-job fit (P-J fit) use difference scores to predict job satisfaction [17, 21], job strain [6, 9], performance, and turnover intentions [11]. Here, we review these studies of IT personnel – as well as other areas of IS research that employ difference scores. Next, we describe some debates that are ongoing in the OB and IS disciplines with regard to the optimal techniques for analyzing difference score data.

In IS research, there are three research streams that use difference scores: IT employee-job fit, IS service quality, and IT strategic alignment, as well as other, miscellaneous studies. In the research stream on employee job fit, most studies examine either "needs-supplies fit" or "demands-abilities fit" [8]. "Need-supplies fit" focuses on the discrepancy between individual employees' needs and how well the job environment satisfies such needs. In contrast, demand-abilities fit identifies the gap between employees' abilities and the skills or personal attributes required by the job [8]. Both areas use difference scores to measure the size of the discrepancy – either between personal needs vs. job supplies (e.g., job security) or between the job's demand for specific skills and individual abilities (design skills).

A second IS research stream that uses difference scores is research on IS service quality. Since an organization's IS department is a type of service provider, Pitt et al. [16] proposed to use the well-known SERVQUAL instrument (first developed in the marketing literature) to assess the performance of companies' IS departments. SERVQUAL has a long history in marketing and was adapted to the domain of IS service quality, as reflected by the five standard dimensions of service: reliability, responsiveness, empathy, assurance, and tangibles. Research on IS service quality uses difference scores to identify the gap between users' expectations for the quality of IT systems, data, and services vs. their self-reports of perceived quality along the same dimensions. Kettinger and Lee [12] were first to adapt the SERVQUAL instrument to address the limitations of older user information satisfaction (UIS) measures from the 1980s. They claimed that the older UIS measures were inadequate to capture all facets of services provided by a firm's IS department, in part, because such service roles have expanded over time. Based on a survey of students who relied on their university's IS department, Kettinger and Lee found that the five dimensions of SERVQUAL and the standard UIS measures were correlated (especially if the *tangibles* dimension was omitted); however, two SERVQUAL dimensions (*reliability* and *empathy*) were statistically significant in explaining students' satisfaction with services provided, above-and-beyond the older UIS measures. This implies that these dimensions (*reliability* and *empathy*) are unique aspects not captured by the older UIS instruments.

Pitt et al. [16] also argued that traditional UIS measures were problematic, and they agreed that SERVQUAL was superior for evaluating IS service quality. To assess the validity of SERV-QUAL, the authors collected data in three countries (South Africa, the U.K., and U.S.), and concluded that SERVQUAL should be used for evaluating the quality of systems and computer-based information, but also for measuring the quality of service provided by people (i.e., technical support). While they advocated greater use of SERVQUAL, Pitt et al. found that the *tangibles* dimension of SERVQUAL had low reliability, and they cautioned against including this dimension of SERVQUAL.

A third area of IS research that employs difference scores is work on IT strategic alignment [2-4], where the fit between IT strategy and business strategy is sometimes operationalized using differ-ence scores. In one study of IT strategic alignment, Chan et al. [4] used the *matching alignment* approach (which employs difference scores) to represent the alignment of a firm's business strategy with its IT strategy. In addition, they used the *moderation*

alignment approach (which employs mathematical product scores, instead of difference scores), and compared the results of the two approaches. Using data from 170 firms, Chan et al. [4] found that the *moderation alignment* approach provided a better explanation of firms' IT effectiveness and business performance, relative to the *matching alignment* (i.e., difference score) approach. The authors argued that, due to the way that difference scores are computed, the *matching alignment* approach was incapable of capturing the relative importance of a given business strategy – but which the *moderation alignment* (i.e., product) approach was able to handle.

Finally, there are several studies using difference scores in a host of other contexts such as trust among virtual team members [18], IT adoption [27], electronic data interchange [26], feedback systems [28], and collaboration software [1]. One study [10] used difference scores to assess the degree of personality "fit" between a user and decision-support software. In this study, Hess et al. [10] explored the effect of various system features (e.g., multi-media vividness), personality attributes, and individual traits (e.g., computer playfulness) on users' decision involvement and on the quality of the decision. Using *similarity-attraction theory*, Hess et al. [10] argued that a high degree of fit between the "personality" of a technology and the user led to higher involvement in decision-making and, in turn, to better decision outcomes. Based on an experiment with students tasked with choosing an optimal housing arrangement with the assistance of an automated decision tool, the authors concluded that the fit between users' personality and attributes of the decision tool increased their level of involve-ment in decision making and, in turn, their satisfaction with and understanding of the automated decision tool.

Most relevant for our purposes, the authors acknowledged problems with using difference scores. They used more sophisti-cated analytic techniques, which yielded similar results to the difference score approach; however, the newer methods yielded stronger effect sizes for the effect of personality fit on the depen-dent variable (involvement), as well as larger explained variance.

Having described four IS research streams that employ difference scores, we discuss the controversies that have emerged in the OB literature with regard to difference scores in recent years.

2.1 Controversies in Organizational Behavior

Several problems have been identified with regard to the use of difference scores. Edwards and Harrison [8] conducted a study on the relationship between person-environment fit and job strain by replicating the data analysis from French et al [9]. In the initial study, French et al. identified five permutations of fit measures.[1] Because the original constructs used difference scores, Edwards and Harrison [8] observed various statistical problems, and replic-ated the original analyses to demonstrate them. The problems they expected to find were: first, difference scores will create a "confound relationship" when computing a difference between environment (E) and person (P) data, since E and P are distinct constructs; second, that difference scores would add constraints to

---

[1] They labeled these as *fit* (where the difference score, E – P, is used for all factors); a *deficiency* model (with deficiency defined as E – P when E ≤ P, but zero when E > P); an *excess* model (with excess = E – P when E ≥ P; zero otherwise); a model labeled *poor fit* (based on the absolute value of E – P); and a *squared fit* model (the squared value of E – P, so that large differences carry more weight, regardless of sign).

the overall model (e.g. the coefficients of E and P being opposite in direction), thus reducing what should be a three-dimensional model (consisting of P, E, and strain) to a two-dimensional model (fit and strain only). As a remedy, they advocated including *all* three variables (P, E, and strain) to resolve such problems. Doing so required that they enter P and E separately into the regression equation, rather than including P and E variables in the form of a difference score. They argued that doing so would free the extra constraints on coefficients and would allow for higher-order terms in the model – such as E^2, P^2, as well as the product of E times P.

In replicating the original analyses, Edwards and Harrison [8] performed confirmatory and exploratory analyses to clarify the relationship between P, E, and strain. Overall, they found little value in difference scores; instead, they recommended that P and E be included as separate predictors, which led to a large increase in amount of explained variance. Edwards and Harrison [8] advised researchers to avoid difference score calculations in their data – instead modeling the independent effects of all predictor variables.

2.2 P-J Fit Research in the IS Literature

Since the research stream with the greatest use of difference score data in the IS literature is IS personnel research – and since the dataset that we analyze below, belongs to this stream – we discuss this research stream in greater detail, before stating our research objectives and planned analyses. We summarize a stream of research initiated by McLean and his colleagues in 1991 and also presented in a series of SIG CPR (the predecessor to SIG MIS) conference papers. Their body of work examined "need-supplies" difference scores and their downstream consequences.

During the first step of a longitudinal study of self-perceptions and job preferences of IS professionals, McLean et al. [15] profiled nearly 1,000 recent IS graduates from 37 universities who were entering the IS job market. In addition to demographic data, they collected data about the recent graduates' job preferences (a measure of "needs"), using the Job Preference Inventory (JPI). Their factor analyses of the JPI instrument alone[2] revealed five factors: *hygienic* environment, which included items representing compensation, benefits, and job security; *motivational* environment, which included items related to *motivational aspects* – such as preference for challenging work; *interpersonal* environment, regarding social interaction with peers, and expectations for the amount of teamwork required; *task autonomy* (whether subjects preferred to be dependent on others or to work alone); and last, *advancement* environment, which dealt with promotional opportunities. Interestingly, McLean et al. [15] found respondents' preferences for each factor to be related to their gender, age, their grade point average (GPA), and the degree received.

In a subsequent study, McLean et al. [14] extended the prior work by analyzing other information regarding the attributes of IS academic programs, which they collected from faculty at each institution. They explored the effect of self-efficacy and IT career certainty on respondents' self-reported job preferences using data from 791 undergraduate students. After factor analyzing the JPI data, they identified three factors: a *hygiene* factor (i.e., extrinsic rewards, fairness in evaluation, and amount of supervision); *motivation*, comprised of items associated with challenging work,

as well as work that is creative, allows independence, and offers a sense of accomplishment); and an *interpersonal factor* (the degree of interaction with peers, system users, etc.).

In a third study conducted after the employees had worked full-time for two years, Smits et al. [24] assessed whether these new employees regarded their prior expectations as being met by the present jobs. Based on 287 responses from the same respondents who had participated in the prior studies, the authors computed difference scores by subtracting subjects' perceptions of their current jobs (using the JCI items) from their pre-employment JPI scores for each pair of analogous items, resulting in a difference score for each item pair. They then used these difference scores to predict respondents' job and career attitudes. Smits et al. [24] found that, in general, respondents perceived their jobs as meeting their pre-graduation preferences in terms of income, fairness of rewards, and challenging work. Moreover, the difference scores that Smits et a computed for each item pair showed a significant effect on respondents' overall job satisfaction, and on specific job attitudes: employees' perception of pay fairness; beliefs about having meaningful work, work that utilized their abilities; and work that provided enough opportunity to take personal initiative.

In a separate research stream focused on IT employees, Jiang and Klein [11] computed difference scores between IT employees' needs and supplies. Grounded in *discrepancy theory* and using Schein's nine career anchors [19],[3] Jiang and Klein [11] posited that achieving better fit between employees' preferences for certain career anchors and the reality of their current jobs would explain their level of career satisfaction and their turnover intentions. Based on data from 153 IT employees, they found that just one of Schein's nine career anchors (creativity/entrepreneurship) yielded a difference score that their subjects' career satisfaction and turnover intentions. In contrast, for the other eight career anchors, there was no significant relationship between the difference scores and career satisfaction or turnover intentions.

Chilton et al. [6] conducted a study to determine whether the cognitive style fit of person and environment (i.e., the cognitive style required by the job) was related to job strain and performance among software developers. Based on Adaption-Innovation Theory, they posited that a better "match" between a person's cognitive style and the cognitive style demanded by the job would explain their level of job strain and performance. Instead of using difference scores to measure person-job fit, Chilton et al. [6] followed the confirmatory analysis procedures that Edwards and Harrison [8] suggested. They regressed each dependent variable (strain and performance) on the person and environment items *separately*. In addition, they allowed for higher-order terms (i.e., P^2 and E^2), since they expected to find curvilinear effects for both person and job factors. Based on the new analytic methods – including response surface analysis – they found that high P-E fit in terms of employees' cognitive style led to lower job strain and higher performance.

In a later study, Chilton et al. [5] examined how the change of technology in the job environment affected job strain and performance. The newer study focused on the effects of "relative" P-E fit, which they conceptualized as how well the current work environment aligns with a worker's ideal environment compared

[2] In this paper, the authors did not analyze difference scores, but instead they considered just employees' "needs" (i.e., their JPI items).

[3] Schein identified nine career anchors: managerial competence, technical competence, job security, autonomy, challenge, service, geographical security, creativity/entrepreneurship, and lifestyle integration.

to how they aligned in the past. Using data from 124 employees in firms that were migrating their software development methods from procedural programming to object-oriented development, and using polynomial regression and surface response analysis (as suggested by Edwards and Harrison [8], Chilton et al. [5] found that employees whose desired level of role ambiguity and need for supervision were met by the environment exhibited lower levels of job strain and higher levels of performance.

3. RESEARCH OBJECTIVES

The purpose of our study is to analyze a dataset containing difference score items – first, according to traditional difference score methods (i.e., where each pair of items is used to compute a difference score), and then according to newer methods suggested by Edwards [7] in the OB literature, and by Chilton et al. [6] in IS. We replicate the analyses provided in earlier studies, in order to show the benefits of analyzing the person and job factors separately (rather than through a difference score, P–J), by allowing for curvilinear effects (e.g., P^2 and J^2), and use of response surface methods to capture three-dimensional effects.

4. RESEARCH METHODS

We start by describing our data collection procedures and survey measures. Next, we describe the types of analyses that we plan to conduct with our data. We first created a computerized survey and distributed it to 220 IT professionals in two large organizations in cities on the U.S. east coast. Although the survey contained over 100 items, we mention just the items relevant to this submission. Publications based on the dataset (using other constructs, and not based on difference scores) have been previously published. First, we measured employees' job preferences using a 21-item version of the Job Preferences Inventory (JPI), and 21 comparable items for the Job Characteristics Inventory (JCI) [22]. The JPI captures respondents' needs, while the JCI items capture respondents' perceptions of the degree to which their needs that are fulfilled (or not) by the current job. In addition to the standard items that McLean and colleagues [14, 15] included in their longitudinal studies of IS students and employees, we added some extra job preference items recommended by IS researchers, such as IS employees preference for having a job with high learning potential [20], as well as providing the opportunity to learn about specific areas of the business and about IT project management.

We measured job satisfaction using 12 items from the "satisfaction with work" scale of the Job Descriptive Index [23], plus a 4-item scale to capture subjects' turnover intentions, and a 21-item scale to measure respondents' job performance (Goldstein 1988).[4] We also included items to capture demographic data (gender, age, level of education), as well as respondents' tenure in the company, job and IT workforce. We received responses from 120 out of 220 employees in two firms (a 56% response rate).

To illustrate the different results from using the difference score approach and Edwards' [7] polynomial regression approach, we computed a difference score for skill latitude by subtracting the JPI score of the items loading on skill latitude from the JCI equivalent items. We expected that job satisfaction would be a function of the discrepancy between actual skill latitude and the

level of skill latitude that respondents identified on the JPI. We expected to find a linear relationship such that when the desired level of skill latitude exceeds the actual skill latitude, job satisfaction would increase as the size of this gap (difference score) decreases. As the actual skill latitude exceeds the desired level of skill latitude, job satisfaction would continue to increase as the size of the gap in increases. We expected to find the opposite relationship for turnover intention. We first conducted regression analyses using the difference score as the predictor variable, and job satisfaction and turnover intention (separately) as the dependent variables.

In order to demonstrate the advantages of the newer methods, we also used polynomial regression, as suggested by Edwards [7]. We identified the unconstrained model – whereby the employee's preferences and her perceptions of the actual job are entered separately into the regression, rather than in the form of a difference score. The unconstrained equation is represented as follows with the actual level of that attribute ("A") and the desired level of a given job attribute ("D") entered separately:

$$Z = B_0 + B_1A + B_2D + e$$

where Z indicates the dependent variable, D indicates the desired level of a specific job attribute, and A represents the actual level of the attribute. After estimating the unconstrained equation, we evaluated specific conditions based on Edwards' [7] suggestions to determine whether or not to reject the constrained model by checking: whether the constrained model explains a significant amount of variance in the dependent variable; whether the two coefficients of the unconstrained are non-zero and in the opposite direction (as expected); whether the constraints that Edwards [7] had specified (i.e., the size of the two coefficients being the same) were met in the unconstrained model; and whether additional variance was explained by higher-order terms in the unconstrained model, such as A^2, AD, and D^2. Failure to achieve any one of these conditions leads to rejecting the constrained model, meaning that job satisfaction (or turnover intentions) is better explained by the newer methods (i.e., the unconstrained model) than by the traditional difference score approach. We considered the higher-order terms to ensure that the current model is sufficient for representing the complexity of the relationship between the two separate components of the difference score and the dependent variable. After identifying the appropriate model, we also employed response surface analysis methods (similar to Chilton et al. [6]) to represent the relationship between the two difference score components and the dependent variable.

5. RESULTS

Descriptive statistics and correlations for the separate difference score components and the outcome variables appear in Table 1.

Table 1. Descriptive Statistics and Correlations

Variable	Mean	SD	1	2	3
1. Actual Skill Latitude	5.41	0.93	-		
2. Desired Skill Latitude	5.85	0.59	0.35	-	
3. Job Satisfaction	53.48	8.61	0.63	0.08	-
4. Turnover Intention	3.72	1.31	-0.16	0.18	-0.38

---

[4] The 21-item job performance scale has the potential to be used as a self-assessment or to be completed by an employee's supervisor. We plan to use both approaches in our future data analysis.

The results from the difference scores approach appear in Table 2. For both job satisfaction and turnover intentions, the difference score approach yielded significant regression coefficients and R^2 values. The results show that job satisfaction increases as the actual level of skill latitude approaches employees' desired level of skill latitude. This linear pattern continues as the actual level of skill latitude exceeds the desired level. In our dataset, job satisfaction reaches a maximum when employees' actual skill latitude exceeds their desired skill latitude by 2 points on a 7-point scale. On the other hand, the level of job satisfaction is lowest when the actual level of skill latitude falls short of the desired level of skill latitude by 5 points. For the other dependent variable (turnover intention), the relationship is the exact opposite. Two-dimensional plots of these relationships appear in Figures 1 and 2.

Table 2. Regression Results Using Difference Scores for Skill Latitude[a]

Dependent Variables	Difference Score Coefficients	R^2
Job Satisfaction	5.61***	0.36***
Turnover intention	-0.40**	0.07**

a.   *: $p < 0.05$, **: $p < 0.01$, ***: $p < 0.001$

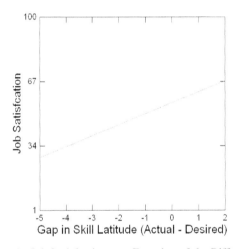

Figure 1. Job Satisfaction as a Function of the Difference Score between Actual and Desired Skill Latitude

In using polynomial regression, we regressed job satisfaction and turnover intention on the two difference score components separately (i.e., actual skill latitude and desired skill latitude). The results for the unconstrained models appear in Table 3.

For both dependent variables, the unconstrained model yielded significant R^2 values. The coefficients were significant and in the opposite direction, as expected. The higher-order terms in the unconstrained model failed to explain any additional amount of variance for either dependent variable (job satisfaction or turnover intentions), indicating that the linear model is sufficient to explain the effect of the two components of the difference score calculation (actual skill latitude and desired skill latitude). For job satisfaction, we found that the additional amount of variance explained (i.e., change in R^2) was significant between the difference score approach and the newer, "unconstrained model." This highlights the benefits of the newer approach vis-à-vis the older,

difference score approach. Of course, this does not imply that the newer approach will be better for *all* combinations of predictor variable and outcome variables.

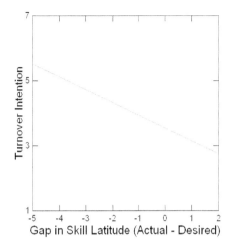

Figure 2. Turnover Intentions as a Function of the Difference Score between Actual and Desired Skill Latitude

Table 3. Regression Results for the Unconstrained Model[a]

Variable	Job Satisfaction	Turnover Intention
Actual Skill Latitude	6.36***	-0.35*
Desired Skill Latitude	-2.35*	0.58**
R^2	0.42***	0.09**
F_C[b]	13.42***	2.21
F_{II}[c]	0.10	0.99

a.   *: $p < 0.05$, **: $p < 0.01$, ***: $p < 0.001$
b. F_C indicates the test of difference in R^2 values for the constrained and unconstrained model.
c. F_{II} indicates the incremental F for the higher-order model with quadratic terms.

In fact, when we analyzed the different models for the influence of skill latitude on turnover intentions, there was no benefit to the newer approach, based on the amount of change in R^2 — which did not differ significantly for the two models. This implies that the difference score approach is sufficient for explaining the relationship between turnover intentions and the "gap" between subjects' desired vs. actual skill latitude. These results show that there are benefits in using the new method (i.e., entering the desired level vs. actual level of a specific job attribute separately) for explaining one outcome variable (job satisfaction) but not another outcome (turnover intentions).

Next, we use response surface methods to illustrate the relationship between actual skill latitude, desired skill latitude, and job satisfaction. Response surface analysis focuses on "estimating and interpreting three-dimensional surfaces relating two variables to an outcome" [7]. This approach can provide more insights with regard to the effect of two analogous items for the same attribute (i.e., desired level vs. actual level of skill latitude) on an outcome variable (in our case, satisfaction and turnover intentions). This method may also be useful for modeling higher-order terms. The benefit of being able to add higher-order terms is that researchers can visibly detect non-linear effects for any predictor variables.

Figure 3 shows the three-dimensional response surface plot of job satisfaction (the vertical axis), which is generated using the results from the unconstrained model in Table 3. The three-dimensional plot shows the level of job satisfaction for all possible combinations of actual and desired levels of employees' skill latitude.

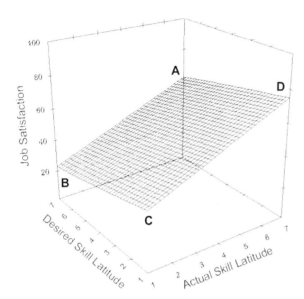

Figure 3. Response Surface for the Unconstrained Model of Job Satisfaction

Point B and point D represent the two extreme cases of misfit: point B (where desired skill latitude is far greater than actual) and point D (where actual level is far greater than desired), where the discrepancy between actual and desired skill latitude is maximized. At the point where desired skill latitude is highest and the actual level of skill latitude is lowest (i.e., point B), employees report the lowest level of job satisfaction. Conversely, when the actual skill latitude is highest and the desired skill latitude is lowest (point D), employees experience highest level of job satisfaction. At the midpoint on the diagonal line that connects points B and D, we observe the "point of perfect fit," where the actual and desired levels of skill latitude are identical or matched.

Point A and point C represent the highest level of perfect fit and lowest level of perfect fit, respectively. The diagonal that connects points A and C represent all possibilities where actual and desired skill latitude are matched. We can observe that the level of job satisfaction increases as the nature of this "match" increases over the length of this diagonal line. In other words, employees will experience different levels of job satisfaction at different points along this line that represents a "match" between actual and desired skill latitude. An employee whose preferred and actual levels are both "7" (extremely high) on a 7-point scale exhibits higher job satisfaction, compared to another employee whose preferred and actual levels are both "5" (moderately-high), and in turn, the latter employee is more satisfied than a third employee whose actual and desired levels of skill latitude are both "3" (moderately-low). Despite the fact that all points on the line

between A and C represent a "match," we see that job satisfaction increases as (both) values for desired and actual skill latitude increase from "1" (extremely low) to "7" (extremely high).

This important relationship can be overlooked when using the older, difference score approach, as the extra constraints imposed by difference scores (i.e., the coefficients of the two components must have the same magnitude, but be opposite in direction) lead prevent us from seeing the variations that can occur within the "plane." As shown in the response surface plot of the constrained model (Figure 4), we can observe that the level of job satisfaction is the same across the diagonal connecting point E and point G, which represents the line of perfect fit.

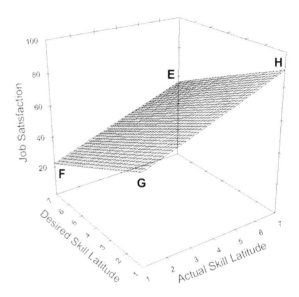

Figure 4 Response Surface for Constrained Model of Job Satisfaction

6. CONCLUSION

In this paper, we demonstrated the use of polynomial regression and response surface methods suggested by Edwards [7] in the context of P-J fit for IT professionals. We find support for the result reported in previous research – namely that including both components of the difference score separately in the regression equation leads to a higher amount of explained variance in the dependent variable (employee job satisfaction). We also achieve greater insights into different combinations of high and low levels of the actual versus the desired level of a given job attribute: higher levels of job satisfaction are associated with "high" perfect fit than with "low" perfect fit. It is not possible to observe these different options when using the conventional difference scores. So far, we provided results for just one predictor variable (i.e., skill latitude) and two outcome variables (job satisfaction and turnover intentions), and it is possible that other advantages may become apparent for other predictor variables. One limitation of our analysis is that we considered only linear equations without any higher-order terms of interaction effects. We plan to conduct further analyses to identify other combinations of predictor and outcome variables – including models with higher-order terms – to illustrate the benefits of response surface analysis.

7. REFERENCES

[1] Banker, R.D., Bardhan, I. and Asdemir, O. 2006. Understanding the impact of collaboration software on product design and development. *Information Systems Research*, 17 (4). 352-373.

[2] Byrd, T.A., Lewis, B.R. and Bryan, R.W. 2006. The leveraging influence of strategic alignment on IT investment: An empirical examination. *Information & Management*, 43 (3). 308-321.

[3] Chan, Y. and Reich, B. 2007. IT alignment: What have we learned? *Journal of Information Technology*, 22 (4). 297.

[4] Chan, Y.E., Huff, S.L., Barclay, D.W. and Copeland, D.G. 1997. Business strategic orientation, IS strategic orientation, and strategic alignment. *Information Systems Research*, 8 (2). 125.

[5] Chilton, M.A., Hardgrave, B.C. and Armstrong, D.J. 2010. Performance and strain levels of it workers engaged in rapidly changing environments: a person-job fit perspective. *SIGMIS Database*, 41 (1). 8-35.

[6] Chilton, M.A., Hardgrave, B.C. and Armstrong, D.J. 2005. Person-Job Cognitive Style Fit for Software Developers: The Effect on Strain and Performance. *Journal of Management Information Systems*, 22 (2). 193-226.

[7] Edwards, J.R. 2002. Alternatives to Difference Scores: Polynomial Regression Analysis and Response Surface Methodology. Drasgow, F. and Schmitt, N. eds. *Measuring and analyzing behavior in organizations: Advances in measurement and data analysis*, Jossey-Bass, San Francisco, CA, 2002, 350-400.

[8] Edwards, J.R. and Harrison, R.V. 1993. Job demands and worker health: Three-dimensional reexamination of the relationship between person-environment fit and strain. *Journal of Applied Psychology*, 78 (4). 628-648.

[9] French, J.R.P., Caplan, R.D. and Harrison, V.R. 1982. *The mechanisms of job stress and strain*. Wiley, Chichester Sussex and New York, 1982.

[10] Hess, T.J., Fuller, M.A. and Mathew, J. 2005. Involvement and decision-making performance with a decision aid: The influence of social multimedia, gender, and playfulness. *Journal of Management Information Systems*, 22 (3). 15-54.

[11] Jiang, J.J. and Klein, G. 2002. A Discrepancy model of IS personnel turnover. *Journal of Management Information Systems*, 19 (2). 249-272.

[12] Kettinger, W.J. and Lee, C.C. 1994. Perceived service quality and user satisfaction with the information services function. *Decision Sciences*, 25 (5,6). 737.

[13] Klein, G., Jiang, J.J. and Cheney, P. 2009. Resolving difference score issues in IS research. *MIS Quarterly*, 33 (4). 811-826.

[14] McLean, E.R., Bryan, N.B., Tanner, J.R. and Smits, S.J. 1993. The structure of job attitudes among entry-level I/S professionals: a path-analytic analysis *Proceedings of the 1993 Conference on Computer Personnel Research*, ACM, St Louis, MO, 27-36.

[15] McLean, E.R., Tanner, J.R. and Smits, S.J. 1991. Self-perceptions and job preferences of entry-level IS professionals: Implications for career development *Proceedings of 1991 Conference on SIGCPR*, ACM, Athens, GA, 3-13.

[16] Pitt, L.F., Watson, R.T. and Kavan, C.B. 1995. Service quality: a measure of information systems effectiveness. *MIS Quarterly*, 19 (2). 173-187.

[17] Rice, R.W., McFarlin, D.B. and Bennett, D.E. 1989. Standards of comparison and job satisfaction. *Journal of Applied Psychology*, 74 (4). 591-598.

[18] Robert, L.P.J., Dennis, A.R. and Hung, Y.-T.C. 2009. Individual swift trust and knowledge-based trust in face-to-face and virtual team members. *Journal of Management Information Systems*, 26 (2). 241-279.

[19] Schein, E.H. 1990. *Career anchors: Discovering your real values*. University Associates, San Diego, CA, 1990.

[20] Sein, M.K. and Bostrom, R.P. 1991. A psychometric study of the job characteristics scale of the job diagnostic survey in an MIS setting *Proceedings of 1991 Conference on SIGCPR*, ACM, Athens, GA.

[21] Siguaw, J.A., Brown, G. and Widing, R.E., II. 1994. The influence of the market orientation of the firm on sales force behavior and attitudes. *Journal of Marketing Research*, 31 (1). 106-116.

[22] Sims, H.P., Jr., Szilagyi, A.D. and Keller, R.T. 1976. The Measurement of Job Characteristics. *Academy of Management Journal*, 19 (2). 195-212.

[23] Smith, P.C., Kendall, L. and Hulin, C. 1969. *The measurement of satisfaction in work and retirement*. Rand McNally, Chicago, IL, 1969.

[24] Smits, S.J., Tanner, J.R. and McLean, E.R. 1993. Job characteristic preference-reality discrepancies and job and career attitudes of I/S professionals *Proceedings of 1993 Conference on Computer Personnel Research*, ACM, St Louis, MO, 120-130.

[25] Szajna, B. and Scamell, R.W. 1993. The effects of information system user expectations on their performance and perceptions. *MIS Quarterly*, 17 (4). 493-516.

[26] Truman, G. 2000. Integration in Electronic Exchange Environments. *Journal of Management Information Systems*, 17 (1). 209-244.

[27] Venkatesh, V. and Goyal, S. 2010. Expectation disconfirmation and technology adoption: polynomial modeling and response surface analysis. *MIS Quarterly*, 34 (2). 281-303.

[28] Zhou, M., Dresner, M. and Windle, R. 2009. Revisiting feedback systems: Trust building in digital markets. *Information & Management*, 46 (5). 279-284.

Understanding and Applying Participant Observation in Information Systems Research

Jo Ellen Moore
Southern Illinois University Edwardsville
Department of Computer Management and
Information Systems, School of Business
Edwardsville, IL, USA 62026-1106
1-618-650-5816
joemoor@siue.edu

Susan E. Yager
Southern Illinois University Edwardsville
Department of Computer Management and
Information Systems, School of Business
Edwardsville, IL, USA 62026-1106
1-618-650-2917
syager@siue.edu

ABSTRACT

We take stock of accepted wisdom regarding the use of participant observation. This research technique is defined and viewed in relation to two spectrums of roles that researchers can take in field studies. Issues associated with covert vs. overt observation are considered and the current prevailing wisdom acknowledged. We outline a fundamental methodology for conducting a participant observation study, and then apply the methodology in presenting a research design for a study in progress. We conclude with identification and discussion of key challenges in participant observation research.

Categories and Subject Descriptors

K.4.3 [**Computers and Society**]: Organizational Impacts – *Employment*

General Terms

Documentation, Management, Measurement

Keywords

IT worker turnover, Participant observation, Voice

1. INTRODUCTION

Participant observation is a field research method that produces rich findings, yet it is seldom employed, particularly in IS. Having recently developed a conceptual model regarding the "dissatisfied IS worker," we wondered if participant observation would be an appropriate methodology for testing the model and for more fully developing it. Uncertainty in how to go about a participant observation study led to this paper. We share with you what we have learned and how we are applying it in the research design of our field study.

2. OVERVIEW: PARTICIPANT OBSERVATION

By definition, "the participant observer gathers data by participating in the daily life of the group or organization he studies" [2, p. 652]. The participant observer watches people to see what situations they encounter and how they behave in those situations. Through participant observation, researchers actually go "out beyond the ivory towers of employment and comfort to live with and live like those who are studied" [23, p. 242].

Gold [11] identified four theoretically possible roles for sociologists conducting field work: complete observer, observer-as-participant, participant-as-observer, and complete participant. In a complete observer role, the field worker does not interact at all with those being observed and the observation is inherently covert. Examples include eavesdropping or reconnaissance of any kind. Observer-as-participant is most commonly represented by the field worker conducting interviews. The last two roles in Gold's [11] framework – complete participant and participant-as-observer – differ in regard to revealing the true identity and purpose of the field research. In a complete participant role, this is not revealed to the people being observed; in participant-as-observer, it is.

In their discussion of distance and engagement in IS research, Nandhakumar and Jones [18] noted that IS researchers tend to adopt relatively distant methods, meaning that IS researchers have tended to avoid intensive and extended interaction with their subjects. Nandhakumar and Jones [18] contend that data collection methods vary in the extent of interaction between researcher and the research phenomena: from "distant" methods where there is no direct contact between the researcher and people in the research context, to "engaged" methods that involve intensive and often extended engagement between researchers and the people in the research context. Figure 1 (next page) reflects the distance-engagement range of data collection methods put forth by Nandhakumar and Jones [18].

To clarify three of the data collection methods in this framework, Nandhakumar and Jones [18] classify experimental lab studies as passive observation. In action research, the researcher actively intervenes in the research context to try to achieve particular outcomes, which is different from participant observation where the researcher seeks to act as a normal member of the research context.

Figure 1. Distance-Engagement Classification from Nandhakumar and Jones [18]

DISTANCE   ENGAGEMENT

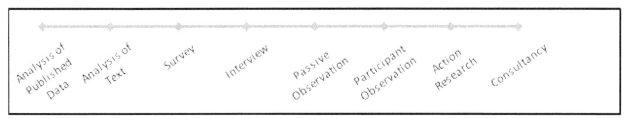

Going forward, we focus on the specific technique of *participant observation*, or participant-as-observer in Gold's [11] terminology. While participant observation originated in ethnographic studies of culture, this data collection method can be used to build theory and test theory on varied sociological concepts and issues. When employed in building theory, a grounded theory approach is generally taken and there may be little *a priori* guidance in deciding what data to collect [18]. When testing theory, the researcher has distinct constructs in mind and can define, *a priori*, indicators to look for and record during participant observation. Once immersed, additional indicators may emerge, ones that the researcher had not anticipated but that are deemed to be valid indicators of a construct of interest.

Participant observation may be conducted in an overt or covert manner, i.e., with or without revealing the researcher's identity and purpose. Requirements of informed consent are making covert participant observations rare, but many argue that such secret observation is often not even necessary – that research objectives can be achieved by overt observational study [3, 13]. Bulmer [3] states that many accounts of observational research maintain that success depends on the acceptance of the individual by those being studied as someone they can trust, rather than depending on elaborate fronts and role pretence. Bulmer notes that Polsky [20], in studying criminals, is adamant that researchers should not spy or try to be one of them, but instead should focus on becoming accepted while making clear the distinction between self (interested researcher) and those being studied. Moreover, Bulmer cites instances where ostensibly closed institutions have opened themselves up to researchers who were up front about their research purpose, including the British higher civil service [12] and the mafia [15].

3. PARTICIPANT OBSERVATION IN IS RESEARCH

The use of participant observation in IS research is scant. Zuboff's [24] classic book on "the age of the smart machine" is the major illustration of participant observation in the realm of IS. In IS research journals, some articles that mention the use of participant observation are in fact using a series of interviews [8], a combination of interviews with passive observation of meetings and testing sessions [19], or action research that is affecting the development of the organization in an intended way [22].

The study by Nandhakumar [17] is an authentic application of participant observation. He immersed himself in an IS development team for six months to examine ways in which time was experienced and managed by team members. Nandhakumar

worked as a full-time employee on an IS development project alongside five other team members. In the observer portion of his role, he recorded information related to time usage and time management. Nandhakumar operated overtly, signing a confidentiality agreement stating that the company would not be identified and that all reports would be cleared by the team leader [17, 18].

Why is there not more participant observation research in IS? Is it that we don't need it? This is doubtful, as in IS we commonly research organizational phenomena (e.g., enterprise-wide system implementation) as well as workplace attitudes and behaviors (e.g., role ambiguity, turnover intention, technology use). Observation can reveal elements beyond what can be achieved through interviews and surveys. Giddens [9] contends that people know more than they can say, and Altheide and Johnson [1] call attention to unarticulated understandings that manifest in nods, silences, humor, and such. Participant observation can enhance our understanding of IS phenomena by adding "thick description" of, for example, reactions to new technologies, decisions to leave the job, and the like.

Or perhaps the reason for the scarcity of participant observation research in IS is uncertainty about how to conduct such a study. We believe this may be a barrier; it was an initial hurdle for us. Thus, we sought to identify a documented methodology for conducting participant observation research.

4. IN SEARCH OF A PARTICIPANT OBSERVATION METHODOLOGY

Long ago, Becker [2] urged field observation researchers toward greater formalization and systematization so such research could become more a "scientific" and less an "artistic" type of endeavor. But according to van Maanen [23], there still is not much of an established technique for participant observation, despite decades of trying to arrive at a standard methodology. Serious researchers seem to agree, however, that participant observation is NOT just hanging out. It consists of "more than merely immersing oneself in data and 'having insights'" [2, p. 660].

Drawing from the literature on participant observation, we formulate a six-phase process for conducting a participant observation study: 1) selecting and defining concepts and indicators, 2) gaining entry and informed consent for overt observation, 3) preparing for data collection, 4) collecting data, 5) drawing conclusions, and 6) verifying and refining conclusions. We are still finding sources of insight and expect to "progressively elaborate" the methodology as we learn more.

Phase I. Selecting and Defining Concepts and Indicators
1. Identify the constructs, or phenomena, to be observed. Also identify hypothesized relationships, especially if testing rather than building theory.
2. For each construct or phenomenon, identify indicators that can be seen or heard that reflect that construct or phenomenon (e.g., specific behaviors, types of statements, certain words or phrases).
3. Enlist knowledgeable others to review the list of indicators for each construct and report face validity; refine and repeat as needed. Knowledgeable others include:
   a. Individuals familiar with the domain of the construct or, in the case of a new construct, familiar with how similar constructs have been examined by researchers.
   b. Individuals familiar with the type of context the participant observer will be entering, e.g., types of formal interactions the participant observer is likely to experience, types of informal interactions, hierarchical structure of the portion of the organization the participant will be entering, etc.
4. Define criteria to be used to assess the validity of observations (drawn from [2]):
   a. Does the informant have reason to lie or conceal some of what he is saying or doing?
   b. Does vanity or expediency lead the informant to misstate his role in an event or his attitude toward it?
   c. Did the informant actually have the opportunity to witness the occurrence he describes?
   d. Do the informant's feelings about a person or issue under discussion lead him to alter his story in some way?
   e. Was the statement made independently of the observer (i.e., the statement was volunteered) or was it directed by a question from the observer? (Common wisdom is that we can be more sure of a statement that is volunteered.)
   Note that even if an observed statement/behavior is defective on one of these five dimensions, it still provides important information – but these nuances of perspective should be documented with the observation.

Phase II. Gaining Entry and Informed Consent
1. Market the contribution the participant observer can make in the area of the organization he or she would be employed; market the value of the research being conducted, how the results can inform practice.
2. Work with University Institutional Review Board (IRB) staff to abide by informed consent regulations – see example at Collaborative Institutional Training Initiative [4].
3. Determine forms/signatures needed for IRB informed consent and obtain signatures.

Phase III. Preparing for Data Collection
1. Given the concepts and indicators to be recorded, define how the participant observer will record observations, for example:
   a. Spreadsheet: Design the sheet and column structure, remembering to capture the "validity of observations" criteria noted in Phase I.
   b. Journal: Design the structure and style to be used, e.g., entries by day? keywords to be used to signal that a

journal entry relates to a particular construct? capture thoughts and happenings that are not necessarily related to the constructs?
2. Pilot the data collection by having the participant observer use the defined data collection system in a similar setting. Refine the system as needed.

Phase IV. Collecting Data
1. Conduct participant observation.
2. Employ sense-making throughout the observation period. If adjustments to research questions or procedures are made, document in detail the change made and why.

Phase V. Drawing Conclusions
1. Quantify observations as much as possible.
2. Express confidence in each conclusion according to the evidence you have. For example, from Becker [2], your statement might take one of these following forms:
   a. "*Every member* of the group said, in response to a direct question, xxx"
   b. "*Every member* of the group volunteered to an observer that xxx"
   c. "*Some proportion* of the group's members either answered a direct question or volunteered that he shared this perspective, but none of the others were asked or volunteered information on the subject"
   d. "*Every member* of the group was asked or volunteered information, but some given proportion said they viewed the matter from the differing perspective"
   e. "No one was asked questions or volunteered information on the subject, but *all members* were observed to engage in behavior or to make other statements from which the observer inferred that the perspective was being used by them as a basic, though unstated, premise"
   f. "*Some proportion* of the group was observed using the general perspective as a basic premise, but the rest of the group was not observed engaging in such activities"
   g. "*Some proportion* of the group was observed engaged in activities implying the general perspective while the remainder of the group was observed engaged in activities that implied a different perspective"
3. Participant observation triangulation
   a. As with other methodologies, the participant observation researcher can be more confident in a conclusion being drawn if multiple kinds of evidence converge to support it. For example, the researcher can report stronger confidence in a conclusion that is supported by statements from group members as well as observable behaviors.
4. Model of conclusions
   a. If theory building, model the elements and relationships that emerged from the participant observation.
   b. If theory testing, show the proposed constructs and relationships that were supported by the observational data.

Phase VI. Verifying and Refining Conclusions
1. Search for "negative cases," i.e., items of data that do not fit the concluding model. Document as a direction for future research or apply these items to further refine or extend the concluding model.
2. Search for relationships that were not anticipated or not hypothesized. Document as a direction for further

research or apply them to refine or extend the concluding model.

3. Is there an alternative explanation – other than your concluding model – for the findings? Does the evidence collected refute the alternative explanations? If not, acknowledge as a direction for future research.

5. APPLYING THE PARTICIPANT OBSERVATION METHODOLOGY

Rosen [21] contends that "to understand social process one must get inside the world of those generating it." Turnover is certainly a social process, and it is a continuing matter of concern in IS organizations and in our IS research community, as evidenced by the theme of this year's CPR Conference. We are designing a participant observation study to examine the role of voice in IS worker turnover. Our study will test portions of a conceptual model recently proposed by Moore [16] and will also seek to discover additional hypotheses specific to managerial behavior and organizational events. The Moore [16] model is presented in Figure 2.

Figure 2. Voice and Exit of the Dissatisfied IS Professional [16]

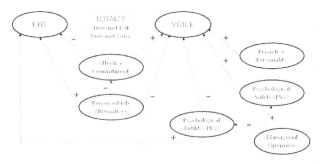

The model in Figure 2 is grounded in the work of Hirschman [14] and summarizes the role that voice is posited to play relative to exit for dissatisfied IS professionals. Because Hirschman's exit-voice-loyalty framework assumes a dissatisfying situation, this model applies to *dissatisfied* IS workers (making worker dissatisfaction a boundary condition for the model).

Following from Hirschman [14], *voice* is defined as: "verbal behavior that is improvement-oriented and directed to a specific target who holds power inside the organization" [6, p. 870]. *Exit* is the act of leaving an employing organization and is typically assessed as actual turnover or turnover intention. *Loyalty* is choosing not to exit and choosing not to voice. Because loyalty is defined as the lack of exit and voice actions, it is represented within parentheses in the model.

The "voice" portion of the model is delineated by dotted lines in Figure 2 and includes constructs drawn from psychology and management research. *Proactive personality* is defined as a disposition toward taking personal initiative to influence one's environment [5]. Two constructs pertinent to voice that are developing in the management literature are psychological safety and psychological futility. *Psychological futility of voice* is defined as the belief that engaging in voice will not lead to desired outcomes [16], and Detert and Burris [6] define *psychological safety of voice* as the belief that engaging in voice will not lead to personal harm. The construct of *managerial*

openness is defined as subordinates' perceptions that their boss listens to them, is interested in their ideas, gives fair consideration to the ideas presented, and at least sometimes takes action to address the matter raised [6]. Reasoning and support for all of the relationships posited in Figure 2 can be found in Moore [16].

We are excited about the potential for participant observation to elucidate nuances that will help explain a worker's decision to voice, or put up with the dissatisfaction, or leave the job. The second author will be the participant observer in an IS group at a large corporation for six months in 2012. She will market herself as a faculty intern, able to bring past experience and solid foundational knowledge to a job in business analysis. Her previous industry experience and current teaching areas are grounded in business analysis, planning, and monitoring; requirements elicitation, analysis, management, and communication; and solution assessment and validation. She is prepared to collect rich data through observation — "the minor grunts and groans as (they) respond to their situation... their gestural, visual bodily response to what's going on around them" [10]. Analysis of the data is expected to provide new insights into the experiences of IT professionals as they make decisions to leave, to stay, and to try to change dissatisfying elements of their work environment.

6. CHALLENGES IN PARTICIPANT OBSERVATION RESEARCH

We continue to study and learn about participant observation research, and continue to update our list of challenges and potential solutions. We will present these issues at the conference. At this point, we note challenges identified related to getting access to conduct a participant observation study, and challenges in maintaining objectivity when the research is underway.

Getting access for participant observation:

- Unless the researcher has skills that are valuable in the work group, there is little incentive for the company to give permission [18].
- Difficulty for an academic to have the extended period of time necessary to immerse in the full-time role of participant-observer.
- Given the present state of IRB informed consent, the option of covert observation is unlikely.
- The issue of "hierarchy of consent" [7] comes into play in corporate organizations. Does top management consent mean that all employees must consent? What if a subordinate wishes to NOT consent – how would that be handled? If many people are encountered casually in the observation setting, is it practical to obtain consent from each without causing disruption?

Maintaining objectivity:

- When the researcher and informant begin to act as ordinary friends, they tend to jeopardize their roles:
  - The risk of "going native": When the participant observer over-identifies with the informants — assumes the values, premises and standards of his informants — and thereby starts to lose researcher perspective [11].
  - Problems can occur in the opposite direction as well: The informant may become too identified with the researcher to continue functioning as a mere informant, instead becoming a fellow observer [11].

7. MOVING FROM RESEARCH-IN-PROGRESS TO RESEARCH

At conference time, we plan to present the participant observation research methodology, details of how we have applied that methodology in the design of our study, key challenges in participant observation and potential solutions we have identified and/or enacted.

8. REFERENCES

[1] Altheide, D., and Johnson, J. 1994. Criteria for assessing interpretive validity in qualitative research. In N. Denzin and Y. Lincoln, *Handbook of qualitative research* (485-499). London: Sage.

[2] Becker, H. 1958. Problems of inference and proof in participant observation. *American Sociological Review*, 652-660.

[3] Bulmer, M. 1980. Comment on 'The Ethics of Covert Methods'. *British Journal of Sociology*, 59-65.

[4] Collaborative Institutional Training Initiative (CITI). 2010, June 22. *CITI*. Retrieved March 7, 2011, from CITI Collaborative Institutional Training Initiative: https://www.citiprogram.org/

[5] Crant, J. 2000. Proactive behavior in organizations. *Journal of Management, 26*, 435-462.

[6] Detert, J., and Burris, E. 2007. Leadership behavior and employee voice: Is the door really open? *Academy of Management Journal, 50*(4), 869-884.

[7] Dingwall, R. 1980. Ethics and ethnography. *Sociological Review, 28*(4), 871-891.

[8] Duhan, S., Levy, M., and Powell, P. 2001. Information systems strategies in knowledge-based SMEs: The role of core competencies. *European Journal of Information Systems, 10*, 25-40.

[9] Giddens, A. 1984. *The constitution of society*. Cambridge: Polity Press.

[10] Goffman, E. 1989. On fieldwork. *Journal of Contemporary Ethhography, 18*(2), 123-132.

[11] Gold, R. 1958. Roles in Sociological Field Observations. *Social Forces*, 217-223.

[12] Heclo, H., and Wildavsky, A. 1974. *The private government of public money*. London: Macmillan.

[13] Herrera, C. 1999. Two arguments for 'covert methods' in social research. *British Journal of Sociology, 50*(2), 331-343.

[14] Hirschman, A. 1970. Exit, Voice, and Loyalty: Responses to Decline in Firms, Organizations, and States. Cambridge, MA: Harvard University Press.

[15] Ianni, F., and Ianni, E. 1972. A family business: Kinship and social control in organised crime. London: Routledge.

[16] Moore, J. E. 2011. Illuminating the Other Road: The Role of Voice in IT Turnover. *Proceedings of the Hawaii International Conference on Social Sciences* (p. 244 Abstracts). Kauai, HI: IEEE Computer Society Conference Publishing Services.

[17] Nandhakumar, J. 2002. Managing time in a software factory: Temporal and spatial organization of IS development activities. *The Information Society, 18*, 251-262.

[18] Nandhakumar, J., and Jones, M. 1997. Too close for comfort? Distance and engagement in interpretive information systems research. *Information Systems Journal, 7*, 109-131.

[19] Pollock, N., and Cornford, J. 2004. ERP systems and the university as a 'unique' organisation. *Information Technology & People, 17*(1), 31-52.

[20] Polsky, N. 1971. *Hustlers, beats and others*. Harmondsworth: Penguin.

[21] Rosen, M. 1991. Coming to terms with the field: Understanding and doing organizational ethnography. *Journal of Management Studies, 28*(1), 1-24.

[22] Smith, S., Winchester, D., Bunder, D., and Jamieson, R. 2010. Circuits of power: A study of mandated compliance to an information systems security De Jure Standard in a government organization. *MIS Quarterly, 34*(3), 463-486.

[23] Van Maanen, J. 2009, August 19. *A song for my supper: More tales of the field*. Retrieved November 4, 2010, from Organizational Research Methods: http://orm.sagepub.com/content/13/2/240

[24] Zuboff, S. 1988. In the age of the smart machine: The future of work and power. Oxford: Heinemann.

The Impact of Media Selection on Stakeholder Communication in Agile Global Software Development: A Preliminary Industrial Case Study

Biyagamage Agra Junius Fernando
Brunel University, Uxbridge, UB8 3PH, UK
bajfernando@gmail.com

Tracy Hall
Brunel University, Uxbridge, UB8 3PH, UK
tracy.hall@brunel.ac.uk

Anthony Fitzpatrick
Pitney Bowes
Watford, WD25 7GS, UK
anthony.fitzpatrick@pb.com

ABSTRACT

This paper investigates the selection of appropriate communication media in agile global software development. Frequent communication between project stakeholders is core to agile software development. Furthermore the choice of media is fundamental to effective communication. In a global software development environment the challenges that distance creates must be addressed in the choice of media. The wrong media for the wrong task can cause many problems. We apply Media Synchronicity Theory to the selection of communication media in a global software company which uses Scrum. Our results show that the theory is helpful in highlighting the important factors in choosing an appropriate media for 'conveying' and 'converging' communications. However the theory does not cover all important factors. We confirm previous findings that media availability, media familiarity and infrastructure capabilities also need to be taken into consideration.

Categories and Subject Descriptors

D.2.9 [**Software**]: Software Engineering – *management*

General Terms

Management, Human Factors.

Keywords

Global software engineering, communication, media

1. INTRODUCTION

The adoption of agile within global software development (GSD) has been steadily increasing. However the challenges involved in implementing agile GSD include: communication, coordination and control. These challenges are largely as a result of distance. Communication is reported to be one of the key processes in software development and there is evidence that it is heavily linked to the effectiveness of coordination and control (e.g. [6],

[16], [17]). Therefore maintaining effective communication is important and even more so in a distributed setting.

A widely accepted practice to overcome the challenge of reduced communication in GSD is to adopt an agile development method which promotes frequent and regular communication (e.g. [20], [14], [22], [33]). Although frequent communication is reported to help decrease temporal, geographical and socio-cultural distance issues in GSD, it brings with it the problem of appropriate communication media choice (e.g. [22], [23], [33]).

The choice of appropriate media however, is proving challenging and using the wrong media for the wrong task has been reported to cause many problems (e.g. [25], [31], [19], [1]). Therefore it is vital that appropriate media is chosen for tasks in order to achieve effective communication [30].

This research applies Media Synchronicity Theory (MST) to the selection of communication media. Media Synchronicity Theory analyses the type of communication within tasks and uses this to drive the selection of media. We evaluate Media Synchronicity Theory using the practices and media choices at a global software company currently using Scrum. Our results show the extent to which Media Synchronicity Theory can be applied to assist appropriate media choice in agile GSD.

The main aim of this research is to understand how best to exercise appropriate communication media choice and therefore achieve effective communication in agile GSD. To achieve this aim the following research questions (RQ) are addressed:

RQ1: How and when do agile GSD teams communicate?

RQ2: Can Media Synchronicity Theory be effectively used to improve appropriate media choice in agile GSD?

2. BACKGROUND
2.1 Global Software Development

GSD is becoming increasingly popular with organisations reporting many benefits including reduced development costs [3]. By globalising, software organisations can leverage on more cost-efficient workforces, located in lower-cost countries. Furthermore adopting GSD has the benefit of having access to a global pool of skilled labourers [2]. This means that organisations can expand their software development activities with a globally distributed workforce and create virtual global corporations.

Distance makes developing a global software team with distributed members challenging. Furthermore, distance has been reported to impact on communication within a team [17]. Communication is a crucial process in software development in general but has been shown to be even more so in a distributed setting (e.g. [6], [16], [17]). Distributed team members have fewer opportunities for communication and the frequency of communication decreases with physical separation among team members ([13], [12]).

2.2 Agile GSD

Agile methods promise reduced development times, shorter response times, better quality, decreased development costs and improved communication within teams and between participants [24]. Studies show that information exchange between distributed project sites has been improved by using agile development methodologies which encourage frequent communication (e.g. [14], [33], [23], 16], [20]).

Agile team members have been shown to communicate through media such as web pages, instant messaging, wikis, telephone, teleconference, videoconference, email and desktop-sharing (e.g. [23], [15], [14]). The effectiveness of communication between distributed sites however, has been shown to be dependent on the appropriateness of the media (e.g. [17], [21]). Choosing inappropriate media for a specific task or situation can create communication issues (e.g. [25], [31], [1]).

2.3 Media Synchronicity Theory (MST)

Dennis & Valacich [10] introduced Media Synchronicity Theory (MST) to explain effective task performance when making use of various media for team functions or communication processes. MST identifies predictors of communication performance [9]. Media synchronicity is defined as the extent to which individuals work together on the same activity at the same time [10]. MST focuses on the capability of media to support synchronicity and hypothesises that communication will be enhanced when the synchronicity that a given medium can support appropriately matches the synchronicity that a communication process requires [8].

A differentiation is also made between synchronous media, such as face-to-face, video-conferencing or telephone conferencing, where all participants communicate at the same time, and asynchronous media, such as email or fax, where participants do not work together at the same time [8]. There are 3 main dimensions of MST.

The first dimension of MST distinguishes between two fundamental communication processes: conveyance and convergence. Conveyance is the exchange of information. Lower synchronicity allows for more time between messages so that the receiver has time to cognitively process the message. Therefore low media synchronicity is suitable for conveyance [10]. Convergence is the development of shared meaning for information. The convergence process typically requires fewer cognitive resources than conveyance because most of the information has already been conveyed. The discussion focuses on already processed information and its meaning. Therefore high media synchronicity is preferred for convergence [10].

MST's second dimension defines five media capabilities (shown in Table 1) which provide a measure for media synchronicity [8].

Table 1. MST media capability definitions [8]

Immediacy of feedback	How quick feedback is received from the recipient
Symbol Variety	The number of ways information can be encoded
Parallelism	The number of effective simultaneous

	conversations that can be established
Rehearsability	The ability to fine tune a message before sending
Reprocessability	The ability to retrieve and process a received message for better understanding

MST's third dimension defines the team functions of production, group well-being and member support. This dimension stresses that social needs have to be considered to improve communication [8].

Media with strong capabilities to support conveyance typically lack strong capabilities to support convergence and vice versa [8]. As a task is usually made out of converging and conveying processes, MST suggests the use of a set of media and encourages media switching [17].

MST has been used and tested in various settings. Ramesh & Dennis [26] apply MRT and MST to coordination and communication processes in global virtual software development teams. Lanubile [17] focuses on effective communication during software requirements gathering in distributed settings. Niinimaki et al [21] apply MST to investigate factors that affect text and audio-based communication in a GSD setting. Studies also evaluate MST in distributed or virtual team settings [7]. Studies investigating MST in agile GSD settings remain scarce.

3. RESEARCH METHODOLOGY

3.1 Research approach

In this study a case study approach [34] is used with data collected by means of semi-structured interviews, non-participant observations and document reviews.

3.2 Case Study Background

Pitney Bowes is one of the world's leading providers of integrated mail and document management systems. Pitney Bowes has sites in 130 locations and employs over 36,000 people worldwide. The company has grown through acquisitions, and globalisation plays a big part in its evolution. To cope with the challenges of globalisation but also take advantage of its benefits, Pitney Bowes has adopted GSD and uses agile development methods.

This case study is focused on one development team who use Scrum. The team consists of 7 globally distributed members, with a product manager based in The Netherlands, a development manager and a senior developer based in the UK, and further developers based in the US and India. The customised version of Scrum implemented in the team has 2 formal communication cross points: "daily stand ups" and "weekly progress meetings". The team makes use of a wide range of communication media.

3.3 Data Collection

Data was collected over the 8 weeks in July and August of 2010 that the first author was based at the company as a researcher.

3.3.1 Semi-structured interviews

The prime method for gathering data was semi-structured interviews. Core questions and follow-on probes were defined (the interview script is provided in Appendix One). The interview script consists of 16 questions focused on discussing communication cross points and the media used. The initial interview questions were piloted [28]. This identified various refinements to the interview that were subsequently implemented.

A pre-interview questionnaire was sent to participants prior to the interview. This focused on identifying communication cross points and the media used. The interview follows this up by focusing on which task-media combinations work well or don't work well and why. A post-interview questionnaire was sent to participants asking them to rate the importance of MST media capabilities in relation to the communication cross points they identified.

In total 4 team members were interviewed, 2 interviews were conducted on a one-to-one basis in the UK and 2 were conducted via telephone, as the interviewees were based in India. The remaining 3 team members were unavailable for interview. Interviews lasted between 18 and 28 minutes.

3.3.2 Non-participant observation

A non-participant observatory role was adopted to collect second degree data [29]. One of the key benefits of choosing observation as a data collection method is the ability to observe and listen to participants carrying out activities in their natural environment [4]. In addition it provides data that is not based on the interviewee's perception and also is an effective means of validating the information gained from participants during the interview sessions [27].

All observations were logged and documented in observation sheets. Data was collected from observation settings that are key communication cross points in agile GSD. In total 7 observations took place, 5 of which were daily stand-up meetings, lasting 15 minutes on average and 2 were weekly progress (sprint) meetings, lasting 45 minutes on average.

3.3.3 Document review

To achieve triangulation by collecting data from multiple sources [34] content analysis was carried out on documents relevant to the case study. Analysing these documents allowed the corroboration of data gathered in the interviews and observations [32].

3.4 Data Analysis

The qualitative data gathered is analysed using guidelines suggested by Miles and Huberman [18]. The analysis process includes the transcription of the tape recorded interviews, followed by coding to classify and categorise the transcriptions.

3.5 Threats to validity

The following limitations should be considered:

- Detailed data was collected on only one GSD team. This limitation restricts the generalisability of our findings.

- Only 4 of the 7 team members were interviewed. There is a risk that the data collected is biased.

- No observations were conducted for the communication cross point "ad hoc communication". This means that we cannot supplement the data collected in interviews relating to this cross point.

4. RESULTS

Tables 2, 3 and 4 analyse the communication processes within three communication cross points (daily stand up, weekly progress meeting and ad hoc communications). We identify the media used for each communication process used in these 3 cross points. We also apply MST classifications: "conveying" or "converging" to each communication process.

Table 2. MST Results: daily stand up

Data source	Communication Processes	Communication process type	Media used
Document Review	A quick stand up where everyone explains what they are currently up to and what if anything is inhibiting progress	convey & converge	No data found
Interview & Observation	Report daily activities, impediments and work to be done	convey	Conference Call
	Discuss any activities done, impediments and planned work	converge	
	Decide on which issues will be discussed in detail after meeting (on a one-to-one basis)	converge	

Table 2 shows that the daily stand up consists of three communication processes, which are currently communicated via the media "conference call". No data was found in the document review regarding the communication media to use for a daily stand up. Table 2 also shows that the "conference call" media is used to communicate both types of MST processes. Dual use of a media is counter to MST which specifies that a media can effectively support either conveying or converging communication.

Table 4 shows that there are several ad hoc communication processes and four types of media used to support these. Although ad hoc communication is identified by all participants as a key communication cross point, no data was found in the document review about the communication processes within ad hoc communication, nor was any data found on media choice. This suggests ad hoc communication may be a communication cross point lacking structure and support and therefore more subject to miscommunication. Table 4 also shows that the process "query solving" is associated with all four communication media. Table 4 identifies converging as well as conveying communication processes are identified during ad hoc communications with desk top sharing and conference call media used for both types of communications.

Table 4. MST Results: ad hoc communication

Data source	Communication Processes	Communication process type	Media used
Document Review	Plan the duration and deliverables of the upcoming sprint	converge	No data found
	Review weekly development reports and hear news from the business	convey & converge	
	The team demonstrates the deliverable completed during the sprint	convey	
	The team reflect on the sprint and suggest improvements for future sprints	converge	
Interview & Observation	Invite participants	convey	Email
	Report and share meeting summary at the end	convey	
	Demonstrate software	convey	
	Discuss demo	converge	Desktop Sharing
	Report weekly progress	convey	
	Discuss weekly progress	converge	Conference Call
	Report field updates	convey	
	Training and knowledge sharing	converge	
	Discuss and decide on future activities	converge	
	Additional 1-2-1 comments during demos direct	convey & converge	Instant Messaging

MST media capabilities	Media: Conference call	Participant media capability expectations (Participants: 1-4)			
		1	2	3	4
Immediacy of Feedback	H	H	H	H	H
Parallelism	L	H	H	L	H
Symbol Variety	L	L	L	L	H
Rehearsability	L	H	H	H	H
Reprocessability	L	L	L	L	L

Note: H=High; L=Low

Table 5 compares the MST media capabilities of the "conference call" media with participants' expectations of the communication media during the daily stand up. Table 5 shows a degree of agreement between the media capability of a conference call and participants' expectations of communication in the daily stand. The major disagreement is rehearsability. All participants expected rehearsability to be "high" for the daily stand up, whereas the conference call media has low rehearsability according to MST.

Appendix Two compares the MST media capabilities of all four media used during weekly progress meetings with participants' expectations of the communication media during those meetings. Table 6 shows that the wide range of media used during weekly progress meetings between them cover the expectations of participants. For example, participants' high expectations of "immediacy of feedback" and "parallelism" for example, are covered by the use of "conference call", "email" and "desktop sharing".

Appendix Three compares the MST media capabilities of all four media used during ad hoc communication with participants' expectations of the communication media during those communications. Appendix Three also shows that the wide range of media used during ad hoc communication between them cover the expectations of participants.

Another issue was identified during interviews related to query solving within ad hoc communication. Email media was typically used for query solving, with chains of emails often leading to miscommunication and confusion. However two participants reported practising the use of multiple media in this situation. These two participants report using email to highlight the problem and identify a suitable person to communicate with, then switching to either instant messaging, phone and even desktop sharing to solve the problem. This suggests that by breaking down the task "query solving" further, conveying as well as converging communication processes are identified and suitable media can be used.

Finally, data was also collected during the interview related to why particular media was chosen for particular tasks.

Tables 5, 6 and 7 compare the capabilities that MST identifies for a particular communication media to the expectations participants have of that media in specific communication cross points. The expectations of participants were collected in the post-interview questionnaire.

Table 5. MST media capabilities and participant expectation: daily stand up

Table 6. Additional media choice factors

Additional factor	Example quote
Media familiarity	"Number one would be to go with the corporate recommendation [...] other than that use whatever works and you know [...]"
Media availability	"Well there is media that is there and available [...] we just choose those that are readily available."
Infrastructure capabilities	"Some of the phone quality is terrible [...] and can be very poor coming from India. The quality is poor and sometimes a connection can't be made. Having a decent set up (infrastructure) is important and is considered when choosing media"

Table 6 shows that participant responses fall into three categories. These additional media choice factors do not directly relate to MST but were mentioned frequently during interviews. All participants acknowledge these factors influence their media choice.

5. DISCUSSION

Our results show that there were several strong communication cross points in place for the team we studied. They communicated frequently using daily stand ups, weekly progress meetings and ad hoc communication. Although this communication framework was provided the formal documents supporting this framework did not provide media choice guidelines for the team. Just as importantly the formal documents also did not set out the nature of ah hoc communications. The lack of guidelines may have contributed to the media task issues identified in the interviews and observations.

Our results show that MST allowed a richer analysis of communication at Pitney Bowes. For example, according to MST a task typically consists of converging as well as conveying communication processes. Furthermore a media with strong capabilities in one process will typically lack capabilities in the other process. MST therefore promotes media switching [17]. This suggests that using a "conference call" to communicate both conveying and converging processes during a daily stand up is not appropriate. This media has high synchronicity and therefore is more suitable for converging communication processes. In addition the "conference call" media lacks rehearsability and therefore is not ideal for conveying communication processes according to MST. Our results suggest that the team studied would improve the effectiveness of its communication by using a wider range of media to support the multiple communication processes involved in the daily stand up.

Indeed Hossain et al [15] suggest that team members email daily scrum questions (What they are currently doing/ What could inhibit progress/ What they are planning to do next) to each other in advance of the daily stand up. This means that the conveying processes are communicated via email, which according to MST is more appropriate and the converging processes are covered by the conference call. This practice also supports media switching, as two types of media are used to communicate the respective processes. The "rehearsability" capability of email will give participants time to compose suitable answers. This will allow for a more effective daily stand up where the focus will be on briefly conveying and then converging about issues that are relevant.

Our use of MST to analyse the use of email in "ad hoc communication" suggests that the use of emails for "query solving" is not appropriate. Email is an asynchronous medium most appropriate for a conveying task. Furthermore, our results suggest that there are two aspects to query solving, each of which involves different communication processes: stating the query involves conveying and solving the query involves converging. MST classifies emails as a medium with low synchronicity most suited to conveying processes. This means that emails are not ideal for solving queries. Synchronous media such as instant messaging, desktop sharing and conference calls are most suitable for solving queries. However email remains suitable for stating the query. This suggests that the most effective approach to query solving involves media switching.

Although MST cast light on the effective use of media for specific tasks, our results suggest that the theory may need to be extended. Our results suggest that the theory does not suitably account for "media familiarity", "media availability" and "infrastructure capabilities". All of which were significant drivers of media choice. Previous researchers (e.g. [21]) have also identified additional factors that affect media choice.

6. CONCLUSION

Our results provide insight into the communication habits and media choices of a contemporary agile GSD team. In particular we answer the following research questions:

RQ1: How and when do agile GSD teams communicate?

Our findings show that there are a variety of communication cross points used by the team studied. These include daily stand ups, weekly progress meetings as well as ad hoc communications. A variety of media is used to support communication during these cross points including conference calls, email, instant messaging and desk top sharing. However we found that the documentation available to the team gives no guidance on selecting the most effective media for each communication cross point, nor does the documentation elaborate on ad hoc communication.

RQ2: Can Media Synchronicity Theory be effectively used to improve appropriate media choice in agile GSD?

Our results suggest that analysing agile GSD communication in terms of MST provides rich insights into the performance of media at specific communication cross points. In particular, our use of MST identified cross points where a greater range of media was needed to support all types of communication in a task. For example our use of MST suggests that query solving comprises both conveying and converging types of communication. This means that query solving is not adequately supported by only email communication media (currently adopted in the team we studied) as email does not effectively support converging communication.

However are results also confirm Niinimaki et al's [21] findings that MST does not cover all important aspects of media choice. Our findings suggest that "media availability", "media familiarity" and "infrastructure capability" are additional important factors driving media selection

7. REFERENCES

[1] Cannizzo, F., Marcionetti, G. and Moser, P. (2008), "Evolution of the Tools and Practices of a Large Distributed Agile Team", Agile 2008 Conference, pp 513-518

[2] Conchuir E., Holmstrom H., Agerfalk P.J., Fitzgerald B. (2006) "Exploring the Assumed Benefits of Global Software Development", IEEE International Conference on Global Software Engineering, pp159-168

[3] Conchuir, E.O., Agerfalk, P.J., Olsson, H.H. and Fitzgerald, B. (2009), "Global software development: where are the benefits?", Communication of the ACM, 52 (8), pp.127-131

[4] Coolican, H. (2009), "Research methods and statistics in psychology", London, Hodder Education

[5] Daft, R. and Lengel, R. (1986), "Organizational information requirements, media richness and structural design", Management Science, 32 (5), pp.554-571

[6] Damian D., Izquierdo L., Singer J., Kwan I. (2007), "Awareness in the wild: Why communication breakdowns occur ", International Conference on Global Software Engineering, pp. 81-90

[7] DeLuca, D. and Valacich, J. (2005), "Outcomes from conduct of virtual teams at two sites: Support for media synchronicity theory", 38th Annual Hawaii International Conference on System Sciences, pp. 1-10

[8] DeLuca, D. C. and Valacich, J.S. (2006), "Virtual Teams In and Out of Synchronicity" Information, Technology & People, 19 (4), pp. 323-344

[9] Dennis, A. R., Fuller, R. M. and Valacich, J. S. (2008), "Media, Tasks, and Communication Processes: A Theory of Media Synchronicity," MIS Quarterly, 32(3), pp. 575-600

[10] Dennis, A. R., and Valacich, J. S. (1999), "Rethinking Media Richness: Towards a Theory of Media Synchronicity", Procs of the 32nd Hawaii International Conference on System Sciences, 1(1), pp1-10

[11] Fruchter R., Bosch-Sijtsema P. and Ruohomäki, V. (2010), "Tension between perceived collocation and actual geographic distribution in project teams", AI & Society. 25 (2), pp. 183-192

[12] Herbsleb J. and Mockus A. (2003), "An empirical study of speed and communication in globally distributed software development", IEEE Transactions on Software Engineering, 29 (6), pp. 481-494.

[13] Holmstrom H., Conchuir E., Agerfalk P.J and Fitzgerald B. (2006a), "Global Software Development Challenges: A Case Study on Temporal, Geographical and Socio-Cultural Distance, International Conference on Global Software Engineering, pp. 3-11.

[14] Holmstrom H., Fitzgerald B., Agerfalk P.J. and Conchuir E. (2006b), "Agile Practices reduce distance in global software development" Information Systems Management, 23 (3), pp. 7-18

[15] Hossain E, Barbar M.A. and Paik H. (2009), "Using Scrum in Global Software Development: A Systematic Literature Review", IEEE International Conf on Global Software Engineering, pp75-184

[16] Korkala M. and Abrahamsson P. (2007), "Communication in distributed agile development: A case study", 33rd EUROMICRO Conference on Software Engineering and Advanced Applications, pp203-210

[17] Lanubile F. (2009), "Collaboration in Distributed Software Development", Lecture Notes in Computer Science, Software Engineering: International Summer Schools, ISSSE 2006-2008, Italy, pp74-193

[18] Miles, M.B. and Huberman, A.M. (1994), "An Expanded Sourcebook – Qualitative Data Analysis", London, Sage Publications

[19] Miller. A (2008), "Distributed Agile Development at Microsoft patterns & practices", [Online], available at: http://download.microsoft.com/download/4/4/a/44a2cebd-63fb-4379-898d-9cf24822c6cc/distributed_agile_development_at_microsoft_patterns_and_practices.pdf [Accessed 21st August 2010]

[20] Moe N.B. and Smite D. (2008), "Understanding a lack of trust in global software teams: A multiple-case study," Software Process Improvement and Practice, 13(3), pp.217-231

[21] Niinimaki T., Piri A. and Lassenius C. (2009), "Factors Affecting Audio and Text based Communication Media Choice in Global Software Development Projects", IEEE International Conference on Global Software Engineering, pp. 153-162

[22] Paasivaara M., Durasiewicz s. and Lassenius C. (2008), "Using scrum in a globally distributed project: A case study", Software Process Improvement and Practice, 13 (6), pp. 527-544

[23] Paasivaara M., Durasiewicz S. and Lassenius C. (2008), "Distributed Agile Development: UsingScrum in a Large Project", IEEE International Conference on Global Software Engineering , p.87-95

[24] Phalnikar, R., Deshpande, V.S. and Joshi, S.D. (2009), "Applying Agile Principles for Distriubuted Software Development", International Conference on Advanced Computer Control, pp. 535-539

[25] Powell, A., Piccoli, G., Ives, B. (2004),"Virtual Teams: A review of Current Literature and Directions for Future Research", The Data Base for Advances in Information Systems, 35 (1), pp. 6–36

[26] Ramesh, V and Dennis, A.R. (2002), "The Object-Oriented Team: Lessons for Virtual Teams from Global Software Development", 35th Annual Hawaii Intern Conference on System Sciences, pp212 – 221

[27] Runeson, P. and Host, M. (2009), "Guidelines for conducting and reporting case study research in software engineering", Empirical Software Engineering, 14 (2), pp. 131-164

[28] Robson, C. (2002), "Real World Research (A Resource for Social Scientists and Practitioner-Researchers)", Blackwell Publishing

[29] Silverman, D (2010), "Doing Qualitative Research", London, Sage Publications

[30] Suchan, J. and Hayzak, G. (2001), "The communication characteristics of virtual teams: A case study", IEEE Transactions on Professional. Communication, 44 (3), pp. 174–186

[31] Thissen, M.R., Page, J.M., Bharathi, M.C. and Austin, T.L (2007), "Communication tools for distributed software development teams", ACM SIGMIS CPR conf on Computer personnel research, pp28-35

[32] Travers, M. (2001), "Qualitative Research through Case Studies", London, Sage Publications

[33] Yadav V., Adya M., Nath D. and Sridhar V. (2007), "Investigating an 'Agile-Rigid' Approach in Globally Distributed Requirements Analysis", 11th Pacific Asia Conf on Information systems, pp151-165

[34] Yin, K. R. (2003), "Case Study Research – Design and Methods – Third Edition", London, Sage Publications.

Appendix One. Interview script

Interview Script

(Based on [28])

Introduce myself, Good Afternoon, How are you?

Have you read through the information sheet and the consent form? Do you have any questions?

Introduction:

As stated in the information sheet I am carrying on a piece of research to understand communication challenges in global software engineering and how to overcome them. I am focusing on team X managed by participant A and will therefore be speaking to all of the members.

- state anonymity…

I just wanted to confirm again that you, the respondent will remain anonymous in any written reports growing out of this study and that the responses you give will be treated in strictest confidence.

You may interrupt at any point for clarification purposes for example.

-May I record the interview?

I wish to tape record this interview as it provides a better way of collecting the data and the risk of missing out on information is lower. Also, because it allows us to have a smoother conversation (I won't have to constantly take notes during the interview). The recordings will be only made available to me and my supervisor (at Brunel). After the analysis and write up these recordings will be destroyed. Is this feasible for you?

If NO: Any particular reason why?
- If still No: OK, that's fine, let's carry on
- If Yes: Great , let's get started

Background Questions

Male: ☐   Female: ☐   Job Title:

Experience Level overall:

Experience within Team: "how long have you been working in the Team"   Work location:

1. I would like to know more about the project you are involved in. What is the function of your team? (Manager Question)

2. How many people are involved and what are their roles? What is your specific role? Who is co-located and who is distributed? (Manager Question)

3. What is your responsibility in the team?

4. What is the standard development methodology used?

5. How would you rate your communication experience working in an agile Global Software Engineering Team?

Very Positive ☐ Positive ☐ Undecided ☐ Negative ☐Very Negative ☐

Main Body:

"Thank you for filling out the communication cross point table for me, looking at what you've put in your cross point table..."

6. Which tasks require you to communicate with other members?
6.1 (alt.) When do you have to communicate with other members?
6.2 What is the purpose of this communication cross point? What are you trying to communicate?

Identification of media use
7. What media do you use to communicate?
8. From the listed communication cross-points, which exist due to the methodology you use?
8.1 Do you use more than one media for a task? If yes, please specify.

Identification of media choice rational
9. Why have you chosen a particular media for a particular task?
10. What were drivers behind that choice?
12. Which task-media combinations work well? Why?
13. Which task-media combinations don't work well? Why?

Thank you for your time.
Have you got any questions?
Good Bye

Appendix Two. MST media capabilities and participant expectation: weekly progress meeting

MST media capabilities	Media				Media capability expectations (Participants: 1-4)			
	Email	Desktop Sharing	Conference Call	Instant Messaging	1	2	3	4
Immediacy of Feedback	L	H	H	H	H	H	H	H
Parallelism	H	H	L	L	H	H	H	H
Symbol Variety	L	L	L	L	L	L	L	L
Rehearsability	H	L	L	L	L	L	L	L
Reprocessability	H	H	L	H	H	H	L	H

Note: H=High; L=Low

Appendix Three. MST media capabilities and participant expectation: ad hoc communications

MST media capabilities	Media				Media capability expectations (Participants: 1-4)			
	Email	Instant Messaging	Desktop Sharing	Conference Call	1	2	3	4
Immediacy of Feedback	L	H	H	H	H	H	H	H
Parallelism	H	L	H	L	H	H	H	H
Symbol Variety	L	L	L	L	H	H	H	H
Rehearsability	H	L	L	L	L	L	L	L
Reprocessability	H	H	H	L	H	H	L	L

Co-Adaptive Processes of Stakeholder Networks and Their Effects on Information Systems Specifications

Richard W. Woolridge
Assistant Professor - Department of Management
University of Arkansas at Little Rock
2801 South University Ave., Little Rock AR 72204
(501)-569-8889
rwwoolridge@ualr.edu

Janet Bailey
Associate Professor - Department of Management
University of Arkansas at Little Rock
2801 South University Ave., Little Rock AR 72204
(501) 569-8851
jlbailey@ualr.edu

ABSTRACT

Information System's (IS) requirements inadequacy and volatility are major IS project risks leading to failed, over budget, or over schedule projects. Within requirements determination, an area of focus for the inadequacy and volatility issue is the application domain (i.e., business domain). One step towards better requirements determination methods, techniques, and tools for the application domain would be a theoretically-grounded model for specification emergence and evolution. This paper presents a model of specification emergence and evolution that is confirmed using a case study.

Categories and Subject Descriptors

D.2.1 Requirements / Specifications, F.3.1 Specifying and Reasoning about Programs - Specification techniques, D.2.11 Software Architectures – Domain Specific Architectures, H.1.1 Systems and Information Theory, K.3.2 Computer and Information Science Education – Information systems education, K.6.1 Project and People Management – Systems analysis and design

General Terms

Management, Documentation, Human Factors, Theory.

Keywords

Application Domain, Conceptual Modeling, Categorization, Complex Adaptive Systems (CAS), Requirements Determination

1 INTRODUCTION

Requirements determination is an important part of Information Systems (IS) development [19, 39, 91, 97]. Requirements determination is also one of the most difficult parts of software development to get right [10, 97]. A dynamic business environment complicates requirements determination by causing requirements volatility [1, 17, 101]. Requirements inadequacy and volatility constitute major risks to failed, over budget, or over schedule projects [86, 93].

Within requirements determination, an area of focus for the inadequacy and volatility issue is the application domain (i.e., business domain). IS projects produce solutions for an application domain [32, 48]. Application domain requirements determination (i.e., specification) has long been recognized as important [19, 84]. A lack of application domain knowledge is a major IS development issue [16] and there have been calls to perform more application domain research [26, 27, 100]. Therefore, the application domain is one area to begin understanding the requirements specification inadequacy and volatility issue.

One step towards better requirements determination methods, techniques, and tools for the application domain would be a theoretically-grounded model of specification emergence and evolution, as the understanding derived from such a model may lead to improved requirements determination methods, techniques, and tools. This step then defines the research question for this investigation: Is there a theoretically-grounded model that explains the emergence and evolution of application domain specifications? The answer to this question is sought using a case research method with frequent iteration through data and prior research [22].

2 PRIOR RESEARCH

2.1 Application Domain Research

Over the years, the application domain has been studied from various aspects of software development. Specifically, it has been studied from perspectives of requirements elicitation using various methodological perspectives, utilized in program comprehension, classification of multiple domains, and descriptions of specific domains. Methodological perspectives have focused on goal-centric [18], process-centric [34], data-centric [56], and object-centric [9] perspectives. Within program comprehension research, the presence of developer application domain knowledge comprehension is a controlled variable that improves task performance on certain kinds of tasks [33, 65, 74-76]. Application domain taxonomies have been proposed [25, 26]. Specific application domain research has focused on electronic markets [28], enterprise resource planning [15], and supply chain [20]. Collectively, these studies suggest the application domain is important to development and maintenance, and worthy of classification and description. However, little of this research describes the emergence and evolution of application domain specifications.

2.2 Conceptual Modeling Research

Conceptual models are a means to represent the application domain [48], where conceptual modeling is "the activity of formally describing some aspects of the physical and social world around us for purposes of understanding and communication" [60 p.51]. The application domain is represented by conceptual models that are composed of scripts, contexts, methods, and grammars [95]. Scripts are instances of representations. Script research has focused on quality metrics [47, 52, 59], but these metrics say little about evolution. Contexts describe the setting within which the representation occurs. Context research has focused on individual difference factors [21, 77], task factors [2, 90], and social agenda factors [41], but little research in areas of dynamic multi-stakeholder business environments. Methods provide mapping mechanisms from observations to representation. Methodological perspectives have focused on goal-centric [18], process-centric [34], data-centric [56], and object-centric [9] perspectives, but these perspectives do not account for emergence and evolution. Grammars provide the rules of representation. Grammar research has focused on ontology [94], speech-act theory [5], semiotics [79], and categorization theory [66][1]. Grammar research also does not focus on emergence and evolution. However, categorization theory establishes a cognitive foundation for conceptual models [66-68] and offers the opportunity for a dynamic environment. For this reason, this investigation assumes a categorization theory basis of conceptual modeling.

2.3 Categorization Theory Research

Categorization is flexible and dynamic enabling individuals to modify concepts in response to variations in the environment [44]. Categorization draws non-binding associations between artifacts based on simple recognition of similarities within a context across a set of artifacts [43]. Individuals group artifacts in the world based on their sharing of some similar properties. Recognition of similarities enables individual comprehension within a complex environment [44]. Categorization enables individuals to simplify their environment, reduce memory load, and aid information storage and retrieval. As a fundamental cognitive process, categorization is a major enabler in almost any intellectual endeavor [54 p.11]. Categorization is the process of determining that an artifact is a concept member. A category is composed of three constructs: intension (i.e., specification), extension (i.e., membership), and label (i.e., name) [44]. The constructs of categorization theory provide the context within which application domain specification emergence and evolution will be investigated.

2.4 Complex Adaptive Systems Research

Complex Adaptive Systems (CAS) is a systems theory. In a CAS, individual agents (i.e., stakeholders in this investigation) are defined by their models of the world and these models are called schema, where a schema is defined as used in psychology, to mean a conceptual framework used to grasp information about the world and give it meaning [24 p.17]. A schema in psychology is a category and its associated knowledge [13].

More about the alignment of categorization and CAS will be provided in a later section of this manuscript.

CAS principles have been broadly applied in the IS literature as an analogy, metaphor, and lens. Most relevantly to this investigation, CAS has been applied to IS development from the agile methodology perspective [38, 40, 49, 57, 58, 92, 98], but these agile method studies have not as yet reached a consensus for confirmation or disconfirmation. This investigation does not assume a software development methodology perspective. CAS principles have also been used in: development and implementation participation [55], crisis management [12, 14], information infrastructure [4, 11, 69, 70], software agents [71, 73], architecture [63], open source collaboration methods [62, 64], enterprise application integration [61, 83, 96], enterprise resource planning [51], modeling [53, 80], problem solving [46], modularity [78, 82], design [37], data farming [85], user interfaces [3], enterprise information resource integration [29], requirements engineering [81], customer relationship management (CRM) [30], knowledge sharing [31], enterprise architecture [35, 45, 99], business processes [36], and project management [23]. While as early as 1996 software development has been said to be performed by a CAS [72] and while recently CAS was used conceptually in development approach reconciliation [7], no studies were found utilizing CAS in the domain of specification emergence and evolution.

3 RESEARCH METHOD

3.1 Case Studies

This investigation utilizes a case study method that develops understanding from the dynamics provided within single cases [22]. This investigation seeks to understand the dynamics of specification emergence and evolution within a single case. Case studies may collect data from multiple sources, for example archives, observations, interviews, and questionnaires. The data may be qualitative, quantitative, or both [6]. The data type in this investigation is qualitative and the sources of data are archival and observational.

A case study methodology is highly-iterative and tightly linked to data [22]. Multiple iterations through the case data were performed to confirm the models. Additional iterations were performed seeking disconfirming evidence of which none was found. Lastly, the case data was utilized to provide examples of the model.

A fundamental difference between case study research and other methods is the degree to which there is less a priori knowledge about what the independent and dependent variables are and how they are measured [6]. Little research was found explaining or describing the emergence and evolution of specifications in general, or more particularly emergence and evolution of specifications in the application domain. This investigation is therefore suitable for case study research.

There are four stages of case research where the four stages are: drift, design, prediction, and disconfirmation [8]. Drift describes the process that occurs upon entry into the research field where the investigator becomes familiar with the phenomena, makes initial literature connections, establishing some a priori knowledge about the phenomena's function, and identifies critical phenomena components. Design occurs with the development of a tentative explanation of the phenomena. In design, the objective is to assess and refine the major areas of

---

[1] Categorization replaces classification based on library science literature definitions [44] Jacob, E. K. Classification and categorization: a difference that makes a difference. *Library Trends*, 52, 3 (01/01/ 2004), 515(526).

inquiry suggested by the preliminary explanation. Design is followed by prediction where generalization-formation occurs. Prediction seeks additional different, but similar, cases in order to determine the scope of the explanation. Lastly, disconfirmation attempts to disconfirm the findings with extreme cases where the generalization's limits might be expected to be exceeded. This investigation is part of the drift stage that is concluded by a tentative explanation. In this case, this investigation finds a tentative explanation in CAS theory.

3.2 Case Selection

There were three criteria for case selection. These criteria were observability of phenomenon, observation of emergence and evolution, and application domain focus. The selected case meeting the selection criteria is an application domain framework project for the United States Army Corps of Engineers (USACE). The project developed an Asset Management Framework (AMF) to include the full lifecycle investment strategy for the assets controlled by the USACE. These physical infrastructure assets and the watersheds they impact, are the artifacts analyzed in this case study. The goal was to provide a framework for the transparent integration of preservation, risk mitigation, budgeting, and resource allocation across the range of asset lifecycle decisions (see Table 1). While future IS are anticipated to support this framework, this particular project was a precursor to IS development so the specifications analyzed in this case are fully focused on the application domain. Participation in the project enabled researcher observation of specification emergence and evolution dynamics.

Table 1: USACE Asset Lifecycle Decisions

Asset Decision	Description
Operate	Utilize an asset at a particular level of service
Maintain	Perform some maintenance action on the asset to maintain the desired level of service
Develop	Create, or significantly change, an asset's level of service
Decommission	Cease utilization of an asset and dispose of the asset through demolition, transfer of ownership, or some other mechanism
Investigate	Perform an assessment to determine whether any lifecycle decision should be made for an asset

3.3 Data Collection

The project began January 2007 and ended in May 2008 resulting in the delivery of a report containing recommendations. The project began with a review of archival documents leading to identification of gaps between state of practice and the desired state. These gaps led to a series of nine site visits, fourteen conference calls, two conference presentations, and supplemented by telephone conversations, emails, and document exchanges to create an electronic document repository. In all, over one-hundred USACE executives, managers, and specialists representing a cross-section of the organization from a diverse set of organizational levels, functions, locations, and business lines with a variety of backgrounds and specialties participated in the process. The electronic repository data analyzed in the case focused on

understanding the emergence and evolution of specifications. Specifically, the interest was in identifying the high-level principles impacting the final formulation and not the low-level details of the iterative process steps. Therefore, the data collection started with an instance of a specification and looked back to identify principles influencing emergence and evolution instead of following the detailed development of a specification instance.

4 PROPOSITIONS

The case analysis sought evidence that Complex Adaptive Systems (CAS) theory explains the emergence and evolution of application domain specifications. Maintenance of observational control in the case was achieved in part through the testing of specific propositions. Those propositions were developed through analysis of CAS theory definitions.

CAS is a systems theory where individual agents (i.e., stakeholders in this investigation) are defined by their models of the world (i.e., specifications) [24]. Individual CAS stakeholders (#1 Figure 1) acquire information about their environment, acquire information about their interaction with the environment, identify regularities in the information, convert the regularities into a specification (#2 which is named with a category label #3), and act based on that specification [24 p.17]. Acting based on a specification means that a CAS utilizes (#4) the specification to describe, predict, or interact with artifacts (i.e., behave) (#5) in the world. Results from that utilization are measured (#6) as consequences (#7). The utilization and consequences are recorded (#8) as experience (#9 which includes category membership #10). Consequences are used to determine specification fitness manifested as promotion or demotion (i.e., prioritization #11) in relation to other specifications [24 p.24]. Specifications are created based on identifying regularities in their experience [24 p. 17, 42 p.10].

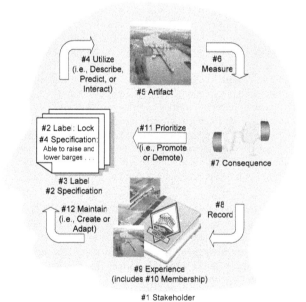

Figure 1: CAS Stakeholder Operation Illustration

Contained image source: U.S. Army Corps of Engineers [87-89])

A CAS is composed of multiple interacting stakeholders [24 p.17]. These stakeholders (Figure 1) form a network (Figure 2), where the network is part of each stakeholder's environment. Stakeholders (#1 in Figure 2) change their specifications as their environment changes and one cause of specification change is a response to another stakeholder's specifications, which is called co-adaptation (#13) [42 p.10]. These models suggest this theory's utility for explaining specification emergence and evolution.

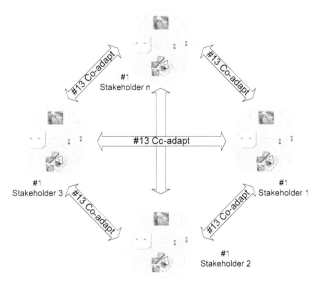

Figure 2: CAS Stakeholder Network Operation Illustration

The propositions used in the case analysis were based on the previously described models. The initial proposition was used to test the connection between categorization theory and CAS theory. The other six propositions are derived from the arrows shown in Figure 1 and Figure 2 as these identify stakeholder actions in the emergence and evolution of specifications.

Proposition 1: Specification (#3 in Figure 1) is the intension of a category, which includes label (#2), specification (#3), and membership (#10).

Proposition 2: Stakeholders (#1) utilize (#4) specifications in artifact (#5) interaction.

Proposition 3: Stakeholders measure (#6) the consequences (#7) of utilizing specifications.

Proposition 4: Stakeholders record (#8) utilization and consequences as experience (#9).

Proposition 5: Stakeholders prioritize (#11) (i.e., promote or demote) specifications (#2).

Proposition 6: Stakeholders maintain (#12) (i.e., create and adapt) using experience (#9).

Proposition 7: Stakeholders (#1 in Figure 2) co-adapt (#13) their specifications.

5 CASE ANALYSIS

5.1 Proposition 1: Intension

The intension proposition states that a specification is the intension of a category, which includes label, specification, and membership [44]. Funded project (i.e., label) is a category at the

USACE whose intension is described by its specification. Its specification is that it identifies a set of structures (i.e., assets) managed by the USACE that are geographically located close together and are funded by a Congressional appropriation. The membership of the funded project category is a set that meets the specification. For example, projects funded under the Estuary Restoration Act of 2000 (PL 106-457, Title I) include: City of Long Beach's Colorado Lagoon, Seal Island Restoration Project, and Half Moon Reef Restoration Project. The intension proposition is confirmed in case data and no disconfirming evidence was found.

5.2 Proposition 2: Utilization

The utilization proposition states that stakeholders use specifications in artifact interaction. Utilization is defined as description, prediction, or action [24 p.24]. The specification for "unsafe dam" provides insight into all three types of utilization. The "DSAC II – URGENT (Unsafe or Potentially Unsafe)" specification describes the requirements for a dam to be placed in this category. The reason why a dam is placed in this category is that it predicts, or predicts the potential for, failure. Failure is defined as issues of structural integrity that in some contexts may lead to uncontrolled release of a reservoir resulting from amount of structural collapse. Behavior is also observed as in the case of the Lower Fox River Dams, the assignment of the "unsafe dam" label to the artifacts De Pere, Rapide Croche, Cedars, Little Chute, and Upper Appleton Dams led to mitigation actions including: sealing concrete cracks around trunnion pins, replace bolts on gate arms, flood inundation mapping, and other actions. The utilization proposition is confirmed in case data and no disconfirming evidence was found.

5.3 Proposition 3: Measurement

The measurement proposition states that stakeholders measure the consequences of utilizing specifications. Measurement is defined in CAS as "results of action in the real world" [24 p.17] and "consequences in the real world" [24 p.24]. Measurement of consequences is illustrated in the same "unsafe dam" example. The USACE Dam Safety Program which was a set of specifications governing the management of dams was measured through an assessment by the Association of State Dam Safety Officials. That assessment resulted in a recommendation regarding existing dam safety policies (i.e., specifications) and suggested additional policies. In addition, dam safety inspections (i.e., measurement) are performed periodically. The measurement proposition is confirmed in case data and no disconfirming evidence was found.

5.4 Proposition 4: Recording

The recording proposition states that stakeholders record utilization and consequences as experience [24]. The definition of experience recording is not well-defined in the CAS literature. Therefore, evidence will be sought using the constructs of the model. These constructs include the used specification, use scenario (e.g., describe, predict, or act), artifacts, measurement scenario, and consequences. For example, the Association of State Dam Safety Officials reviewed specifications and the records for dams. Likewise, the results of dam safety inspections produce the dam records which are utilized to decide required actions for dams. In addition, the damage from Hurricane Katrina is recorded as consequences.

The recording proposition is confirmed in case data and no disconfirming evidence was found.

5.5 Propositions 5 and 6: Prioritization and Maintenance

Due to the close relationship between the evidence for prioritization and maintenance, these two propositions are discussed in this single section. The prioritization proposition states that stakeholders prioritize (i.e., promote or demote) specifications based on consequences and that they maintain (i.e., create and adapt) using experience [24, 42]. For example, the Association of State Dam Safety Officials review of dam specifications and records lead to recommendations for policy (i.e., specification) changes (i.e., maintain). These changes identify a specification that was demoted (prior policy) and specifications that were promoted (new policy). In addition, damage from Hurricane Katrina (consequences) and the policies utilized to maintain the failed structures were utilized to update (maintain) policies. The prioritization and maintenance propositions are confirmed in case data and no disconfirming evidence was found.

5.6 Proposition 7: Co-adaptation

The co-adaptation proposition states that stakeholders change their specifications as their environment changes and one cause of specification change is a response to another stakeholder's specifications, which is called co-adaptation [42]. One high-level example is a change to project selection criteria by commanders post-Katrina. The public demanded better protection post-Katrina. Congress acceded to that demand and in turn made demands from the USACE. The USACE then performed a reality check on what was possible and returned those findings to Congress who adjusted their demands. The USACE took those demands and began operationalizing them through changes in project selection criteria. Those criteria at the headquarters level were issued to divisions, districts, and finally structure managers. At each level, co-adaptation occurred and fed more changes back into the process. The co-adaptation proposition is confirmed in case data and no disconfirming evidence was found.

6 DISCUSSION AND IMPLICATIONS

The case analysis confirmed the seven theoretically-grounded propositions. Through this confirmation, this investigation shows that CAS explains the emergence and evolution of specifications in the application domain. This confirmation, however, has limitations. There are four problems to overcome when using a case study research methodology: controlling observations, controlling deductions, allowing for replication, and allowing for generalization [50]. The control of observations and control of deductions is believed to be sufficient in this investigation though they could be improved with more formal instruments, protocols, and definitions. This investigation was conducted by a single researcher on a single case thus limiting replicability and generalizability.

In addition to research methodology limitations, theory extensions are suggested by the data. The case analysis reveals that additional propositions may be appropriate for exploration. First, a review of the data suggests that the CAS model applies at multiple levels of detail. For example, the CAS model applies at the organizational level as described in co-adaptation proposition section, but it also applies at individual levels of detail suggesting the need for a recursion proposition (i.e., a CAS within a CAS). Second, there is not a proposition in the theory that directly addresses stakeholder contribution. Stakeholders contribute facets, or pieces, of a specification through communication that triggers stakeholder co-adaptation. Without contribution there cannot be co-adaptation.

In addition to extensions to the model, new models are suggested by the case analysis. Case analysis suggests that there is a pattern associated with stakeholder specification interaction, but it was not identified. This pattern is associated with what appears to be common stakeholders (i.e., roles). For example, the specifications have common stakeholders: who pays, who uses, who builds, etc. These common stakeholders contribute comparable facets to the specification; thus suggesting an underlying structural pattern, or patterns, to specifications. While the theories grounding the model do not explain this pattern, those theories also do not exclude the existence of a pattern characterizing the stakeholder specification facet pattern.

6.1 Implications for Practice

The findings provide a reason for an often heard refrain from IS development team members on IS projects. "The users don't know what they want. If they would just tell us what they want, we could build it." The answer suggested by this investigation's findings is that users "do not know" what they want and more profoundly for IS development, this investigation suggests a reason why users "cannot know" what they want. More precisely, this research finds that users cannot predict requirements with any accuracy because, according to the model, users must first utilize the specification encoded in the system with real world artifacts before they can judge the requirements "goodness" through the measurement of consequences. This measurement of consequences drives another iteration of adaptation leading to another potential outcome, which is "even when users know what they want, it turns out that it's not what they want". The model describes a scenario where outcomes of multi-stakeholder co-adaptations are not predictable with any accuracy. This implication explains the evolution of methods in practice towards more iteration and where each iteration concludes with delivery of a prototype or some other level of working product.

6.2 Implications for Academia

The implications of this investigation for academia are threefold. First, the model suggests that the correctness of elicited requirements cannot be easily, or accurately, measured prior to their conversion to a system that has been utilized by the stakeholders. Students need to be prepared for the likelihood that stakeholders from whom they have elicited specifications may change their mind once the system is used. Curriculums should therefore include exposure and practice with iterative prototyping style IS development methods. Second, students need to understand that each stakeholder provides a specification facet, so a good specification must be developed from multiple stakeholder inputs. Curriculums should therefore include lectures, discussions, and exercises identifying the different stakeholders that are commonly associated with IS development projects (e.g., sponsor, user, managers, etc.). Lastly, students need to understand that the integration of specification facets into a completed specification results from inter-stakeholder communication where stakeholders modify their individual facets based on the experience and knowledge shared with them by other stakeholders. Curriculums should therefore include lectures, discussions, and exercises where students must: a) determine requirements during stakeholder interactions, b) control stakeholder interactions so that they can determine requirements, and c) understand how the different stakeholder requirements fit together. In short, curriculums need to focus on iterative prototyping methods that emphasize stakeholder communication and stakeholder interactions.

7 FUTURE RESEARCH

This investigation suggests many avenues of future research. In addition to addressing investigation limitations, future research should address findings not addressed by this investigation. In addition, future research should address implications to practice and academia.

Future research should confirm model extensions suggested by the case analysis. Specifically, the case analysis suggests two extensions to the theoretically-grounded propositions. A contribution and a recursion proposition must be confirmed in theory and in additional cases.

Future research should seek a new model, or models, suggested by the case analysis. Case analysis suggests that there is a pattern associated with stakeholder specification interaction, but it was not identified by the theory. While the theories grounding the model do not explain this pattern, those theories also do not exclude the existence of a pattern characterizing the stakeholder specification interaction. Future investigations are needed to identify the pattern, or patterns, that characterize the stakeholder specification facet pattern.

Future research should leverage these findings for practice. The finding provides a theoretically-grounded explanation for the phenomenon that users don't know what they want, can't know what they want, and will change what they want after the system is delivered. This finding suggests a need for a significant amount of research to increase the number of iterations that can be accomplished within a set timeline. Increasing the number of iterations, according to the theory, is a way to increase development speed and customer satisfaction.

Future research should leverage these findings for curriculum improvements. Based on the theory, research is needed to enable multiple requirements determination iterations within a classroom assignment environment and timeline. Students should see variation in requirements among the iterations. Research is also needed to enable multiple real or virtual stakeholder roles that provide different specification facets to students during requirements determination assignments. Students should start to recognize the roles and the types of requirements provided by the roles. Lastly, research is needed enabling requirements determination by students on assignments from multiple stakeholders simultaneously. Students must identify, document, and integrate requirements specifications during these interactions; students must also be able to control these complex interactions. These curriculum improvements could have a significant impact on students requirements determination proficiency.

8 REFERENCES

[1] Abdel-Hamid, T. K. and Madnick, S. E. *Software project dynamics: an integrated approach* Prentice Hall, Englewood Cliffs, N.J. , 1991.

[2] Agarwal, R., De, P. and Sinha, A. P. Comprehending object and process models: an empirical study. *Software Engineering, IEEE Transactions on*, 25, 4 1999), 541-556.

[3] Alvarez-Cortes, V., Zayas-Perez, B. E., Zarate-Silva, V. H. and Uresti, J. A. R. *Current Trends in Adaptive User Interfaces: Challenges and Applications.* City, 2007.

[4] Amin, S. M. and Horowitz, B. M. Toward Agile and Resilient Large-Scale Systems: Adaptive Robust National/International Infrastructures. *Global Journal of Flexible Systems Management*, 9, 1 (01 2008), 27-39.

[5] Auramaki, E., Lehtinen, E. and Lyytinen, K. A speech-act-based office modeling approach. *ACM Transactions on Information Systems (TOIS)* 6, 2 1988), 126-152.

[6] Benbasat, I., Goldstein, D. K. and Mead, M. The Case Research Strategy in Studies of Information Systems. *MIS Quarterly*, 11, 3 1987), 368.

[7] Benbya, H. and McKelvey, B. Toward a complexity theory of information systems development. *Information Technology & People*, 19, 1 2006), 12.

[8] Bonoma, T. V. Case Research in Marketing: Opportunities, Problems, and a Process. *Journal of Marketing Research (JMR)*, 22, 2 (05 1985), 199-208.

[9] Booch, G. *Object-Oriented Analysis and Design with Applications.* Addison-Wesley Professional, 1994.

[10] Brooks, F. P., Jr. No Silver Bullet Essence and Accidents of Software Engineering. *Computer*, 20, 4 1987), 10-19.

[11] Camorlinga, S., Barker, K. and Anderson, J. Multiagent Systems for resource allocation in Peer-to-Peer systems. In *Proceedings of the Winter International Symposium on Information and Communication Technologies* (Cancun, Mexico, 2004). Trinity College Dublin.

[12] Chen, S.-C., Chen, M., Zhao, N., Hamid, S., Saleem, K. and Chatterjee, K. Florida Public Hurricane Loss Model (FPHLM): research experience in system integration. In *Proceedings of the 2008 International Conference on Digital Government Research* (Montreal, Canada, 2008). Digital Government Society of North America.

[13] Chi, M. T. H., Feltovich, P. J. and Glaser, R. Categorization and representation of physics problems by experts and novices. *Cognitive Science*, 5, 2 (1981/6// 1981), 121-152.

[14] Comfort, L. K., Sungu, Y., Johnson, D. and Dunn, M. Complex Systems in Crisis: Anticipation and Resilience in Dynamic Environments. *Journal of Contingencies & Crisis Management*, 9, 3 (09 2001), 144.

[15] Cotteleer, M. J. and Bendoly, E. Order Lead-Time Improvement Following Enterprise Information Technology Implementation: An Empirical Study. *MIS Quarterly*, 30, 3 (09 2006), 643-660.

[16] Curtis, B., Krasner, H. and Iscoe, N. A field study of the software design process for large systems. *Commun. ACM*, 31, 11 1988), 1268-1287.

[17] Cusumano, M. A. and Selby, R. W. How Microsoft builds software. *Commun. ACM*, 40, 6 1997), 53-61.

[18] Dardenne, A., van Lamsweerde, A. and Fickas, S. Goal-directed requirements acquisition. *Science of Computer Programming*, 20, 1-2 1993), 3-50.

[19] Davis, G. B. Strategies for Information Requirements Determination. *IBM Systems Journal*, 21, 1 (1982 1982), 4-31.

[20] Dong, S., Xu, S. X. and Zhu, K. X. Research Note--Information Technology in Supply Chains: The Value of IT-Enabled Resources Under Competition. *Information Systems Research*, 20, 1 (March 1, 2009 2009), 18-32.

[21] Dunn, C. and Grabski, S. The Effect of Field Dependence on Conceptual Modeling Performance. *Advances in Accounting Information Systems*, 61998), 65-77.

[22] Eisenhardt, K. M. Building Theories from Case Study Research. *Academy of Management Review*, 14, 4 (10 1989a), 532-550.

[23] Eoyang, G. H. Complex? Yes! Adaptive? Well, maybe . . . . *Interactions*, 3, 1 1996), 31-37.

[24] Gell-Mann, M. *The Quark and the Jaguar: Adventures in the Simple and the Complex* W.H. Freeman, New York, NY, 1994.

[25] Glass, R. L. and Vessey, I. Toward a taxonomy of software application domains: History. *Journal of Systems and Software*, 17, 2 1992), 189-199.

[26] Glass, R. L. and Vessey, I. Contemporary application-domain taxonomies. *Software, IEEE*, 12, 4 1995), 63-76.

[27] Glass, R. L. and Vessey, I. *Focusing on the application domain: everyone agrees it's vital, but who's doing anything about it?* , City, 1998.

[28] Grover, V. and Ramanlal, P. Six Myths of Information and Markets: Information Technology Networks, Electronic Commerce, and the Battle for Consumer Surplus. *MIS Quarterly*, 23, 4 (12 1999), 465-495.

[29] Guoling, L., Lei, X. and Xuejuan, H. *Complexity Analysis and Modeling of Enterprise Information Resources Integration*. City, 2007.

[30] Guoling, L. and Shasha, H. *Frame Analysis of Customer Relationship Management in Commercial Bank Based on CAS*. City, 2008.

[31] Guoling, L., Xuejuan, H. and Wei, W. *Building CAS-Based Framework of Enterprise Internal Knowledge Sharing*. City, 2007.

[32] Hale, D. P., Sharpe, S. and Hale, J. E. Business - information systems professional differences: Bridging the business rule gap. *Information Resources Management Journal*, 12, 2 1999a), 16.

[33] Hale, J. E., Sharpe, S. and Hale, D. P. An evaluation of the cognitive processes of programmers engaged in software debugging. *Journal of Software Maintenance: Research and Practice*, 11, 2 1999b), 73-91.

[34] Hammer, M. and Champy, J. *Re-engineering the corporation: A manifesto for business revolution*. Harper Collins, New York, NY, 1993.

[35] Harmon, K. *The "systems" nature of enterprise architecture*. City, 2005.

[36] Hawryszkiewycz, I. *Workspace requirements for complex adaptive systems*. City, 2009.

[37] Hengeveld, B., Voort, R., Balkom, H. v., Hummels, C. and Moor, J. d. Designing for diversity: developing complex adaptive tangible products. In *Proceedings of the 1st International Conference on Tangible and Embedded Interaction* (Baton Rouge, Louisiana, 2007). ACM.

[38] Henry, W. and Stevens, J. *Net-centric system development*. City, 2009.

[39] Hickey, A. M. and Davis, A. M. A Unified Model of Requirements Elicitation. *Journal of Management Information Systems*, 20, 4 (Spring2004 2004), 65-84.

[40] Highsmith, J. and Cockburn, A. Agile software development: the business of innovation. *Computer*, 34, 9 2001), 120-127.

[41] Hirschheim, R. A., Klein, H. and Lyytinen, K. *Information Systems Development and Data Modeling: Conceptual Foundations and Philosophical Foundations*. Cambridge University Press, Cambridge, U.K., 1995.

[42] Holland, J. H. *Hidden order : how adaptation builds complexity* Addison-Wesley, Reading, Mass, 1995.

[43] Jacob, E. K. *Classification and categorization: Drawing the line*. Medford, NJ: Learned Information, City, 1992.

[44] Jacob, E. K. Classification and categorization: a difference that makes a difference. *Library Trends*, 52, 3 (01/01/ 2004), 515(526).

[45] Janssen, M. and Kuk, G. *A Complex Adaptive System Perspective of Enterprise Architecture in Electronic Government*. City, 2006.

[46] Kapur, M., Voiklis, J. and Kinzer, C. K. Problem solving as a complex, evolutionary activity: a methodological framework for analyzing problem-solving processes in a computer-supported collaborative environment. In *Proceedings of the 2005 Conference on Computer Support for Collaborative Learning: Learning 2005:The next 10 years!* (Taipei, Taiwan, 2005). International Society of the Learning Sciences.

[47] Kesh, S. Evaluating the quality of entity relationship models. *Information and Software Technology*, 37, 12 1995), 681-689.

[48] Khatri, V., Vessey, I., Ramesh, V., Clay, P. and Park, S.-J. Understanding Conceptual Schemas: Exploring the Role of Application and IS Domain Knowledge. *Information Systems Research*, 17, 1 (March 1, 2006 2006), 81-99.

[49] Khoshroo, B. M. and Rashidi, H. *Towards a Framework for Agile Management Based on Chaos and Complex System Theories*. City, 2009.

[50] Lee, A. S. A Scientific Methodology for MIS Case Studies. *MIS Quarterly*, 13, 1 (03 1989), 32-50.

[51] Lengnick-Hall, C. A., Lengnick-Hall, M. L. and Abdinnour-Helm, S. The role of social and intellectual capital in achieving competitive advantage through enterprise resource planning (ERP) systems. *Journal of Engineering & Technology Management*, 21, 4 (12 2004), 307-330.

[52] Lindland, O., Sindre, G. and Solvberg, A. Understanding quality in conceptual modeling. *IEEE Software*, 11, 2 1994), 42.

[53] Maciaszek, L. A. Modeling and engineering adaptive complex systems. In *Proceedings of the 26th International Conference on Conceptual Modeling* (Auckland, New Zealand, 2007). Australian Computer Society, Inc.

[54] Markman, E. M. *Categorization and Naming in Children Problems of Induction* MIT Press - Cambridge, Mass., City, 1989.

[55] Markus, M. L. and Ji-Ye, M. Participation in Development and Implementation - Updating An Old, Tired Concept for Today's IS Contexts. *Journal of the Association for Information Systems*, 5, 11/12 (12 2004), 514-544.

[56] Martin, J. *Information Engineering Planning & Analysis: Book 2*. Prentice-Hall, Inc., Upper Saddle River, NJ, 1990.

[57] Meso, P. and Jain, R. Agile Software Development: Adaptive Systems Principles and Best Practices. *Information Systems Management*, 23, 3 2006), 19.

[58] Moe, N. B., Dingsyr, T. and Kvangardsnes, O. *Understanding Shared Leadership in Agile Development: A Case Study*. City, 2009.

[59] Moody, D. L. and Shanks, G. G. Improving the quality of data models: empirical validation of a quality management framework. *Information Systems*, 28, 6 2003), 619-650.

[60] Mylopoulos, J. *Conceptual Modeling and Telos*. Wiley City, 1992.

[61] Narain, S., Vaidyanathan, R., Moyer, S., Stephens, W., Parmeswaran, K. and Shareef, A. R. Middleware For Building Adaptive Systems Via Configuration. In *Proceedings of the ACM SIGPLAN Workshop on Languages, Compilers and Tools for Embedded Systems* (Snow Bird, Utah, United States, 2001). ACM.

[62] Neus, A. and Scherf, P. Opening minds: Cultural change with the introduction of open-source collaboration methods. *IBM Systems Journal*, 44, 2 (03 2005), 215-225.

[63] Nguyen, T. N. The Software Continuum Concept: Towards a Biologically-Inspired Model for Robust e-Business Software Automation. *Communications of AIS*, 2005, 15 (03 2005), 263-288.

[64] Niederman, F., Davis, A., Greiner, M. E., Wynn, D. and York, P. T. Research Agenda for Studying Open Source II: View Through the Lens of Referent Discipline Theories. *Communications of AIS*, 2006, 18 (06 2006), 2-45.

[65] O'Brien, M. P., Buckley, J. and Shaft, T. M. Expectation-based, inference-based, and bottom-up software comprehension. *Journal of Software Maintenance and Evolution: Research and Practice*, 16, 6 2004), 427-447.

[66] Parsons, J. An information model based on classification theory. *Management Science*, 42, 10 (10 1996), 1437.

[67] Parsons, J. Effects of Local Versus Global Schema Diagrams on Verification and Communication in Conceptual Data Modeling. *Journal of Management Information Systems*, 19, 3 2002), 155-183.

[68] Parsons, J. and Wand, Y. Choosing classes in conceptual modeling. *Communications of the ACM*, 40, 6 1997a), 63-69.

[69] Ragab, K., Kaji, N. and Mori, K. *Service-oriented autonomous decentralized community communication technique for a complex adaptive information system*. City, 2003.

[70] Ragab, K., Ono, T., Kaji, N. and Mori, K. *Autonomous decentralized community concept and architecture for a complex adaptive information system*. City, 2003.

[71] Ren, C., Huang, H. and Jin, S. *Specification of Agent in Complex Adaptive System*. City, 2008.

[72] Rule, P. G. *Using Jackson methods to implement software process improvement*. City, 1996.

[73] Schweiger, A., Sunyaev, A., Leimeister, J. M. and Krcmar, H. Information Systems and Healthcare XX: Toward Seamless Healthcare with Software Agents. *Communications of AIS*, 2007, 19 (03 2007), 692-710.

[74] Shaft, T. M. and Vessey, I. Research Report--The Relevance of Application Domain Knowledge: The Case of Computer Program Comprehension. *Information Systems Research*, 6, 3 (September 1, 1995 1995), 286-299.

[75] Shaft, T. M. and Vessey, I. The relevance of application domain knowledge: characterizing the computer program comprehension process. *J. Manage. Inf. Syst.*, 15, 1 1998), 51-78.

[76] Shaft, T. M. and Vessey, I. The Role of Cognitive Fit in the Relationship Between Software Comprehension and Modification. *MIS Quarterly*, 30, 1 (03 2006), 29-55.

[77] Shanks, G. Conceptual data modeling: An empirical study of expert and novice data modelers. *Australian Journal of Information Systems*, 4, 2 1997), 63-73.

[78] Song, Y. Adaptation Hiding Modularity for Self-Adaptive Systems. In *Proceedings of the 29th International Conference on Software Engineering* (2007). IEEE Computer Society.

[79] Stamper, R. *Semantics*. John Wiley and Sons, City, 1987.

[80] Stanton, C. A methodology for grounding representations. In *Proceedings of the 2006 International Symposium on Practical Cognitive Agents and Robots* (Perth, Australia, 2006). ACM.

[81] Sudeikat, J. and Renz, W. *Toward Requirements Engineering for Self - Organizing Multi - Agent Systems*. City, 2007.

[82] Sullivan, K. J., Griswold, W. G., Cai, Y. and Hallen, B. The structure and value of modularity in software design. In *Proceedings of the 8th European Software Engineering Conference held jointly with 9th ACM SIGSOFT International Symposium on Foundations of Software Engineering* (Vienna, Austria, 2001). ACM.

[83] Sutherland, J. and Heuvel, W.-J. v. d. Enterprise Application Integration and COMPLEX ADAPTIVE SYSTEMS. *Communications of the ACM*, 45, 10 (10 2002b), 59-64.

[84] Taggert, W. M. J. and Tharp, M. O. Dimensions of information requirements analysis *Data Base*, 7, 1 (Summer 1975 1975), 5-13.

[85] Tivnan, B. F. *Data farming coevolutionary dynamics in repast*. City, 2004.

[86] Tiwana, A. and Keil, M. The one-minute risk assessment tool. *Communications of the ACM*, 47, 11 2004), 73-77.

[87] USACE *Kaskaskia Lock and Dam, U.S. Army Corps of Engineers*. City, 2009c.

[88] USACE *Lock and Dam 24, Clarksville, Mo., U.S. Army Corps of Engineers*. City, 2009e.

[89] USACE *Locks 27, Granite City, Ill., U.S. Army Corps of Engineers*. City, 2009f.

[90] Vessey, I. Cognitive Fit: A Theory-Based Analysis of the Graphs Versus. *Decision Sciences*, 22, 2 1991), 219.

[91] Vessey, I. and Conger, S. Learning to Specify Information Requirements: The Relationship between Application and Methodology. *Journal of Management Information Systems*, 10, 2 (Fall93 1993), 177-201.

[92] Vidgen, R. and Wang, X. *Organizing for Agility: a complex adaptive systems perspective on agile software development process*. Citeseer, City, 2006.

[93] Wallace, L. and Keil, M. Software Project Risks and Their Effect on Outcomes. *Association for Computing Machinery. Communications of the ACM*, 47, 4 2004), 68.

[94] Wand, Y. and Weber, R. On the ontological expressiveness of information systems analysis and design grammars. *Journal of Information Systems*, 3, 4 (October 1993 1993), 217-237.

[95] Wand, Y. and Weber, R. Research commentary: Information systems and conceptual modeling--a research agenda. *Information Systems Research*, 13, 4 2002), 363.

[96] Wei, D. and Liu, J. *Intelligent Adaptive Services for On-demand Systems Integration*. City, 2007.

[97] Wetherbe, J. C. Executive Information Requirements: Getting It Right. *MIS Quarterly*, 15, 1 1991), 51-65.

[98] Whitworth, E. and Biddle, R. *The Social Nature of Agile Teams*. City, 2007.

[99] Zacarias, M., Caetano, A., Magalhaes, R., Pinto, H. S. and Tribolet, J. *Adding a Human Perspective to Enterprise Architectures*. City, 2007.

[100] Zani, W. M. Blueprint for MIS. *Harvard Business Review*, 48, 6 1970), 95-100.

[101] Zmud, R. W. Management of Large Software Development Efforts. *MIS Quarterly*, 4, 2 1980), 45-55.

Boundary Spanners and Client Vendor Relationships in IT Outsourcing: A Social Capital Perspective

M. Das Aundhe
Louisiana State University
E.J. Ourso College of Business
Baton Rouge, LA 70803
madhu.das@gmail.com

Beena George
University of St. Thomas
Cameron School of Business
3800 Montrose, Houston TX 77006
georgeb@stthom.edu

Rudy Hirschheim
Louisiana State University
E.J. Ourso College of Business
Baton Rouge, LA 70803
rudy@lsu.edu

ABSTRACT

Information technology (IT) outsourcing is one of the key contexts in management in which inter-organizational relationships are studied. Since in an IT outsourcing situation, the client and vendor organizations come together with the stated purpose of creating something new within the dynamics of a business relationship, a social capital perspective of the client-vendor relationship is quite appropriate for the study of the inter-organizational relationship in IT outsourcing. The social capital perspective provides for an examination of the structural, cognitive, and relational aspects of the client-vendor relationship and its effect on the knowledge exchange and outcomes of IT outsourcing. Between the client and vendor organizations, boundary spanners function as exchange agents and are responsible for information exchange and knowledge creation. This study attempts to understand the role of these boundary spanners in creating social capital in client-vendor relationships in IT outsourcing. In this study, the behavioral exchange of the boundary spanner in an organization with their counterparts in the other organization is analyzed from a social capital perspective. Using a case study approach, the roles, the relationship, and the outcomes of IT outsourcing arrangements in ten organizations are being examined to identify the structural, cognitive, and relational aspects of their exchange with their counterparts.

Categories and Subject Descriptors

H.0. Information Systems

General Terms

Management, Human Factors.

Keywords

Boundary spanners, Social Capital, Client-vendor relationship, IT outsourcing.

1. INTRODUCTION

Outsourcing of business-critical IT applications has become a well-established business practice over the past two decades. IT

outsourcing has long played an important role in the field, yet outsourcing relationships are little understood (Lee et al., 2003). IT outsourcing is broadly defined as a decision taken by an organization to contract-out or sell the organization's IT assets, people, and/or activities to a third-party supplier, who in exchange provides and manages assets and services for monetary returns over an agreed time period (Loh and Venkatraman, 1992; Lacity and Hirschheim, 1993).

Transaction cost theory (TCT) (Williamson 1979, 1981) is the most commonly cited theory for explaining the outsourcing phenomenon. TCT adopts an economic view, and at its core views the actor (i.e., person or company) as dealing not with other actors but directly with the market, which in this context of discussing the client-vendor relationship is inappropriate. To explain the outsourcing relationship, more than an economic view is needed; an understanding of the episodes of exchanges from an individual's standpoint which is guided by the contract but might lapse into voluntary exchanges is needed (Hakansson and Snehota, 1995). The core concept of social capital theory addresses the exchange relation between two specific actors (Coleman 1990; Putnam 2000). Nahapiet and Ghoshal (1998) define social capital as the sum of the actual and potential resources embedded within, available through, and derived from the network of relationships possessed by an individual or social unit. The framework focuses directly on the social process of give-and-take in individual's interactions and aims to understand the behavior of each actor/group contributing to the exchange. In the context of an outsourcing venture, the actual operationalization of the contract occurs through these individual exchanges, and it is these exchanges that introduce a certain amount of predictability into the relationship. The key exchanges in this kind of a set-up happen at the boundary of the client and the vendor organizations and depend largely on the exchanges of the relationship manager (boundary spanners) who co-ordinates across the boundaries of the two organizations. This is an exploratory study which uses the social capital framework to understand how these boundary spanners create social capital that facilitates the development and management of client-vendor relationships.

2. RELEVANCE OF SOCIAL CAPITAL IN IT OUTSOURCING

In an IT outsourcing situation, two organizations come together with the stated purpose of creating something new out of the combination of their knowledge pool. Outsourcing (whatever be the nature of projects - applications development, application maintenance, infrastructure management, consulting or research and development) produces value only when the individuals from client and vendor organizations working on the project bring together their skills and knowledge (Tiwana et al., 2003). It is true that one organization, the vendor, comes in with a profit motive, while the other comes in with a business need. However, guided by the objectives of the outsourcing arrangement, these two organizations establish contact and move through the process of establishing a relationship that will facilitate the creation of something that did not exist before in that particular form. While the contract stipulates the organizational structure and interactions necessary to fulfill the objectives of the outsourcing arrangement, a strong relationship characterized by elements such as trust, norms of commitment and cooperation, and shared understanding is necessary to support the activities required to complete the processes required for the outsourcing arrangement. These characteristics of the outsourcing relationship are central to the success of the outsourcing arrangement. And, these are the elements that constitute social capital (Nahapiet and Ghoshal 1998). Hence, it is considered appropriate to build upon the social capital perspective to examine the IT outsourcing phenomenon.

3. PRIOR RESEARCH ON BOUNDARY SPANNING ROLES

Boundaries are a defining characteristic of organizations, and boundary roles are the link between the environment and the organization. Individuals, who operate at the periphery or boundary of an organization, performing organizationally relevant tasks which relate the organization with elements outside it, are called boundary spanners (Leifer and Delbecq, 1978). Since information from the environment must pass through the boundary of the organization before reaching organizational decision makers, boundary spanners function as exchange agents between the organization and its environment (Leifer and Delbecq, 1978). The importance of boundary-spanning roles that serve to link organizations has been confirmed by research in a number of diverse organizational contexts (Allen and Cohen 1969, Allen et al., 1971; Rosenbloom and Woleck 1970; Whitley and Frost 1973; Brass et al., 2004; Doney and Cannon 1997; Sydow 1998). These roles are vital to the effective monitoring of the environment as well as the transfer of technology and information across boundaries (Keller and Holland 1975). IT outsourcing success depends on the integration of knowledge of multiple stakeholders in the client and the service provider organizations; in this context, the boundary spanners have the additional role of facilitating knowledge creation.

According to the Nahapiet and Ghoshal (1998) framework, social capital facilitates the exchange that creates knowledge or intellectual capital. Lane et al (2004) suggest that boundary spanners develop networks of contacts which give them social capital. This social capital confers benefits such as quick access to valuable information and receiving referrals. Thus social capital is valuable to the boundary-spanning individual/manager and to the organization, because it can be used to facilitate and leverage knowledge creation, which leads to continuous innovation and ultimately to competitive advantage for the organization.

The characteristics of the boundary spanning roles, and characteristics of individuals in these roles were the focus of research done in the past (Tushman and Scanlan 1981; Aldrich and Herker 1977; David et al., 1982; Keller and Holland 1975;

Organ, 1971). These studies on the expectations from the boundary-spanning role demonstrate that it would be very difficult to build inter-organizational relationships in the absence of boundary spanners. Tushman and Scanlan (1981) indicate that informational boundary spanning is accomplished only by those individuals who are well connected internally and externally. Boundaries can be spanned effectively only by individuals who understand the coding schemes and are attuned to the contextual information on both sides of the boundary, enabling them to search out relevant information on one side and disseminate it on the other side. Informational boundary spanning, then, must be a two part process; obtaining information from outside units and disseminating this information to internal users (Tushman and Scanlan 1981). Aldrich and Herker (1977) examine the creation, elaboration, and functions of boundary spanning roles, with respect to various organizational environments, and organizational technologies. Based on this they develop eleven hypotheses which are amenable to empirical testing. David et al. (1982) empirically examine demographic and job related characteristics associated with three boundary spanning roles and statistically significant comparisons revealed that stars[1] tended to be white, male, high level managers; isolates to be female with high organizational and job tenure; and liaisons to be white, low level managers with low organizational and job tenure. Keller and Holland (1975) state that since boundary spanners respond to external organizations as well as in their own organization, conflicting and misunderstood expectations for role performance often are sent to the boundary spanner. These conditions have been found to result in strong and conflicting role pressures and tensions for incumbents of boundary-spanning roles, making it a role that cannot be easily carried out by any individual. Organ (1971) has also hypothesized that effective boundary spanners should have relatively high economic and political value orientations, and relatively low aesthetic and religious value orientations as the other organization may require tact and manipulation on issues.

The impact of boundary spanning roles on organizational performance also validates the importance of the boundary-spanning role in understanding the environment and building relationships. Jemison (1979) found that boundary spanning roles are important for strategic decision making. Dollinger (1984) uses the boundary spanning activity of the entrepreneur to examine the strategic management process in small businesses. In a sample of eighty-two owner/operators, intensive boundary spanning activity was strongly related to organizational performance, and information processing capability significantly affected the performance of boundary spanning relationship.

In more recent years, the research focus has broadened to include the roles of boundary spanning individuals as well as teams. A multilevel research approach which combines micro and macro lenses, is being adopted to address the levels of theory, measurement, and analysis required to examine research questions associated with boundary-spanning (Marrone et al., 2007; Hitt et al., 2007) fully. Marrone et al. (2007) examine team boundary spanning and show that greater levels of boundary spanning were associated with higher team performance; their multilevel analysis show that team-level boundary spanning also yielded benefits to individual team members by reducing their

---

[1] Types of boundary spanners - stars and liaisons facilitate organizational communication, while isolates inhibit its flow.

role overload. Kostova and Roth (2003) develop a micro-macro model of social capital formation, explaining how boundary spanners form their private social capital and how this social capital is transformed into public social capital of the subunit.

However, the process of relationship building by these boundary spanners in an IT outsourcing context has not been completely understood yet. This requires a separate examination as boundary spanners in this context, have an additional role of knowledge creation, besides the primary responsibility for information exchange between the organization and its task environment. The implications of this research are extremely important for building, developing, and managing the client-vendor relationship in IT outsourcing.

4. RESEARCH QUESTION

Research has validated that boundary-spanning can effectively facilitate offshore transactions and interactions, reducing the challenges innate in offshore engagements in IT outsourcing (Levina and Vaast 2005, 2008). Krishnan and Ranganathan (2009) also examine the usefulness of boundary spanning in addressing the challenge of teams separated by geographic, organizational and cultural contexts in offshore outsourcing. They focus on the role of client project manager as a boundary spanner, connecting the distributed team members from both client and vendor firms, and facilitating expertise sharing and coordination. They examine organizational capital generated in offshore project teams through boundary spanning, as a potential mechanism through which boundary spanning effects successful project outcomes. We build on the social capital and boundary-spanning research, to understand the role of boundary spanners in creating social capital in IT outsourcing. Therefore, this study addresses the research question: How do relationship managers (boundary spanners) create social capital that facilitates the development and management of client-vendor relationships in IT outsourcing projects? We go on to explore allied research questions: Would social capital be created without boundary spanners? How does one get to know that boundary spanners have created social capital?

Nahapiet and Ghoshal's (1998) social capital framework is used to analyze the interaction between the relationship managers of the client and vendor organizations: The structural, cognitive, and relational aspects of exchange between the relationship managers are examined to determine how this social capital facilitates the creation of intellectual capital in the outsourcing arrangement.

5. DATA AND METHODS

This research adopts a case study method. Ten relationships in the context of IT outsourcing arrangements have been identified, and the relationship managers of both the client and vendor organizations have been interviewed. The client and vendor organizations in these case studies consist of large, small and medium organizations. The vendor organizations include a mix of U.S. based and offshore vendors (based on the location of their headquarters). All offshore vendors in this research are based in India. This research focuses on outsourcing projects consisting of application development and maintenance.

Interviews are semi-structured and questions address the relationship manager's interaction with the counterparts in the other organization. Each relationship manager was interviewed

about his own exchanges, as well as those of his counterpart in the other organization. These interviews have been transcribed and will be analyzed. Since the goal of this research is to determine how the relationship between the boundary spanners contributes to the development of social capital in the outsourcing arrangement, the "relationship between the managers in client and the vendor organizations" is the unit of analysis in this research.

The interview protocols for the individuals in the client and the vendor organization were similar, except for the initial set of questions aimed to capture background information about the organization and the project. One set of questions aimed at eliciting information about the structure of the interaction between the managers in both organizations and the changes in the interaction over time; another set of questions examined the impact of the interactions and the perceptions of the counterpart in the partner organization on the operational and monitoring processes in the outsourcing arrangement, the relationship between the organizations, and the outcomes of the outsourcing arrangement. The interviews were conducted in an open and semi-structured manner, and the interviewees were free to interject their comments or expand on issues they thought were important. Therefore, the protocol is only indicative of the questions that were discussed during the interview.

6. PLAN FOR ANALYSIS

The interactions between the boundary spanners of each organization would be analyzed for indicators for social capital creation. A review of Nahapiet and Ghohals' framework and other social capital research (for example, Adler and Kwon 2002) suggest the following indicators to determine the presence of social capital in the relationship between the relationship managers of the client and vendor organizations: improved information quality, relevance, and timeliness for both organizations, clearer and deeper understanding of the requirements, and solidary of the relationship between the client and vendor organizations. The ten cases taken up would lend themselves for understanding roles of boundary spanners in various types of outsourcing (onshore vs offshore, types of projects, size of projects etc.).

7. CONTRIBUTIONS OF THE RESEARCH

Given the key role played by these boundary-spanning individuals in the success of outsourcing arrangements, this research will provide additional insights into how this role can be performed. Additionally, the analysis of the boundary-spanning role using a theoretical framework that clearly separates the different dimensions of the exchange should further the understanding of the boundary spanning role and the inter-organizational relationship.

8. REFERENCES

[1] Adler P.S. and Kwon S.W., Social Capital: Prospects for a new concept, *The Academy of Management Review*, 2002, Vol 27, 1, 17-40.

[2] Aldrich H., Herker. D., Boundary Spanning roles and Organization Structure, *Academy of Management Review*, 1977, Vol 42, No. 2 , 217-230.

[3] Allen, T. J., and Cohen S. I., Information Flow in Research and Development Laboratories, *Administrative Science Quarterly*, 1969, Vol. 14, 12-19.

[4] Allen, T. J., Piepmeier J. M., and Cooney S., The International Technological Gatekeeper, *Technology Review*, 1971, Vol. 75, 30-37.

[5] Brass, D.J., Galaskiewicz, J., Greve, H.R., and Tsai, W. Taking Stock of Networks and Organizations: A Multi-Level Perspective, Academy of Management Review, 2004, 47, 6, 795-817.

[6] Coleman, J.S., *Foundations of Social Theory*, Belknap Press of Harvard University, Cambridge, MA, 1990.

[7] David F. R., Pearce J. A., Elliott T. C., Characteristics and Internal Orientations of Boundary Spanning Individuals, *Academy of Management Proceedings*, 1982, Vol 08, 191-195.

[8] Dollinger M. J., Environmental Boundary Spanning and Information Processing Effects on Organizational Performance, *Academy of Management Journal*, 1984, Vol. 27, 2, 351-368

[9] Doney, P.M., and Cannon, J.P. An Examination of the Nature of Trust in Buyer-Seller Relationships, *Journal of Marketing* (61:2), Apr 1997, pp 35-51.

[10] Hakansson, H., and Snehota, I. *Developing Relationships in Business Networks*, Routledge, London, 1995.

[11] Hitt M. A., Beamish P. W., Jackson S. E. and Mathieu J. E., Building Theoretical and Empirical Bridges Across Levels: Multilevel Research in Management, *Academy of Management Journal*, 2007, Vol 50, 6, 1385-1399.

[12] Iivari, J., Hirschheim, R., and Klein, H.K. A Paradigmatic Analysis Contrasting Information Systems Development Approaches and Methodologies, *Information Systems Research*, 1998, 164.

[13] Jemison D. B., Strategic Decision Making Influence in Boundary Spanning Roles, *Academy of Management Proceedings*, 1979, 08, 118-122.

[14] Kostova, T., and Roth, K. Social Capital in Multinational Corporations and a Micro-Macro Model of Its Formation, *Academy of Management Review*, Apr 2003, 28, 2, 297-317.

[15] Krishnan P., Ranganathan C., Boundary spanning in offshored ISD projects: a project social capital perspective, *Proceedings of the Special Interest Group on Management Information Systems (SIGMIS CPR '09)*, 47th Annual Conference on Computer Personnel Research, 2009.

[16] Lacity, M.C., and Hirschheim, R., *Information Systems Outsourcing: Myths, Metaphors and Realities*, Wiley, Chichester, 1993.

[17] Lane, H. W., et al, *The Blackwell Handbook of Global Management: A Guide to Managing Complexity*, Malden, MA ; Oxford, UK : Blackwell, 2004.

[18] Lee, J.N., Huynh, M.Q., Kwok, R.C.W., and Pi, S.M., Outsourcing Evolution – Past, Present, and Future, *Communications of the ACM*, May 2003, 46, 5.

[19] Leifer, R., and Delbecq, A., Organizational/Environmental Interchange: A Model of Boundary Spanning Activity, *Academy of Management Review*, Jan1978, Vol. 3 Issue 1, 40-50.

[20] Levina, N., and Vaast, E., Innovating or Doing as Told? Status Differences and Overlapping Boundaries in Offshore Collaboration, *MIS Quarterly* , 2008, 32, 2, 307-332.

[21] Levina, N., and Vaast, E.. The Emergence of Boundary Spanning Competence in Practice: Implications for Implementation and Use of Information Systems, *MIS Quarterly* , 2005, 29 (2), 335-363.

[22] Loh, L., and Venkatraman, N., Diffusion of Information Technology: Influence Sources and the Kodak Effect, *Information Systems Research*, 1992, 4, 3, 334-358.

[23] Marrone J. A., Tesluk P. E., Carson J. B., A Multilevel Investigation of Antecedents and Consequences of Team Member Boundary-Spanning Behavior, *Academy of Management Journal*, 2007, Vol. 50, No. 6, 1423–1439.

[24] Nahapiet, J., and Ghoshal, S. Social Capital, Intellectual Capital, and the Organizational Advantage, *Academy of Management Review* ,1998, 23, 2, 242-266.

[25] Organ, D. W. Linking Pins Between Organizations and Environment, *Business Horizons*, 1971, Vol. 14, 73-80.

[26] Putnam, R.D., *Bowling Alone: The Collapse and Revival of American Community*, Touchstone Books, New York, NY, 2000.

[27] Robert T. Keller and Winford E. Holland. Boundary-Spanning Roles in a Research and Development Organization: an Empirical Investigation, *Academy of Management Journal*, 1975 Vol 18, 2, 388-393.

[28] Rosenbloom, R. S., and Wolek F. W., *Technology and Information Transfer* (Boston-Harvard Business School Division of Research), 1970.

[29] Sydow, J. Understanding the Constitution of Interorganizational Trust, in: *Trust within and between Organizations: Conceptual Issues and Empirical Applications*, L. Christel and B. Richard (eds.), Oxford University Press, 1998.

[30] Tiwana, A., Bharadwaj, A.S., and Sambamurthy, V. The Antecedents of Information Systems Development Capability in Firms: A Knowledge Integration Perspective, *International Conference on Information Systems*, 2003, 246-258.

[31] Tushman M. L., Scanlan T.J., Boundary Spanning Individuals: Their Role in Information Transfer and Their Antecedents, *Academy of Management Journal*, 1981, Vol. 24, No. 2, 289-305.

[32] Tushman M. L., Scanlan T.J., Characteristics and External Orientations of Boundary Spanning Individuals, *Academy of Management Journal*, 1981, Vol 24, 1, 83-98.

[33] Tushman M.L., Special Boundary Roles in the Innovation Process, *Administrative Science Quarterly*, 1977, Vol 22, 4, 587-605.

[34] Whitley, R., and Frost P., Task Type and Information Transfer in a Government Research Laboratory, *Human Relations*, 1973, Vol. 25, 537-550.

[35] Williamson, O. E., Transaction-Cost Economics: The Governance of contractual Relations, *The Journal of Law and Economics* (22), 1979, 233-261.

[36] Williamson, O. E. The Economics of Organization: The Transaction Cost Approach, *American Journal of Sociology* (87), 1981, 548-577.

Panel – Academic Trends, Challenges, and Opportunities for IT Programs in Today's Evolving Environment

Indira R. Guzman
Trident University International
iguzman@tuiu.edu

Michelle L. Kaarst-Brown
Syracuse University
Mlbrow03@syr.edu

Diane Lending
James Madison University
lendindc@jmu.edu

Greg Brierly
United States Army
gregory-brierly@us.army.mil

Chino Rao
University of Texas at San Antonio
chino.rao@utsa.edu

Johanna L. Birkland
Syracuse University
jlbirkla@syr.edu

Categories and Subject Descriptors

K.3.2 **Computer and Information Science Education:** Curriculum; Accreditation; Information Systems education;

General Terms: Human Factors.

Keywords: Curriculum; Accreditation; Education.

1. INTRODUCTION AND MOTIVATION

How do academic programs in information technology (IT) react to the new challenges of the evolving environment and multiple stakeholders (accreditation bodies, types of schools, non-traditional students, to name a few)? As an example, according to CIO.com, in the year 2020, technical expertise will no longer be the sole province of the IT department. Employees throughout the organization will understand how to use technology to do their jobs. This extends IT development issues beyond internal training for the IT department, or even traditional entry level or Master's MIS programs found in business schools. New IT graduates need to have a different set of skills; but in addition, non-traditional entrants to the profession, existing IT employees, and mid-career IT professionals are also seeking development opportunities that our academic institutions aim to address.

In this panel, we will discuss some of the current trends and stakeholder pressures facing programs serving this increasingly diverse group of IT professionals. As a foundation for larger group discussion, our panel will share both practitioner and academic perspectives on five issues based on research and experiences, commenting on curricular challenges and opportunities related to development of IT professionals during different phases of their careers:

A) The IT Professional's View: Why Traditional IT Training and Development is Not Enough (Greg Brierly, Practitioner)

B) Keeping Programs Relevant While Balancing Stakeholders, Standards, and Accreditation (Diane Lending – Business School with dual accreditation)

C) The Ever Expanding Expectations: Curricular Demands on MIS Programs in Business Schools (Chino Rao - Business School)

D) Emerging Programs for Mid-Career IT Professionals - Professional Doctorates and Certificates of Advanced Study (Michelle Kaarst-Brown - Information School)

E) The Face of the New IT Professional - Non-traditional Students and Non-Traditional Programs (Indira Guzman – College of Information Systems)

2. OVERVIEW OF PRESENTATIONS

Johanna Birkland will introduce the panel and its members, summarize the key themes and recent data that highlight the importance of this topic, and moderate the discussion.

Greg Brierly will share the "IT professional's perspective", with a focus on why IT service providers require flexible, modular, vendor- agnostic and multi-disciplinary training in order to provide the levels of service demanded by their customers. Consumers of IT services demand agility from their IT service provider. These demands for agility present IT service providers with challenges in terms of training content and method. He will share some thoughts on why conventional IT training is not enough to create and sustain a professional IT workforce capable of consistently meeting the requirements of the customer and the organization. Greg will also discuss important skills for new and established IT workers and identify challenges organizations face in the development of IT workers.

Diane Lending will address the challenge of meeting industry and professional expectations for skills and training of IT professionals while meeting accreditation standards. She will discuss the differing requirements for a program to be accredited by AACSB, the Association to Advance Colleges of Business, and ABET, the Accreditation Board for Engineering and Technology. Both the challenges and opportunities provided by the often conflicting demands of different stakeholders will be discussed.

Chino Rao will discuss challenges and opportunities in delivering relevant information systems (IS) education. As technology continues to evolve, there is more to be taught in the same limited amount of time. This is compounded by the challenge to the faculty to be productive in research, the topics of which can be quite different from what needs to be taught in the classroom. Even as IS departments and faculty try to cope with these conflicting demands, there are other opportunities. For instance, courses in data mining skills for marketing students, computer forensic skills for criminal justice students and so on are needed. The challenges and opportunities that arise from the

SIGMIS-CPR'11, May 19–21, 2011, San Antonio, Texas, USA.
ACM 978-1-4503-0666-9/11/05.

continually changing technical and social environments will be addressed.

Michelle Kaarst-Brown will focus on a few innovative responses and programs that help meet the demands of the mid-career IT professional. Pressures for different skills for the mid-career professional come from external trends such as outsourcing, but also internal demands for rigor in decision making due to budget and agility requirements. In particular, she will report on emerging value of advanced research skills and doctoral training, as well as advanced certificates in new technologies. Drawing upon her own and other schools' experiences, she will provide some examples of opportunities and challenges in addressing development needs of the more advanced IT practitioner through innovative programs.

Indira Guzman will discuss different educational paths and career options available to information professionals of tomorrow based on perspectives presented in her new book *Information Nation: Education and Careers in the Emerging Information Professions* (Stanton, Guzman and Stam, 2010) as well as recently collected points of view from adult learners in undergraduate and graduate programs in a fully online context. The findings include observations about stakeholder expectations, real world challenges related to technology that happen faster than those in academia, the global dynamics that influence the technology changes, and some examples of how non-traditional academic programs deal with those challenges.

3. BIBLIOGRAPHICAL INFORMATION

Johanna Birkland is currently a doctoral candidate at the School of Information Studies; Syracuse University; Syracuse, NY; USA. She holds a M.S. in Communication Management from Ithaca College and a M.S. in Instructional Design from Syracuse University. Her research interests include older adults and ICT use, generational issues surrounding ICT usage and exposure, and how ICTs can be used in organizations to promote inter-generational understanding and knowledge sharing.

Greg Brierly serves as the strategic planner for a US Army organization responsible for IT services at more than twenty army installations in the continental United Sates. Greg has over fifteen years experience in IT service management, IT project management, and developing IT professionals. He is currently a Professional Doctoral Candidate at Syracuse University.

Diane Lending is an Associate Professor of CIS at James Madison University in Virginia. Her research interests are in information systems education, the adoption of information technology, and medical information systems. Dr. Lending has written papers published in several journals including the Journal of Information Systems Education; the Journal of Computer Information Systems; Computers, Informatics, Nursing; and Data Base. Prior to joining academia, she was a programmer, systems analyst, and manager of systems development projects.

Chino Rao is an Associate Professor in the Department of Information Systems and Technology Management, College of Business, University of Texas San Antonio. His areas of research interest include information systems professional culture,

electronic commerce, and, behavioral issues in computer security. He has published in leading academic journals, such as *MIS Quarterly, Management Science, and Communications of AIS.*

Michelle Kaarst-Brown is an Associate Professor and Director of the Professional Doctorate Program in Information Management at the School of Information Studies, Syracuse University. Drawing upon prior management experience, her research explores the influence of social, cultural, knowledge and generational factors on IT governance and the IT workforce. She has published in a number of top academic and business journals including *MIS Quarterly, Information Technology and People,* the *Journal of Strategic Information Systems,* and *CIO Canada.*

Indira Guzman is an Associate Professor of Business Administration and Information Systems and Director of the Computer Science and Information Technology Management Programs at Trident University International (TUI). Her research work focuses mostly on human resources in IT and the occupational culture of IT professionals. Dr. Guzman has published in academic journals such as *The DATA BASE for Advances in Information Systems, Information Technology and People, Human Resource Management, and Women's Studies.*

4. REFERENCES OF INTEREST

1. ABET 2010-2011. *Criteria for Accrediting Computing Programs: Effective for Evaluations* During the 2010-2011 Accreditation Cycle taken from www.ABET.org, November 5, 2010.

2. Collett, S. (2010, August 23, 2010). *5 Indispensable IT Skills of the Future.* Retrieved, 10/10/10, from the World Wide Web: http://www.cio.com/article/print/605217

3. Stanton, J., Guzman, I., and Stam, K. (2010). *Information Nation: Education and Careers in the Emerging Information Professions.* Information Today, Inc.

4. Hecker, D. (2004). *Employment outlook: 2002-12 - Occupational Employment projections to 2012*: Bureau of Labor Statistics.

5. Hirschheim, R. and Newman, M. (2010) *"Houston, we've had a problem...Offshoring, IS employment and the IS discipline: Perception is not Reality".* Journal of Information Technology. *In Print.*

6. Kaarst-Brown, M.L. (2010) *"Houston we've had a problem" Response to Hirschheim and Newman.* Journal of Information Technology. *In print.*

7. Lending, D. and Mathieu, R.G. (2010). *"Workforce preparation and ABET assessment"* in Proceedings of the 2010 Special Interest Group on Management Information System's 48th annual conference on Computer personnel research on Computer personnel research ACM, New York, NY, USA, 136-141.

8. May, T (2010). *The shape of the IT workforce in 2020.* Retrieved from the World Wide Web: http://www.computerworld.com/s/article/351065/Imagining_the_Shape_of_the_2020_IT_Workforce

Author Index